A
New Essay
concerning the
Origin of Ideas

ANTONIO ROSMINI

A
NEW ESSAY
CONCERNING THE
ORIGIN OF IDEAS

Volume 2

Translated by
DENIS CLEARY
and
TERENCE WATSON

ROSMINI HOUSE
DURHAM

Translated from
Nuovo Saggio sull'Origine delle Idee
Vol. 2, Intra, 1876

Typeset by Rosmini House, Durham
Printed by Bell & Bain Limited, Glasgow

ISBN 1 899093 60 5

Note

Square brackets [ ] indicate notes or additions by the translators.

References to this and other works of Rosmini are given by paragraph number unless otherwise stated.

Contents

SECTION FIVE
Theory of the Origin of Ideas   1

PART ONE
Origin of the Idea of Being

CHAPTER 1. Fact: we think being in all its universality   10

CHAPTER 2. Nature of the idea of being

Article 1. The pure idea of being is not a sensible image   12

Article 2. The idea of anything must be distinguished from some judgment about its subsistence   13

Article 3. Ideas of things never contain the subsistence of these things   15

Article 4. The idea of being presents only simple possibility   15

Article 5. We cannot think of anything without the idea of being

Demonstration   16

Article 6. No other idea is necessary for the intuition of the idea of being   18

CHAPTER 3. Origin of the idea of being   19

Article 1. The idea of being does not come from bodily sensations   19

Contents

§1. *Demonstration 1. From* objectivity, *the first characteristic of the idea of being and its first element*   19

Observations. The difference between sensation, sense perception, idea and intellective perception   21

§2. *Demonstration 2. From* possibility *or* ideality, *the second characteristic of the idea of being and its second element*   23

Observations. The connection between the two general proofs, already given, of the inability of sensations to provide us with the idea of being   23

§3. *Demonstration 3. From* simplicity, *the third characteristic of possible being*   24

§4. *Demonstration 4. From* unity *or* identity, *the fourth characteristic of possible being*   24

§5. *Demonstrations 5 and 6. From* universality *and* necessity, *the fifth and sixth characteristics of possible being*   25

Observation 1. Ens is the source of *a priori* knowledge   26

Observation 2. The idea of being in all its universality and all other ideas without exception possess the characteristics indicated, especially *universality* and *necessity*   26

Observation 3. Origin of the Platonic system of innate ideas   27

§6. *Demonstrations 7 and 8. From* immutability *and* eternity, *the seventh and eighth characteristics of possible being*   28

§7. *Demonstration 9. From* undetermination, *the ninth characteristic of possible being in all its universality and its third element*   29

§8. *A synopsis of the proofs already stated, together with an indication of other special proofs that* a priori *knowledge cannot be deduced from sensations*   31

Article 2. The idea of being does not come from the feeling of one's own existence

§1. *This proposition follows from what has been said*   32

§2. *The distinction between the feeling and the idea of* myself   33

Contents

§3. *The feeling of* myself *gives me only my particular existence* 33

§4. *My own feeling is innate; the intellective perception of my existence is acquired* 34

§5. *The idea of being precedes the idea of* myself 34

§6. *Malebranche's error was his opinion that we directly perceive ourselves intellectively without the intervention of an idea* 34

Article 3. The idea of being does not come from Locke's reflection

§1. *Definition* 35

§2. *Demonstration 1* 37

§3. *Demonstration 2* 37

Article 4. The idea of being does not begin to exist in our spirit in the act of perception

§1. *Demonstration 1. From observation of the fact* 39

§2. *Demonstration 2. From absurdity* 44

Article 5. The idea of being is innate

§1. *Demonstration* 46

§2. *Why it is difficult to be aware that the idea of being is continually present to us* 47

§3. *The theory was known by the Fathers of the Church* 50

PART TWO
Origin of all ideas in general through the idea of being

CHAPTER 1. Given the idea of being, the origin of other ideas is explained by analysis of their elements

Article 1. The link with what has been said above 52

Article 2. Analysis of all acquired ideas 53

Article 3. A twofold cause is needed to explain form and matter, the two elements of all acquired ideas 53

Article 4. The twofold cause of acquired ideas is the idea of being and sensation 53

Article 5. St. Thomas' teaching on the cause of our ideas 54

Article 6. The true interpretation of the Scholastic dictum: 'There is nothing in the intellect that did not first exist in sense' 55

CHAPTER 2. Another way of explaining the origin of acquired ideas: through the formation of human reason
Article 1. The idea of being present to our spirit forms our intellect and human reason 57
Article 2. The teaching of St. Thomas and St. Bonaventure about the formation of intellect and reason 57
Article 3. Corollary: all acquired ideas depend upon the innate idea of being 59

CHAPTER 3. Third way of explaining the origin of acquired ideas in general: by the potencies that produce them
Article 1. Reflection 60
Article 2. Universalisation and abstraction 62
  Observation 1. Why the faculty of abstraction has been confused with the faculty of universalisation 63
  Observation 2. Universalisation produces species, abstraction genera 65
  Observation 3. Plato's theory on genera and species 66
Article 3. Synthesis of ideas 67

CHAPTER 4. Fourth way of explaining the origin of acquired ideas in general: by means of a summary classification of the ideas themselves
Article 1. Classification of our intellections 68
Article 2. The difficulty lies in explaining the three listed classes of intellections 69
Article 3. In forming abstracts, our intelligence needs language as a stimulus 71
  §1. *Our spirit is drawn to the act of perception by sensible things* 71
    Observations. The limits of development attainable by human beings outside society if sensations and bodily images were the only stimuli of their reason 73
  §2. *Corporeal images are sufficient explanation of the spirit's activity in forming ideas separated from perceptions* 74
  §3. *Language provides sufficient explanation of the spirit's activity in forming abstract ideas* 75

Observation 1. An objection drawn from human
freedom 78
Observation 2. Human development by means of
society and language; the necessity of language,
if human beings are to become masters of their
own powers 80
Article 4. Intellective perception explained
§1. *The only intellective perception we have is
of ourselves and of bodies* 81
§2. *Explanation of the perception* 82
§3. *Explanation of the judgment generating the perception of bodies* 82
Observation 1. The teaching of the ancients about
the *word* of the mind 84
Observation 2. Relationship between *idea* and the
word of the mind 86
Article 5. Necessity of intellective perception 86
Observation 1. Is the soul always thinking? 88
Observation 2. How the intelligence is a *tabula rasa* 89

CHAPTER 5. The innate idea of being resolves the general
difficulty of the problem of the origin of ideas
Article 1. The difficulty solved 90
Article 2. Objections and answers
§1. *First objection* 90
Reply to the first objection 91
§2. *The first objection renewed* 91
The reply continued 92
§3. *Second objection* 95
Reply to the second objection 96
Corollary 1. There is an idea which precedes any
judgment whatsoever 99
Corollary 2. Human beings possess an intellectual
sense 99
Observation 1. The difference between corporeal
and intellectual sense 100
Observation 2. The nature of *ideal being* 100

PART THREE
Origin of the First Principles of Reasoning   102

CHAPTER 1. The first and second principles: of knowledge and of contradiction   102

CHAPTER 2. The third and fourth principles: substance and cause   106

CHAPTER 3. The nature of scientific principles in general   108

CHAPTER 4. Origin of scientific principles in general   109

PART FOUR
Origin of Pure Ideas, which derive nothing from Feeling

CHAPTER 1. Origin of elementary ideas or concepts of being presupposed in human reasoning
  Article 1. List of elementary ideas of being   110
  Article 2. Origin of these concepts   110
  Observation   111
  Article 3. St. Augustine's arguments about the ideas of unity and number and similar things confirm the theory I have given   111

CHAPTER 2. Origin of the idea of substance   120
  Article 1. The question relative to the origin of the idea of substance   120
  Article 2. Description and analysis of all that we think about substance
    §1. _The starting point for the study of ideas of substance_   122
    §2. _Definition of substance_   122
    §3. _Analysis of the concept of substance_   122
    §4. _Various modes of the idea of substance_   123
    §5. _Origin of the idea of individual_   126
    §6. _Judgments on the subsistence of substances differ from ideas of substance_   126

Contents xiii

§7. *Summary of all the thoughts the human mind can have about substances* 127
Article 3. The three ideas of substance follow one from the other 128
Article 4. All judgments on the subsistence of substances are explained when one difficulty is overcome 128
Article 5. The explanation of the specific idea of substance depends on the difficulty found in accounting for judgments on the subsistence of substances 129
Article 6. Explanation of the perception of individuals 130

CHAPTER 3. **A further explanation of the idea of substance**
Article 1. Necessity of the explanation 131
Article 2. Systems dealing with the origin of the idea of substance 131
Article 3. Another way of finding the origin of the idea of substance 133
Article 4. First proposition: if our understanding conceives, it conceives something 134
Article 5. Second proposition: everything can be an object of the understanding
§1. *Definition* 135
§2. *Objection to the principle of contradiction* 135
§3. *Reply. — The principle of contradiction defended* 136
§4. *The demonstration concluded* 137
Article 6. Third proposition: the understanding can perceive qualities only in a subject in which they exist 137
Article 7. The distinction between Hume's idealism and Berkeley's 138
Article 8. Hume's idealism refuted 139
Article 9. Origin of the idea of accident 141
Article 10. An observation on the invariability of substance 148
Article 11. Sensible qualities do not exist through themselves, that is, they are not substances 150

CHAPTER 4. **Origin of the ideas of cause and effect**
Article 1. Purpose of this chapter 153
Article 2. Proposition 153

Article 3. The proposition analysed, and the difficulty
uncovered   154

Article 4. Explanation of the difficulty in uncovering
the origin of the idea of cause   156

Article 5. Distinction between substance and cause   159

Article 6. The understanding completes sense perceptions   160

Article 7. Application of the teaching on substance to
internal feeling   162

CHAPTER 5. **Observation on the origin of the ideas of
truth, justice and beauty**   164

PART FIVE

**Origin of *Non-Pure* Ideas, which derive Something
from Feeling**   165

CHAPTER 1. **Origin of the difference between the ideas of
corporeal substance and spiritual substance**

Article 1. The opinion already expressed about substance
and cause   165

Article 2. The subject of the following investigation   167

Article 3. The difference between the idea of cause and
the idea of subject   168

Article 4. A further analysis of sensations

§1. *The purpose of this analysis*   169

§2. *There is in the sentient subject something other
than the act by which sensations exist*   170

§3. *The subject of sensible qualities must be an act involving more than these qualities*   172

Article 5. The difference between the ideas of *substance*
and of *essence*

§1. *Definition of essence*   173

§2. *Specific, generic and most universal essence*   174

§3. *Specific essence*   174

§4. *Generic essences*   177

§5. *A more perfect definition of substance*   179

Article 6. Resumption of the question under discussion 180
Article 7. A perceiving subject, *MYSELF*, exists 181
Article 8. The concept of *MYSELF*, a perceiving subject, is entirely different from the concept of corporeal substance
§1. *There are two series of facts in us, in one of which we are active, in the other passive* 181
§2. *We are cause and subject of active facts but only subject of passive facts* 183
§3. *What we call 'body' is the proximate cause of our external sensations* 183
§4. *Our spirit is not body* 184
Article 9. Simplicity of the spirit 184

CHAPTER 2. **Origin of our idea of corporeal substance**
Article 1. The way to demonstrate the existence of bodies 189
Article 2. The existence of a proximate cause of our sensations 190
Article 3. Any cause different from ourselves is a substance 190
Article 4. The substance causing our sensations is immediately joined to them 190
Article 5. The cause of our sensations is a limited ens 191
Article 6. We name things as we conceive them intellectually 191
Article 7. How to use words without making mistakes 191
Article 8. Bodies are limited entia 192
Article 9. God is not the proximate cause of our sensations 193
Article 10. Bodies exist, and cannot be confused with God 193
Article 11. Berkeley's idealism refuted 193
Article 12. Reflections on the demonstration of the existence of bodies 195

CHAPTER 3. **Origin of the idea of our own body, as distinct from exterior bodies, through the fundamental feeling** 200

Article 1. First classification of the qualities observed in bodies   200

Article 2. Classification of the corporeal qualities which immediately constitute the relationship of bodies with our spirit   204

Article 3. The distinction between life and the fundamental feeling   205

Article 4. Two ways of perceiving our body: subjective and extrasubjective   207

Article 5. The *subjective* way of perceiving our body is twofold: the *fundamental feeling* and *modifications* of this *feeling*   208

Article 6. Explanation of sensation in so far as it is a modification of the fundamental feeling of our body   209

Article 7. Explanation of sensation in so far as it perceives external bodies   210

Article 8. The difference between our own and external bodies   211

Article 9. Description of the fundamental feeling   211

Article 10. Existence of the fundamental feeling   215

Article 11. The origin of sensations confirms the existence of the fundamental feeling   218

Article 12. Explanation of St. Thomas' teaching that the body is in the soul   219

Article 13. Physical relationship between soul and body   220

CHAPTER 4. Origin of the idea of our body by means of modifications of the fundamental feeling

Article 1. The analysis of sensation (contd.)   221

Article 2. Definition of the fundamental feeling; how it is distinguished from the sense perception of bodies   222

Article 3. Origin and nature of corporeal pleasure and pain   223

Article 4. Relationship of corporeal pleasure and pain with extension   224

Article 5. Confutation of the opinion: 'We feel everything in our brain and then refer the sensation to the relevant parts of our body'   225

Article 6. Comparison of the two subjective modes in which we feel and perceive the extension of our own body 226

Article 7. Further proof of the existence of the fundamental feeling 228

Article 8. All our sensations are simultaneously subjective and extrasubjective 228

Article 9. Touch as a universal sense 231

Article 10. The origin of touch 231

Article 11. The relationship between the two subjective ways of perceiving our body 232

CHAPTER 5. **Criterion for the existence of bodies**

Article 1. A more perfect definition of bodies 233

Article 2. The general criterion for judgments about the existence of bodies 236

Article 3. Application of the general criterion 236

Article 4. The certainty of our own body is the criterion for the existence of other bodies 238

Article 5. Application of the criterion to possible errors about the existence of some part of our body 238

Article 6. Response to the idealists' argument based on dreams 240

CHAPTER 6. **Origin of the idea of time**

Article 1. The connection between what has already been said and what follows 241

Article 2. The idea of time derived from consciousness of our own actions 242

Article 3. The idea of time indicated by the actions of others 243

Article 4. Pure idea of time 244

Article 5. Idea of pure, indefinitely long time 244

Article 6. Continuity in time

§1. *Everything that happens, happens by instants* 244

§2. *The difficulty is not solved by the idea of time obtained by observation alone* 245

§3. *We need to consider the simple possibilities of things, which must not be confused with real things* 247

§4. *Granted the same intensity of action, observation presents time simply as a relationship of the quantity of different actions*   248

§5. *The idea of pure time and of its indefinite length and divisibility are mere possibilities or concepts of the mind*   249

§6. *The phenomenal idea of the continuity of time is illusory*   250

§7. *The continuity of time is a mere possibility, that is, a concept of the mind*   254

§8. *Distinction between what is absurd and what is mysterious*   255

§9. *There is no succession in the duration of complete actions and therefore no idea of time, only of continuum, is present*   255

§10. *The idea of being constituting our intellect is not subject to time*   256

CHAPTER 7. **Origin of the idea of movement**

Article 1. We perceive movement in three ways   257

Article 2. Active movement described   258

Article 3. Passive movement described   259

Article 4. Of itself, our movement is not sensible   260

Article 5. Movement in our sense organs is sensible   260

Article 6. Relationship between movement and sensation   262

Article 7. Movement relative to touch-perception   262

Article 8. Movement relative to sight-perception   262

Article 9. Movement relative to aural-, smell- and taste-perceptions   263

Article 10. The continuity of movement

§1. *Observation cannot perceive minute extensions*   263

§2. *Observation provides only phenomenal continuity of movement*   264

§3. *Real continuity of movement is absurd*   264

§4. *Solution to the objection drawn from leaps in nature*   265

§5. *Mental continuity of movement*   266

CHAPTER 8. **Origin of the idea of space**

Article 1. Distinction between the ideas of space and of body   267

Article 2. Extension, or space, is limitless 267
Article 3. Space or extension is continuous 268
Article 4. The real continuum 270
Article 5. The continuum has no parts 271
Article 6. The continuum can have limits 271
Article 7. How the continuum can be said to be infi-
nitely divisible 272

**CHAPTER 9. Origin of the idea of bodies by means of the
extrasubjective perception of touch**
Article 1. Analysis of the extrasubjective perception of
bodies in general 273
Article 2. All our senses give us a perception of some-
thing different from us 273
Article 3. All our senses give us a perception of something outside us 274
Article 4. Touch perceives only corporeal surfaces 275
Article 5. Touch together with movement gives the idea
of three dimensional space 276
Article 6. A review of the ways we perceive solid space 277
Article 7. It is easier for us to think about the idea of
space acquired by touch and movement than by the
fundamental feeling and movement 277
Article 8. Space perceived by the movement of touch-
sensation is identical with space perceived by the
movement of the fundamental feeling 278
Article 9. Identity between the extension of our body
and of an external body is the basis of the communication between the idea we have of each of them 279
Article 10. Continuation 279
Article 11. The subjective sensation of our body is the
means of corporeal, extrasubjective perception 280
Article 12. The extension of bodies 281
  §1. *Multiplicity is not essential to corporeal nature* 281
  §2. *The composite unity of our sensitive body* 282
  §3. *We cannot err about the unicity of our body* 282
  §4. *The multiplicity of the feeling of our body* 282
  §5. *Our perception of multiplicity in external bodies* 283
  §6. *The distinction between a body and a corporeal
  principle* 284

§7. *Granted that corporeal sensation terminates in a continuous extension, a continuous real extension must also be present in the bodies producing it*   285

§8. *The sensitive parts of our body do not produce a feeling extending beyond themselves*   288

§9. *The extension of external bodies is neither greater nor smaller than the sensations they produce in us*   288

§10. *Phenomenal continuity is present in our touch-sensations*   288

§11. *Elementary sensations are continuous*   289

§12. *Elementary bodies have a continuous extension*   291

§13. *Argument against simple points*   292

Article 13. The definition of bodies completed   293

Article 14. We perceive external bodies by touch and movement   293

Article 15. Origin of the idea of mathematical body   295

Article 16. Origin of the idea of physical body   295

CHAPTER 10. The particular criterion for the existence of external bodies

Article 1. The criterion for external bodies is an application of the general criterion for the existence of bodies   296

Article 2. Applications of the criterion for the existence of external bodies   296

CHAPTER 11. The subjective and the extrasubjective content in external sensations

Article 1. The necessity of this distinction   298

Article 2. Some truths recalled   298

Article 3. The understanding analyses sensations   299

Article 4. The general principle for discerning what is subjective and what is extrasubjective in sensations   299

Article 5. Application of the general principle to determine the extrasubjective part of sensations   300

Article 6. The difference between primary and secondary properties of bodies   301

Article 7. Application of the general principle to determine the subjective part of sensations   301

Article 8. Resistant extension felt by touch   304

Article 9. The extrasubjective sensation of the four sense
organs   306

CHAPTER 12. **Origin of the idea of bodies through the extrasubjective perception of sight**
Article 1. The eye perceives a coloured surface   311
Article 2. The coloured surface is a corporeal surface   311
Article 3. The coloured surface is identical with the
light-affected surface of the retina of the eye   311
Article 4. The coloured surface we perceive is as big as
the retina touched by light; but the colours are distributed in that surface in fixed proportions   312
Article 5. The coloured surface cannot furnish the idea
of solid space, even through the movement of colours
taking place in space   313
Article 6. Colour sensations are signs of the size of
things   313
Article 7. Our sight, associated with touch and movement, perceives the distances and qualities of movement of our body   318
Article 8. Smell, hearing and taste compared with sight   320

CHAPTER 13. **The criterion of bodily size and shape**
Article 1. The criterion of the size of bodies is the size
perceived by touch   322
Article 2. Application of our criterion to illusions about
the visible size of things   323
Article 3. Application of the criterion to visual illusion
about the distance of things   327
Article 4. Application of the criterion to illusions about
the position of things   329
Article 5. The criterion of the shape of bodies is their
shape as perceived by touch   332
Article 6. Errors about the shape and size of bodies occasioned by sight   333

CHAPTER 14. **The extrasubjective perception of bodies by
means of the five senses considered in their mutual relationship**

Article 1. The identity of space unites different sensations, so that one body is perceived   334
Article 2. Our attention is chiefly engaged by the visual perception of bodies   335
Article 3. Whether sensation gives us the species of corporeal things, or we perceive things themselves   337
Article 4. Reid mistakenly denies all sensible species in the perception of bodies   339
Article 5. Reid's distinction between sensation and perception   339
Article 6. Galluppi improves Scottish philosophy   340
Article 7. The contribution to Galluppi's theory of the foregoing analysis of sensation   342

CHAPTER 15. The relationship between intellective and sense perceptions of bodies
Article 1. The distinction between intellective perceptions and sense perceptions   345
Article 2. Locke confuses sense perception of bodies with intellective perception. Criticisms levelled against Locke   347
Article 3. Reid recognised better than others the activity of the spirit in the formation of ideas, but fell into the same error   349
Article 4. Continuation   352
Article 5. Whether we perceive bodies through the principles of substance and cause   354
Article 6. Intellective perception was confused with sense perception even in the case of internal feeling and *MYSELF*   356

CHAPTER 16. The natural disharmonies between the perception of our body as co-subject, and as agent foreign to the subject
Article 1. The difference between the two principal ways of perceiving our body, that is, as co-subject and as an agent foreign to the subject   358
Article 2. The similarity between the impression of external things and the sensation that follows   359
Article 3. Materialism rebutted   362

Article 4. The dividing line between physiology and
psychology 367

Article 5. Systems concerning the union of soul and
body 369

Article 6. The relationship between the *external* body
and the body as *co-subject* 370

Article 7. Matter of the fundamental feeling 371

PART SIX
Conclusion

CHAPTER 1. Epilogue of the Theory 380

CHAPTER 2. The question concerning the origin of ideas 384

CHAPTER 3. Learning to understand what has been said
about the origin of ideas 389

Appendix

1. D'Alembert, Falletti and Galluppi on the feeling of
myself 391

2. St. Thomas on knowledge 393

3. Reid's analysis of sensation 394

4. Intellective and sense perception 396

5. Philosophy and mysteries 397

6. St. Thomas on the union of the spirit with the idea of
being 398

7. Plato and the idea of being 400

8. St. Thomas on intellect and phantasms 403

9. St. Thomas' illustrated phantasms 405

10. Plato's species and genera 406

11. Plato's ideas and Pythagoras' numbers 408

12. Reflection 408

13. Language and abstract ideas 409

14. St. Thomas on natural and scientific knowledge 410

15. The *tabula rasa* 414

16. Logical impossibility in things 415

17. Solid foundations needed in philosophy   416
18. St. Thomas on ideas and phantasms   417
19. St. Thomas and innate principles   418
20. St. Thomas on substance   419
21. The action of St. Thomas' acting intellect   420
22. Sensations and the meaning of words   423
23. St. Thomas and Locke on reflection   428
24. Locke and the philosophy of sensation   429
25. Extrasubjective perception of bodies   431
26. St. Thomas and phantasms   433
27. Galluppi and sensation of distant bodies   436
28. Idea relative to subsistence of things   437
29. Judgment about the identity of a body   439
30. Extension misunderstood   440
31. Reid and the concept of body   441
32. Tradition and the subjectivity of sensations   442
33. Advertence and senses   444
34. Indication and perception in sensation   446
35. Primary and secondary qualities   447
36. Error and habitual judgment   448
37. Sight relative to touch   449
38. Erroneous judgments about sensations   450
39. Reid on judgment and sensation   451
40. Ideas and the need for intellectual activity   453
41. Reid and the meaning of idea   455
42. Galluppi's and Descartes' perception of self   458
43. Reid's censure of other philosophers   459
44. Malebranche's basic difficulty   460
45. Descartes' mistaken criterion of certainty   461
46. Being in potency and in act   462

Index of Persons   465

General Index   467

Commonebo, si potero, ut videre te videas
[If I can, I shall help you see that you see]
St. Augustine, *De Trinitate*, 11: 12

SECTION FIVE

Theory of the Origin of Ideas

Objectum intellectus est ens vel verum comune [The object of the intellect is ens or universal truth]

St. Thomas, *S.T.*, I, q. 55, art. 1

385. So far we have considered the principal systems concerning the origin of ideas, looking for the one system which might satisfactorily explain ideas. But the search has been fruitless: some theories have failed by defect (Section Three), others by excess (Section Four). Some grant in the mind too little that is innate, others too much. We must now delve more deeply into the difficult investigation and try to find the golden mean between these two extremes. Nothing innate must be granted without necessity; nor must we allow any preconceived antipathy, perhaps to the simple word 'innate', to cause us to reject the little that has been established as the necessary condition for the fact of our ideas (cf. 26–28).

But, to know how far we still need to go and the path we have to follow, let me summarise the journey so far.

I began by positing the difficulty, which I presented as clearly as I could in its most general form: 'In the system of those who consider all ideas man-made, we must establish an order among the actions necessary for forming ideas. In this order either a *judgment* precedes an *idea* or an idea precedes a judgment; there is no middle path. But both these processes are impossible. We cannot therefore suppose in any way that all our ideas are man-made' (cf. 41–45).

386. Sensists, and generally those who claim that all ideas

without exception are formed by us, did not even glimpse this difficulty. This explains the tenacity of their opinion. Those who see and feel the force of the difficulty must inevitably renounce their belief that all our ideas are made by us. Consequently the disagreement between philosophical schools about the origin of knowledge originates solely from whether we see this difficulty or not.

However, even those who did not clearly see the problem sometimes caught a vague side-glimpse of it; if they did not see it at all, it still stood out (for the clear-sighted) at the heart of their argument, which it rendered inconclusive and ineffective.

As we saw, Locke, for example, in describing the development of sensitivity, continuously introduced *judgments*. Unaware of them, he did not think it necessary to explain their origin or possibility (cf. 112). Similarly, we saw him claim elsewhere that *ideas* were undoubtedly prior to judgments. Nevertheless, he did not investigate or even suspect that the act with which ideas are formed might be a judgment whose function as cause must precede ideas as effects (cf. 68–69).

But if Locke did not at this point see the difficulty I have explained, he did glimpse it in other places, although weakly. For example, he is aware that we cannot have *knowledge* without *judgment* (cf. 113–114). Again, when he comes across the idea of substance, the difficulty is so great for him that he confesses *substance* to be inexplicable in his system. However, his imperfect, partial understanding of the difficulty prevented him from feeling its importance. After stating that every cognition is preceded by a judgment, he drew no other conclusion and, finding the idea of substance very troublesome, swept it away as non-existent (cf. 48–62).

387. Sometimes philosophers noticed the difficulty (always under some particular form) in other people's arguments without noticing it in their own. Condillac, for example, rightly reproaches Locke for introducing unexplained judgments into his explanation of the actions of sensitivity (cf. 68–69). But Condillac himself, in order to sweep away this faculty of judgment, attributed it also to the senses and thus monstrously confused the principle that *feels* with the principle that *judges* what is felt (cf. 70–71).

On the other hand, Condillac does not see Locke's other

error of supposing that ideas are first formed in us without *judgments*. He begins from ideas without noticing that he introduces an act of judgment into their formation. Nor does his system offer any suitable explanation for the origin of the *universality* of ideas, although universality is an essential characteristic of all ideas and no judgment could be formed without it (cf. 86–96).

388. Reid, seeing further than Condillac, clearly notes that Locke was introducing something impossible when he claimed that ideas were formed first and then judgments (with the help of ideas). In fact, no idea can be formed without a judgment. Reid therefore established that the first operation was a *judgment*, not an *idea* (cf. 115–117).

But how can we conceive the possibility of making judgments without having an idea? Reid replies that the judgments are made instinctively.

This is purely an hypothesis, or rather a gratuitous affirmation. Moreover, the statement does not in any way answer the difficulty. Indeed, instinct cannot undertake the impossible, which would be the case if someone without ideas undertook to make judgments; ideas are simply the means and elements of judgments. Instinct can of course explain why I undertake to use my power of judgment rather than leave it inactive, but it cannot constitute the power or explain its origin; it can only move it. Nor can the power of judgment set itself in motion unless it has something to judge and some means of judging. In other words, it must have ideas, the indispensable conditions of judgment itself (cf. 121–129).

Reid and his disciple Stewart, driven by the difficulty they saw, although imperfectly, went even further. Instinctive judgments, even granted the power attributed to them, could never produce truly universal ideas. Consequently these two philosophers took the shortest but most desperate route: they denied the existence of ideas (cf. 104–108, 160). Locke himself had taught them this kind of summary justice against defenceless ideas, whose only guilt lay in hiding the mystery of their origin from these philosophers. As we saw, Locke had decreed that the idea of substance, inimicable to his system, no longer existed.

Because the difficulty had so little effect on these ideologists, they failed to see that the actions of our spirit could not in any way explain the production of all ideas. They either did not see the difficulty, or saw it only partially and vaguely.

389. But there were other, more incisive philosophers who fully saw how difficult, indeed how impossible, it was to admit that all ideas were formed by sensations and reflection, or more generally by some operations of our spirit. They understood that these actions, which should form ideas, cannot take place without ideas. I have listed the highest and most extreme intellects among these thinkers: Plato, Leibniz and Kant (cf. Section Four).

All these great men agreed unanimously that 'if we do not admit that the human spirit possesses of itself some innate, natural, intellective element, distinct from a pure, simple faculty, our spirit would never begin to think and therefore never form ideas.' This opinion of the deepest, most learned thinkers of the nations is constant and very solid.[1]

390. The sharpest minds fully agreed about the negative part of the problem: it is impossible for all ideas, whole and entire, to be formed by us. But they have different opinions about the positive part, that is, about the definition of the nature of this necessary element, connected naturally to our spirit, and making it capable of intellective operations.

The reason is this. Some thought that the innate element necessary to our intellect should be greater; others, less. These great men were certainly not ignorant of the principle of method I posited at the start: 'In explaining facts of the human spirit, we must not assume more than necessary to explain them' (cf. 26–28). But the difficulty consisted in finding the

---

[1] Until recently, France was known only through the thought of Condillac, but it was also the fatherland of Descartes and Malebranche, and today favourably welcomes many doctrines of the Alexandrian school. Germany, after hard work and deep thought, showed its unanimity in affirming as impossible that all ideas in all their elements are man-made. What shall we say of Italy? We must remember that Italy was laying the immovable basis of doctrine (called *italic* after her) before other nations could even stammer philosophically. The sole purpose of this doctrine was to explain the noble, hidden nature of ideas and show them to be so infinitely superior to the senses and to the human being that they could not proceed from either one or other. During the centuries, this national heritage has never been entirely forgotten. Let us hope that it is not forgotten.

minimum sufficient to explain ideas while avoiding superfluity. This innate element grew smaller as philosophy drew closer to the solution of the problem. At the same time, it was shown to be sufficient, because what I laid down was certain: 'Of all the complete explanations of the facts of the human spirit, the simplest and that requiring the fewest suppositions is to be preferred' (cf. 26–28).

Indeed there was progression among philosophers who agreed that something innate must be granted if we are to explain the origin of ideas. More recent philosophers have sought to remove what was superfluous from the earlier theories by demonstrating that ideas could originate even if we granted less that was innate than earlier thinkers had done (cf. 361–362).

391. Plato, for example, was convinced that all ideas are innate, although dormant. This was the only way he could explain why a child replies truthfully to questions on many things it has never heard of, but which apparently it sees intellectually as present to it. For Plato, those ideas had always been present to the child's spirit, although it had never paid any attention to them or thought about them. The child, when asked about these things, but without being instructed about them, is roused and motivated to look at truths which it does not know it possesses. In this way, the child discovers truths which no one has communicated to it.

392. Leibniz realised that this was too much; it was unnecessary to posit so much to explain the ideas which we gradually acquire by ourselves. According to him it was sufficient if there were only very light traces of ideas in the spirit, in the way that a statue can be outlined in a block of marble; the colour of the streaks in the marble would precisely outline the statue in the block (cf. 278–279).

393. Kant, who came next, added a more accurate, deeper analysis of cognitions and found that they result from two elements, one of which is traced back to what is sensible, while the other cannot in any way be traced back to what is sensible. According to him, the former need not be innate in any way, and the origin of the latter must be found in what we have within us. He correctly called the first element *matter* of knowledge, and the second, *form*. Hence, he did not posit innate ideas

either in themselves, as Plato did, or in their traces, as Leibniz did. For him, the *formal* part of ideas is innate so that *all* ideas are man-made, but not *totally*. This was a notable step forward for philosophical science (cf. 324–325).

394. But there was still need for simplification: the *formal part* of knowledge, now known to be given necessarily by nature and not formed by ourselves, that is, the seed sown in our souls by the Creator, had to be reduced to a minimum so that the great tree of human knowledge might grow from it. Our predecessors had seen that this part, essential to the intellective spirit, could only be something very small. They expressed this beautifully by saying that 'God, in the act of creating our souls, allows them for a moment to catch a glimpse, so to speak, of the immense treasure of his eternal wisdom'.[2]

395. After Kant's efforts the problem was still 'to determine the *minimum* knowledge or *light* rendering the soul intelligent and therefore suitable for intellective actions'. This minimum is barely a heavenly spark snatched from the sun; it is what we can snatch of the truth by means of a slight, instantaneous glimpse of it.

Kant did not in fact find this minimum. He had extended the *formal* part much further than it extends in reality. Instead of

---

[2] These words are found in a truly Italian, classical book available to everyone (*Saggi di Naturali Esperienze fatte nell'Accademia del Cimento sotto la protezione del Serenissimo Principe Leopoldo di Toscana, e descritte dal Segretario di essa Accademia*, Florence, 1691, at the new printing works of Giovanni Filippo Cecchi). To understand better how those people thought (in Europe they were masters of the art of experimentation and greatly helped the progress of the physical sciences), I will quote the entire piece from which I took the quotation: 'The sovereign beneficence of God, in the act of creating our souls, allows them to catch a fleeting glimpse, as it were, of the immense treasure of his eternal wisdom. Our souls then adore these first lights of truth, like precious jewels. We see that this is true because of the information these lights contain, information which we could not have gained here below. It must therefore be said that our souls have received it from elsewhere' (*Proemio*). Leaving aside the Platonic imagery, introduced to make the statement more attractive, and keeping to the basic teaching, we see in these words of the Secretary of the Academy of Cimento that 1. we know we have some part of knowledge which cannot in any way be formed by us and which therefore must be given us by nature, and 2. this part must be only a very tiny particle, as much as we can absorb, as it were, in a rapid glimpse at eternal wisdom.

moving from a single, simple principle, he divided the formal part into many independent forms, two of which he allotted to internal and external sense, four, each of which had three modes, to intellect, and three to reason (cf. 357–358). He did not see that sense has nothing pertaining to formal knowledge, and that all the forms he attributed to intellect and reason are reduced to one, very simple form, that is, *possibility*, or its equivalent, *ideality*. All other forms easily stem from this, as from a tiny seed. Consequently, positing many forms is superfluous; granted this one form in our spirit, it easily produces others, not equal to it but posterior and subordinate (cf. 363–380).

Lack of such simplification damaged Kant considerably. He remained ignorant of the nature of the one, true form, which is *objective*, sublime, independent of the soul itself, immune from every mode and therefore from all manipulation; anything incapable of undergoing a variety of modes cannot be manipulated. Consequently Kant could not give a solid basis to knowledge, to truth and to human certainty (cf. 327–329, 379).

396. I think I have demonstrated all this, as I was obliged to do if I wished to continue the work of philosophers who had flourished up till now, and to take advantage of what they had done. It was right for me to make my own the two truths they had brought to light:

1. The necessary distinction between the *formal* and the *material* parts of knowledge.

2. The *formal part* alone is given by nature.

But because these philosophers had not found the *unknown* part of knowledge, that is, the *formal part* contained in the second proposition, I then had to make use of this rich heritage to attempt to determine this part, taking great care not to include in addition anything from the *matter* of knowledge. I had to isolate the formal part in its mode of primal, most simple being, leaving aside the modes which clothe it when it is applied. I carried out this investigation with the following result: 'In its primal, original state, the formal part of knowledge consists in a single, natural and, in us, permanent intuition of *possible being* (cf. 363–380, 52–54, 115–120).

397. This is what I attempted in the first volume. I must now indicate the purpose of the present volume.

My intention is to present in regular order my theory of the origin of ideas. I will begin by examining the intuition of possible being. This intuition, on the basis of what has been said, is the most solemn and important idea of all ideas; indeed, it alone merits the name of idea. The whole difficulty I have presented in so many different ways is reduced to this one idea.

None of the sensist philosophers could give a satisfactory explanation of the origin of this idea, which lay before them like a reef on which they would come to grief. The operations of the spirit, which according to these philosophers produce ideas, depend continually without exception on this idea. Despite the philosophers' claim that all ideas are produced by actions of the spirit, every idea without exception requires *this* idea. But given this idea, intellective activity can begin and carry through its work unhindered

It is impossible therefore to begin from any starting point other than this idea. If it is not explained, other ideas become impossible. To form other ideas we must act in an intellective way, and every intellective act, as I have said, presupposes and makes continual use of this idea.

If I succeed in taking this difficult step, the way will be open for discovering the origin of all the principles of human cognitions and of all other ideas, or rather, concepts, which are easily generated with the help of this idea.

Hence, I will first show that *being* shines naturally as light to our souls. I will then explain the *first principles* of reasoning. A careful analysis of them will indicate that they can be called only *modes* of the application of this single idea of being which adheres immovably to us. In doing this, I will have explained how we can reason, because the principles of knowledge and contradiction, and the other first principles, are instruments of reasoning, without which human understanding does not take a single step.

After seeing how human beings become *intelligent* and *reasoning*, it will be easy to show how they are authors of their many concepts, which can be formed easily with the use of reasoning.

Amongst the concepts, the first that come to hand are those closest to the source from which they derive; these are *pure concepts*, containing nothing of real feeling but stemming from the innate, primal idea alone.

[397]

I will descend from this sublime height by deducing *non-pure concepts* which receive matter in varying degree from feeling. I will then be able to show how the concepts of the two kinds of substance, corporeal and spiritual, are formed.

Next, I will discuss the origin of the concept of body. This presents itself to our intellect in two ways: as *body animated* by our spirit and as *inanimate body*. I will first analyse the concept of our body, but cannot deal with the concept of external body without investigating the three difficult concepts of *time, movement* and *space*. These concepts are necessary if we are to formulate completely the concept of external body. I will then conclude with an analysis of this concept. The whole of the present Section therefore is divided into the following parts:

1. Part One: Origin of the idea of being.

2. Part Two: Origin of all concepts in general through the idea of being.

3. Part Three: Origin of the first principles of reasoning.

4. Part Four: Origin of pure concepts, that is, those which contain nothing proper to feeling.

5. Part Five: Origin of non-pure concepts, that is, those which for their formation take something from feeling.

6. Part Six: Conclusion.

PART ONE

Origin of the Idea of Being

CHAPTER 1
Fact: we think being in all its universality

398. I begin with a simple, very obvious fact, the study of which forms the whole theory of this book: we think being in a universal mode.

This fact, no matter how we explain it, cannot be called into doubt.

To think being in a universal mode simply means thinking of the quality common to all things, while ignoring all other qualities, generic, specific or proper. I can will to fix my attention on one element of a thing rather than on another, and in concentrating exclusively on being, the quality common to all things, I am said to be thinking *being* in all its universality.

To deny that we can direct our attention to being as common to all things, while ignoring or rather abstracting from all their other qualities, contradicts what is attested by ordinary observation of our own actions; it would mean contradicting common sense and violating ordinary speech. When I say: reason is proper to humans, who have feeling in common with animals, and vegetable life in common with plants, but being in common with everything, I am considering this *common being* independently of everything else. If humans did not have the ability to think *being* separately from everything else, this statement would be impossible.

This fact is so obvious that to mention it would be sufficient, if it were not for the doubt prevalent in modern thinking. Yet it is the extremely simple foundation of the entire theory of the origin of ideas.

[398]

399. To think being in a universal mode means that we have the idea of being in all its universality, or at least presupposes that we have it; without the idea of being, we cannot think being.

Our task, then, is to identify the origin of this idea. But if we are to discover its source, we must first examine its nature and character.

CHAPTER 2
Nature of the idea of being

Article 1
The pure idea of being is not a sensible image

400. Because the argument has to be free from every possible ambiguity, I must first point out that in affirming human capacity for possessing the *idea of being*, isolated and separate from all other ideas (cf. 394–395), I do not wish to say that we form for ourselves a *sensible image* of that idea. A sensible image cannot be formed of anything unless the thing itself is: 1. determined and individualised; 2. corporeal, and perceived by the senses.

401. Some modern philosophers have denied abstract or undetermined ideas simply because it is impossible to form images of them.

This is a material reason unknown to true thinkers who understand the necessity of observing nature and acknowledging all it presents. The existence of something cannot be denied just because it does not conform with laws imposed *a priori* on the nature of things by our fantasy. Simple, unprejudiced observation would have easily recognised three series of thoughts within the human spirit:

1. Thoughts representing *undetermined ideas*, that is, objects which cannot be presented under the form of images, nor exist in reality on their own, but which can nevertheless be considered on their own;

2. Thoughts about spiritual entia which have everything required for *subsistence* but offer no basis for sensible images;

3. Thoughts about bodies or corporeal qualities which alone are capable of being expressed by sensible imagination.

The existence of these three classes of thoughts is a fact, independent of any system and must be admitted even by those who deny the *existence of spiritual beings*, an altogether different question from that implied by *concepts of spiritual beings*.

To establish gratuitously the principle, 'What we cannot imagine sensibly, we cannot even think', and to draw from this gratuitous assertion the consequence: 'Hence, universal and abstract ideas do not exist', is a false method. Its starting point is a prejudice to which we wish to subject the facts; it implies a determination to dictate laws to nature, rather than a desire to listen to nature, and interpret it wisely.

Article 2

The idea of anything must be distinguished from some judgment about its subsistence

402. We must also distinguish the *idea* from the *judgment about the subsistence* of things. This is a cardinal distinction in ideology.

When we form the *idea* or *concept* of an ens, we can possess a perfect concept of the ens, with all its essential and accidental qualities, without *judging* that it really exists. This is sufficient to assure us that, when intuiting the *idea*, we perform a different operation from that involved in making a *judgment* about the subsistence of an ens.

Let us take the idea or concept of a horse containing every individual internal and external feature necessary for its existence (body, head, neck, legs, and so on), and imagine that this could really exist, if I were capable of creating it, without need of any addition to the particulars contained in the idea that serves me as its exemplar or type.

If I wished to bring this horse into existence, and were capable of doing so, and if my concept still did not present all the minute particulars of the individual horse I intended to make, I would be obliged as I went ahead with my work to think of the parts lacking to the concept, which I would gradually perfect as the external reality was formed.

Let us imagine now that the concept has been perfected, and that the horse has been materialised in such a way that it corresponds exactly with the concept used to bring it to this state and make it exist. There is no doubt that the material horse would

depend upon the thought and concept from which I had copied
it.

403. The next step is to ask whether my perfect concept has
received anything from the real subsistence of the horse.
Undoubtedly, it has not. The concept had to be perfect before
the horse could exist in order that I might have a standard or
exemplar from which to produce and forge it. The concept
derives nothing from the perfected horse, nor can it do so,
because its own perfection first comprises without exception all
the particulars of the horse. So much is evident.

404. This fact throws light on the nature of ideas which are
independent (as far as their nature is concerned) of the *real*
existence of individuals in such a way that they can be perfect
irrespective of the real existence of individuals. Moreover, when
individuals come into existence, their subsistence adds nothing
to their idea or concept. Whatever grade of perfection the individual has is already contained in its concept.

405. This truth concerning the independence of the idea of an
external thing (we are speaking about the nature of the idea, not
its origin) enables us to grasp the difference between possessing
an *idea*, and *judging* that the thing of which we have the idea
really exists.

This second operation of thought is a *judgment* on the subsistence of the thing we are thinking about and as such is
entirely different from its *idea* or concept.

As we said, our *idea* of anything is equally perfect and complete whether the thing subsists or not, whether we judge of its
real existence or not, whether we make this judgment in one
way or another.

The *judgment* of a thing's subsistence supposes the *idea* of the
thing, the judgment, therefore, is not the *idea*, and does not add
anything to it.

Such a judgment forms within us only a *persuasion* of the *subsistence* of the thing we judge to exist in real mode. *Persuasion* is
only *assent*, an operation *sui generis* which must not be confused in any way with the *intuition* of the idea.

Article 3

Ideas of things never contain the subsistence of these things

406. I call the *subsistence* of anything its real, actual existence.

407. The heading of this Article is, therefore, a corollary of the preceding Article which affirmed the essential distinction between the *idea*, and the *judgment* we make on the real existence of things.

In fact, if the *idea* is complete and perfect without its containing any thought of the real, actual existence of things (cf. 399–400 [402–407]), it cannot help us in any way to know things as *subsisting*. It presents them to us only as *possible*. The subsistence of things is known by means of another operation of our spirit, called *judgment*, which is essentially different from the intuition of the idea.[3]

Article 4

The idea of being presents only simple possibility

408. 'Idea of being' does not mean the thought of some subsistent ens whose qualities, apart from actual existence, are unknown or abstract, like *x, y* and *z* in algebra. Nor does it mean *judgment* or persuasion about the subsistence even of an undetermined ens; it simply means *idea of being*, mere possibility. This is a corollary of the preceding Article.

After the last possible abstraction on an ens as thought, *possibility* remains. If we think of a subsistent ens without knowing

---

[3] I will have the opportunity to analyse the operation of judgment when I attempt to explain the origin of our idea of body.

Note: the observation I have made here about the distinction between *ideas*, and *persuasion* of the subsistence of something, confirms what I said (cf. 177) about the false teaching of those who claim that ideas *take* and *enclose* subsistent things themselves — on the contrary, ideas present only mere *possibilities* of things.

These philosophers exchange one truth for another. There is indeed a faculty in us which *grasps* and *encloses*, as it were, subsistent things. This is not the *faculty of ideas* but the faculty of *feeling* joined with the rational operation of *judgment*, a faculty totally distinct from that of intuiting ideas.

its qualities, we can still abstract from it the *persuasion* of its subsistence while retaining the thought of its possibility.

409. The most universal idea of all, therefore, which is also the last abstraction, is *possible being*; we can call it simply *idea of being*.

Article 5

We cannot think of anything without the idea of being

Demonstration

410. Although this obvious statement needs little consideration, few people have given it sufficient attention.

Modern philosophers (cf. 50–57, 278–282) have been at pains to analyse the *faculties* of the spirit, although few have analysed their *product*, that is, *human cognitions*. Faculties are known only by their effects which, therefore, must be analysed first; we examine the faculties after investigating cognitions. The opposite way is taken by Locke, Condillac and generally by those who begin by examining the faculties and then move on to cognitions.

This inversion of the process is possibly the principle source of their errors.

I have started from the effects and tried to analyse a known fact. By doing this I have endeavoured to find the cause of the fact, that is, to determine the faculties necessary for producing all human knowledge in all its parts.

411. Now the analysis of any cognitions we have always gives the same result: 'We cannot think of anything without the idea of being.'

Indeed we can have no knowledge or thought separate from the idea of being. *Existence* is the most common, universal quality of all.

Take any object you wish. First, abstract its particular qualities, then its less common qualities, then its more common qualities and so on. In the end, the last quality will be existence, by means of which you can still think something, an ens, but without its mode of existence; the object of your thought is a perfectly undetermined something, unknown as regards its qualities, an *x*. But it *is* something because existence, although undetermined, remains; it is not nothing, because nothing has no existence, not even possible existence. Either you are thinking that an ens exists, or can exist, with all the qualities necessary for its existence, although these remain unknown to you, or you are not thinking of them. Nevertheless what you are thinking is indeed an idea, although totally undetermined.

On the contrary, if you finally take away *being*, the most universal of all qualities, nothing is left in your mind; all thought has disappeared and along with it any idea of the ens.

To give an example. Let us take the concrete idea of a particular person, Maurice. Now when I take away from Maurice what is particular and individual to him, I am left with what is common to human beings. Next, by a second abstraction, I remove the human elements such as reason and freedom, and now I have a more general idea, that of an animal. Abstracting animal qualities I am left with a body that has vegetable life without sensitivity. After this I take away all physical organisation and vegetable life, fixing my attention on what is common to minerals; my idea is now that of body in general. Finally I withdraw my attention from what is proper to body; my idea is now of an ens in all its universality. But during this process of abstraction, my mind has dealt with something, and has never ceased thinking; it has always had an idea as the object of its action, although this idea has become consistently more universal until my mind arrived at the most universal of all ideas, the idea of an *ens*, undetermined by any quality known or fixed by me. I can finally think that this ens is an ens because it has *being*. Abstraction can go no further without losing every object of thought and destroying every idea in my mind. The idea of being, therefore, is the most universal idea, and remains after the last possible abstraction; without it, all thinking ceases and all other ideas are impossible.

Article 6

No other idea is necessary for the intuition of the idea of being

412. This statement is the converse of the preceding statement and follows naturally from what has been said (cf. 406).

We have seen how the idea of any ens whatsoever can be broken down, as it were: first, the particular qualities are removed, then the less common and finally the most common. After reducing it to its bare minimum, we are left only with *being* as the basis of all the other qualities and the most abstract of ideas: take this away and every other thought and idea becomes impossible. Yet this single, bare idea, revealed by our abstractions, remains in the mind as an object of contemplation. Able to be intuited and known of itself, it needs no other idea for its intuition.

This consequence is of supreme importance.

CHAPTER 3

Origin of the idea of being

413. After establishing the existence and learning the nature of the idea of being, we must now investigate its origin, that is, how it is given in our mind.

I will first indicate where it does *not* come from and then where it *does* come from.

Article 1

The idea of being does not come from bodily sensations

414. To see the truth of this statement clearly, we must examine the special characteristics of the idea of being, which are very different from anything sensations can present to us.

Because each of these characteristics is inexplicable in any system claiming to derive the idea of being from sensations, they provide an irrefutable demonstration of the invalidity of this claim.

§1. *Demonstration* 1

From *objectivity*, the first characteristic of the idea of being and its first element

415. When we think of an ens in all its universality or even of some particular ens, we are thinking of it only in itself, that is, as it is.

Its relationship with us or with anything else is not part of our thought;[4] we think of it absolutely.

---

[4] If this way of conceiving things in our mind, that is, as they are in themselves, were only apparent because their existence was in fact relative to us, the argument would still be valid. But apparent or not, we would still have to explain the fact that things seem to be perceived in themselves, objectively. On the other hand because the discussion is solely about the way we perceive

This way of perceiving things as they are in themselves, independently of any relationship with anything else, is common to everything our mind can conceive; we perceive things impartially, as it were, just as they are and with their own grades of being. The thought by which we perceive them as they are can be reduced to the following formula: 'This thing (that I conceive in my mind) has such a grade or mode of existence.' Existence, the sole term of reference of such a mental conception, is common to everything we perceive; it is also the term to which everything experienced in our feeling is related. It is equally common to all perceived things because all are perceived and conceived as entia, that is, as having existence in a certain degree or mode indicated to us, let us say, by our senses.

416. But sensations, I maintain, are incapable of making us perceive *objectively*, in the way characteristic of intellectual perception.

In fact, sensations are only particular modifications or experiences in our own make-up; what is felt exists as such only relatively to us.

Sensations, therefore, can make us feel only the relationship to us of external things (if there are any, but I am not discussing this yet), and the power they have to modify us. If we were limited to sensations alone, the *subject* of this power could never be present to us as it is in itself. Existence in itself is not felt by us because the expressions 'to exist in itself' and 'to be felt' indicate what is absolute and what is relative, opposite concepts which directly exclude one another.

In fact, the mere existence in itself of a thing does not require and imply any sensation produced in some other thing; sensation, which does not include the idea of something *existing in itself*, indicates only our experience and its term.

Sensations, therefore, cannot make us perceive a thing as it is in itself but only in relationship to us: *sensation* means simply

things, the difference between what is apparent and what is true is irrelevant. We cannot deceive ourselves about the way we conceive an object in our mind: to say 'I conceive the object in this way' means only that I conceive it in the way I do and nothing more. Whether the external thing corresponds to my concept or not, does not concern us here; I will deal with this question later. This footnote should dissipate any doubts raised by my argument in the followers of transcendental idealism.

[416]

some modification in us, while *idea* means *mental conception of something that exists*, independently of any modification or experience in another being.

The idea of being, therefore, is not given to us in any way by sensations.

Observations
The difference between sensation, sense perception, idea and intellective perception

417. To avoid confusion, we define our use of certain words:

1. *Sensation* is a modification of a feeling subject.

2. *Sense perception* is sensation (or more generally any feeling) considered in so far as it is united to a real term.

3. *Idea* is being, or ens in its possibility, intuited as object by the mind.

4. *Intellective perception* is the act by which the mind apprehends a real thing (something sensible) as object, that is, in the idea.

Sensation therefore is *subjective*, sense perception is *extra-subjective*; idea is *object*; intellective perception is *objective*.

418. It is difficult for us to separate sense perception from intellective perception because, as reasoning beings, we habitually make the second follow immediately on the first; the two are naturally linked in us and taken as one so that very accurate observation is needed to distinguish them.

419. Another reason for our extreme difficulty in separating *sensations* from *ideas* and forming an exact concept of each without confusing them, is our need for an intellective perception or an idea in order to know or reason about anything. If we have no idea of a thing, we have no information about it, we cannot think or talk about it. We see therefore that in order to know a *sensation*, think about it and discuss our thought, we need an idea or intellectual perception of a sensation, which of itself is unintelligible, an object neither of thought nor of reason.

Every time we intend to talk about sensations, therefore, we necessarily unite some idea with them. This necessity of thinking about sensations by means of an idea makes it very difficult for us to understand the need to isolate a sensation from its idea in order to gain a clear concept of it.

420. It is a fact that we particularly resist the strenuous mental effort of isolating whatever is foreign to sensation, even the idea by which we conceive it, because sensation by itself is unintelligible. This rarely perceived difficulty is found in our knowledge of material entia, or of any ens that is not an *idea*. In themselves such entia are obscure and incomprehensible; separated from ideas, they have an existence impossible for us to understand.

421. In addition to the difficulty we meet in forming a clear concept both of bodies and of sensations, there is a special difficulty connected with the concept of sensations.

Sensations, once separated from the ideas with which they are conceived, are unknown, as I said. But this fact is very hard to accept. Because sensations, as modifications felt essentially by our spirit, are always accompanied by pleasure or pain, it seems impossible for them to be unknown. This great difficulty comes precisely from what we said earlier about our habit of perceiving sensations intellectually as soon as we have them; we are entia endowed with intellect and reason, and what we feel is also apprehended intellectively.

Furthermore, even if we were to have a pure sensation without any accompanying idea — as seems to happen when we feel something without being aware of it because our mind is occupied with other things — such a sensation could not help us form an exact concept of itself because we would have neither understood it nor considered it; relative to our understanding it would not exist at all, and could not, therefore, be thought or reasoned about.

422. The concept of a sensation unaccompanied by an idea can be formed only indirectly as follows: 1. we perceive a sensation intellectually, for example, the colour red; 2. in this sensation we have joined intimately the idea and the sensation: the idea is essentially *knowledge*, the sensation something made *known*; 3. we then analyse this act of our intellectual perception, that is, we analyse our *idea of the sensation of red* and separate the *idea* that makes the *sensation* known from the *sensation* known through the idea; 4. we conclude that the *sensation*

without the *idea* can only be an *unknown entity*; it is known only through the *idea*, and by separating the idea, we have removed what makes the sensation present to our mind — in a word, we have removed the *form* of that knowledge and left only its *matter*; 5. finally we direct our attention to this *matter* and see that it is a *sensation*, a *modification* of our spirit different from external bodies which, as such, are not only *not known per se* but *not even felt*.

§2. *Demonstration 2*

From *possibility* or *ideality*, the second characteristic
of the idea of being and its second element.

423. The simple idea of being is not the *perception* of some subsistent thing (cf. 406–409), but the *intuition* of possible beings, the possibility of things.

Our sensations provide only modifications of our spirit coming from subsistent things; merely possible things have no power to act on our organs and produce sensations in them. Sensations, therefore, have nothing in common with our idea of being and cannot in any way furnish us with it.

As we saw, the same reason determines the impossibility of any *image* of the idea of being (cf. 396–397).

Observations
The connection between the two general proofs,
already given, of the inability of sensations to provide us
with the idea of being

424. The idea of being comprehends or at least implies two elements so united that the idea could not exist without either of them. These elements are: 1st. *possibility*; 2nd. *some undetermined thing* to which possibility can be referred.

Just as it is impossible to think of *anything* which is logically *impossible*, it is also impossible to think of *possibility* alone, without understanding it as the *possibility* of *something*.

Hence the idea of being, although perfectly simple and indivisible in itself, has or implies two *mental* elements, that is, elements assignable by the mind alone.

425. Examination of the nature of one of these elements (existence, or something undetermined) has provided the first demonstration; examination of the other element (possibility) has provided the second demonstration.

The first element, *existence*, or anything whatsoever in so far as it has a mode of existence, cannot be perceived by sense, which perceives a being not in so far as it *exists*, but only in so far as it *acts*. The second element, *possibility*, cannot be perceived by sense because what is merely possible cannot produce sensations: that which does not yet actually exist cannot act.

§3. *Demonstration 3*

From *simplicity*, the third characteristic of possible being

426. We must now consider *possible being* on the one hand and *sensation* on the other.

Every organic sensation, with its root in an extended organ, will be found to have some extension. On the contrary, anything *possible* intuited by the mind is perfectly *simple* and free from bodily solidity.

This characteristic of *simplicity* consists in the absence of anything material or of any likeness with matter, and in the absence of anything extended or of any likeness with extension. It is directly opposed to the nature of real sensation which cannot therefore be a source in any way of the extremely simple light of the mind.

§4. *Demonstration 4*

From *unity* or *identity*, the fourth characteristic
of possible being

427. We shall continue our comparison between *possible being* and concrete *sensations*.

[425–427]

Every concrete sensation resides in a single place, cut off from and incommunicable with other sensations. For example, the pain I feel in one of my fingers has nothing to do with a similar pain experienced by someone else in the same finger. The two sensations are separated by the limitations imposed by place and real subsistence.

On the contrary, being, or an ens which shines before the mind in a state of mere possibility, is not in one place rather than another. It can be actuated in many places if its reality is such as to occupy space; it can be multiplied indefinitely even if its nature is not subject to the limitations of place.

For example, the mind can contemplate the human body in its possibility. This possible body remains present to the mind even if its subsistence is actuated in various places, and multiplied indefinitely. *Real bodies* are multiple, while the *concept* or idea of body remains constantly one. The mind — several minds, if you wish — sees it as identical in all the infinite human bodies that can be thought of as subsisting.

The nature of real things, therefore, to which *sensations* belong, and the nature of the simple *idea* are opposed to one another. The latter cannot be found in the former, nor can it be produced by them.

§5. *Demonstrations* 5 *and* 6

From *universality* and *necessity*, the fifth and sixth characteristics of possible being

428. Every ens, considered in its logical possibility, is *universal* and *necessary*.

There is no repugnance in the thought of an indefinite number of real, subsistent entia, all in conformity with my one idea. Every idea is a light in which I can know any number of entia that subsist or will subsist in correspondence with it. Every idea therefore is universal, *infinite*.

On the other hand, every single sensation is particular: everything I feel in it is limited to that sensation. It is impossible to find the universal in sensation, or to draw the universal from it.

429. Something similar can be said about the characteristic of

necessity; what I contemplate as possible is also *necessary*, because it is impossible to think that what is possible could ever be impossible. Real sensations, however, can be or not be. They are accidental, contingent, and without any element which would prompt the mind to think of some absolute *necessity*. Consequently, the idea of being, or of possible ens, cannot be drawn from sensations.

Observation 1
Ens is the source of *a priori* knowledge

430. The two characteristics of *universality* and *necessity*, laid down by Kant and prior to him by ancient thinkers as the criteria of *a priori* knowledge (cf. 304–309, 324–326), that is, knowledge that cannot come from our senses, are not the ultimate criteria of *a priori* knowledge. They are partial criteria, derived by an exact analysis from the *idea of being*, the unique form of knowledge and the source of all *a priori* knowledge.

Observation 2
The idea of being in all its universality and all other ideas without exception possess the characteristics indicated, especially *universality* and *necessity*

431. This proposition, a corollary of what has already been said, is very helpful for making known the nature of ideas.

We have already seen that we think only *possibility* in the pure idea, which indicates nothing about the *subsistence* of things. Subsistence is proper to another faculty of the human spirit, different from that of ideas (cf. 405–406). We have also shown that the possibility of something extends to its unlimited repetition, and that it cannot be thought not to be. The characteristics of *universality* and *necessity*, therefore, are contained in that of possibility (cf. 428–429).

Consequently every idea is universal and necessary.

It is always the idea of being, clothed with determining

qualities drawn from experience, which provides us with a quantity of more or less determined ideas or *concepts*. These concepts, however, represent merely possible, non-subsistent entities.

For example, generic and specific ideas, such as the concepts of *human being, animal, tree, stone,* and so on, which do not indicate individuals in any way, are only the idea of *possible ens* clothed with the determinations and qualities common to human beings, animals, trees, stones, etc., and given to us through experience. If the idea were clothed with these ultimate qualities, (for example, if the idea of a tree were endowed with all the qualities necessary for its subsistence), it would still remain void of the act of *subsistence* itself, and therefore something possible.

All these more or less general ideas, therefore, represent merely possible entia, not real entia, and share: 1. *universality* and 2. *necessity*, the characteristics of possibility.

In fact, every idea is both *universal* in relationship to the possible, infinite individuals that can be formed on the model offered by that idea, and *necessary* for the same class of individuals because no individual of the class can exist without possessing what is presented by the idea. It would be absurd to imagine an individual in a given class without attributing to it the constitutive qualities of the same class.

Observation 3
Origin of the Platonic system of innate ideas

432. From this observation we see more clearly the origin of Plato's system of ideas.

He had noted that our ideas of things contain some *necessity* and *universality* and concluded that our ideas had to be innate because sensation offers nothing necessary and universal.

But his conclusion was too hasty. He had not discovered how to break ideas down, separating what is formal in them from what is material. Such an analysis would have revealed to him that all our ideas are indeed endowed with some *necessity* and *universality*, which however is participated *necessity* and *universality*.

If he had gone further still, he would have seen that these two admirable characteristics, *necessity* and *universality*, are drawn from a single idea, superior to all other ideas. This *one idea*, essentially containing within itself the two characteristics of *necessity* and *universality*, without drawing them from other ideas, is *being*. All generic and specific ideas are simply this one idea clothed with various determinations received as a result of the experience of our internal or external sense. If Plato had seen this, he would have discovered that:

1. All ideas are composed of two elements: *a*) an *invariable* element, common to all ideas, the idea of being, and *b*) a *variable* element, that is, the determinations added to the idea of being.

2. The part which could not come from the experience of the senses was not the ideas as a whole, but their first element, the invariable part. Consequently, only a single innate idea need be granted in the human spirit to explain the origin of all our ideas.

3. The variable part in ideas[5] could be occasioned by the senses. Hence this part need not be qualified as innate, as seems to be the case in Plato's system.

I say, 'seems to be the case' because in some places he comes near to my theory.

This observation of mine about his system will either show what is exaggerated or erroneous in the system, or at least offer a guideline (if others accept it as such) for interpreting this great philosopher more accurately than has been done so far.

§6. *Demonstrations* 7 and 8

From *immutability* and *eternity*, the seventh and eighth characteristics of possible being

433. The mind which contemplates *being*, or any *possible ens* whatsoever, cannot think of it in any other way, and thus change

---

[5] The important question whether all the possible modes and determinations of entia emanate from the idea of being alone, when perfectly comprehended, pertains to the ontological sciences.

it. It can only turn its attention from one possible ens to another. All possible entia, therefore, present themselves to the mind as *immutable*. It follows that the mind cannot think of any time in which a possible ens might not have been what it is now and always will be. The impossibility of thinking of change or limitation of time in a possible ens is what we call the *immutability* and *eternity* of the *possible ens*. These characteristics are not found in changeable, passing sensations. Sensations therefore cannot in any way enable the mind to think of them.

§7. Demonstration 9

From *undetermination*, the ninth characteristic
of possible being in all its universality and its third element

434. By analysing the idea of being in all its universality, and separating two elements within it, we have shown that it cannot come from the senses. These two elements consist of: 1. the notion of *something*; 2. the notion of the relationship of *possibility* (cf. 415–426).

Our analysis shows that the idea of being is furnished with the characteristics of *simplicity*, *identity*, *universality*, *necessity*, *immutability* and *eternity*, each of which allows us to demonstrate that the idea of being is not given to us by sensations (cf. 426–431). The same conclusion can be deduced from the third constitutive element of the idea of being in all its universality, that is, its total *undetermination*.

The arguments used hitherto are indeed valid for all ideas, and show that none of them, considered *purely* as an idea, can derive from sensations. Every idea is an ens intuited in its essence or possibility, without concrete existence (cf. 402–407), but furnished with all the characteristics we have indicated and distinguished (cf. 430–431). However, the idea of being in all in its universality provides another argument, which can be deduced from its *undetermination*.

435. A pure idea is constituted when the mind intuits an ens without reference to its *subsistence*, although the ens can have qualities which posit it in some particular *genus* and *species*.

Being in all its universality, however, is not only devoid of *subsistence*; it is also free of any differentiation and determination dependent upon *species* and *genus*. While other ideas are universal because they respond to an infinite number of equal, possible individuals, being in all its universality is even more universal because it extends to all possible *species* and *genera* without being limited by any of them.

Our real sensations cannot possess any likeness whatsoever with this kind of ideal being because they are all perfectly *determined*. Sensations are produced by real, existing things which, like their effects, must be furnished with all the particular determinations and qualities necessary for their real, actual existence.

The idea of being in all its universality and sensations are, therefore, contrary to one another and mutually exclusive. Perfect *undetermination* is essential to the idea of merely possible, universal being; perfect *determination*, without which they would lack individuation and subsistence, is essential to sensations and the agents producing them. A stone, for example, could not exist without determined form, weight, and so on. On the other hand, when we think of being in all its universality, we prescind from all such accidental and essential qualities of particular entia. The being I have in mind is not particular, but universal to the highest degree. It is, in other words, only the possibility of various entia, the possibility of infinite modes and grades of real existence which we do not enumerate, reflect on, or reach out to. Thinking of their possibility, we are in fact thinking of *existence* without reference to its *modes*, although we are satisfied that these modes, whatever they may be, will be found in really existent entia.

436. Nor can it be said that I am in possession of an *undetermined ens* if I abstract the special determinations which individuate a particular agent from the qualities perceived by the senses alone. As we have seen repeatedly, sensations enable me to perceive only what is particular and proper, without any relationship, without what is common considered as common.

Sensations, therefore, do not bring me to know sensible things as entia, that is, as existing in themselves with their own grades of existence, nor as related to the common existence in which they share. With my sense I perceive only their action upon me, their sensible quality and the effect left in my sensory make-up where particular agents are separated from one another. Moreover, each action of an agent stands on its own, separate from every other action, because sense, which cannot refer an action to anything else, cannot experience an action except in isolation, nor extend itself beyond the limits of an action. If I had only sensations of sensible entia, without simultaneously perceiving them with my understanding, and then wished to abstract everything particular from the sensations, I would find myself left with nothing at all, rather than with an undetermined ens. As the sensations and their causes vanished, I would remain bereft of everything. We have to understand this fact carefully, and consider it attentively, if we wish to form a correct idea of the human spirit and its way of acting.

But, as I said, this is extremely difficult because we never possess sensations alone (cf. 417–420). When we experience them, we perceive what is real and external with both sense and understanding. We do not analyse our *sensations*, therefore, but our *ideas* of bodies, and through abstraction find in them the existence, possibility and undetermination of ens. Although we think we find these things in pure *sensations*, they are found only in our *ideas*. We are not aware of having put them there because our understanding, as we have hinted elsewhere, perceives sensible things and all other entia in themselves, that is, in relation to being in which they all participate. This cannot be achieved by sense. Because of the outstanding importance of this truth, we shall deal with it again later.[6]

§8. *A synopsis of the proofs already stated, together with an indication of other special proofs that* a priori *knowledge cannot be deduced from sensations*

437. So far, our analysis of the idea of being has shown it to contain three inseparable elements, interconnected in such a way that one cannot be thought of without the others. These elements are: 1. *something* (ens); 2. the *possibility* of this something, of this ens; 3. *undetermination*. We have seen that none of

[6] In passing, we note that *undetermination* is the effect of our imperfect vision of being; it is not something inherent in *being itself*.

these elementary concepts, or elements of a single idea, can be proffered by sensations because they are essentially different from them, to the point of mutual exclusion. On this basis, we gave three fundamental demonstrations of the following proposition: 'The idea of ens cannot be derived from sensations' (cf. 414, 424, 433, 435). Further analysis of the first two elements, especially that of possibility, showed it to contain other characteristics, all equally impossible to be deduced from sensation (cf. 426–433). If we were to analyse possible *being* further, we would find other things incompatible with sensation, and have more proofs that this idea cannot be found in or derived from sensation.

In this case we would encounter all those particular difficulties which confronted different philosophers in their search for the origin of ideas. I discussed these difficulties in the preceding two Sections and laid out the history of the problem, that is, the difficulty of determining the origin of the idea of substance, cause, relationship, etc. Carefully examined and analysed, these ideas ultimately come down to the one difficulty of finding what is present in the idea of being from which and on which all other ideas derive and depend.[7]

However, these ideas, which have occupied the minds of philosophers, will be dealt with later when I can better demonstrate how they originate from the idea of being joined with sensible experience. For the moment I will omit these further developments of proofs which could confirm the above proposition.

Article 2

The idea of being does not come from the feeling of one's own existence

§1. *This proposition follows from what has been said*

438. If the *idea of being*, and consequently all other ideas,[8]

---

[7] The derivation arises through the different applications and uses of which the idea of ens is capable. Cf. vol. 1, 55–62, 86–96, 109–114, 134–135, 161, 180–188, 226–228, 250, 278–282, 341; this volume, 385–397.

[8] Article 1.

cannot come to us from *external sensations*, it follows that it cannot come from *feeling*, which is simply a permanent, interior sensation. Although feeling is characterised by special qualities, the arguments already employed to prove that *the idea of being* cannot come from bodily sensations are applicable to it [*App.*, no. 1].

§2. *The distinction between the feeling and the idea of* myself

439. The internal feeling of *myself*, therefore, has to be distinguished from the idea or intellectual perception of *myself*. The feeling of *myself* is simple. The idea, on the other hand, is made up of: 1. the feeling of *myself*, which is the matter of knowledge; and 2. the idea of *being*, the form to which the mind refers the feeling of *myself* and thus knows it, that is, considers *myself* as an *ens*, and thinks it objectively, as it is in itself.

Myself is subject, and as such is wholly particular, related only to itself, a real, determined ens. In order to know this subject or have an *idea* of it, I must conceive it objectively, that is, as referred to being, not to myself, just as I consider any other particular, sensible thing. Ens is, as it were, the common measure, and when I have referred what I feel to this standard, I *feel* and I *know* what I feel.

§3. *The feeling of* myself *gives me only my particular existence*[9]

440. The feeling of *myself* gives me, therefore, the sensation of my existence, but not the idea of existence in all its universality. This feeling is indeed my own existence, but not therefore the intellective perception of my existence. This arises early within me, but comes about through an act by which I consider my own feeling as an ens with the same impartiality with which I would consider anything else. Classifying myself amongst

[9] Here, *myself* expresses the proper, substantial feeling of a person, not the additions provided by reflection carried out from the moment when the human being pronounces the monosyllable 'I'.

entia, I find myself in their midst, and distinguish myself from others through the feeling of *myself* that marks me. Through the judgment made by my reason, I refer the idea of existence to this feeling.

§4. *My own feeling is innate; the intellective perception of my existence is acquired*

441. Hence, although the feeling expressed by the pronoun *myself* is innate (because I must be innate to myself), the intellective perception of myself is acquired, and cannot be confused with my subsistence nor with the feeling constituting it.

§5. *The idea of being precedes the idea of* myself

442. The universal idea of *myself* is formed through the intellective perception of my own *myself* which, in turn, is formed through the idea of being (cf. 436).

In the order of ideas, therefore, the idea of being precedes the idea of *myself*. The former is necessary for the production of the latter.

This is a corollary following immediately from what was established when we showed that the first thing understood by our intellect in any object is *being* [*App*., no. 2].

§6. *Malebranche's error was his opinion that we directly perceive ourselves intellectively without the intervention of an idea*

443. Those, therefore, who make the idea of *myself* precede the idea of *being* in all its universality, seem to fall into this error because they have confused the intellective perception of *myself*, from which the general idea of *myself* is extracted, with the feeling present in *myself*. This feeling precedes acquired ideas, which are even more necessarily preceded by the idea of being.

[441–443]

Hence, Malebranche's error when he says that our soul comes to know itself only through *feeling*, not through *idea*.

He is quite right in maintaining that feeling and idea are two different things, but fails to see that feeling, unable in itself to form a cognition, certainly cannot form an intellective perception. Malebranche simply grants the matter of some cognition, which is informed by the *idea* of being in all its universality.[10]

If we had nothing but a feeling of ourselves, we could not reason about our soul and see it as an *ens*, that is, an object of our thought.

Article 3

The idea of being does not come from Locke's reflection

§1. *Definition*

444. By *Locke's reflection* I understand the faculty by which our spirit fixes its attention on our external sensations or internal feeling (feeling includes here all the *operations* of our spirit felt by us). Such attention may be directed to the whole or any part of sensation and feeling, without however adding anything to it and creating a new object.

445. This way of explaining Locke's *reflection* is justified by comparing what he says about reflection with what he says about innate ideas, that is, I use Locke to explain himself. Indeed, his definition of reflection as 'the perception of the operations of our own mind within us, as it is employed about the ideas it has got (from the senses),'[11] is too equivocal to be of any systematic use. If it is simply the perception of the operations of our spirit on ideas given by our senses, ideas are presumed to be already formed; and because we cannot have ideas without the idea of being, this awkward *idea* must also be presumed, which is the point at issue. The difficulty has been overcome by a simple supposition, or rather has neither been seen nor faced. As a result Locke's reflection can proceed rapidly

[10] *Recherche de la vérité*, bk. 3.

[11] *An Essay concerning Human Understanding*, bk. 2, c. 1, §4.

without trouble. But let us go back and look for a moment at the difficult path it has taken.

The first *ideas* were formed from *sensation*, but Locke does not tell us how and he is in no hurry to explain; he finds it enough to say: 'Our senses do convey all these ideas into the mind,' adding as his only words of explanation: 'I mean the senses from external objects convey into the mind what produces there those perceptions.'[12] This is not a satisfactory explanation; it is not even a satisfactory description of the fact of sensation. Locke is not interested in explaining how our sense causes the act by which our spirit first perceives sensibly and then intellectively. It is as if he were saying: 'Our sense produces the act by which our spirit feels and also the act by which it understands and forms ideas; I have no intention of embarrassing myself by showing you the difference between *feeling* and *understanding*, or by seeking what is needed for understanding to follow feeling. Whatever is required for producing these two facts and the difference between them, I start from the principle that all ideas come from sensation and reflection!' — this principle is the fundamental postulate of all Locke's philosophy. He seems to be saying: 'Let me use these two words, *sensation* and *reflection*, without having to define them accurately. Let them express all the causes of ideas with any meaning necessary for doing this. So, starting from this postulate, let us list all the ideas we have and refer them all to their source, *sensation* and *reflection*.'

A genuine analysis of Locke's *Essay* shows that the preparation of such a list is the sum total of the book that has caused such a stir in the world.

446. Our analysis shows the whole question of innate ideas to have been bypassed by Locke, as he would seem to have intended, had he not introduced matter extraneous to his argument and used the whole of the first book to refute every innate idea and principle. What he says at such length in his first book, however, gives us the right to determine the sense of his *per se* equivocal and, for our purposes, inconclusive definition of reflection. If there is no innate idea or principle in the human spirit, *reflection*, without adding anything to *sensations*, can

[12] *Ibid.*, bk. 2, c.1, §3.

only fix its attention on them to discover what they contain. And, as we said when commenting on Locke's definition, this is characteristic of Locke's reflection.

§2. *Demonstration* 1

447. It is clear from what I have said that the idea of being does not come from Locke's reflection. I pointed out: 1. that the idea of being is not contained in any way in external sensations (cf. 414–436); 2. nor in our internal feeling (cf. 437–443); 3. that Locke's reflection is a faculty for observing and finding what is in our sensations or feeling without adding anything to either (cf. 444–446).

It follows, therefore, that Locke's reflection, unable to discover what is not present in our sensations or feeling, is incapable of finding the absent *idea of being*. Consequently, this idea has to come from some other source.

§3. *Demonstration* 2

448. If I show that Locke's reflection is in fact impossible, I also show that the idea of being cannot come from it. If we recall the definition (cf. 444), it is not difficult to prove that his reflection is impossible. We have seen that it is 'the faculty by which our spirit fixes its attention on the whole or parts of our external or internal sensations, without adding anything and creating a new object.' It is true our attention can be held at random by the pleasure we have in sensations, but this is not Locke's reflection, whose aim is to acquire ideas, not to experience pleasure or enjoy it more easily. His reflection is a force of our spirit directed to and fixed on a part or complex of our feelings with the intention of finding new ideas in them. But can our spirit come to reflect in this way on its internal and external sensations without already possessing the universal ideas it is looking for?

Any similar reflection purposing to analyse sensations and extract ideas from them, has to divide, compose and find similar and dissimilar parts; in a word, it has to classify. But we cannot classify anything unless we presuppose the presence of the general idea constituting the class: it is impossible to compare and know what is similar or dissimilar in two individuals without first having the abstract idea common to both of them. Without this idea we would perceive two similar individuals, two red flags for example, but we would not think or reflect at all about their similarity. The two red sensations, perceived by our sensories, would remain separate, at least in time and place, as long as they were simply sensations with different, incommunicable existence (cf. vol. 1, 180–187). Locke's reflection, therefore, is impossible. How can we reflect on our sensations for the purpose of extracting ideas from them if we have no ideas to direct our spirit or enable it to unite and analyse sensations, and to move its attention freely from reflection to sensation?

449. When our spirit has only sensations but no ideas, *instinct* enables it to concentrate on any sensation for greater pleasure. This is not reflection properly speaking, but a reinforcement of attention on the part of our senses, not of our understanding. In fact, rather than *attention* it would be better to call it *an application of instinctive, animal force*, naturally captivated by the pleasant sensation. I do not have time to take this further, but what has been said is sufficient to distinguish it from *intellectual attention*, the sole source of reflection. In passing, let me add that *sensible attention* does not differ from the feeling faculty, and could, if necessary, be called a natural actuation of this faculty.

Such attention could have caused Condillac's error: he tried to reduce *attention* to *sensation* (cf. vol. 1, 73–74). He seems unaware that attention with this meaning is of two kinds: sensitive (that is, instinctive) and intellective (that is, willed). Having overlooked this observation, he came to the conclusion that all attention could be regarded as a mode of sensation.

450. We conclude that it is impossible to conceive mentally any reflection which is 1. directed to the formation of ideas, and 2. begins to act before there are any ideas to direct and regulate it. Reflection of this kind contains contradictory elements because it requires the formation of ideas without ideas.

But if Locke's reflection is impossible and absurd, neither the idea of being nor any other idea (which will always contain the idea of being) may be derived from it. This is what I intended to demonstrate.

Article 4

The idea of being does not begin to exist in our spirit in the act of perception

§1. *Demonstration* 1
From observation of the fact.

451. Bodily sensation does not contain the idea of being (cf. 409–433), and cannot therefore offer it for our reflection, which only notes what is present in sensation without adding anything to it (cf. 444–450). We have yet to see whether the idea of being presents itself to our spirit in the act of sensation or reflection in such a way that its sudden appearance to our mind draws us to conceive and possess it.

452. Before dealing with the possibility of such an extraordinary phenomenon, we must note carefully whether it actually occurs or not.

Reid, for example, insists that he wishes simply to describe the fact of human knowledge without attempting to explain it. Having separated its parts, and taken all its circumstances into account, he has no doubt that, related to the existence of bodies, the fact is composed of three totally unconnected parts: 1. an *impression* on our bodily organs; 2. *sensation*; 3. *perception* of the existence of bodies, which follows immediately upon sensation (cf. vol. 1, 109 ss.). He believes he has observed a law of constant succession between these three occurrences: given the first, the second follows; given the second, the third follows. But, he continues, the first is unlike the second, the second unlike the third; moreover, none is connected with the other as cause and effect. Having described the fact, he now affirms that it is inexplicable and totally mysterious. This description of the perception of bodies certainly indicates his philosophical concern and effort, but we may doubt whether it is rigorous and complete. Let us examine it briefly.

453. I have no doubt that the three events are successive, and have to be distinguished from one another [*App.*, no. 3]. Reid's

account leaves no room for doubt here. I agree that the events bear no likeness to one another, and that one cannot be impressed on the other. Certainly, the *impression* made on the bodily organs is of its nature essentially different from sensation, while *sensation* has no likeness whatsoever with the *perception of ens* proper to our understanding [*App.*, no. 4]. One event cannot therefore cause another by reproducing its own impression or copy. But does this entitle us to say that the fact under consideration is entirely inexplicable and mysterious in all its parts? [*App.*, no. 5].

454. Reid maintains: given the *sensation*, I have a *perception of existing bodies*, although sensation is totally different from perception. This is inexact. Although we have seen that *existence in all its universality* is different from and opposed to *sensation* (cf. 402–429), our previous analysis of perception (cf. 411–417) shows that *intellective perception* is not totally different from sensations.[13]

I am not speaking here of the way in which a sensation takes place in us on the occasion of an external impression. That is outside our scope at present. I want to insist on the last part of the fact, that is, on the way in which the *perception of bodies* as existing things arises in the soul on the occasion of *sensations*. Reid considers this inexplicable, because he has not submitted it to sufficient analysis. Let us try to complete his work.

Thorough analysis indicates that intellective perception is not simple, like sensation, but made up of distinct parts. If it were simple, an inexplicable appearance in our souls would offer the only possibility of understanding its presence; a creation would be carried out in our spirit whenever a sensation occurred. But if it consists of different parts, it is not sufficient to declare it inexplicable. First, it should be split up into its parts; then, the relationship of the parts should be examined. Are they simultaneous or successive? How are they connected and so give rise to our perception of bodies?

I. As we have already seen, intellective perception is composed of three parts: 1. *sensation*, in which particular sensible qualities, separated from the predicate of quality and

---

[13] I include in *sensation* here what I have called *corporeal sense perception* (cf. 417, [*App.*, no. 4]).

every other abstract notion, are terms of our sensory capacities; these sensible qualities establish the sign to which our thought turns its attention; 2. *the idea of existence in all its universality*: to conceive of a body mentally as something existing means classifying it amongst existent things. This in turn presupposes the idea of existence in all its universality which forms the class, as it were, of that which exists; 3. *judgment, the relationship between sensation and the idea of existence*, in which existence, known in the idea (predicate), is attributed to the *force acting* in the sensations and drawing them together in an ens. This final act of the spirit is the proper source of the *intellective perception of bodies*. We also saw that the spirit achieves this in virtue of its perfect unity, that is, of the identity between the feeling and understanding subject. In a word, the same subject, on receiving sensations and seeing ens in them, possesses the energy to turn towards itself where it beholds what it undergoes in its feeling related to the agent whose existence it affirms. In this way it sees the thing in itself, *objectively*.

455. II. If we now ask whether these parts are of their nature simultaneous or successive, we can see that naturally and temporally they have to be found in the following order. First, the idea of being must be present; this is followed by sensation; finally, judgment, by joining the idea of being and sensation, generates the perception of the existence of bodies. Such perception is simply the application of existence (a quasi-predicate) to bodily agents which, in the self-same application, become *objects*.

It is surely obvious that no judgment can take place unless it is preceded by its two terms (subject and predicate). Moreover, careful observation of these terms of judgment will show that the idea of being must precede sensation. Most obviously of all, we see on reflection that the idea of being must be present in all our ideas, and therefore in all our judgments (cf. 405, 417). Granted that we have made a judgment or obtained an idea, it must also be granted that we have made use of the idea of existence which we must already possess.

456. Observation will clarify the matter further for those wishing to understand it better. The question, 'Does the idea of being precede sensations or not?' can only be asked about the

first judgment we make on entering this world. By noting the *essential* laws governing judgment, which must be applicable to our first judgment, we shall be in a better position to answer the question.

In every judgment made as we feel something, we think of the existence of a particular, sensible thing; this is a constitutive law of judgment. But what does 'thinking of the existence of a sensible thing' mean? It does not mean receiving, but making use of, the idea of existence. Using the idea, however, presupposes it. How can one make use of something which is non-existent?

457. Whoever takes observation as a sure guide to the presence of facts in nature will notice something relevant to our argument in the way he makes use of the information he already has about existence. He is certainly not conscious of receiving this information by suddenly passing from a state in which he does not possess it to one in which he does. He is conscious, however, of using it as something already stored in his mind when he comes to employ it on the occasion of some sensation. He is not surprised that he knows what existence is, nor has he any new awareness as he uses it. He sees it as something already familiar to him, and understood independently of other things. Careful observation of the act by which we affirm to ourselves the existence of external things shows precisely this.[14] Although in judging the existence of things we unite existence to the bodily force we feel, the idea of existence is so well-known that it escapes our attention. This, of course, makes it very difficult to observe.

It seems to me rather rash modesty, therefore, to maintain that the *perception of bodies* succeeds *sensation* in a mysterious, inexplicable manner. In saying this, the possibilities of explanation are restricted to the limits of one's own observation. But are these limits the ultimate criterion? We do not always have to believe philosophers who declare on their own authority that

---

[14] This observation did not escape the ancients. Relative to the principles of reason one very acute author notes that our mind *eis assentiat, non tamquam* DE NOVO *percipiat, sed tamquam sibi innata, et* FAMILIARIA RECOGNOSCAT [although our mind assents to them, it does not perceive them as SOMETHING NEW but as innate to itself, and ACKNOWLEDGES THEM AS FAMILIAR] (*Itiner. Mentis, etc.*, c. 3).

philosophical investigation can go no further simply because
they themselves can make no progress. I have no doubt that
there is a mystery involved in intellective perception, but it is
not to be found where Reid put it.

458. The intellective perception of bodies is only the application of an idea, that is, of some information known prior to
bodily sensations. Confirmation of this may be obtained from
the very words we use, which according to Condillac[15] are an
analysis of our thoughts. 'Perception of the existence of bodies'
includes and expresses *the idea of existence* applied to *bodies*.
The perception of the *existence of bodies* is therefore generated
by the preceding idea of *existence*, which precedes the perception and is applied on occasion of *sensations*. The resulting
object is called 'body'.

459. We may conclude: the idea of being does not begin to
exist in our spirit in the act of *perception*. Self-observation provides no awareness of any sudden presence of this idea in us, nor
of any instantaneous illumination; it tells us nothing of the
immense leap necessarily required if our spirit is to pass from
non-possession to possession of this idea; it provides no recol-
lection of a time when we did not possess it and when we did.
On the contrary, we are conscious only of the continual use
made of this idea which we have always considered as our own.

---

[15] Condillac defines languages as *analytical methods*, that is, as methods
which break down ideas. Such methods can certainly be called analytical, but
Condillac fails to see that just as every *analysis* supposes a previous *synthesis*,
so languages are first *synthetical* and secondly *analytical* methods; they first
unite and then break down. When I use a noun, for example, 'body', I unite
several ideas, all bound together in this single sign, 'body'. If I state a
proposition, for example, 'A body is possible', I break down the idea of
'body'. In fact, in this word, I already express a possible essence which I
separate out as possibility when I add 'is possible'. I have therefore the idea of
possible existence, contained in 'body' and separated out in 'possible'. 'Body'
is a synthesis, while the proposition, 'A body is possible', is an analysis.
Universally, all *nouns* are *syntheses*, and the propositions of which they form
part are *analyses*. Now, just as individual words precede propositions, which
are composed of individual words, so *synthesis* precedes *analysis*. This is true
for both vocal and purely intellectual discourses. Languages therefore are
faithful presenters of thoughts (just as they are a great help to thought) and are
not merely 'analytical' but 'synthetico-analytical' methods. This expression
embraces everything, and avoids what is partial and systematic.

We have no right, therefore, without further proof, to assert as fact the extraordinary, interior, instantaneous creation within us of an idea which bears no relationship to exterior, corporeal things.

§2. *Demonstration 2*
From absurdity

460. Let us now suppose that the idea of being did enter our mind either on the occasion of a sensation or immediately afterwards, and that we perceived the existence of bodies by applying this fortuitous idea to the bodily force felt in sensations. Such an occurrence would be a miracle: an idea unconnected with sensations and appearing to our mind is either a creation or at least a unique, isolated event, connected with nothing and without analogy in nature. This consideration would be enough to exclude the hypothesis as unnecessary, since there is an easier, more ordinary way to explain the origin of ideas.

461. Moreover, the idea of being, if created instantaneously in our soul, could result from only one of two causes: either from an ens outside us (God) producing the idea on the occasion of sensations, or from the nature of the soul itself emitting and creating the idea according to some necessary, physical law.

The first of these hypotheses is the system of the Arabs, which I refuted above; the second is Kant's system.

The Arabs said that Aristotle's acting intellect was separate from us; it was God. But Aristotle's potency, by which the ideas of things are produced in us, is simply that which presents being to us. The claim that that which makes us see ens in sensible things (in other words, the acting intellect) is God, means that God, on the occasion of sensible phantasms, makes ens appear to our mental vision.

Similarly, in the case of Kant. Although he failed to consider being in all its universality, because he was more occupied with ens clothed with certain forms, the tendency of his philosophy is entirely directed to making everything we perceive, and therefore ens, come from the intimate depth of our spirit, as

root, trunk, branches, foliage and blossom are all said to come
from a seed.

462. The supposition, made by the Arabs, that human beings
lack a complete faculty of thought and that, on the occasion of
sensations, God himself has to create in our mind the idea of
being, which makes us thinking beings, is a strange, unsupported hypothesis, unlikely to attract many followers, especially today.

463. However, is Kant's principle, any more true, that is, that
the soul is capable of drawing the idea of being from itself when
sensation occurs? Such an extraordinary occurrence would be
an emanation or creation, both of which are inexplicable and
gratuitous.

If the idea of being were indeed an emanation, it would
already be present deep in the soul and therefore innate. This
would be a kind of revelation made by the soul itself on the
occasion of sensation. In this case, the soul would not begin to
have the idea because this already pre-existed. How this emanation takes place does not concern me; what does concern me is
that we are dealing either with a pre-existing idea (this would
seem to be the real case), or with the soul as producing the idea,
an absurd hypothesis unsupported by observation.

If the idea of being is entirely different from sensation, how
can sensation give rise to it? We have to turn to the system of
pre-established harmony or of occasional causes, that is, to systems which require an agent external to nature. But this is contrary to Kant's system.

Let us suppose then that sensation cannot give the idea of
being but can move the subject in such a way that, following the
laws of its nature, the subject is drawn to see the idea immediately before it. Would we not be aware of such a change?

464. But the fallacy of the hypothesis is shown above all by
the following consideration. If the idea of being does not
pre-exist, the subject cannot produce it of itself. A subject is
particular, contingent and real, like all bodies and the sensations
deriving from them; the idea of being is universal, necessary and
possible. In a word, they are opposites: a subject is *subject*, the
idea is *object*, (cf. 415–416).

465. Let us consider this last point for a moment. *Myself,
subject*, sees the idea of being, *object*. This is the undeniable

result of observation which tells us that our mind is indeed conscious of *seeing*, but not of *producing* what it sees.

When we produce something, we are conscious of the effort made in producing it. When we simply gaze, we are conscious of not acting: the object of our vision is independent of us and has not been placed there by our eye. Similarly the idea of being stands before us as something seen, not made or produced: its essence is as independent of our spirit as a star is independent of the astronomer.

466. Finally, it is not difficult to show by means of the sublime characteristics obtained from our accurate analysis of the idea of being (cf. 414–433) that the production of this idea is beyond the strength of any finite being, even of the human mind. But I think I have said enough to prove my point. I shall return later to this second, more rigorous, demonstration.

Article 5
The idea of being is innate

§1. *Demonstration*

467. That the idea of being is innate follows from what has been said already. For:

1. if the idea is so necessary and essential to the formation of all our ideas that the faculty of thought is impossible without it (cf. 410–411);

2. if it is not found in sensations (cf. 414–439), nor extracted by reflection from internal or external sensations (cf. 438–447);

3. if it is not created by God at the moment of perception (cf. 461–462);

4. if finally its emanation from ourselves is an absurdity (cf. 463–464);

then the only possibility left is that the idea of being is innate in our soul; we are born with the vision of possible being but we advert to it only much later [*App.*, no. 6].

468. This proof by exclusion is final if no other case is possible. That there is none, is shown by the following.

The fact to be explained is the existence of the idea of being in all its universality.

If it exists, then either it was given to us by nature or produced later; there is no middle term.

If it was produced later, either we produced it or something else did; again there is no middle term. Production by us is excluded; anything else producing it must be either sensible (the action of bodies) or insensible (an intelligent *ens* different from us, God, for example, and so on), and again there is no middle term. But these two cases were also excluded.

The list of possible cases therefore is complete because it has been reduced to alternatives with a middle term excluded as absurd. But if all the cases which consider the idea of being as given to us after we come into existence are impossible, it remains that the idea of being is innate and not produced. This is what we had to prove.

§2. Why it is difficult to be aware that the idea of being is continually present to us

469. People unused to reflecting on themselves, usually make the following objection: 'How can we have the intuition of the idea of being without being aware of it, without knowing we have it or without stating it?' This constant objection was resolved by Leibniz in reply to Locke's book; it was the Achilles' heel of Locke's arguments against innate ideas. Although I have discussed it in the chapter on Leibniz's system (cf. vol. 1, 288–292), I will add a few thoughts here.

The person who makes this objection should first ask himself what happens when he thinks about something that absorbs his attention; does he simultaneously reflect on all the other ideas acquired during life and stored in his memory? Is he actually aware of having them? He would say, I believe, that he can think or talk of one thing only at a time. Yet all kinds of topics and arguments are stored in his mind, ready to be taken out when needed.

This fact implies two things:

    1. Many ideas can be in our mind without our giving them

a thought or actually being aware of them, as if they were not there at all.

2. We cannot turn from one idea to another without some act on our part by which we disregard what we are now thinking of in order to attend to what was indeed stored in our mind but lay neglected and unnoticed.

I do not need to explain here how this is possible; observation tells us it is, and this is sufficient for the present. Nor do we need to discover the nature of facts or ideas lying unnoticed in the memory — this is irrelevant. Nothing more is required than ordinary observation which attests to the two points we have noted.

But if we need a new act of attention in order to be aware of and enunciate new ideas, it follows that some ideas must remain unobserved and unnoticed in our spirit until some stimulus directs our attention to them. It is neither absurd nor strange, therefore, that the *idea of being itself* lies in our soul unobserved and unenunciated in the first moments of our existence. It cannot be otherwise, for what in fact do we observe about ourselves when we are born? So even the idea of being remains unnoticed until our reflection is stimulated to find it and contemplate it. But after reflection has sufficiently distinguished it, the idea can be enunciated and stated without hesitation.

470. This is what happens in fact. In the first moments of our existence, our spirit has nothing to excite and direct it to reflect on itself; it has no interest nor stimulus in turning inward. Indeed everything that affects our spirit draws it away from itself by directing its attention to external, sensible things. From the beginning our sense organs are struck from all directions by countless new impressions; the baby's eyes are enchanted by light, his palate and stomach cry out for nourishment; he has no interest in his spirit; he is totally unaware of his thoughts and ignorant of his nobler part. Philosophy and profound self-knowledge do not begin in the cradle, where even the body remains in great part unknown. Yet the baby has an intellect and heart as well as a body.

As the child grows, and reflection is stimulated, he begins to philosophise (philosophy is nothing but a kind of inner reflection). The philosopher's very effort to discover what takes place within him is sufficient to confirm that feelings and ideas take place unnoticed in our spirit and intellect where they do indeed exist, although we pay no attention to them nor mention them to others.

In fact, to be aware of an idea in our mind, we must not only note it attentively but be drawn to do so by some special need or curiosity, although even when stimulated in this way we do not find and determine the idea quickly, always or effortlessly. If all the ideas and events in our spirit were continually present to us, human philosophy would be a waste of time; everybody would be a philosopher or, rather, would be intimately informed about the spirit without the accurate, philosophical meditations required to ascertain what is in us. No philosopher would know more than another, nor correct another's observations, nor affirm about our spirit what a colleague had denied. To sum up, no matter how strange it may seem, observation forces us to conclude that an idea may exist in our mind without conscious advertence, awareness, affirmation or declaration on our part; we could be unaware of it and unable to affirm it to ourselves or others.

This objection, therefore, does not dissuade us from positing the idea of being as innate. It is certain that in the first moments of our existence, and for a long time after, we are unable to observe this idea because: 1. our attention lacks a reason or stimulus for concentrating interiorly on our spirit rather than on external matters, or for focusing on what is happening within when everything draws it outside; 2. our attention, even when sufficiently stimulated in early adulthood to search for what is present and taking place in our spirit, cannot easily discover this idea of pure being. If we wish to see the idea directly as it is, there is nothing to draw our attention to it; if we want to find the idea of pure being in the ideas we already have, which are ideas of bodies, a very difficult abstraction is required to isolate it from the other elements composing these ideas. We reach this idea only through a final abstraction, after all the accidents, forms and modes of being of an object have been distinguished and separated from it (cf. 408–411).

The spirit needs much practice to be sufficiently capable of prolonging a series of abstractions to the final point where it discovers the idea of being. Very few people have the ability and time to do this [*App.*, no. 7]. Many give up, abandoning the path that would lead to the discovery of the reflex idea, if only they had the courage to follow it. Kant, one of the most experienced in abstraction, stopped half-way at the forms of space and time, the twelve categories and his schemata. These, as we saw,[16] are simply somewhat general determinations, modes of the idea of being which, however, lies a little further beyond them, entirely immune from all determinations.

§3. *The theory was known by the Fathers of the Church*

471. The fact that a long time passed before the theory of being was known and acknowledged is only to be expected.

Although we use the idea in all our thoughts, we give it no attention whatsoever. Moreover, it is extremely difficult to place the idea before ourselves in all its purity and free from every addition, and then observe its strict relationship with all other ideas, whose own origin is from and through it. Indeed, as I have mentioned earlier, a thorough examination of the matter shows that all other ideas are in fact only the same idea related to the passive experiences we have in our (internal and external) senses, and generally speaking, to varyingly broad or very precise determinations such as the sensible qualities of bodies. Nevertheless this first, innate idea, this form of other ideas which enlightens all minds, was clearly seen by many noble spirits of antiquity. In particular, Christian society has for a long time held these teachings which are found in the books of its wise men.

472. In proof of this, I need quote only the following passage of a book attributed to St. Bonaventure where the author notes so well the distinction between *seeing* an idea (as the intellect does) and *considering it*, that is, turning our attention to it so that we are aware of seeing it. He applies this distinction precisely to the theory of the idea of being as the mother-idea which we use to form all other ideas although we pay attention to it only later, and with greater difficulty than to other ideas.

[16] Cf. vol. 1, 368–384.

The blindness of the intellect is extraordinary:[17] it does not *consider* the very first thing *it sees* and without which it cannot know anything else. Just as our eye, when noting differences of colour, does not see the light by which it sees the differences,[18] or if it does, does not advert to it, so the eye of our mind, intent on particular and universal entia,[19] does not see ENS ITSELF OUTSIDE EVERY GENUS. But this ens comes to our mind before all other things, which come to our mind through it, although our mind does not advert to it. Thus, we can very truly say that the eye of our mind relative to the most obvious things of nature is like the eye of a bat relative to light.[20]

---

[17] Our intellect needs to reflect on itself in order to be aware of what it sees. This arises from the limited nature itself of the human intellect. The fall of humankind however made our spirit inert and sluggish in turning back on itself, and uncertain in its reflections. This defect is fittingly called 'blindness'.

[18] When I discussed Aristotle's teaching, I showed how he had come to know that the human understanding, although without any *knowledge*, nevertheless had to have an innate *light* which made it capable of illuminating sensible things and *knowing them*. If we wish to keep to the path of Aristotle's thought and move forward in his line of reasoning, we simply have to explain in appropriate terms the meaning of that mysterious, innate *light*. I myself began the investigation at the point where Aristotle had left it. I was convinced that the light could only be the *idea of being* in all its universality. I showed that this idea is the true light of the mind by which all sensible things are illuminated, that is, are perceived and known (cf. vol. 1, 262–275). This very thing was taught six centuries ago and presented as free from all doubt.

[19] *Universal entia*, that is, *genera* and *species*. Being, however, is the *most universal* idea, and very fittingly said to be 'outside every genus', because the idea of being has no difference or determination of any kind, which constitutes it as a kind of special *genus*.

[20] *Mira igitur est caecitas intellectus, qui non* considerat *illud quod prius* videt, *et sine quo nihil potest cognoscere. Sed sicut oculus intentus in varias colorum differentias, lumen, per quod videt caetera, non videt, et si videt, non tamen advertit; sic oculus mentis nostrae intentus in ista entia particularia et universalia, IPSUM ESSE EXTRA OMNE GENUS, licet primo occurrat menti, et per ipsum alia, tamen non advertit. Unde verissime apparet, quod sicut oculus vespertilionis se habet ad lucem, ita se habet oculus mentis nostrae ad manifestissima naturae* (Itiner. Mentis in Deum, c. 5).

PART TWO

Origin of all ideas in general through the idea of being

CHAPTER 1
Given the idea of being, the origin of other ideas is explained by analysis of their elements

Article 1

The link with what has been said above

473. In explaining the origin of acquired ideas through the idea of being which is not acquired but bestowed by nature, I have not been guilty of empty theorising. My first step has enabled me to prove the existence of this one idea, which can now serve to explain all others.[21] Because all ideas are derived from the single idea of being, I now have to show that, granted this idea, all other ideas are readily explained.

[21] Newton notes that two conditions are necessary if a hypothesis is to explain facts: 1. the thing assumed to be the cause of the facts really exists, and is not itself a hypothesis; 2. this thing is *capable* of producing the facts it is intended to explain.
In addition to Newton's two conditions, my own way of explaining the origin of ideas fulfils a third condition enabling it to be classed as solid theory rather than hypothesis. Not only do I prove that the idea of being exists with its *capacity* for generating all other ideas, but I also show that it does in fact generate them. Careful analysis demonstrates that the *formal* part of ideas consists only in the idea of being. But while I prove that this idea is the (formal) *cause* of all other ideas, I also show that this cause is a *fact*. My teaching on the origin of ideas can therefore claim a place amongst the rigorous sciences.

Observation itself tends to indicate the idea of being in all its universality as the source of other ideas. Of all ideas it is the simplest and, as we have seen, the least innate element that can be admitted if we wish to explain the origin of ideas (cf. 368 ss.).

Article 2

Analysis of all acquired ideas

474. A careful analysis of our ideas has led us to the following conclusions:

1. All contain essentially the mental conception of being in such a way that we can have no idea of anything without first conceiving *possible existence* (cf. 408–409), which constitutes the *formal, a priori* part of our knowledge (cf. 304–309, 325–327).

2. If an idea contains something other than the mental conception of being, this can only be a *mode of being*. It follows that any idea whatsoever is either ens, conceived regardless of mode, or ens more or less determined by its modes. The determination forms *a posteriori* knowledge or the *matter* of knowledge.

Article 3

A twofold cause is needed to explain form and matter, the two elements of all acquired ideas

475. In order to explain the origin of ideas, two things have to be accounted for: 1. the mental conception of ens; 2. the different determinations of which ens is susceptible.

Article 4

The twofold cause of acquired ideas is the idea of being and sensation

476. Having shown that the mental conception of *being* is

naturally innate in our spirit, there is no difficulty[22] in indicating *sense* as the source of the determinations of being.

Let us imagine that we have to explain how we think of a corporeal ens of a given size, form and colour — a football, for instance. When I think of a football, I think two things in my idea: 1. something that can *exist*, because I could never think a football without thinking at the same time some possibly existing thing; 2. something possessing a given size, weight and shape. Granted I have the idea of possible existence, what have I to do now to explain the way in which I begin to think this football? I have to show how intuited, possible ens is determined by means of weight, shape, size, colour and so on.

This is not difficult; it is clear that such determinations of ens are suggested to my spirit by the exterior senses which perceive them, and that I remember what I have perceived.

Article 5

St. Thomas' teaching on the cause of our ideas

477. St. Thomas is far from declaring *sense* alone as the cause of human cognitions. He too distinguishes between the *material* and *formal* cause of ideas. He grants that sense is the *matter of their cause* but makes the intellect the quality of being truly their *formal cause*:

> We cannot say that sensible knowledge is the perfect and *total cause* of intellectual knowledge; rather it is in a certain way the MATTER OF THE CAUSE.[23]

[22] Part One. — St. Thomas also says: 'The intellective soul remains in potency to the DETERMINED likenesses of knowable things (that is, the natures of sensible things). These determined natures of sensible things present us with PHANTASMS' (*Contra Gentiles*, II, 77).
According to me, *sensations* proffer the determinations of things present; *images*, those of things not present. In St. Thomas, 'phantasms' refer to both.

[23] *Non potest dici, quod sensibilis cognitio sit totalis et perfecta causa intellectualis cognitionis, sed magis quodammodo est* MATERIA CAUSAE (*S. T.*, I, q. 84, art. 4). In St. Thomas' system, *sense* is only a secondary agent in the formation of ideas, not the principal agent. His actual words are: *In receptione qua intellectus possibilis species rerum* (that is, ideas) *accipit a*

Article 6

The true interpretation of the scholastic dictum: 'There is
nothing in the intellect that did not first exist in sense'

478. According to St. Thomas's teaching, therefore (cf. 477),
sense provides only the *matter* of human cognitions; the second
element, *form*, depends upon the intellect. Hence, to interpret
the scholastic dictum, 'There is nothing in the intellect that was
not first in sense', as though it meant that sense were the only
source of human cognitions, is to misunderstand the saying.
This is the error of modern sensists. The authentic meaning of
the saying, as it must have been understood by the great scholastics, could only have been: 'Everything *material* in human
cognitions has its source in sense.'[24] I have already explained

phantasmatibus, se habent phantasmata ut agens instrumentale et
SECUNDARIUM, *intellectus vero agens ut agens* PRINCIPALE ET PRIMUM
[When the possible intellect receives from the phantasms the species of
things (that is, ideas), the phantasms are considered the SECONDARY,
instrumental agent, and the acting intellect, the FIRST, PRINCIPAL agent] (*De
verit.*, q. 10, art. 6, ad 7). Like St. Thomas, the author of the *Itinerary of a Soul
to God* also recognises a double cause of ideas and clearly distinguishes them:
*Non solum habet (memoria) ab exteriori formari per phantasmata, verum
etiam a superiori suspiciendo et* IN SE HABENDO *simplices formas quae non
possunt introire per portas sensuum et sensibilium phantasias* [Not only has
the memory to be formed from outside by means of phantasms, but also
from above by its reception and POSSESSION of simple forms which cannot
enter through the doors of the senses and the phantasies of sensible things]
(*Itin. mentis in Deum*, 3).

[24] Nevertheless, 'sense' remains insufficient when understood solely as
'external sense' (the five sense organs). It must also be understood as the
internal feeling which the soul has of itself. In fact, how could we form ideas
of an intellective being and its operations unless they were supplied by the
feeling of ourselves? St. Thomas teaches this expressly in his *Contra Gentiles*:
'We could not know, either by demonstration or by faith, that separated
substances were intellectual substances unless our soul first knew from itself
what an intellectual ens is. We must begin from a principle, from knowledge
of the understanding in our soul, if we are to arrive at what we know about
separated substances' (bk. 3, c. 46). According to St. Thomas, therefore, two
sources supply us with the *matter* of our cognitions in this life: 1. our
external senses; 2. the internal feeling of ourselves.

For him, sensation and reflection are in no way the source of knowledge (as
Locke claimed), but solely the source of the material part of our knowledge.
St. Thomas derives his teaching from St. Augustine (cf. St. Thomas, *loc. cit.*).

what is to be understood by 'everything material' when I said that in all our ideas we think: 1. being, as the *formal* element of ideas; and 2. a *determined mode* of being as their *material* element. The meaning of the scholastic dictum, therefore, must be: 'The intellect cannot think a determined *mode* of ens unless it is administered to it by sense.'

479. As long as we think undetermined being alone, we are not thinking anything that subsists or merits to be called 'real thing'. All knowledge of what is real is suggested by the senses; *subsistence* determines being in such a way that it can rightly be called *real thing*.

The teaching is clearly ancient, and assured by a long, respectable tradition.

[479]

Another way of explaining the origin of acquired ideas: through the formation of human reason

Article 1

The idea of being present to our spirit forms our intellect and human reason

480. We receive the *matter* of our cognitions from sensations (cf. 476). This *matter* is not of itself knowledge, but becomes such when *form*, being, is added to it. This means that our spirit, simultaneously sensitive and intellective, considers what it feels with its sense in relationship to being which it sees with its intellect and then discovers in what it feels something (an ens) that acts upon it.

481. We have defined *intellect* as the faculty of seeing undetermined being, and *reason* as the faculty of reasoning and hence primarily of applying being to sensations. Reason sees ens determined to a *mode* offered by the sensations, and unites *form* to the *matter* of cognitions. But if *being* is the essential object of both intellect and reason, these two faculties (intellect and reason) can exist in us only through our permanent vision of being.

482. *Being* as object, therefore, draws our spirit to that essential act we call *intellect*, making it capable of beholding being itself in relationship to the particular modes provided by sensations. We call this capability, *reason*. In a word, the idea of being joined to our spirit is that which forms our *intellect* and our *reason*; it makes us intelligent entia, rational animals.

Article 2

The teaching of St. Thomas and St. Bonaventure about the formation of intellect and reason

483. I believe that the teachings which St. Thomas and St.

Bonaventure derived from ancient tradition agree with what I have said so far.

St. Thomas, it seems to me, clearly knew that intelligence was simply the power to see being. In other words, he knew that being forms intelligence, for he states expressly that the proper object of the intellect is ens or common truth: *objectum intellectus est ens, vel verum commune.*[25]

St. Thomas teaches that the object determines the faculty. *Ens* therefore must be the constitutive element of the intellective faculty.

Again we note that St. Thomas did not neglect in any way the analysis of ideas, an analysis which showed him how the first thing we conceive in any idea whatsoever is *ens* which, therefore, he calls the *first intelligible thing.*

484. Here, we must look at my argument, based on the teaching of the great doctor.

St. Thomas describes the *form* of a thing as the element which can be mentally discerned in the thing. By means of this element the thing is in act at its first moment.[26]

If *ens* is the first thing our intellect understands in any of its intellections, we have to say that we understand nothing prior to seeing ens in a thing; intellection does not yet exist for us. On the other hand, as soon as we have understood ens in anything whatsoever, intellection is in act; we have already understood something. Ens is therefore the form of intellective knowledge because from the first moment it posits knowledge in act, that is, makes it exist.

Now, if the intellect is the faculty of positing the *form* of cognitions, and this *form* can only be *ens* (as St. Thomas teaches), the first thing seen by the intellect, the first thing that puts it into act, must be the idea of ens which *forms* human intelligence.[27]

[25] *S.T.*, q. 55, art. 1. — He says 'ens', I say 'being'. I do not think it necessary to explain the difference between these two words. It is sufficient to note that the ancients often used one for the other.

[26] The scholastics define form as: *Quod in unaquaque re primo agit* [that which acts first in anything whatsoever].

[27] Aristotle calls the intellect *species specierum* [the species of species]. The commentators who were keen to remove all suspicion of innate things from the minds of Aristotle's readers, readily interpret the Aristotelian expression

485. The author of the *Itinerary* came to the same truth. He teaches that '*being* is that which first occurs in the mind; this being is pure act',[28] because it posits the mind in act, that is, informs it.

Because being, present in the mind, is truth, he says with St. Augustine: 'The mind is formed by truth.'[29]

Article 3

Corollary: all acquired ideas depend upon the innate idea of being

486. All philosophers agree that ideas belong to our faculty of knowledge. But this faculty receives its existence from the union of the idea of being with our spirit (cf. 470–485).[30] Therefore, the idea of being, the principle of the faculty of knowledge, is also the principle of all the ideas acquired by this faculty — which is what we had to prove.

as meaning the kind of intellect which is a *habit of principles* and acquired. I do not wish to become involved in a philological question, but will simply observe that the phrase, 'the species of species', would be very suitable to describe the *idea of being in all its universality*. This most universal idea itself presents all others to our spirit.

[28] *ESSE igitur est quod primo cadit in intellectum, et illud esse est quod est purus actus.* The explanation, according to Bonaventure, is the clear fact of the matter: *Si non ens non potest intelligi nisi per ENS* (*Itin. mentis etc.*, c. 5).

[29] *Cum ipsa mens nostra IMMEDIATE AB IPSA VERITATE FORMETUR* etc. (*Itin. mentis etc.*, c. 5). This teaching is repeated almost word for word from Christian antiquity. St. Augustine says precisely that the human mind *nulla substantia interposita, ab IPSA FORMATUR VERITATE* [IS FORMED by TRUTH, without the mediation of any substance] (cf. the Book of 83 Questions, q. 61). In Section Six I will show that the *idea of being in all its universality* is precisely that which everyone calls *truth*; human intelligence is created by union with it.

[30] The way in which the idea of being in all its universality adheres to our spirit will be explained later (cf. 534–535).

CHAPTER 3

Third way of explaining the origin of acquired ideas in general: by the potencies that produce them

Article 1
Reflection

487. I have said that *reflection*, which can produce ideas, differs from sense-instinct, found also in irrational animals as the means by which the animal responds to sensations with its potency of feeling, seeking and concentrating on a pleasant sensation so as to enjoy it fully (cf. 448–450).

Reflection is a function of *reason* and differs from simple *perception*[31] in the following way.

Perception is limited to the *object perceived* and does not go beyond it; in so far as I *perceive* a thing, I know nothing outside it. In *reflection* however I direct my attention to things *perceived*. As a result my reflection is not limited to the object of a single perception; it can review many perceptions at once and make a single object of several objects and their relationships. Relative to *perception*, *reflection* is *general*, because it is not limited to any number of perceptions for its object; *perception*, relative to its corresponding *reflection*, is *particular*. Hence *reflection* could be called a *general perception*, a *perception of many perceptions*. Therefore when I *reflect*, I act at a higher level than when I perceive. From this vantage point I observe the objects below me as I contemplate, compare, join or separate my different perceptions, creating natural or even absurd compositions as I like.[32] I am reflecting when I turn my attention to

[31] I recognise two kinds of *perception*: *sense perception* and *intellective*. [Cf. *App.*, nos. 3, 4, 5].

[32] We can say that all this teaching is contained in the following passage of St. Thomas Aquinas: *Intellectus enim* UNICA VIRTUTE *cognosit omnia quae pars sensitiva diversis potentiis apprehendit* (perceives), *et etiam* ALIA MULTA; *intellectus etiam quanto fuerit altior* (that is, the higher the reflection), *tanto* ALIQUO UNO *plura coognoscere potest, ad quae cognoscenda intellectus*

the ideas in my mind and say to myself: 'I have some cognitions', and then reason about them, put them in some order, deduce one from the other, and so on.

488. If I concentrated on only one of my ideas, would I be *reflecting*? We must distinguish. If I have some definite *end* for concentrating on that idea, my concentration is an act of *reflection*. However, such a case is contrary to the hypothesis which says: 'If I concentrate on only one idea.' When I concentrate for some end, I am no longer concentrating on one idea because the idea of the end is also present: I am considering both the idea on which I concentrate and the end to which the idea is directed. I am considering the idea and its *relationship* with the end.

On the other hand, if I concentrate on the idea involuntarily, captivated by the pleasurable action of its light in the same way that sense-pleasure delights and instinctively captures the activity of my feeling, then my concentration is not *reflection*, but simply direct *attention* drawn to and held naturally in a more intense act. This *heightening* of activity must be carefully distinguished from *reflection*.

'*Reflection* therefore is *voluntary attention* to our concepts,' an attention governed by an end, which supposes an intellective ens capable of knowing and pursuing a purpose (cf. 73–74).

489. *Reflection* therefore enables us to form *ideas of relationship*, grouping them together (synthesis) or dividing them (analysis). When I use *reflection* to analyse an idea, separating what is *common* from what is *proper* in it, I am carrying out an *abstraction*. All these actions are functions of reflection.

---

inferior (a lower reflection) *non pertingit nisi per multa* [The intellect knows WITH A SINGLE POWER everything that the sensitive part apprehends (perceives) with its different powers. The intellect also knows MANY OTHER THINGS. The higher the intellection (the higher the reflection), the more the intellect can know many things WITH ONE INTELLECTION. A lower intellection (a lower reflection) would know these things only through many things] (*C. Gentiles*, I, q. 31).

Article 2

Universalisation and abstraction

490. *Abstraction* is quite different from *universalisation* and many errors have been caused by confusing them. In *abstraction*, something is subtracted from knowledge, for example, its particular characteristics; in *universalisation*, something is added [*App.*, no. 8], and knowledge is universalised. Subtraction and addition are opposites.

491. In *universalisation* we add *universality* (*intentio universalitatis*, to use the scholastic expression) which, as I have shown, is only the *possibility* of the thing (cf. 418–419). A precise description of universalisation would be: I receive a sensation; I add the idea of an ens that is causing the sensation (*intellective perception*); I consider this ens as possible; it is therefore universalised (*pure idea*). For example, let us suppose the ens is a dove. When I universalise the dove acting on my senses, I certainly do not remove anything from it: while I still have a vivid image of the dove before me with all its physical features clearly defined, I can add the possibility of other real doves corresponding in every detail to that phantasm. My representation of the dove is universal although it has remained entirely as it was before I universalised it. It has both the essential and the accidental characteristics of doves; only the reality is missing.

492. But if I had mentally taken away its colour, shape, movement, in fact, all its accidental qualities, replacing them with only what is essential to the genus dove, I would have also carried out an *abstraction*. My representation of the bird would be pure, abstract thought; it would be incomplete, imperfect and deficient.

493. Bearing in mind this distinction between *universalisation* and *abstraction*, we can say that all ideas are *universal* but not *abstract*. It is helpful to keep this distinction clear so that we may distinguish ideas which, because of their affinity, can be easily confused.

Observation 1
Why the faculty of *abstraction* has been confused
with the faculty of *universalisation*

494. The reason for the confusion is that in every *universalisation* we set aside our judgment on the *subsistence* of the thing; this resembles *abstraction*.

495. However I think it is clearer not to use the word *abstraction* in this sense, because universalisation does not take anything away from the representation. It will help if I clarify the matter further.

The difference between the *idea* of a thing and *judgment* on its subsistence (cf. 402–407) has been pointed out: I can have the full idea of a thing without judging that it subsists. But when I judge that a thing subsists, I have at the same time the *idea* of it, and the *judgment* of its subsistence. The *idea* of the thing accompanied by the *judgment* is what I call *intellectual perception* of the thing (cf. 417).[33]

Intellectual perception certainly requires the *idea* of a thing but it also determines and fixes the idea on an individual actually felt. The idea, applied to something felt, *illuminates* it [*App.*, no. 9], enabling the perception within it of an ens which we call 'body'.

If we consider the *idea* alone (one of the elements of *perception*), we see that it is *universal*; this *universality*, considered as an element of *perception*, exists in the idea. But the *universality*

---

[33] The distinction between these two mental operations, *idea* and *judgment*, did not escape the great St. Thomas. In the following passage, where he makes the distinction, he calls *knowledge* what I call *perception*, and *apprehension* what I call *idea*: Ad cognitionem duo concurrere oportet, scilicet APPREHENSIONEM, et JUDICIUM de re apprehensa [Two things are necessary for knowledge: APPREHENSION, and JUDGMENT of the thing apprehended] (*De Veritate*, q. 10, art. 8). Whenever I can, I very happily quote similar passages, from Aquinas and others. In the present work, it is often sufficient to express the teachings of antiquity in contemporary language. Furthermore, St. Thomas' use of 'judgment' refers not only to subsistent things but to anything which is affirmed as such after it has been perceived. The *word* in our mind also has this extension of meaning because everything we affirm is considered an *ens*, according to the law to which, as we saw, our mind is subject.

lies unnoticed in perception because it is considered in its relationship to the particular thing perceived by sense.

When I detach an *idea* from complete perception in order to consider it by itself, I seem to have abstracted it because I have removed its bond with the image and with the real thing; I have dismissed the *subsistence* of the thing. In this action, as I have said, there is apparently a kind of abstraction which could be called *abstraction from subsistence* or judgment.

When, in *intellectual perception*, I separate judgment about subsistence from an idea and retain only the idea, I do not remove the core, as it were, of the idea but only those things that are not its own and adhere to it without forming its nature. The persuasion of the subsistence of the thing represented by the idea is not the idea nor anything belonging to it. So the idea itself does not undergo the slightest abstraction or change; it remains just what it was when joined with the persuasion of the subsistence of the thing.

Strictly speaking, therefore, *abstraction* has not taken place; what abstraction there was concerned only the *intellectual perception* and not the *idea*, a part of the perception. If we wish to keep the word *abstraction* in this case, we must say that the idea was obtained by an abstraction carried out on the perception.

496. Again, if nothing is abstracted from the idea which is an element of intellective perception, the nature of the idea does not change when considered separately. If it is universal when contemplated separately from the perception, it was also universal in the perception, and not universalised through abstraction. Universalisation took place at the moment of the intellectual perception before the apparent abstraction (cf. 90–97).

497. This process, inappropriately called *abstraction*, concerns the *perception*, not the *idea*. In it the following three steps must be noted:

1. Corporeal *sensation*, phantasm, sense perception.

2. *Union* of what is felt corporeally with the idea of being in all its universality; this takes place in our own unity, as thinking subjects (intellective perception); thus: a) a *judgment* about the subsistence and b) the intuition of the particular ens or *idea* of the thing, take place in intellective perception simultaneously and with one operation.

3. *Abstraction*, or separation of the *judgment* from the *idea*, which gives the pure idea alone. Although the idea was *universal* from the first moment of its existence in the perception, it was considered still bound to the subsisting individual; dissolved from this bond, it stands alone in its universality.

498. *Universalisation* therefore is the faculty that produces ideas,[34] while *abstraction* is a faculty that changes their form and mode of being.

Observation 2
Universalisation produces *species*, abstraction *genera*

499. The whole of the ancient world classified things in two ways, as *genera* and *species*. Such a universal consensus suggests that the classification was not arbitrary but followed a distinction actually found in the faculties of the human spirit. This is in fact the case; close investigation shows that *species* and *genera* correspond to the faculties of *universalisation* and *abstraction*. The faculty of *universalisation*, which is the faculty of forming *ideas*, is the faculty relative to *species* (hence *species* are also called *ideas*);[35] to form *genera*, the faculty of *abstraction* is also needed.

[34] Note how all the greatest philosophers of antiquity were aware that human *knowledge* is simply *universal* apprehension. Both Plato and Aristotle expressly say this in many places. In the *Metaphysics*, for example, Aristotle says, *Quatenus universale quid est, eatenus omnia cognoscimus* [In so far as there is something universal, we know all things] (bk. 3, less. 9). St. Thomas comments, *Sic igitur scientia de rebus singularibus non habetur nisi in quantum sciuntur universalia* [Knowledge of individual things is totally dependent on their being known universally]. We must therefore have something universal in us, if we are to know individual things. This explains why, in full agreement with antiquity, I make the faculty of *universalisation* the source of knowledge.

[35] Originally 'species' meant 'aspect', 'something seen', 'representation', 'idea', etc., but it came to mean certain classes of things because every *idea*, being universal, is the foundation of a class.

Observation 3
Plato's theory on *genera* and *species*

500. We now have the key to understanding an important theory of Plato on *ideas*. We must note that *ideas*, which he understood to be substances separated from things and subsistent in themselves, were *species* and not *genera* [*App.*, no. 10]. This makes me suspect that he had some notion of the difference between *universalisation* and *abstraction*.

Plato included *types* of individual things among his *ideas*. Now the type according to which a craftsman, for example, models his product must be complete in all its parts (cf. 398–401): it must have not only what is essential but also all the accidents due to it. The accidents may vary, but the product must have at least some of them —were the craftsman to have only the idea of an abstract thing without being able to add anything to it mentally, he could never produce it in reality.

501. But such an explanation would still not be enough for a proper understanding of Plato's *ideas* or for forming a true concept of the nature of *species*. We have to know more than that. Plato noticed that every ens in this universe is capable of greater or less perfection; he said that we can mentally assign to any ens its final and complete perfection, or at least that it is not absurd for us to be able to do that. Every ens, therefore, has a *concept* that can represent it in its full, natural perfection without defect. For Plato there could be only *one* such full and absolute *concept*; no ens could be thought of as having its final perfection except in one way only. This sort of intellectual *optimism* does in fact seem probable. However, leaving aside an investigation into the truth of the matter, which is the subject of ontology, I offer the following consideration.

If an ens has two forms of natural perfection, it has two *primal concepts*, two types, two ideas, which form two *species* of things. In this sense, the opinion that the individual of a species has only one form of natural perfection is true; if it had two, it would be two species or would belong to two *species*. All the *ideas* then that represent some defective ens are reduced to this *idea* of the ens that constitutes its ideal perfection; they are all the same idea more or less deficient and imperfect.

502. If a craftsman had in his mind the perfect idea of the product, he could produce a perfect work from it, and produce imperfect objects even more easily, since these are relative to the perfect idea, as everything imperfect is relative to its perfect form.

503. We can now see how the *species* of a thing originates. It is constituted by the most perfect idea, which contains all the accidents of the thing. This idea, being the type of perfection, requires and determines these accidents because, from among all accidents, they are demanded by its perfection. However, the idea also has an infinite number of other ideas subject to it, which represent the ens in its various states of imperfection without forming a new *species*. They are not truly other *ideas*, but the most perfect idea without some part or endowment which lessens but does not change it.

Article 3

Synthesis of ideas

504. Besides the faculties mentioned above, we also have the power to devote our attention to several ideas at once and reduce them to unity by means of their relationships. This means that we can form *composite ideas*.

CHAPTER 4

Fourth way of explaining the origin of acquired ideas in general: by means of a summary classification of the ideas themselves

Article 1

Classification of our intellections

505. I define *intellection* as every act of the mind terminating only in an idea, or in an idea joined to something else, or forming a mode of an idea.

506. All our intellections are classified as follows:

I. *Intellective perceptions.*
II. *Ideas* properly so-called.
III. *Modes of ideas.*[36]

Intellective perception is the judgment I make persuading me of the *subsistence* of something (cf. 491). It springs from two elements, *judgment* on the subsistence of the thing, and the *idea* of the thing.

507. It will be helpful if we distinguish *modes of ideas* from *ideas*, retaining the word *idea* for the *complete species*, as Plato did (cf. 501) [*App.*, no. 11] and the phrase *modes of ideas* for *abstractions* and *composite* ideas.

508. Normally, however, these modes are also called ideas, whether *abstract* or *composite*. Thus there would be three classes of ideas: 1. ideas properly so-called; 2. abstract ideas; and 3. composite ideas. In this case, the sources of the three classes are the three faculties already listed: the faculty of *universalisation*, which produces *ideas* properly so-called, one of which is the perfect idea (cf. 503); the faculty of *abstraction*, which produces

---

[36] *Memory* and *imagination* form part of these intellections. Memory is concerned with past intellections, the imagination with intellections formed in the likeness of others already experienced. But examining them here would complicate matters.

abstract ideas; and the faculty of *synthesis of ideas,* which produces *composite ideas.*

509. However, *abstract* and *composite ideas* do not contain
more than *full ideas* (cf. 507). All three kinds of ideas are distinguished only by the different way in which our mental attention
focuses upon them. Ideas are *full*[37] if we think of them as they
first show themselves; *abstract* when we consider any part of
them, disregarding other parts (abstraction, analysis); *composite*
when they are considered as joined to other ideas (synthesis).
These names indicate three *modes* of intellectual attention, and
hence three *modes* of ideas which are objects of attention; but
strictly speaking, they do not indicate three classes of *ideas.*

Article 2
The difficulty lies in explaining
the three listed classes of intellections

510. Our mind carries out three successive operations: 1. it
perceives intellectually; 2. it separates the idea from the perception; 3. it draws abstracts from ideas, that is, the bonds which
unite ideas and produce composite ideas.[38] The first operation is
carried out by means of *universalisation,* the second by an
abstraction exercised on the perceptions, the third by an *abstraction exercised on ideas* already formed.

511. No faculty of *reflection* [*App.,* no. 12] is necessary for
universalisation. Universalisation is a direct, natural action of
our spirit which, abandoning the judgment on subsistence that
forms part of perception, retains the *determined idea,* that is,
the union between what is felt and the idea of being, brought
about by the unity of the sentient subject intuiting the idea of

---

[37] *When first generated,* the ideas of things are *full species* (that is, they
possess all the substantial and accidental constitutives of things), but they are
not *perfect species* because they are not produced by perfect things. Species
are perfected by another operation of the spirit which I call *integration.*

[38] Composite ideas are brought about by *reflection* after the formation of
abstract ideas. After explaining *reflection* and *abstract* ideas, it is not difficult
to understand how *composite* ideas come about, and hence unnecessary to
explain them further at this point.

being. The determinable idea of being and the thing felt that
determines the idea happen to find themselves together in the
same subject and are joined by identity, as it were, of place.

512. *Abstraction* on the contrary is an operation belonging to
the faculty of *reflection*. It is clear that I cannot abstract anything from my perception unless I turn back on it, just as I cannot abstract anything from my idea until I consider it
reflectively.

513. The *primal synthesis* containing *universalisation* is not
deliberately thought out, although it is bound up with an external element. It is carried out, or at least helped, by an alert
understanding inserted in human beings by nature. It is as
though the human being, through his essential understanding of
being, had an eye open to everything passing before him. In this
case, it is not difficult to understand that, given sensations, the
primal synthesis is achieved spontaneously by the soul which,
relative to the synthesis, is already active by its own power.
There is no need for me to explain how the spirit moves towards
universalisation once its first, essential activity has been demonstrated and established. It would be like explaining at length
how the sun illuminates an object on which it shines when it is
already known that the sun radiates light continually on everything around. But it is still necessary for me to describe universalisation accurately, and analyse it into all its parts.

Abstraction, on the contrary, is an act of reflection, which is a
faculty dependent on the will and of itself remains motionless
until activated by the will. We have to find, therefore, a *sufficient
reason* to explain the will's desire to reflect upon perceptions
and ideas, to abstract ideas from perceptions, and to draw
abstract ideas from ideas. Lack of a sufficient reason for the
movement towards reflection would leave unexplained the acts
of the faculties, the origin of *abstract* ideas, and the *composite*
ideas springing from them.

In attempting the explanation, we suppose that *perceptions*
are already formed. But we shall come back to them later, and
show how they can be brought about by means of the primal
synthesis.

Article 3

In forming abstracts, our intelligence needs
language as a stimulus

514. Our reasoning faculty has no energy of itself independently of external stimuli. This truth can be shown from experience, and from the nature of human intelligence.

> If we were left solely to ourselves and to the internal forces arising from our nature, without our being affected in any way by forces foreign to us, we would be incapable of activating ourselves or carrying out any intellective operation. If the Almighty were to keep us in this state of isolation from other entia for thousands of years, we would remain motionless without a single thought. We would be totally at rest, with inactive minds, because stimuli and terms would be lacking; our life could be compared only to non-existence. This kind of life, may I say in passing, is a worthy object of philosophical consideration, and a key for explaining marvellous secrets in the study of human beings.
>
> *Theodicy*, no. 90

Summing up, therefore, we have to see what kind of stimulus is needed for: 1. perception; 2. ideas; and 3. abstract ideas. We must also discover how the reason is activated relative to all three.

§1. *Our spirit is drawn to the act of perception by sensible things*

515. Our spirit cannot perceive anything not present to its perceptive faculty.[39]

Thus the human being can neither feel nor think unless some term is presented to this faculty; without this term, he remains

---

[39] Not as bodies are present to one another, but as the terms of acts are present to the spirit that carries them out.

in the first state of immobility described above, bound by one of the limitations of human intelligence.

It follows that the action of our spirit is limited by its term. But although it is the term that draws our intelligent spirit to act and find rest after acting, we also have to say that the presence of a term provides an explanation only for the special activity of the spirit to which it gives rise and offers repose.

A term is incapable of explaining any activity of a different nature or grade higher than that which is carried out in the term.

516. According to these principles, bodily elements experienced by our senses can move the spirit only to *perception*, not to abstraction or some other act. Although sensations present sensible things to our spirit and give rise to a new activity beyond the innate activity of seeing being, the activity of our spirit is limited and finalised by the terms themselves. The activity of our spirit stimulated by sensible things cannot therefore exceed and surpass sensible things. Thus sensible things cannot provide sufficient explanation for the formation of abstracts, which are insensible objects, by our spirit.

If sense presents me with something corporeal, I have no difficulty in understanding how my intelligence can be attracted and moved to see such a corporeal ens. Because my intelligence is naturally awake and active, the appearance of a term is sufficient to stimulate attention and vision. But what meaning is to be attached to 'the presentation of such a term to the intelligence'? What is it that presents the term to the intelligence? Only feeling; nothing else can do it. As sensitive beings we receive the action of corporeal agents in us by means of our sense organs. Because the agent is in us through its activity on us, it is present where it can be seen by our understanding. It is not difficult to grasp how we see that which is in us. As I have said, we have already opened the seeing eye of our intellect to the vision of all that takes place within us, in so far as it operates through the senses (cf. *Theodicy*, no. 153).

In a word, we can understand how sensible things are capable of attracting our spirit to themselves, and how what is felt can be grasped by us. Everything needed by our mind for such an operation is present. We have: 1. the *faculty*, intelligence; 2. the *terms* presented to us, which stimulate our intelligence to an act terminating in them. Granted sensations, there is no difficulty in understanding that intelligence forms for itself perceptions of corporeal individuals.[40] In other words, what is felt requires nothing more than itself in order to be perceived by us intellectually.

517. We can go a step further. People do not always mistake the *corporeal images* of what they see for subsisting things themselves; they understand the difference, whatever it may be, between real things and their images. It is at least probable, therefore, that these *images* stimulate us to form *pure ideas*, devoid of any *persuasion* of the actual presence and subsistence of *entia*. Thus, just as *sensations* occasion *intellectual perceptions*, so weaker images occasion *ideas* of corporeal entia, devoid of persuasion and judgment about their subsistence. This kind of *abstraction*, which separates *ideas* from *perceptions*, seems to find its explanation in *phantasms* or *corporeal images* in the same way that *perceptions* of bodies have their explanation in *sensations*.

Observations
The limits of development attainable by human beings
outside society if sensations and bodily images were
the only stimuli of their reason

518. *Intellective perceptions* and full, specific *ideas* follow *sensations* and *phantasms*. *Sensible* things, therefore, granted their presence, provide sufficient explanation: 1. for all the *activity* unfolded in human beings through *feeling* and *corporeal imagery*; 2. for all the activity manifested in human beings through the laws of *animal instinct* corresponding to those two faculties; finally 3. for all the activity shown in the formation of *perceptions* and *full, specific ideas* of corporeal things.

Let us consider briefly the nature and limitation of this third kind of activity. *Intellective perceptions* and *full, specific ideas* of material things are such that they follow and are indivisibly

[40] I am speaking of external sensations. The same can be said about internal feeling.

joined to *what is felt* and *what is imagined*. *Intellective perception* contains a judgment that what is felt subsists, but nothing more. It terminates in a particular felt thing, and is therefore an *idea* joined with *sense perception*, to which it adds *judgment about subsistence*. *Idea* and *sensation* are bound together in *intellective perception* and obliged to move in harmony like a pair of human eyes. More accurately, we could say perhaps that the idea is like an impetuous horse yoked to a plodding ox whose lumbering pace it has to tolerate.

An *idea* joined to a *sensation* cannot extend beyond the limits of the sensation; by this kind of idea, human beings are confined to the sphere of movements and actions common to animal sense and instinct. This explains why people separated as infants from society and left without human companionship or language are in a pitiable state when found later after years in which their only stimulus has been natural sensations. They have been unable to rise above the sensible things comprising animal life, and their only guide has been instinctive behaviour. They are not without reason which, however, follows instinct instead of guiding it. Their way of life could not be called human in the sense used of life amongst people born and reared in society. The same is true, more or less, of the uneducated deaf and dumb, and is what we would expect on the basis of the principle established above: 'The action of our spirit is limited by its term' (cf. 515).

As long as the term of the spirit is limited to corporeal elements (which in this case we presume not to have reached the status of signs), the human being, whose activity is limited to and completed by them, can think only of *bodily, individual* things. His ideas are always tied to sensations and images, from which they cannot be separated. The spirit can go no further; sensations and instincts are its sole guide.

§2. *Corporeal images are sufficient explanation of the spirit's activity in forming ideas separated from perceptions*

519. *Abstraction* is carried out in two ways on what is present in our intelligence. Broadly speaking, it is exercised on our

perceptions by separating *ideas* from them; strictly speaking, it is exercised on *ideas* from which it produces *abstract ideas* (cf. 494–498). Both operations may be carried out by *reflection*, which is however indispensable for the second.

Abstraction exercised on *perceptions* consists in fixing one's attention solely on the *apprehension* of a thing (idea), to the exclusion of *judgment* on the thing's subsistence. Exercised on *ideas*, abstraction consists in *reflecting* upon them while fixing attention on a single part of what is contained and thought in the idea. The part reflected upon may be an essential or an accidental element of the whole ens considered in the idea. The first type of abstraction leaves the idea whole and entire, still a complete object with all its parts; only *persuasion* about the object's subsistence is lacking.

520. *Persuasion* about the subsistence of anything can be disregarded not only through reflection, but naturally, as we have indicated, by means of the *corporeal images* remaining in us and reactivated according to certain animal laws governing our internal sensibility. Such images are not always sufficiently vivid, complete, consistent and coherent to prevent human beings from knowing them as different from the real, present things actively impressing themselves on our external sensory organs.

§3. *Language provides sufficient explanation of the spirit's activity in forming abstract ideas*

521. How then is reason activated to form abstracts? If *sensations* and *images* are incapable of activating it for this purpose, what other stimulus will draw it to the growth and development implied in its possession of abstracts?

First, in order to remove possible objections, we must note that 'the natural act of the intelligent spirit in focusing on being is totally insufficient to turn the mind to abstractions.' Being is the ever-present *object*, holding our spirit in a *first act* constituting human intelligence. But the spirit's activity ends and comes to rest in its object, not outside it (cf. 515). The object, *being in all its universality*, instigates in the spirit only the activity of terminating and resting in it. This primal activity of our spirit, therefore, is an immanent act, unmoved by any accidental disturbance; it is a firm, uniform, continuous vision of being, and nothing more. As an immobile, direct act, it provides no explanation of the spirit's activity in applying itself to particular entia and their (abstract) modes.

As we shall see immediately, our mind is moved to make abstractions by signs. An *abstract idea* is only *part of an idea*. Hence, our spirit's activity in forming *abstract ideas* will be explained if we can show what motivates it to suspend its attention from the idea as a whole and concentrate exclusively on a part of it. It is this discriminatory activity which needs causal explanation.

Let us take as an example the abstract idea of *humanity. Sense* offers our understanding the matter with which to perceive *real human beings*. The general notion of *humanity*, however, deprived of all the accidents proper to single individuals, does not fall under our senses nor possess any sensible elements. *Images* of human beings already perceived will be activated in us (with varying degrees of vividness) by similar sensations either accidentally or through some internal movement in the nerves. They will provide some impetus for my intelligence, but only enough for me to form a full *idea* of one or more human types. The idea of *humanity* is altogether different: it is not a sensation, not a corporeal image, not an object of perception, nor an idea detached from perception. How then can it be explained?

The law we have discovered and established about forces that move our attention may be stated thus: 'Our spirit is drawn to the act of perception by the terms presented to it' (cf. 515). But can *humanity* which is not real and does not exist be presented to us in person? Obviously some *vicarious sign* of it is needed. Humanity has no existence outside the mind and cannot draw the mind's attention to itself except through a sensible *sign* which, existing outside the mind, can take the place of that idea and in some sense cause it to subsist. The mind cannot be stimulated to think *abstract ideas* which have no corresponding realities, unless sensible signs replace, represent or activate such realities in our minds. But how can *signs* perform this task?

Both *natural* and *conventional signs*, especially words,

[521]

express everything added to them by tacit or express agreement. They are equally suitable for indicating a subsistent thing, a sensation, an image, a complete idea or part of an idea, or a single quality common to several objects and isolated from them, even though this quality does not subsist outside the mind in which it has its existence as an ideal object. If words can do all this, as we see they can, it is obvious that in the same way as they draw our attention to what subsists by indicating and expressing it, so they can draw our attention to any other meaning they may have. When they are used to indicate abstract ideas, they can draw us to them in such a way that our attention is limited to and concentrated upon the abstract qualities signified by the words; anyone listening wants to understand what the word says, and nothing more.

522. Note that I do not intend to deal with questions of fact about the divine or human origin of language, nor with the philosophical question of the possibility of language [*App.*, no. 13]. I take language as it is transmitted by the society in which we are born, and proceed to affirm that it is suitable for stimulating the attention of the child, who hears language from the moment of its birth, to discover the meaning of the sounds, and to find amongst the different meanings the ideas of qualities and relationships continually named and expressed by the words.

Nor is it my intention to describe in detail the fact I have in mind, or to show how *natural language* is the child's first key to its understanding of *artificial and conventional language*. Daily experience is sufficient to show clearly that children first understand words expressing subsistent, real things related to their needs, instincts and affections, and then come to understand and speak the whole language. This is enough to remove any doubt about language's capacity for drawing attention to abstract ideas, that is, to forming them, because in every language and reasoning and judgment, the most noble and important part is formed by abstractions.

If language can achieve what is impossible to sensations, images, and the idea of being, it follows that the child's development towards the use of *abstractions* is totally dependent upon the assistance provided by language. A good negative example of what I mean is found in human beings lost as children, and later rediscovered as adults incapable of speech. They give no sign whatsoever of having conceived abstractions mentally, nor of being raised in any way above the level of material, individual objects. The same can be said about uneducated deaf-mutes.

Observation 1
An objection drawn from human freedom

523. It may be objected that free, human activity, which renders human beings master of their own powers, can direct attention where it wills, and specifically to ideas in their entirety, or to parts of ideas. This intrinsic activity, by which human beings deliberately restrict their attention to part of an idea and to a single common quality, could enable them to form abstract ideas without need of *signs* determining and fixing these qualities and parts by removing and separating them from the whole.

524. Careful observation of the laws and conditions according to which our free activity is employed is sufficient to overcome this objection.

First, we certainly know that human activity is stimulated in two ways, *instinctively* and *deliberately*.

So far we have spoken of the *instinctive* stimulation of activity: the act is drawn out physically, as it were, by its term when the *impression* made by an agent draws the sense to feel, and the sensation stimulates the imaginative faculty. All this depends upon *sense instinct*. But there is also *rational instinct*,[41] drawn naturally by sensation to the *perception* of the corporeal agent, and by the *phantasm* to the *idea*, that is, to the object, without added persuasion of its subsistence.

I grant that instinct also leads human beings to express outwardly, by words, gestures and even sounds, what they feel and understand inwardly. Moreover this instinct, in so far as it is sense instinct, generates inarticulate noises and exclamations, expressive of feeling; in so far as it is rational instinct, it will proffer a few articulate words, signs of perceptions and ideas.

---

[41] The active faculty of *rational instinct* corresponds to the receptive faculty of being (intellect). *Spontaneity* properly speaking means the mode of operation of sense instinct, rational instinct or moral instinct.

But such instincts will never bring human beings to express what they have not yet mentally conceived, such as abstractions. *Sense instinct* and *rational instinct* have these limits beyond which they cannot progress. Can *free will* make these instincts go further, without the stimuli and assistance human beings receive from the society of their fellows?

Free will is conditioned by a law requiring it to have an end as sufficient reason for its acts.

Free, intelligent will cannot therefore do anything without having an end in view that enables it to be active and mobile. The aim bringing me to restrict my intellectual vision to a quality common to many objects, whilst ignoring all other qualities, is my natural desire to produce *abstract ideas*.

But can I propose to form *abstract ideas* for myself if I do not have or know any, and am unable to see how they can help me, or what value they have for me? It is certain that no one can propose for himself an aim of which he is ignorant, and in which he sees no advantage or need. In our case the necessary *condition* enabling the free will to impel itself to discover abstract ideas is lacking. The sufficient reason, the *end* from which it gains its motivation, is unknown, as is the *good* obtainable from this end. Thus there is no knowledge to interest and move the will to abstract ideas.

My free will cannot urge and direct my intelligence to *abstract mental concepts* without its first possessing some abstract mental conceptions.

It cannot *move* the intelligence to an abstract idea if it is ignorant of all abstract ideas: *voluntas non fertur in incognitum* [the will is not borne towards the unknown]; it lacks all *stimulus*. Nor can the free will *direct* the intelligence because it lacks any notion of the proposed object to serve as a *rule* with which to guide the intelligence. But if our free will needs abstract ideas before it can form abstract ideas, we have to conclude that it is impossible to explain the formation of these ideas by free, human activity without language.

Observation 2
Human development by means of society and language;
the necessity of language, if human beings are to become
masters of their own powers

525. We have seen that signs are needed if human free will is to
motivate itself to form abstract ideas. We must now add that
abstract ideas are always necessary to our will if it is to be able
deliberately to move the other powers.

The will does not, in fact, decide to move its powers, the
attention, for example, except for some *good* which it understands.

But activating oneself for some good presupposes an abstraction, that is, some *relationship* of end to means, which of its
nature is an abstract idea.

526. Moreover, how can I deliberately move my attention
from one idea to another except through a *relationship* binding
together in some way the ideas to which I successively move my
attention? Every *relationship* between two things or ideas is an
abstract, that is, neither the one idea nor the other, but a connection that each has with my mind as it thinks them; every *relationship*, therefore, is an *abstraction*.

Let us imagine that I decide to go to a spa for health reasons.
As I deliberate, I think of the *suitability* of the spa for a cure; I
think of the journey in front of me, and the *means* I shall need to
reach my destination. This *suitability* and these *means* are both
abstract ideas.

I could also imagine myself thinking through all the new
knowledge I have gained from conversation with some cultured
person. What binds together the series of thoughts running
through my mind? I cannot distinguish them from all other
thoughts, and look upon them as a class in themselves except
through an abstract idea, a *relationship* common to all the
knowledge acquired through my conversation. This common
quality or relationship enables me to review on its own the
knowledge acquired in this conversation.

If I make up my mind to think, and decide to choose one
argument from the many which could presently exercise my

intelligence, I must be acting for an end, for a reason, for some idea bound up with that argument; and this *bond* is an abstract.

Without *abstracts*, therefore, I cannot use my free will, nor can I direct my intelligence in one way rather than another. *Abstracts* bind together my particular ideas, and provide a passage from one to another. Without abstracts, ideas would remain totally divided and separate from one another. My attention would be fixed upon each of them individually without its being able to turn towards them as a group and embrace them collectively in a general view. There would be no reasoning because the whole operation of understanding would end where feeling itself ends. Abstractions are of the utmost importance.

527. We have seen that abstracts are obtained with the help of language coming to us through human society.

The proposition I set out to demonstrate is, therefore, true and irrefutable: 'Language is necessary to make us masters of our own powers'; and every great advance made by mankind is due to this immense benefit which we receive from the society of our peers.

Article 4

Intellective perception explained

§1. *The only intellective perception we have is of ourselves and of bodies*

528. At our birth, nature endows us with the intellective perception of ourselves and of bodies.

In fact the only way we can *perceive*[42] *the subsistence* of an ens, is when we feel its action in us.

Feeling therefore is necessary for the intellective perception of some subsistent thing.

Now the only *feeling* we have is: 1. of ourselves; 2. of bodies.

---

[42] We can *believe* and be persuaded that other beings subsist but this must not be confused with *perception*, which takes place directly through our external and internal senses.

Therefore we have *intellective perception* only of ourselves [*App.*, no. 14] and of bodies.

§2. *Explanation of the perception*

529. If one of the two kinds of perception is explained, the explanation of the other will follow. Let us take the explanation of the perception of bodies.

We recall that we are 1. affected by *sensations* which 2. immediately tell us that something exists (*judgment*) and 3. is determined by the way it affects us (*idea of bodies*).

There is no need to explain *sensation* (the first part) in this sequence because we start with it as a simple, basic fact.

Nor do we need to explain the nature of the *idea* of bodies (the third part), that is, the *way* something judged to exist is limited and determined by sensations. I shall try to do this in a later chapter when I examine our idea of bodies.

What must be done here is give a satisfactory explanation of the *judgment* we make as a result of sensations: 'Something different from us exists.' This judgment gives rise to the *perception* of bodies, that is, the persuasion of their actual particular existence (subsistence).

§3. *Explanation of the judgment generating the perception of bodies*

530. The idea of being in us does not by itself make us know any particular ens but only the possible existence of any ens.

Existence means actuality, because the concept of existence is only the concept of a *first action* (cf. 350–352). So it is impossible for me to conceive existence mentally without conceiving an *act of existing*, since both these expressions mean exactly the same. The *act of existing* can be thought in two ways, either by not applying it to anything real or by applying it to something real.

If I think the *actuality* of existence without applying it to anything real, I think the *possibility* of entia and nothing more, existence in something real, I think of what I call *subsistence* or real ens. This is the *judgment* that produces *intellective perception* and is what I want to explain.

When I make this judgment I add nothing to the idea of existence (cf. 402–407); all I do is concentrate on the existence I have thought of in something real. Such an action of my spirit takes place when I think of actual existence in all its universality. To think of actual existence means to think a first *action* (cf. 530). Sensations are *actions* in us of which we are not the authors. As *actions*, sensations suppose a *first action*, an existence. Sensations are also determined actions and therefore suppose a *determined first action*. A *determined first action* is an ens existing in a determined way. If we compare the *experience* we have (through sensations) with the *idea of actual existence*, we find that this *experience* is a particular case of what we were thinking previously with the idea of *existence*. We were thinking an *action* with this idea but not affirming or determining it. In the sensation, or more correctly in what is felt, we know a determined ens, a definite body.[43] But because we naturally think of the *action* in itself (existence), so in experiencing an action (a sensation) our spirit notes the action itself in its limitations. We recognise it precisely through what we were previously thinking by saying to ourselves: 'This is one of the actions (or a grade and mode of action) that I was thinking with my spirit.' The act of noting this particular case, of recognising what is happening in us as part of what we were previously thinking, forms the perception of the real thing, that is, the judgment we are examining.

In this judgment we focus our spirit (which previously had nothing to concentrate on but rested immobile in empty and uniform *possible being*) on a particular, limited ens in which it finds being realised. It notices what it already knows, it finds, we may say, what it was seeking. This explains how we make a comparison and judgment between *what is felt* and the *idea of*

---

[43] Thus it is very easy for a child to pass from sensations to making a judgment on subsisting entia. This judgment is only an intellective perception carried out by the very nature of the child's intelligence. In many theories the judgments made by children in their early years on the existence of substances and causes are inexplicable.

being. It also explains how what is felt becomes the *subject* in so far as it is contained in the idea of being, the *predicate*.

To understand this more clearly, let *sensation* and *undetermined existence*, the two things we wish to compare, be reduced to the same terms. Both are *actions*, but *undetermined existence* is *action* void of real conditions; *sensation* is *action* limited by real conditions and determinations. There is nothing extraordinary then in my noticing and recognising a *particular action* when I already possess the notion of *universal action*. From *action* it is easy to come to *ens*, which, as I have said, is nothing but *first action*. If there is an action there must be a first action, for no second action can exist without first action.

Observation 1
The teaching of the ancients about the word of the mind

531. This description of *perception* can, it seems to me, throw light on the meaning of the *word* of the mind, mentioned by the ancients. When we have the idea of a thing, we do not know whether it *subsists*.[44] Granted that we make a *judgment* with which we affirm the subsistent thing, this act is the *word* of the mind.[45]

[44] When I speak about the *idea* of a *thing*, it seems I am positing two elements: 1. idea, and 2. thing. But this is not so. There is a single object, but with two relationships, in the thought of something possible. If I consider in itself the object I am thinking about, I say it is *something* or essence; if I consider it relative to the mind, I call it *idea*. Hence the simple *idea* (species) does not contain the *word*, which is the the *subsistent thing* as *pronounced*, that is, affirmed as subsistent. The *thing I am thinking about* can be considered in itself, not because it exists without reference to a mind but because it acts as *exemplar* with which an intelligent ens can imagine or even produce. *Idea* of a thing therefore means simply *possible thing*, *exemplar*, according to which the intelligent ens thinks and acts.

[45] The word of the mind exists when I fix my mind on something subsistent and assent to its subsistence. Hence I can think 1. about an actually subsistent thing (*perception*); 2. about a thing that was subsistent and perceived by me (*memory of the perception*); 3. about a thing which I did not perceive as subsistent but *believe* on another's authority (*faith* about subsistence) — in all these three operations, whether I err or not, I always form a *word* of the mind, that is, I say and pronounce *a subsistent thing*; and

532. This *word* is produced by means of the efficacy of the will which fixes and determines what I am thinking of by assent to the belief that the thing subsists. Hence, it is not a simple *idea* or *species* but the *affirmation* of something determined which corresponds to an *idea* as its type or exemplar.[46]

533. If my mind possessed only pure *ideas* or *species*, it would intuit only pure possibility without affirming anything or *saying* anything.

External language, as well as the internal language of the mind, begins only when the mind notes some subsistent ens. As long as the mind does not think of an ens as *subsistent*, it says nothing and pronounces no word; it contemplates in perfect silence, still totally dumb.

Only the impulse of internal and external sensations draws the mind out of its silence to say that something subsists. Sensations are therefore the starting point of every *discourse* and word of the mind.[47]

4. I pronounce a *word* even when I consider subsistent that which in itself is not subsistent, either mistakenly or in my imagination or because my reasoning is aided by *suppositions*.

[46] St. Thomas says, 'The *species*, and the *word* generated by the species, are accidents because the soul is their subject. Nevertheless, the *word* rather than the species takes on the likeness of substance' (this must be the case because the word is an assent to a determined subsistence). In fact, 'the word, which is precisely what can be *formed* interiorly by means of the *species*, comes closer to representing the (subsistent) thing than the bare species itself because 1. the intellect strives to arrive at the quiddity of the thing, and 2. the quiddity of the substance' (the subsistence of the thing) 'is virtually in the *species* in a spiritual mode' (that is, as possible) 'in such a way that it' (the thought of subsistence) 'can be accurately formed from the species' (*Opusc.* 14). Clearly, nothing more is required to form the *word* than the *species* and idea of a thing. We can in fact *imagine* a thing corresponding to the idea we have. For example, the sculptor imagines the statue in the block of marble before him, so that even the *human imagination* has in some way its own word. This is the sum total of the creative power in our sense-powers.

[47] Aquinas, following St. Augustine, defines *word* as 'a kind of emanation of the intellect' (*S.T.*, I, q. 34, art. 2). Elsewhere he says, 'Strictly speaking, a word is that which the intelligent being forms by understanding' (*Opusc.* 13). This is the *definition*, or any *enunciation* whatsoever about something.

Observation 2
Relationship between idea and the word of the mind

534. That which is conceived only as possible by the *idea* is pronounced as subsistent by the *word*.[48]

The *thing as thought* (idea) stands in relationship to the *real as thing* (expressed by the word) as *potency* to *act*.

This is why I said that the ideal object and the real agent are reduced to one, single nature (cf. 530). The subsistent ens is the first action conceived by us (with the idea). This action, however, needs to pronounce it in its *real mode*.[49]

Article 5

Necessity of intellective perception

535. Must our spirit immediately perceive some ens when it has sensations?

This question of fact is not relative to my purpose at the moment; I am concerned with a different kind of necessity

---

[48] This observation is expressed in scientific, scholastic language as follows: 'Universal knowledge' (that is, the *species*, which is always universal) 'makes us know a thing in potency rather than in act' (St. Thomas, *Contra Gent.*, I, 50). To say that we know a thing *in potency* means simply thinking the thing as possible. As a result, many scholastic expressions which are now obscure and even awkward and clumsy, contain clear, excellent matter when divested of their antiquated form.

[49] Anyone who notes this distinction between *idea* and *word* will in my opinion understand Plato's distinction between *true opinion* and *knowledge*. The latter was about ideas, possibles; the former, about existent particular things (word). When we affirm something as true or false, we are using attributes of *opinion*, not of *knowledge* which, according to Plato and St. Augustine, is always true (*De Trin.*, bk. 50). In the *Timaeus*, Plato distinguishes *knowledge* from *true opinion* when he says that 'the first is insinuated by *teaching*, the second by the *persuasion* we form'. In fact, when we judge something as subsistent, we do not acquire a new *teaching*; we already knew the thing, of which we had the idea. But we do acquire a new *persuasion* of its subsistence by assenting to its subsistence. An acception must be made however in the case of necessarily subsistent being, that is, essential being, in the perception of which word and idea are identified.

relative to *perception*. I maintain that if our spirit understands something, it must understand in the way I have described, that is, by the primal judgment through which it recognises that the being it is thinking has a subsistence in the way determined and limited by the sensations it has received.

What I have said so far demonstrates this necessity. I have shown that the essence of understanding subsistent things is nothing other than giving such assent or forming the judgment I have described.

In fact, granted that our spirit has the idea of being and necessarily always sees it; granted that this idea is what forms our intellect and reason (cf. 480–485); and granted therefore that the nature of intelligent spirit consists in intuiting being, then the law of intelligence is: 'Not to conceive anything except as an ens, a thing.'[50]

536. This law of intelligence is neither *subjective* nor arbitrary; it is necessary in that its contrary cannot be thought.

Indeed, it would be a contradiction in terms to say our spirit knows things presented to it without its conceiving anything. But to conceive something is the same as conceiving an ens.

The general formula therefore that expresses the necessary nature of intellectual perception is: 'Judging, affirming, being persuaded that an ens subsists with its determinations.'

To clarify the matter further, let us suppose that we have received sensations from bodies but do not have the interior power to see an ens and therefore could not consider the sensations in relationship with being. In this case our spirit would have been modified by corporeal sensations without their appearing as determinations of being; we would not perceive a determined ens, a subsisting thing, a body. To perceive a body is to perceive a determined ens. The sensations would not be perceived by our understanding; they would remain only in our feeling, and therefore we would know nothing. To be able to

[50] The famous statement of the Schools, is in harmony with this teaching: *intellectus habet operationem circa ens in universali* [the intellect has an action relative to ens in all its universality] (cf. St. Thomas, *S.T.*, I, q. 79, art. 2); St Thomas, too, is of the same mind: *intellectus respicit rationem entis* [intellect beholds the nature of ens] (*S.T.*, I, q. 79, art. 9). We see again the scholastics' teaching that *quod non est, non intelligitur, nisi per id quod est* [that which is not, is understood only through that which is].

know a *body* (the name 'body' itself was invented as a result of intellective perception) as well as feel it, we must have the power to see a determined ens where the sensation is.

The intelligent spirit therefore does not know except by means of the idea of being. To know is only to conceive a *determination* of possible or common *being*, a determination that makes possible being an individual ens.

Observation 1
Is the soul always thinking?

537. What has been said answers the Cartesian question, 'Is the soul always thinking?'

The soul is intelligent because it has continually the vision of being (cf. 535).

Intelligence, therefore, is an essentially active,[51] thinking faculty, not because it has present to it all ideas, but solely the first idea, being. With this idea, which is its light,[52] it sees and

---

[51] St. Thomas, following in the footsteps of Aristotle, solves the question in the same way. As I have said, he applies to the intelligent spirit the famous principle: *nihil agit, nisi secundum quod est actu* [nothing acts except in so far as it is in act] (*S. T.*, I, q. 76, art. 1). From this he deduces the necessity that the spirit is essentially in act, and that we would have no power to understand if it were not in act. When Aristotle says, 'This kind of intellect is not such that sometimes it understands and sometimes does not understand', he means that it always understands (*De Anima*, 3). I do not see why this cannot apply to the *acting intellect* rather than the *acquired intellect* (*intellectus adeptus*). St. Thomas does not deny that the statement can be understood of the *acting intellect*. He says: 'In every act of our understanding, the action of the acting intellect goes hand in hand with that of the possible intellect. — Now, the acting intellect, relative to our ability to think, has everything necessary for continual understanding on our part. This is not the case with the possible intellect, whose content is only the intelligible species extracted from phantasms'(*De Verit.*, q. 10, art. 8). The reason why we continually understand, relative to the acting intellect, is that the *acting intellect* 'receives nothing from outside' but draws everything from itself, that is, the *form* of knowledge, being in all its universality.

[52] Norris, in England, developed Malebranche's system. In his work *Essay towards the Theory of the ideal or intellectual World*, he tries to defend the following proposition, among others: 'If material things were perceived through themselves, they would be a real light to the mind because they

distinguishes what the senses provide (in the way I have explained), and understands when other reasoning *entia* speak.

I have also explained (cf. 469–470) why we remain for a long time unaware of the idea of being, even though it is joined inseparably with us from the first moment of our existence.

Observation 2
How the intelligence is a *tabula rasa*

538. We can now see clearly why I used the ancient likeness of the *tabula rasa*[53] to describe the state of our intelligence at the first moment of our existence.

This likeness, understood in the following way, fits the argument well.

The *tabula rasa* is undetermined being, present to our spirit.

Because this being has no determination at all, it is like a perfectly uniform board devoid of all writing. As a result, it receives any kind of sign and impression made upon it. This means that the idea (totally undetermined being) is determined and applies equally to anything felt, to any form or mode presented to us through the external or internal senses. From our birth, therefore, we do not see characters but a clean sheet of paper devoid of any writing; there is nothing at all on this paper for us to read; it is a sheet which has only susceptibility (potency) to receive any writing, that is, any determination of particular existence [*App.*, no. 15].

would take on the intelligible form of our intellect, which they would perfect and to which they would be superior.' Norris rightly finds the proposition erroneous and absurd.

[53] Aristotle made this likeness famous when he used it in the third book of *De Anima*.

CHAPTER 5

The innate idea of being resolves the general difficulty of the problem of the origin of ideas

Article 1

The difficulty solved

539. I have reduced the difficulty contained in the problem of the origin of ideas to one, simple question: 'How is the first judgment possible?' (cf. 41–45). In Locke's hypothesis, which derives all ideas from the senses, the difficulty is insuperable. But granted and proved that a totally universal idea naturally exists before we experience sensations, there is no difficulty in understanding how the first judgment is formed.

Article 2

Objections and answers

§1. *First objection*

540. Nevertheless, we have to examine objections to our conclusion.

First: the judgment said to be necessary for the formation of ideas was shown to be the same as the conception of ideas, which must be brought about through judgments.

If this is true, an innate, totally universal idea offers no solution to our difficulty because it too requires a judgment in order to be conceived mentally. To say that this idea is innate resolves nothing; it can only mean that it is conceived mentally by us through our natural powers from the first moment of our existence.

If this is the case, all ideas will be conceived mentally through judgment, and we find ourselves face to face once more with the difficulty: 'How can we make the judgment enabling us to conceive the most universal idea?'

Reply to the first objection

541. The objection depends upon a false supposition: 'A judgment is necessary for the conception of all ideas.'

It is true that a judgment is needed for *ideas which we form*, such as those of bodies, which unite predicate to subject. Here we find two elements, one of which must be universal. But it is not the case with an idea comprising one element only, which does not require a judgment in order to be possessed and conceived. Judgment, we remember, is always an operation of the mind bringing together two terms. The presence of one term alone would not require any kind of *judgment*, which would indeed be impossible because pre-empted by an immediate *intuition*.

Amongst the ideas we possess, only one, the idea of being, has this unique characteristic of utter simplicity. Not composed of predicate and subject, it is the one idea needing no judgment in order to be conceived mentally. It cannot, therefore, be formed by means of some mental operation, but only *intuited*. Equally, it cannot be intuited unless present to our spirit. Thus we have a new, very clear demonstration that the idea of being is given to human beings by nature.

§2. *The first objection renewed*

542. Nevertheless, I accept that it is very difficult to understand how the idea of *being* can be intuited without admixture of some kind of judgment in the intuition itself. At first sight, it would seem that the idea of being could be expressed in the following proposition: 'Anything can exist.' But this is a judgment. We conceive this proposition by judging: 'Something is possible.' Such a judgment, however, would be included in the idea of being, as our own analysis of it shows (cf. 424). There we found the idea of being to comprise three elements, two of

which are: 1. the idea of something; and 2. the possibility of something. In these two elements we seem to have come across the kind of predicate and subject necessarily expressed in the proposition: 'Something is possible.' *Possibility* is the element providing the predicate, while the undetermined *thing* is the element forming the subject. We must now confront this difficulty.

The reply continued

543. The difficulty rests upon the uncertainty presented by the concept of *possibility*, which requires further analysis.

We first note that we must not confuse this *logical possibility* of which we are speaking with *probability*. The two things are quite different.

What is *logical possibility*? By a *possible* entity we mean an entity that *can* subsist, that is, can be thought as subsisting.

Everything not involving contradiction is said to be possible. The mind can always think it exists, and can, whenever it wishes, imagine it to exist.

For a thing to be declared *impossible*, the mind must possess a necessary reason excluding the possible existence of the thing, so that either the reason must be shown to be false or the thing must be declared impossible. A reason acknowledged as necessary cannot be false, and the thing under discussion must be declared impossible.

The contrary of *impossible* is *possible*. When we rightly state that something is impossible, we must possess a necessary concept contradicting the very thing we are considering. On the other hand, the *possibility* of something requires only the absence of any concept rendering it incoherent and contradictory. If there is no necessary reason to the contrary, everything is *per se* possible.

It is characteristic of our mind and language that the word *possibility* takes on a positive meaning. Language expresses both positive and negative beings by words, that is, positive signs. This makes for confusion. For example, when we say 'nothing', we exclude the existence of everything, although we think we have said something because the sign for *nothing* is a word.

[543]

What is said about *possibility* cannot be said of *probability*. While *possibility* indicates only the absence of contradiction, *probability* adds some positive reason to the mental entity which renders the entity's present or future existence probable. The reason may be the number of times the thing has happened, or the knowledge of a special, subsistent power capable of producing it.

It is clear that we take *possibility* in its absolute, logical sense, not in the approximate sense of ordinary conversation. People say: 'It is impossible for this tree to be in the garden without the presence of a seed from which it grew.' This is a physical impossibility, and as such clashes with the physical law requiring plants to grow from seeds. Again, people say: 'Granted the risks you take, it is impossible for you to escape serious injury.' This so-called impossibility is in fact improbability, because in the ordinary course of events it clashes with the chances of remaining uninjured. But we are not thinking about impossibility that clashes with physical laws, nor about the impossibility of avoiding the natural consequence of actions, nor about the impossibility of breaking moral laws; we are dealing with impossibility that conflicts with the laws of thought in such a way that one term of a given proposition cannot be conceived as existing along with the other term. Everything not involving such a contradiction we call possible [*App*., no. 16].

544. The *possibility* of a thing is not, therefore, positive in itself, outside the thing. It is, as they say, a mental entity or an observation made by the mind about some essence in which it cannot find intrinsic repugnance. We express this lack of ideal, intellectual repugnance through the word *possibility*, giving the impression of something separate from the mental entity, although this is not the case.

All mental entities are in fact the fruit of observation by which we notice some lack, or relationship, or quality, etc. Considered separately and of themselves, they cannot be present to our mind from the beginning of our existence; they can be noted and considered by us only as our understanding develops.

We conclude that the *possibility* of things, as a mental entity capable of being expressed through a word, is not innate in us, but observed through an act of our mind. *Possibility*, as simple lack of repugnance, tells us only that the *idea of being* contains no repugnance. As a consequence, there is no repugnance in anything we behold in this idea; possibility therefore is not something distinct from *ideal being* itself.

It follows that our only innate element is the idea of being in all its simplicity. Possibility, as a predicate, adds nothing to this idea but excludes something from it (repugnance) and serves to simplify it, allowing it to be recognised in its utter unity and simplicity.

545. Granted these principles, the proposition, 'Something can exist', is inexact if used to point to what is innate. The proposition supposes that we have mentally extracted *the idea of possibility*, a purely mental entity, from the simple idea of being and given a positive form, such as a thought or a word, to what is negative by nature. In other words we have changed the idea of possibility into an apparently positive predicate.

If we wish to analyse the proposition, 'Something can exist', in order to discover its innate elements, we need to strip it of all that has apparently been added to it by the way we conceive and express something. We first need to change the statement, 'It is innate to us that something is possible' to 'It is innate (that is, it is naturally present to our spirit) that the idea of being is free from repugnance', or to 'The idea of being is innate; reflecting upon it, we see it is without repugnance'. Because the idea of being, as objective form, constitutes our intelligence, intelligence can be defined as the faculty of seeing being. Further reflection shows that if the vision of being were removed, our intelligence would cease. Being therefore cannot be eliminated or removed from the mind. But removing being and leaving being is a contradiction which our intelligence cannot tolerate. Our intelligence can understand only that which does not involve contradiction; this alone is intelligible and thinkable.

546. It is only *a posteriori* that we observe the many determinations taken by being in the real entia we behold. This leads us to declare that the possibility of things is contained in the essence of being. But this, in turn, simply means 'There is no repugnance between the idea of undetermined being and its determinations and realisations.' The concept of possibility involves a *relationship* with the *determinations* of being, which are initially unknown to our spirit until we apprehend them through experience.

[545–546]

Summing up, we may say that after observing *being* to be devoid of determinations (this is a negation, not a positive predicate), we conclude (after reflection) that real *entia*, undetermined in quantity, are possible and thinkable as determinations and realisations of the essence present to our spirit. In other words, these real *entia* involve no contradiction with the idea itself, while the idea accepts them in itself without repugnance. The concept of mere possibility is, therefore, *acquired* as our faculties develop. There is nothing innate except its foundation, that is, the ideality and undetermination of being.

The idea of being, the innate element devoid of any predicate whatsoever, is itself the universal predicate. Deprived of all determination and real action, it unites and applies itself as predicate to determinations and actions which thus become subject. The idea of being includes no judgment, therefore, but constitutes the *possibility of all judgments* in so far as we can judge anything that we feel by means of the idea of being, the common predicate within us.[54]

§3. *Second objection*

547. The previous objection was based upon *possibility*, one of the two primary elements of the idea of being (cf. 423). Its solution depended upon showing that this element is negative when conceived separate from being, and hence takes nothing from the simplicity of the idea of being which it serves to express.

The second primary element, that is, *something*, or being, gives rise to another difficulty in understanding how the idea of being can be present to us without the intervention of a judgment. It may be stated as follows: 'Two terms are distinguished in my conception when I intuit being: *myself* who intuit, and being as intuited. During this act my consciousness tells me: I perceive being. But this is a judgment, and it would seem therefore that judgment must be present in every objective mental

---

[54] According to St. Thomas, *knowledge supposes a measure*, a *rule*, for he says: *Intellectus accipit cognitionem de rebus MENSURANDO eas quasi ad sua principia* (*De Verit.*, q. 10, art. 1).

conception that is something more than mere subjective modification.'

Reply to the second objection

548. Our answer lies in an observation that cannot be overlooked, despite its subtlety [*App.*, no. 17].

The act of intuiting being is entirely different from the act by which I say: 'I intuit being.'

Note that I am not asking whether this act follows or must necessarily follow from the other. It is only necessary, at the moment, to know if *intuiting an idea* and *judging that an idea is intuited* are different acts of the spirit.

Intuition is the act by which I fix my attention on an idea. Weak and inconsistent attention, dispersed over many objects, does not change the nature of the act which, it is important to note, is essentially one in so far as its object is one. Wandering attention, although it may associate other unique, entirely different acts with it, does not destroy the uniqueness of the act; each act considered in itself remains unique. Our task is to examine the simple, unique act of attention to an idea, independently of all other acts which may be found mingled with it. Of itself, the act with which I fix my attention on an idea is essentially restricted to the object in which it terminates.

549. First, let us try to find some state in which our spirit concentrates all its force of attention on a single point. This will help us to consider one act of attention separated from every other. Let us imagine that the object of our attention is something we love so much that all our powers of concentration are totally focused on it. As our contemplation grows and reaches a certain point of intensity something strange occurs. Enthralled by the desired object, we have no energy for anything else. Absorbed by this one object, we are in a state of ecstasy where we forget ourselves and everything else; external things no longer exist for us. All our thinking and loving energy is captivated and exhausted by what we behold. Such alienation, experienced probably by all human beings although at different levels of intensity, is a fact, and lesser degrees of alienation in our own lives enable us to form some notion of the total experience.

The question we have to put to ourselves is this: if a person finds himself in such a state, will he pay attention to himself? Will he be capable of reflecting upon his own state? We say that this capacity for reflecting upon himself will be no more than that of a baby totally absorbed in its feed. He cannot carry out this kind of reflection on himself and his own state of self-forgetfulness unless he has come to himself and woken, as it were, from his absorption. His energies, previously occupied and almost lost for his own purposes, are now available for self-reflection. However, if his heart and mind are fully and completely immersed in the ecstasy, there is no immediate connection with any following act. All his energies have been exhausted in the ecstasy itself, forcing him to rest before acting once more. There is no connection with his previous intense action, which he cannot even remember. Dante noted this peculiar state when he wrote:

> Now near its aim, our mind
> is so enthralled that memory
> falls incapable behind.[55]

550. What we have said helps us to realise that reflection on the operations of our spirit is an act entirely different from the operations themselves.

We can state, therefore, that human beings can think an object, such as being for example, without *reflecting* upon themselves or realising that they are thinking.

Now it is clear that no one can make the judgment 'I intuit being' without reflecting upon himself, paying attention to his state of mind, and making it the object of his attention. *My state*, however, is not the same object as *being*, and I need to perceive my own state by means of an act different from that by which I intuit being. I intuit being through an act of attention directed at being; I perceive myself with an act of attention directed towards myself. When I intuit being, my attention is fixed simply on a mere *object* very different from *myself*. Perceiving *myself*, my attention has as its object the very *subject* which intuits. Finally, the first act is an *intuition,* the second *a perception* relative to myself, a *reflection* relative to being. The act,

[55] *Par.* 1.

therefore, by which I intuit being is simple, primary and spontaneous; the act by which I judge myself to be intuiting being is complex (it is a judgment) and subsequent. The intuition of being can be innate; the reflective judgment cannot be innate although the second act may follow more or less closely upon the first. The first is intrinsic and necessary; the second can simply be acquired and voluntary.

551. Distinguishing these two acts, I referred to the state of a person totally occupied by a single object. I did this in order to assist comprehension of the fact at issue, not to prove the distinction made between the two acts. In a state of mental concentration, the energies of our intelligence are all reduced to a single point of focus,[56] and it is easy to see how one act, normally accompanied by another, can stand on its own. My purpose here, however, does not require me to show one act of attention as temporally distinct from the other. It is enough to indicate that one is not the other in order to prove that one can be innate, and the other not.

My argument would be considerably strengthened were I to insist upon a truth known to the ancient philosophers, that is, that the understanding can perform only one act at a time, and that *being* (or anything conceived mentally) and *myself* intuiting are two objects requiring two acts of understanding in order to be grasped. In this case, it would be absurd to think they could be grasped simultaneously, or to imagine that in understanding one object I also *know* that I understand it. The argument would be strengthened still further were I to prove the

---

[56] Human absorption in the contemplation of an object gives me an opportunity of commenting on a very common false judgment. When a person has difficulty in remembering something, or experiences a sensation without noticing it, or pays only little attention to it, it is often said that the impression or sensation made upon him must be rather weak. But the explanation could be exactly the opposite. The sensation, and we can say the same about the act of contemplation, could have been intense without its being noticed or reflected upon. It seems to me that when sensation or contemplation is intensified to the maximum, the person experiencing it knows, notices and remembers nothing of his experience: he is no longer present to himself, but constrained by the experience itself. The relevance of this remark for understanding what takes place deep within the human spirit will best be seen by those accustomed to serious reflection on matters of this kind.

evident truth that the second act, having as object the first act, could not begin to exist without presupposing the first as already complete. This would clearly indicate the contradiction inherent in claiming as simultaneous the act by which we know something, and know that we know it.

Corollary 1
There is an idea which precedes any judgment whatsoever

552. From what we have said, it follows that a first, natural intuition within us precedes any judgment whatsoever. This intuition makes us intelligent beings, and forms our faculty of knowledge. The object of the intuition is *ideal being*, the idea.

Corollary 2
Human beings possess an intellectual sense

553. Being, therefore, is intuited by our spirit without mediation, just as sense receives a direct impression of what is sensible. The immediate presence of being to the spirit enables us to speak of an *intellectual sense* possessed by human beings.

Our intelligence can be called a *sense* (different in kind from the corporeal senses, however) in so far as it intuits being. But in so far as it judges, or notices the relationship between what is felt and being in all its universality it carries out a mental operation very different from that of sense.

It no longer receives sensations but, pronouncing and synthesising, produces cognitions and persuasions.[57]

---

[57] This enables us to understand St. Thomas' opinion that *intellectus est vis passiva* (receptive, strictly speaking), *respectu totius entis universalis* ['the intellect is a passive' (receptive, strictly speaking) 'power, relative to total, universal ens'] (*S.T.*, I, q. 74, art. 2). Aristotle says: 'In the case of anything separate from matter' (in other words, in the case of what is purely form, precisely like the idea of being) 'that which is understood is the same as that with which it is understood' (*De Anima*, bk. 3, com. 15). I think that this

Observation 1
The difference between corporeal and intellectual sense

554. The difference between *corporeal* and *intellectual sense* lies in the diversity of their terms. Corporeal sense has determined, real, corporeal terms; intellectual sense has a purely spiritual and perfectly undetermined term.

The difference between these terms gives rise to another distinction between the two senses. Although the nature of *sense* in general requires an action done in a subject, or a modification undergone by the subject, in corporeal sense the object is not communicated as object, but as an *acting* force. In intellectual sense, the *object* is manifested as object, not as agent, because an object is characterised properly speaking by presence and manifestation, not by action. Consequently, intellective sense does not first sense itself, but immediately understands ens. Only afterwards does it experience joy from its understanding of ens (intelligence). We can say, therefore, that intellective sense follows intelligence.

Being in all its universality is idea; but the subject intuiting it, *produces for itself* intellectual sensations from this idea [*App.,* no. 18].

Observation 2
The nature of *ideal being*

555. From what we have said, it can easily be seen that besides the form of being possessed by subsisting things (REAL being, as I have called it) there is another, entirely distinct form, constituting the foundation of the possibility of things (the IDEAL form). IDEAL BEING is an entity of such a nature that it cannot be confused with either our spirit, or with bodies, or with anything belonging to REAL BEING.

556. It is a serious error to believe that IDEAL BEING or THE IDEA is nothing because it does not belong to the category of

opinion can also be applied to the *innate idea* of being, which makes us know everything, including ourselves.

things common to our feelings. On the contrary, *ideal being*, the *idea*, is an authentic, sublime entity, as we saw when we examined the noble characteristics with which it is endowed. It is true that it cannot be defined, but it can be analysed, or rather we can express our experience of it and call it the LIGHT of our spirit. What could be clearer than light? Extinguish it, and only darkness remains.

557. Finally, from what has been said we can form a concept of the manner in which the idea of being adheres to our spirit. We realise that it neither asks nor demands our assent or dissent, but *presents* itself to us as pure fact (cf. 398), because such an idea neither affirms nor denies; it simply constitutes our possibility of affirming and denying (cf. 546).

PART THREE

Origin of the First Principles of Reasoning

558. So far we have seen how the intuition of ideal being is proper to the intelligent spirit and necessary for its existence (Part One). Granted that *ideal being* is present to the spirit, we have shown how the origin of other ideas is explained by means of *sensation* and *reflection*. We have also shown that ideas as a whole originate in this way, and have applied the argument to certain broad, general classes of ideas (Part Two). We must now deduce in another way various ideas and cognitions strengthening our theory and making it easier to use. For the sake of clarity, let us begin with necessary, basic cognitions. They are: 1. the *first principles* of reasoning; and 2. certain *elementary* and very abstract ideas always taken for granted in human reasoning, without which reasoning is impossible. Once possessed, these *first principles* and *elementary ideas* become instruments enabling our mind to perform its noble operations and produce new ideas and knowledge. We begin therefore with the supreme principles of human reasoning.

CHAPTER 1

The first and second principles: of knowledge and of contradiction

559. Principles are expressed by propositions which, in order to be analysed, must be reduced like mathematical formulae to their simplest expression. When dealing with a formula, mathematicians may reduce it to the expression most suitable for their purposes, provided they do not change the value of the formula or alter the equation.

Origin of the First Principles of Reasoning   103

560. A *proposition* expresses a *judgment*, that is, a relationship between two terms, *predicate* and *subject*.

Because the *principles* of reason are judgments, they comprise a predicate and a subject. Therefore the simplest and most natural expression of the principles of reason is that which directly indicates the predicate with one distinct word (or phrase), the subject with another, and the connection between them with a third. Let us take the principle of contradiction as our example.

561. The principle of contradiction, in its simple form, is: 'That which is (being) cannot not be.'

'That which is' is the subject; 'not be' is the predicate; 'cannot' is the copula expressing the relationship between the two terms.

In this judgment, the relationship between *being* and *not-being* is *impossibility*.

We have seen that logical *impossibility* cannot be thought and is in fact *nothing*.

The principle tells us that *being* (that which is) cannot be thought at the same time as *not-being*. When *being* and *not-being* are put together therefore, we have both an affirmation and a negation, that is, nothing; not-being cancels previously posited being, and all thought disappears.

The principle of contradiction is simply the *possibility of thought*.

562. Without this principle, therefore, investigation of other matters is impossible. We cannot doubt its existence, validity or effectiveness. Like any other thought, this doubt presupposes the principle as already valid and effective; we cannot begin to think, to question or reason without presupposing thought, questioning and reasoning. In this way the principle of contradiction is completely safe from any attack. Attacking it demands thought but, in order to think, thought has to be *possible*, and this is precisely what the principle of contradiction states: we cannot think without thinking! If we think at all (no matter what we think) we admit the principle of contradiction, which states: 'I think or I do not think; there is no middle term, because to think without thinking is impossible.' The principle of contradiction therefore is independent of all human thought and opinion, which is possible only with this principle.

563. Someone might say to me: 'I deny the possibility of thought.' I would reply that to deny the possibility is to think

it! I would ask: 'Do you think at all? Your answer is either that you think or do not think; whichever it is, you confirm the principle of contradiction. To invalidate the principle, you would have to reply: "I am thinking while I am not thinking", and this would be ridiculous and meaningless.'

564. But let us return to the analysis of the principle of contradiction, which is a proposition expressing the following fact: 'Being cannot be thought at the same time as not-being'; in other words, 'Thought does not exist unless it has being for its object.'

This fact which I have observed and, it seems to me, proved beyond doubt, is the idea of being informing and producing our intelligence (cf. 473–557). Thus we often define intelligence as 'the faculty of seeing that which is' (being). The phrase 'being together with not-being' expresses *nothing*, and *nothing* is the opposite of *something*, of *being*. By showing that our intellect and reason is the faculty for seeing being, I have also shown conversely that it is not possible to see *nothing*, which is all that the principle of contradiction affirms.

This principle therefore draws its origin from the idea of being, the form of our reason; it is simply the *idea* of being considered in its application.

565. As Thomas Aquinas and Bonaventure have said, the principle of contradiction is in a certain sense innate [*App.*, no. 19]. According to them the principle reveals itself from deep in the human spirit at our first use of reason. However, it seems more strictly true to say that while the foundation of the principle is innate, the principle itself is not. The reason is as follows.

Principles take the form of *judgments* and are expressed by *propositions*. Any principle may presuppose some reasoning except for the absolutely first principle which is not under discussion here. In fact the principle of contradiction can be deduced from a preceding principle, which I call the *principle of knowledge*, expressed by the proposition: 'The object of thought is being or ens' (cf. 535–536). I reason as follows: 'The object of thought is being; but the phrase "being and not-being" expresses *nothing*, and *nothing* is not *being*. Therefore *being and not-being* is not an object of thought.'

566. Hence, for the *idea* of *being* to have taken the form of the principle of contradiction, I must have used it, that is, have

begun to judge and reason. I must have formed a mental *ens*, *nothing*, and acquired the ideas of *affirmation* and *negation* by thinking, and seen that negation plus affirmation equal nothing.

Judgment and reasoning, although naturally and closely tied to the idea of being and carried out promptly, are only the *idea of being in its application*, disguised and accompanied by relationships. Our reason needs to be released like a spring from its initial state of complete inactivity. But anything in us resulting from such contingently intellectual movement is *acquired*. Such is the principle of contradiction in its explicit form of a judgment.

CHAPTER 2

The third and fourth principles: substance and cause

567. The principle of contradiction depends on the principle of knowledge (cf. 565), which is a necessary fact expressed as follows: 'The object of thought is being.' It is the principle of all principles, the law of intelligent nature, and the essence of intelligence.

The second principle is that of *contradiction*, derived directly from the first: 'Being and not-being cannot be thought at one and the same time.'

The third is the principle of *substance*: 'Accidents cannot be thought without substance.'

The fourth principle is *cause*: 'A new entity cannot be thought without a cause.'

568. *Accidents* are perceived through actions on us and can also be called by the general name, *happenings*, which is very appropriate because they are something that happens to substance without being necessary to it. There is no difference between *accidents* and *effects* except that *accidents* are considered as one thing with the substance and terms of it, while *effects* are considered separate from their cause, and proper to some other ens. With that understood, the way we deduce the *principle of cause* will serve as an example for deducing the *principle of substance* (cf. 52–54), which the reader can deduce for himself.

569. The principle of cause derives from the *principle of contradiction*, and hence from the *principle of cognition*, in the following way. The principle of cause can be stated as: 'Every happening (anything that begins) has a cause that produces it.' We found this expression elsewhere and analysed it; at this point we must recall the analysis.

'Every happening has a cause that produces it.' This proposition means exactly the same as the following: 'It is impossible for our intelligence to think a happening without thinking a cause that produced it.' To show that 'a happening without a cause cannot be thought', we must show that 'the concept of a happening without a cause involves contradiction.' Once this is demonstrated, we will have deduced the principle of cause from the principle of contradiction.

The demonstration is as follows: to say 'What does not exist, acts' is a contradiction. But a happening without a cause means 'What does not exist, acts.' Therefore a happening without a cause is a contradiction. The proofs follow.

As regards the major: to conceive mentally an action (a change) without an ens, is to conceive without conceiving, which is a contradiction. Indeed, the principle of knowledge states: 'The object of thought is ens'; therefore without an ens, we cannot mentally conceive. To conceive an action without conceiving an ens that performs the action, is to conceive without conceiving. Therefore to apply the action to something that does not exist is a contradiction in terms, which was to be proved.

As regards the minor: a happening is an action (a change). If this action has no cause, it is conceived by itself, without belonging to an ens; there is then an action without ens or, which is the same, what does not exist, acts. Thus the minor is proved (cf. 350–352).

The principle of cause therefore derives from the principle of contradiction, and both derive from the principle of knowledge, which is only the *idea of being in its application*. As such, this idea takes the form of a principle and is expressed in a proposition, when considered in relationship with human reasoning, of which it is the formal cause.

CHAPTER 3
The nature of scientific principles in general

570. We have seen that the principles of knowledge, contradiction, substance and cause are only the *idea of being in its application*, that is, the law governing its application expressed in a proposition.

This observation opens the way to understanding the nature of all the *principles of reasoning* which in general are only *ideas* used for making judgments.

The application of these ideas can always be conceived as a judgment, and expressed in a proposition.

The proposition serves as a norm for forming a series of more particular judgments, virtually contained in the first, most general judgment to which they are subordinate. This first judgment is a *principle* relative to others deduced from it. Such deduction is called reasoning.

571. For example, the *idea of justice* becomes the *principle* of ethics when we reason and systematise its applications; the *idea of beauty* becomes the principle of aesthetics when it is considered as directing, regulating and indeed originating all our reasoning about what is beautiful.

Hence the *definition of beauty* is only the proposition resulting from an application of the idea of being, and is the first principle of any reasoning about what is beautiful.

572. Generally speaking, then, the *essence* of things is the *principle* of our reasoning about them.

573. The principle of each science therefore is the *definition* that expresses the essential idea of the subject of that science. From this truth comes the *art of classifying* the sciences correctly and reducing them to unity. They are no longer mere collections of disconnected information but well ordered treatises, each regulated by a single principle from which other truths are clearly seen to originate as rays of light from a common source.

CHAPTER 4
Origin of scientific principles in general

574. We have seen that principles are purely *applied ideas* (cf. 570–575), that is, ideas used as norm and exemplar according to which we can make more particular judgments. The origin of principles is therefore reduced to the origin of ideas. The latter explain the former.

PART FOUR

Origin of Pure Ideas, which derive nothing from Feeling

CHAPTER 1
Origin of elementary ideas or concepts of being presupposed in human reasoning

Article 1
List of elementary ideas of being

575. The elementary concepts conditioning all human reasoning are principally the concepts of: 1. unity; 2. numbers; 3. possibility; 4. universality; 5. necessity; 6. immutability; 7. absoluteness.

Article 2
Origin of these concepts

576. All these concepts, contained in *ideal being*, are its characteristics and natural qualities. As a result, they are given to our mind together with being itself. We simply have to note them one by one, distinguish them within being, and assign each a name. We do this through various uses of the idea of being, and of reflection.

577. This explains why such concepts, although so far removed by nature from material determinations that their

formation would seem to require a long, difficult process of mental operation, are familiar to all human beings and presupposed by them. In fact, they are the most obvious, easily known and available of all human concepts.

Observation

578. Taken individually, these abstract concepts are an element of an idea rather than an idea itself. Of themselves, they provide no content to our knowledge. For this reason, I call them *elementary concepts* of ideal being. Generally speaking, *abstract* ideas are said to be *elementary concepts* of the idea from which they are abstracted.

Article 3

St. Augustine's arguments about the ideas of unity and number and similar things confirm the theory I have given

§1

579. Because these elementary concepts appertain to *ideal being*, we should not be surprised at the difficulty of knowing and explaining them through sensations.

Indeed, great thinkers were always struck by their appearance and extraordinary nature when they came upon any of them. Aware of the difficulty of explaining information which has nothing similar in the sensible world, they paid more attention to these concepts than people normally do when encountering problems. Each concept was used by some great philosopher to elevate his thought from nature and from the sphere of visible things to the infinite. However, because their meditation was limited to one concept, it did not lead them to the origin of all the elementary ideas in being. If they had grasped undetermined, ideal being, they could have explained the great ideological problem in its entirety.

It will be helpful therefore, while discussing these concepts, to give an example of how any one of them could be sufficient to stimulate and guide great minds to rise above the highest peaks of human things and discover many of the truths I have explained. I choose the elementary concept of unity and numbers, and quote St. Augustine as the mind which reached such great height in these concepts.

580. He deals with this problem in his dialogue with a friend, Evodius. The dialogue, set in Rome (where it perhaps took place) is found in book 2 of his *On Free Will*. He begins by noting the difference between the *individuality of our powers* and the *universality of truth* shining equally in all human beings. He writes:

Augustine: I first ask whether the feeling of my body is the same as yours or whether mine is only mine, and yours only yours.

Evodius: I fully grant that each of us has particular senses of seeing, hearing and other sensible operations, although they are of the same kind.

Augustine: Would you say the same about the internal sense?

Evodius: I would.

Augustine: But what about reason? Don't we each have our own? Certainly, I can understand something which you don't. And you cannot know whether I understand or not, although I myself certainly know whether I understand.

Evodius: Yes, we have our own particular mind.

Augustine: But can you say perhaps that we also have our own particular visible sun, our own particular light, star and such things, although we each see them with our own sense?

Evodius: No, I wouldn't say that.

Augustine: A group of us therefore can see one, single thing, although each of us has our own particular sense with which we all sense that thing and simultaneously see it. Although my sense is not yours, I see the same thing as you; the same thing is present to and seen simultaneously by both of us.

Evodius: Yes, that's clear.

Augustine: We can also hear the same voice, although my sense is not yours. But my hearing does not receive one part and yours another; we both hear the total sound whatever it is.

[580]

Evodius: Right.[58]

Augustine: Now, tell me, do all who reason (each of course with his own reason) see anything in common? What is seen by the eye is, as we said, present to all; it is not changed in use by those to whom it is present for their use, like food and drink; it remains entire and incorrupt whether seen or not. Or do you think that nothing of this sort exists?

Evodius: On the contrary, I see there are many things like this. It is sufficient to recall one: the explanation and truth of number. Number is present to all who can count[59] in such a way that each strives to apprehend it with his own reason and intelligence. Some do this easily, others with more difficulty, and some not at all. Nevertheless it presents itself equally to all who can understand it. Moreover, when understood, it is not changed into food, as it were, for its perceiver, nor altered.[60] Even when someone makes a mistake in calculation, the explanation and truth of number remains true and complete although the person making the calculation is more involved in error the less he sees the truth.

Augustine: Quite right. I see you have some experience of

---

[58] In St. Augustine's time, the analysis of sensations was not as developed as it is now. We must not be surprised, therefore, if no distinction seems to be made here between the sun perceived by our senses and perceived by our understanding. Strictly speaking, our senses do not perceive the sun but only its partial action. The sun's action on different people, although similar and of the same kind, is numerically different. Thus, although we can say that different senses perceive different suns in a particular way, it would be more accurate to say that, strictly speaking, the sun as such is perceived only by the understanding, which perceives the *sun-ens*. Sense perceives only the *agent* in its various, separate actions.

[59] Note how carefully St. Augustine distinguishes between *subject* and *object* and between *reasoning power* and *truth* perceived by reason. The differences he notes are clear and undeniable. Nevertheless we still hear of people who claim to make knowledge and *truth* one with the human *mind*; for them, knowledge and truth are simply an effect or emanation of the mind.

[60] Note that subject who understands is varied, changeable and defective. Truth (object) does not suffer anything from the various conditions of the subject endeavouring to contemplate it. These last words of St. Augustine destroy every system which claims that knowledge is informed by the qualities of the subject. This cannot be true at all, because knowledge is by nature immutable.

these matters and can reply immediately. But what would you say if someone claimed that numbers were not impressed in the spirit in virtue of their nature, but by the things we perceive with our corporeal sense, as if numbers were images of visible things? Do you think this could be the case?

Evodius: No, I don't. Even if I perceived numbers with my corporeal sense,[61] this could not explain how they can be subtracted or added. Only through this light of my mind do I correct a person who makes a mistake in adding or subtracting. I may not know the duration of everything I perceive with my bodily sense, like the sky, earth and everything in them, but I do know that seven and three make ten, and that this is true now and for ever; there never was and never will be a time when seven and three do not make ten.[62]

Augustine: I agree entirely; there is no doubt about that. But note, not even the ideas of numbers are abstracted from corporeal senses. You will see this easily if you consider that every number is a composite of unity. For example, the number which is twice one unity is called two; that which is three times one unity, is three, and that which is ten times, ten. In other words, each number receives its name according to the number of times it has one. Now, anyone who truthfully thinks what one is finds that it certainly cannot be felt by the corporeal senses. Everything perceived by bodily sense shows itself as many, not one, because it is a body, which has innumerable parts. But without getting involved in such small, inarticulate parts of bodies, I say that whatever the size of a body, it certainly has left, right, higher and lower parts, or sides and an end and a middle part. Such things are clearly present in every size of body, no matter how small. We must grant therefore that no body is truly and purely *one*, although in order to number all the things in it we would have to distinguish them by means of our knowledge of unity. When I look for unity in a body and certainly know I cannot find it, I nevertheless know beyond all doubt what I'm looking for, although I do not and cannot find it, or rather it is

[61] Although Evodius seems to grant here that numbers can be perceived by sense, St. Augustine immediately rejects this as impossible.

[62] These are the characteristics of immutability, necessity and eternity, noted by St. Augustine in the properties of numbers.

not there to be found. Thus knowing that *one* is not body pre-supposes that I have the idea 'one'. If I do not know what one is, I could not number the *many* things of the body. Furthermore, whenever I know one, I certainly do not know it through bodily sense. This gives me knowledge only of body, which never shows itself as truly and purely one.[63] If however we do not know unity through bodily sense, we cannot know any number with that sense — I mean numbers seen with our understanding.[64] In fact, all numbers are named by the quantity of unity within them — unity which is not perceived by bodily sense.

St. Augustine goes on to discuss the properties and relation-ships of numbers, and shows them to be eternal and independ-ent of anything temporal.

581. He says:

> Moreover, if we look at the order of numbers, we see that two comes after one and is the double of one. But the double of two does not come immediately after two. To obtain this double, which is four, we have to place another number, three, between two and four. This fact, which ap-plies to all numbers, is governed by the following most certain, immutable law: the quantity of a given number must be repeated in order to find its double. This charac-teristic, which we see to be immutable, firm and incorrupt and valid for all numbers, does not come from our senses, because nobody can perceive with his bodily sense all

[63] Granted also that there is some kind of *unity* in the body, as in the case of extended continua, I must, in order to know the unity of a body, always perceive the body first as *ens* and then as *one*, that is, objectively. Sense itself, however, can receive only the *action* of things, and feels this action in its own feeling, not the things in themselves and outside its own feeling. Moreover, the unity of what is extended is not perfect because the *possibility* of division and multiplicity is never excluded.

[64] Shallow-thinking people are convinced that it is very easy to conceive multiplicity. *Conceiving it* is indeed easy, but *explaining how it is conceived* is difficult. They confuse the fact of the conception with its theory, the facility of the conception with the difficulty of its explanation. On the other hand, anyone who considers the matter deeply will see that 1. we cannot conceive the *many* unless the idea of the *one* is already in us, and 2. we cannot conceive the *one* unless the idea of *ens* is already in us.

[581]

numbers, which are innumerable.[65] How then do we
know that this law is valid for all numbers? What phantasy or phantasm enables us to see a totally reliable truth
about numbers applicable with complete certainty to an
innumerable series of things, if we do not see this truth in
interior light, a light unknown to bodily sense?

He concludes:

> These and many other teachings constrain those whom
> God has gifted with skill in argument and whose minds are
> not darkened with prejudice, to confess that the explana-
> tion and truth of numbers does not pertain to the bodily
> senses, that this truth is inflexible and always clear, and a
> common object given to be seen by all who reason.[66]

§2

582. St. Augustine now introduces similar arguments for all
unassailable truths whatsoever. He shows how they are completely alien to the senses, like the truths concerning numbers,
and how they must proceed from a source higher than sensible,
temporary natures. I will make use of one passage from these
arguments to reveal more clearly the mind of such an authority,
and to confirm more securely the truth discussed in the whole
of this work, namely, that the formal part of knowledge cannot
come from the senses. I shall continue his discussion with
Evodius at the point where he moves from numbers to other
truths.

Augustine: We maintain that wisdom exists, and everyone
wishes to be wise and happy. How do we see this? I am sure you
see it, and see that it is true. But do you see this truth in the same
way as you see your thought of which I am ignorant, unless you

[65] Here we see how St. Augustine realises that our reasoning about
possible, necessary things exceeds all experience.

[66] *His et talibus multis documentis coguntur fateri, quibus disputantibus
Deus donavit ingenium et pertinacia caliginem non obducit, rationem
veritatemque numerorum et ad sensus corporis non pertinere, et invertibilem
sinceramque consistere, et omnibus ratiocinantibus ad videndum esse
communem* (*De lib. Arbitrio*, 2, 8).

tell me what it is? Or rather, do you see the truth and are at the same time aware that I also can see it, even if you do not reveal it to me?[67]

Evodius: I am certain that you can yourself see the truth, even if I do not want you to.

Augustine: Well, if we both see the same truth with our own individual minds, it must be common to us.

Evodius: I agree.

Augustine: Now let's take another, similar proposition. I think you will accept as true the proposition that human beings must apply themselves to the study and love of wisdom.

Evodius: Certainly.

Augustine: Can we deny that this truth is one, and is commonly visible to all who know it, even though each person sees it with his own mind and not mine or yours or anybody else's?

Evodius: We certainly cannot deny it.

Augustine: Would you not agree that we must live justly, that inferior things take second place to better things, that equal things must be considered equally, and that every ens must be given what is due to it? And if you agree, are not all these opinions true and present in common to me, yourself and all who see them?

Evodius: I fully agree.

Augustine: You will also not deny, I am sure, that what is incorrupt is more valuable than what is corrupt, and what is eternal, more than what is temporary, and what is inviolable, more than what is violable?

Evodius: No doubt about it.

Augustine: Can anyone call this truth his own when it is there to be contemplated, resplendent in an unchangeable light, by all who are capable of doing so?

Evodius: No one would truly say it is their own; it is as much one and common to all as it is true.

Augustine: Right. You agree with me and grant as certain that these rules and lights of virtue, as we may call them, are both true and immutable and, whether taken singularly or all together, are present in common ready to be intuited by those able

---

[67] This is a very acute, accurate observation and greatly helps us to distinguish between knowledge of contingent and of necessary things.

to intuit them, each with his own reason and mind. In your opinion therefore, do these things appertain to wisdom?

Evodius: Certainly.

Augustine: Well then, the rules of wisdom are just as true and unchangeable as those of numbers, whose explanation and truth are present unchangeably and in common to all who gaze upon them. I have taken a few of the rules of wisdom and questioned you about them individually. You replied that they are true and clear, and granted that they are contemplated in common by all who are capable of doing so.[68]

Evodius: I certainly did.

Augustine: You conclude that you cannot deny that there is an *unchangeable truth* which contains all these things that are immutably true, a truth that you cannot call your own or mine or anybody else's. You say in fact that it is ready to offer itself to be seen in common by all who can see immutable truths; it is, in a wonderful way, a kind of hidden and simultaneously public light.

Evodius: Everything you say is very true and clear.

Augustine: Let me ask you something. This *truth* we have been discussing for a long time and in which we see so many things, do you think it is more excellent than our mind, or equal or inferior to it?

Evodius: Perhaps inferior.[69]

Augustine: If it were inferior, we would judge it just as we judge inferior bodies rather than judge by it; we often say not only that they are this or that, but that they *ought* to be different in this way or that. We say the same about our spirit: not only do we know what it is, we often know what it *ought* to be. In the case of bodies, for example, we judge, 'It is not as white as it should be', or 'It is not truly square', and so on. In the case of a spirit, 'It is not disposed as it should be', or 'It is not gentle enough', or 'It is far too listless', according to the demands of

---

[68] Note how St. Augustine proves that moral and metaphysical sciences are grounded on unshakeable foundations, just as much as those we call exact, rigorous sciences.

[69] To help the reader understand the argument better, I have interrupted Augustine's words here, and Evodius' reply further on, but the substance of the teaching is in no way disturbed.

custom. We judge these things according to the internal rules of
the truth we all see in common. But no one judges the internal
rules in any way. If someone says that eternal things are more
valuable than temporal, and that seven and three make ten, no
one will say it has to be like that. Instead, knowing that the thing
is like that, he does not correct it as though he were inspecting it,
but delights in it as though he had discovered it.

Evodius: Well, if the truth is not *inferior* to the mind, I presume it is *equal* to it.

Augustine: If that were the case, the truth would be changeable, just as our mind is.[70] Our minds, which sometimes see
more, sometimes less, must be accepted as changeable. When
the truth is constant in itself, it does not develop because we see
it better, nor regress because we see it less. Complete and
incorrupt, it satisfies with its light those who turn to it and pun-
ishes with blindness those who withdraw from it. This is so true
that we judge even our minds *according to it*, although we cannot judge *it* in any way. We quite rightly say a person does not
understand, or understands sufficiently. The mind is governed
by this law: it understands in exact proportion to its nearness
and attachment to immutable truth. We must conclude therefore that the truth is neither *inferior* nor *equal* but *superior* to
the mind and of a more excellent nature.[71]

Such is Augustine's teaching.

---

[70] All these arguments are most effective in clearly demonstrating that the
truth is not a product of the mind (of the subject) but an *entity* superior to the
mind and to the human subject. It comes to the mind and to the human
subject from a source infinitely superior to the human being. It is sad that
Galluppi did not see this.

[71] *De libero arbitrio*, 2: 7–12.

CHAPTER 2

Origin of the idea of substance

583. So far I have shown that ideas taken as a whole, together with the principles of reason and in particular the ideas which I called *elementary concepts of being* that serve as conditions for the use of reason, have their origin, on the occasion of sensations, in a first idea naturally present to our spirit. As we saw, this theory overcomes the difficulty of the origin of ideas on which so many philosophers, and philosophy itself (cf. 539–551), foundered.

I also noted that the difficulty, set out by me in a general way, presented itself under particular forms to others who attempted to explain the origin of special classes of ideas. It would be helpful, therefore, if I carried on to show how the theory could resolve not only the general difficulty but also its individual manifestations. This implies that all special ideas, which have caused endless trouble to so many philosophers, can be deduced from the supreme idea of being.

I have, however, already dealt with the elementary ideas of being. I can turn, therefore, to the ideas of substance and cause as the closest to the first ideas, and the most difficult and necessary to examine.

Article 1

The question relative to the origin of the idea of substance

584. The difficulty encountered in indicating the origin of the idea of substance is compounded by the inexact, confused concept of substance many philosophers have created for themselves. They confuse the idea of substance as a genus with the ideas of specific substances. For example, they maintain that because we cannot know the substance of bodies, we cannot have the idea of substance. This is far from being a rigorous argument.

It is also clear that we could have the idea of *substance as a genus* without knowing intimately any *substance* connected with particular things. It is as though we saw a weight suspended from a column without knowing whether its support was a piece of chain or a length of rope. We could be ignorant of the material and shape of what holds the weight and nevertheless realise that there must be some kind of support.

Our own case is somewhat similar. In order to know that a substance must be present, it is not necessary to know that it is the substance we call 'body' nor do we need to understand its nature fully. Conversely, we do not have to conclude that in general we have no notion of substance if we do not know what forms substance in bodies. Indeed, we could not know that some substance was necessary to bodies if we had no notion of substance.

585. As someone said not long ago, to demonstrate that we possess the notion of substance is to beg the question.[72] We have to ask those who deny the existence of the notion of substance how they can deny what they do not know.[73] As I have noted many times, the idea of substance is a fact witnessed to by the human race, including those who deny it in words. Even if mankind were deceiving itself, and believed it possessed an idea that it did not in fact have, it would still be necessary for it to think it had it. But thinking it has an idea, and having one, are equivalent because an apparent idea is no less an idea than any other. Further than this one cannot go.

[72] 'I know I am guilty of begging the question when I discuss such a matter. I set out to see if the notions of substance and cause are present to the human spirit while I, a human spirit, suppose these notions before me; furthermore, I posit them after defining them. It is clear that I am begging my own question, just as it is clear that I am objecting to myself. As Pascal put it so well: "Evidence is not to be proved"' (Cousins, *Fragments philosophiques*, p. 425).

[73] Sceptics create their own difficulty in imagining that *idea* is external, and mediated. On the contrary, it is totally interior and immediate and, as such, outside controversy. In other words, a fact.

Article 2

Description and analysis of all that we think about substance

§1. *The starting point for the study of ideas of substance*

586. First, we must ascertain the facts by verifying our cognitions and thoughts about substance. It is these cognitions or thoughts which must be explained.

One fact is this: the mind thinks of substance. To say: it is an illusion, or it is a false thought, gets us nowhere and is irrelevant to our discussion. Our mind has its thoughts, true or false, illusory or real, and it is our task to explain their origin. The philosopher must indicate the cause of what the mind *thinks* it does, as well as what it does. When we find the origin of the thoughts that we believe we have about substance, we shall be able to weigh their value and decide what legitimate use we can put them to. Their origin determines their authenticity and truth, or shows them to be spurious illusions — at least in their applications (it is impossible for them to be illusions *per se*). Our first step, therefore, is to analyse everything the human mind conceives about substance.

§2. *Definition of substance*

587. Substance is 'the energy by which an ens and all that it possesses actually exists', or 'the energy in which the actual existence of the ens is grounded'. The relationship between *substance* and *accident* is not fully developed in this definition, and will have to be dealt with later.

§3. *Analysis of the concept of substance*

588. Let us analyse the concept to find how many ways the mind conceives this energy.

We note two elements: 1. the act of existence, or that energy by which an ens exists;[74] 2. the ens itself that exists (essence).

The distinction depends upon an abstraction, which is exactly what we need because we are speaking of what exists in the mind, not outside it. What is in the mind is not seen separately from other things except by means of abstraction which is incapable of producing division in things subsisting outside our spirit. Abstraction is a fact, an operation of the spirit. It is also a fact that many thoughts can be abstracted from a single thought. Although our attention is first directed to one entire thought through a single act, attention can then split into as many acts as there are parts of the thought to turn to. It would be unreasonable to object here, as modern sophists often do, that we are abusing abstraction in order to create imaginary entia. The objection is an attempt to evade the core of the question which requires us to explain the fact of abstraction and its products. We cannot prescind from abstraction, nor avoid noting and describing the different thoughts and concepts it forms and originates in our spirit. Whether ideas respond or not to something outside the mind, they remain ideas, and we have undertaken to explain them all as the title of this work indicates.

§4. *Various modes of the idea of substance*

589. What modes can be assumed by our idea of substance?

1. We can think the *energy*, by which entia exist, in all its universality. In this case, we do not think any particular ens, but any possible ens whatsoever, without any determination except that necessary for its existence. This is the idea of *substance in all its universality*.

2. We can think the *energy* of an ens furnished with some generic determination. This is the idea of *generic substance*.[75]

---

[74] *The energy that constitutes the actual existence of entia* and *the energy by which they exist* are one and the same. The first expression explains the second. In a word, we must not make two things of the *energy* we are speaking about and the *actual existence* of entia. The *actual existence* is the *energy* itself.

[75] It is necessary to recall what has been said about *genera* and species (cf. 499–500), and the way in which we mentally conceive these classifications.

3. We can think the *energy* predicated of a *specifically* determined ens. In this case, we think the actual existence possible to the individual of a determined species furnished with everything necessary to its existence, that is, with what is common and proper. When the mind thinks the possibility of such an individual's actual existence, without knowing whether it really exists, it has the idea of *specific substance* which is either an idea-exemplar or can be reduced to the state of idea-exemplar.

590. Before going further, let us examine carefully these three more or less abstract ideas of substance. We have called them: *idea of substance in all its universality, idea of generic substance,* and *idea of specific substance.*

In all three of these conceptions we think an individual, that is, a single, undivided ens, furnished with everything necessary for existence. The difference between the conceptions lies in the mode according to which each one is thought, that is, with or without its determinations.

A question may help to clarify the matter: when I think substance in all its universality, what am I thinking? What is comprised in this idea of *substance in all its universality*?

I think any ens whatsoever (an individual, therefore) that possesses the energy called actual existence. I am not asking to which class, or genus, or species it belongs; I think only its energy or actual existence. Along with this, I think implicitly that the ens is determined with everything required for existence, without, however, mentally determining these determinations or properties or asking what they may be.

The idea of *substance in all its universality* contains, therefore: 1. the thought of actual existence; 2. the thought of the individual which exists; 3. the thought in all its universality of the determinations it must have in order to exist, that is, the thought that it must be complete, with everything necessary for existence. But there is no attempt to know what is necessary for making it a determined ens, a complete type.

Similarly, these three elementary thoughts can be distinguished in the idea of *generic substance*: 1. the thought of an energy constituting its existence; 2. the thought of an ens possessing this energy in itself; 3. the thought of the determinations necessary in order that this ens be complete relative to existence, that is, an individual.

[590]

The third part of these two ideas is variable, and the different modes in which we mentally conceive the third element accounts for the difference between the two ideas.

In the idea of *substance in all its universality* we think the ens as having in itself all the determinations or properties necessary for existence, but without specifying these determinations in any way. In the idea of *substance as a genus*, however, we think certain generic determinations of the ens. For example, we think of a spiritual or corporeal substance. We are not thinking of an individual in all its universality, but of an individual of a determined spiritual or corporeal genus.

Finally, the idea of *specific substance*, if *full*, contains the individual with all its determined generic and proper characteristics. If I think the substance of an individual tree, and not of any tree whatsoever, I must think a tree furnished with all its distinct notes and characteristics.[76]

In all three ideas of substance, therefore, we think something totally determined in its relationship to being. This thing, which lacks nothing except subsistence, I call 'individual'. An architect who designs a house with all that it needs for existence thinks a perfect house. Building it, he adds nothing to its idea, which already embraces every part of the house; what is new is the house itself which is given existence in itself without loss to the ideal existence in the mind of the person who has conceived and thought it out in all its details.

Hence, we can think the individual in all its universality when we think all that is necessary for an ens to exist, but without determining any of its characteristics.

We can think the generic individual when, in addition to what is necessary in general for its existence, we begin to think of the generic qualities of an ens.

Finally, when we add specific to generic qualities in addition

[76] We shall see later (cf. 646–659), in dealing with genera and species, that it is not necessary for me to offer another class of ideas of substance to accommodate imperfect individuals in a species. Ideas of this kind are ideas of perfect individuals (specific, complete idea) from which certain valuable characteristics have been removed.

Moreover, we are not speaking here of any affirmation about *subsistent* individuals; we think these not with ideas alone, but with our judgment. We shall speak of subsistent individuals later.

to what is necessary in general for its existence, we can think the specific individual. In a word, we can think 1. any individual whatsoever, 2. an individual of a determined genus, and 3. a special individual.

If I think the energy by which an individual can subsist, I think substance in all its universality; thinking the energy by which an individual of a given genus can exist, I think substance as genus; thinking the energy by which an individual of a given species can exist, I think of special substance. The idea of substance in all its universality, of generic and of specific substance are always ideas of *energy* constituting actual existence, which can only pertain to *individuals*.

§5. Origin of the idea of individual

591. I cannot think the actual existence of an ens unless I think simultaneously that this ens receives every determination necessary for its existence.

The idea of *individual*, therefore, is intimately connected and associated with the idea of substance. Explaining the origin of the idea of substance presents us with the explanation of the origin of the idea of individual.

But there can be no other ideas of substance or individual in our mind except the three we have listed: substance in all its universality, generic substance and special substance. Our next task is to describe the origin of each of them.

§6. Judgments on the subsistence of substances differ from ideas of substance

592. Nevertheless, we have not yet explained all our thoughts about substances.

Besides *ideas*, we form *judgments* on the real subsistence of substances.

Like the architect with a complete idea of the house he is about to construct, we present ourselves with an (as yet) non-subsistent ens in our idea. As long as we think only of the possible subsistence of the individual, we have still not embraced anything that really subsists.

But let us grant that an individual corresponding to our idea really subsists, and that we can perceive it. How does our perception take place? We have already seen that we affirm, by means of a judgment, the subsistence of the individual we think of in the idea.

Let us be quite clear that the act by which we say, 'Such a thing subsists', is an operation of the spirit essentially different from simple intuition. It unites to the idea of the thing a *persuasion* or belief in the subsistence of what has previously been thought as possible.[77]

It follows that as there are three ideas of substance, so there are three judgments that we can make about the subsistence of these substances in so far as we can judge: 1. that a substance subsists; 2. that a substance of a given genus subsists; 3. that a substance of a given species subsists.

§7. *Summary of all the thoughts the human mind can have about substances*

593. Our thoughts about substances consist in *ideas* and *judgments*, both of which embrace three species: the idea of substance in all its universality, the idea of generic substance, the idea of special substance; judgment about the subsistence of a substance in all its universality, judgment about the subsistence of a substance of a given kind, judgment about the subsistence of a special substance.

We have to describe the origin of all these ideas and judgments, showing how they are possible to the human mind.

---

[77] To object that in doing this we acquire a new idea, the idea of subsistence, would be out of place because this was already present; without it, we cannot think 'An ens *can* subsist.' *Persuasion* about real existence is something entirely distinct from *mental conception*; the nature of persuasion is totally different from that of ideas.

[593]

Article 3

The three ideas of substance follow one from the other

594. Let us see if we can facilitate our study by avoiding separate treatment of each of the ideas and judgments we form about substances. First, we can lighten our work by noting the connection which binds the three ideas in such a way that one gives rise to another. If, therefore, we can explain the origin of one of them, we have explained the origin of the other two.

Let us take for granted the idea of special substance. In order to possess the ideas of generic substance and of substance in all its universality, it is now sufficient to abstract them from the idea of special substance which provides us with the idea of the actual existence of an ens, fully determined in its common and proper characteristics. If we set aside its special characteristics we are left with generic subsistence; setting aside generic determinations, we are left with the universalised idea. In a word, the ideas of generic substance and of substance in all its universality are only abstractions of the idea of special substance. When we have explained this, we will have explained the other two.

We have already used this method in clarifying the *status quaestionis* (cf. vol. 1, 41–44): explain one idea, and the rest can be explained by means of abstraction. If we restrict the problem to that of substance, it can now be stated as follows: 'We need to explain the idea of specific substance; the explanation of other ideas of substance will then be clear.'

Article 4

All judgments on the subsistence of substances are explained when one difficulty is overcome

595. What is the origin, therefore, of the idea of special substance?

As we search for the origin of this idea, we find it connected with the judgments we make on the subsistence of entia. If we focus our attention on this connection and penetrate its meaning, we notice that a single explanation will satisfy two questions: what is the origin of the idea of special substance? and what is the origin of the judgments we make on the subsistence of substances?

We have already pointed out that we make three judgments about the subsistence of substances. If we consider their connection, we shall see how the same difficulty is present in all three.

In judging the subsistence: 1. of any individual ens whatsoever, 2. of an individual of a certain genus or 3. of a certain species, we have to be prompted by some reason which determines us to affirm the subsistence of individuals.

This reason is our perception of the individuals, and once found it explains how these judgments are formed by our spirit. In all three kinds of judgments, therefore, the single difficulty we have to solve consists in showing what prompts us to say 'Such an individual subsists.'

Article 5

The explanation of the specific idea of substance depends on the difficulty found in accounting for judgments on the subsistence of substances

596. We must, therefore: 1. indicate the manner in which we form the idea of specific substance; 2. show the reason leading us to judge of the subsistence of these substances. This is our problem, stated simply (cf. 594–595). But granted the connection between the two questions, it can be put even more simply if we take account of the reason prompting us to posit the subsistence of an individual.

We say to ourselves, 'Such and such an individual subsists.' Included in the perception of this individual is the idea of substance. But substance is simply the energy by which an ens exists. We cannot therefore conceive a subsistent ens without conceiving it together with the energy by which it exists, that is, with its substance.

Hence the two questions can be reduced to one: how can I judge that an ens subsists? If I make such a judgment and perceive this ens, I inevitably perceive its substance and easily form or rather have already formed an idea of it.

Article 6

Explanation of the perception of individuals

597. We have already explained carefully how intellective perception of individuals takes place, and how we form our ideas about them as we make the judgments affirming their subsistence (cf. 528–534). We are now in a position, therefore, to sum up and resolve our present question:

1. We form ideas of individuals by means of the judgment we make about their subsistence.

2. We can draw the abstract idea of special substance from the intellective perception of individuals. From this idea we can draw the more abstract idea of generic substance, from which in turn we can draw the idea of substance in all its universality.

3. The intellective perception of individuals has already been explained.

No difficulty remains, therefore, in explaining both the origin of the three ideas and of the judgments we make about substances.

CHAPTER 3

A further explanation of the idea of substance

Article 1

Necessity of the explanation

598. What has been said so far could seem more than sufficient. However, granted the times, it may not be sufficient for everybody. It will certainly not suffice for those who have already accepted any of the various opinions about the origin of the idea of substance and grown used to them. Their opinion will be as tenacious as it is ingenious, like that of the German school, which is rapidly establishing itself in France and Italy, and could extend to the whole world if it puts down strong, vigorous roots here.

I will therefore explain further the teaching I have given, which alone I believe to be true. I will try to make it clearer so that even the prejudiced who do not find it wholly convincing (a very difficult task) will see it as strong and unassailable.

Article 2

Systems dealing with the origin of the idea of substance

599. In the course of this work I have already touched upon four systems offered by philosophers to overcome the difficulty of the origin of the idea of substance. They are:

I. Some philosophers, unable to extricate themselves from the maze, denied the existence of the idea. Their argument can be reduced to the following: 'I cannot explain the origin of the notion of substance; therefore it does not exist.' The reader will know how to answer these philosophers.

II. Some tried to extract the idea from sensations. They claim to follow the facts, and argue as follows: 'All ideas *must* come from sensations because this alone is the source of all the knowledge we recognise in a human being. Therefore the idea of substance also must come from sensations.' Is this really the most perfect type of rigorously philosophical method in its search for facts?

III. Some said that the idea of substance must be innate because it could neither be denied nor come from sensations.

IV. Finally some, who saw that innate ideas today encounter very strong opposition, thought a third system possible, in addition to the systems which make the idea come from the senses or make it innate. The connection between the idea of substance and the idea of accidents (or accidental qualities) was, for them, so close that these ideas could not be separated. They took this as a primal fact; the human spirit therefore could not conceive one without the other. But the source of their argument is a *psychological* law, a law of the spirit itself. They do indeed call the connection between substance and accidents *ontological*, that is, *self-contained*, but mean that this connection *appears* such to the human spirit through a necessity intrinsic to the spirit. When they consider the connection relative to the human spirit which conceives and forms it, they call it *psychological*. In other words, 'The human spirit makes the idea of substance emanate from itself when it perceives accidents, but in such a way that the connection to the accidents appears necessary.' The necessity is objective but only *apparently* so, which means that it is not objective. It appears objective to the spirit because the spirit cannot see it in any other way. The necessity is *subjective objectivity* and, they say, we can go no further than this.

A recent disciple of this system (which in the last analysis is Kant's, whatever its modifications), speaks about universal notions, among which he includes the notion of substance. He says: 1. 'These notions have a psychological, not a logical origin'; 2. 'No one can ever find the explanation of any of these truths', and 3. 'As soon as I conceive the truth, I conceive it as immutable, eternal, absolute'. Hence he describes it as coming from the soul, but offers only necessity, fact, as the sole explanation of its origin. The nature of the spirit is such that of itself it extracts the idea or somehow sees the idea when it sees the sensible qualities. In the eyes of critical philosophy, this mysterious fatalism is where human research ends. In plain language, these philosophers are saying: 'The general notion of substance does not come from the senses, nor is it innate, nor can we say it is nothing. It is therefore an appearance (real only relative to us) which emanates from the nature of our spirit.'[78]

600. This system, whatever its guise, is idealism and scepticism. It rests finally on this argument: 'There are only four systems capable of explaining the idea of substance. The first three are untenable. Therefore the last is true.'

The argument would be acceptable provided the absurdity of a fifth system were demonstrated. Unfortunately, this does not occur to the mind of our philosophers. But if they do not show the absurdity of a fifth system to explain the idea of substance, their method is not an example of modesty but of incredible presumption, though they see themselves as the first to restrain philosophical self-confidence and make philosophy solid and circumspect. Consequently they forget to add 'as far as we know' to the first part of their proposition. This little rider would have been sufficient to make them choose a totally different route.

In my opinion, a modest, discreet philosopher would argue as follows: 'As far as I know, there are only four systems capable of explaining the idea of substance. The first three raise very serious difficulties; the fourth results in idealism and scepticism, which is repugnant to rational natures and therefore flawed. Consequently, I must admit that I am unable to explain the idea of substance.'

Article 3
Another way of finding the origin of the idea of substance

601. But there is indeed a fifth system, which I have explained and which avoids all the difficulties of the four systems known to and exhausted by modern philosophy.

The idea of substance comes from the *form* of human cognitions, that is, from the idea of being.

In this system the idea of substance is neither denied, nor

[78] Even Galluppi has gone along with this, like all subjectivists.

deduced from sensations, nor seen as innate nor proclaimed as apparent and subjective. It is deduced from the first, essential idea of all ideas which alone is innate and, as we shall see better elsewhere (Section 6), justified of itself because it is truth itself.

Hence, the idea of substance is conceived precisely when we have occasion to deduce it from the first idea. This occasion is given us at the very moment of our first sensations and perceptions. Although we do not conceive it abstractly, isolated and free of every other addition, we nevertheless conceive it. Only later, when we begin to philosophise and make abstractions from our concepts, do we acquire it in its abstract, pure form.

This idea therefore has *logical* as well as *psychological antecedents*, as Cousin puts it; it does not, as it were, emanate through blind fatalism from the soul. It is deduced, and can be assigned an explanation which justifies it and proves it true. I will now give a more detailed explanation of this idea of substance.

Article 4

First proposition: if our understanding conceives, it conceives something

602. This has already been demonstrated: 'conceiving nothing' and 'not conceiving' mean the same thing.

If our understanding cannot conceive and operate without an object, it must conceive either an ens (through the principle of knowledge, cf. 565) or something. These words are the most universal of all; their opposite is nothing. As we saw, our understanding is 'the faculty of conceiving ens, that is, something having an existence of its own' (cf. 480–482).[79]

[79] The intellect is the faculty of conceiving things as having an existence of their own. It can certainly be mistaken about the real existence of things. But even when mistaken, it conceives them as having an existence of their own.

Article 5

Second proposition: everything can be an object of the understanding

§1. *Definition*

603. Consequently, 'everything can be an object of the under-standing' because everything has a species of existence proper to itself. To say that a thing exists but has no existence is a con-tradiction in terms (principle of contradiction).

Whatever has no existence either in itself or in another is not thinkable; it is not an object of the understanding. We can, therefore, say frankly that it does not exist, because 'having no existence' and 'not existing' mean the same thing; it is nothing.

§2. *Objection to the principle of contradiction*

604. At this point it is most important for the reader to see the validity of my argument.

Followers of the fourth system will, I am sure, retort: 'You invoke the principle of contradiction to show that the intellect, the faculty of being, can conceive everything. But how do you prove the force of this principle? According to the ancients, the proof was complete because rooted in the principle of contra-diction; granted the force of the principle, it was impossible to proceed further. However, we find the argument gratuitous and deny it *a parte sui*. Furthermore, the nature of the argument requires you to justify the principle of contradiction. In your desire to convince the sceptics, you show that the idea of sub-stance is something objectively true, not merely subjective and apparent, nor a blind, fatal emanation of spiritual nature. If you now introduce the principle of contradiction into your argu-ment as something objectively true, you are supposing that objective truth exists. On the contrary, we maintain that the idea of substance is ultimately subjective and apparent, because there is no possibility in the human being of any knowledge whatsoever endowed with really objective truth. If you begin by begging the question, we are not surprised at your later adding to the idea of substance the same objective truth that you gratuitously bestow on the principle of contradiction.'

§3. *Reply. — The principle of contradiction defended*

605. The objectors fail to note that I deduced the principle of contradiction from the idea of being by showing it to be one with this idea. They have not felt the force of this idea, which is justified by itself, and with its light satisfies and conquers all the doubts of those who gaze directly upon it. Without wishing to repeat what I have already said or anticipating what I will say in Section 6, let me use a more gentle but equally capable way of persuading (if that is possible) our sceptics. This will reinforce and profit the truth I am defending, which becomes clearer and more resplendent the more we see its many sides and aspects.

The only postulate I must be granted is 'the use of language'. If I am forbidden this, I could not add one more word. My adversaries would have rather unkindly forced me to silence, while they themselves could proclaim with full voice that they are right, as if language, or certainly proclamation, was reserved solely to them.

Granted then the use of language, when I say 'a thing', 'a thing' has to be understood; if on the contrary 'a non-thing, nothing' were understood, then the language allowed me would simply be mockery. The use of language demands that what is said is said. When I say 'bread', I say 'bread' and when I say 'stone', I say 'stone'.

If I say a word and immediately retract and deny it, I have not said anything; I have recalled and cancelled what I said. If I draw a line on paper and then erase it, the paper is clean again. If you allowed me to draw something provided that I immediately erase it, no one would say I have been allowed to draw. Similarly, if you grant me the use of language only on condition that every word I say must be immediately withdrawn and cancelled, I have not been granted the use of language. Language is not a casual conjunction of sounds; it is an order of sounds indicating ideas. The possibility of my use of language requires that I avoid contradictory, contrasting expressions. A language composed of expressions of this kind is not the language whose use is granted me.

Hence, if I speak about 'a thing that does not exist in any way', I am not concerned whether the phrase is logical or not. I am saying that it is not language because it says nothing. I am saying that the person who says it, is making noises, not words, and making noises even better than the person who retracts and denies the word he has spoken. In fact, the meaning attached to the word 'thing' is precisely the idea of some existence. When I say 'thing' therefore, I express the idea of some existence, and when I add, 'that does not exist in any way', I destroy the idea I first posited. The word 'thing' is now as if I had never said it; the phrase is similar to the algebraic formula $a\text{-}a$, which equals *zero*.

§4. *The demonstration concluded*

606. Granted all this, my proposition that 'everything can be the object of the understanding',[80] seems clear; every system, because it requires only one postulate, must be granted by all who speak. Sceptics indeed have never shown themselves disposed to silence, any more than all the other classes and kinds of philosophers.

Article 6

Third proposition: the understanding can perceive qualities only in a subject in which they exist

607. The reason is that the understanding's proper mode of perceiving is to perceive things in the existence with which they are endowed (cf. 602).

[80] I think that even those who deny objective truth must accept my definition of *understanding* and the proposition that it can conceive everything, even though they are compelled to give these two propositions a subjective truth, as they call it, that is, apparent to the subject.

Sensible qualities, however, do not have any existence in themselves, but in a subject different from us.

The understanding therefore (which can perceive anything whatsoever because anything whatsoever has some kind of existence (cf. 603–606)) must, in perceiving sensible qualities, perceive them together with the subject in which they exist. Otherwise it would not perceive them; they would be imperceptible — they are perceptible only because their subject is perceptible.

On the other hand, let us suppose that the understanding does perceive them. In this case it would perceive something (cf. 602). If it perceives something, it perceives an existence, something existing. But something existing is the same as saying a substance, because substance is the act by which an ens exists (cf. 587).

Article 7

The distinction between Hume's idealism and Berkeley's

608. My argument runs counter to the idealists of Hume's school.

Hume, unlike Berkeley, was not satisfied with positing the doubt that bodies may be nothing more than ideas. He went further and wondered whether perhaps ideas could exist by themselves, without any subject, so that the whole universe was simply an infinite number of ideas in random motion, like waves of a great ocean or atoms in an immense vacuum.

There are two questions therefore: 1. can sensible qualities (whether ideas or anything else) be conceived without a subject? 2. is the subject of sensible qualities (whether mere acts of the spirit or not) the human spirit or something different from the spirit (bodies)?

Berkeley is content to say that sensible qualities (which for him are synonymous with sensations) exist only in the spirit. Our spirit is therefore the only subject of sensible qualities, and there are no sensible qualities outside the spirit. This means that Berkeley recognises the need for a subject; sensible qualities

[608]

could not naturally exist alone. Consequently, they can be thought only in something else, that is, in a substance.

Hume however, in contrast to Berkeley, decisively rejects the need for substance. We must therefore first refute Hume's idealism and show the obvious contradiction inherent in his opinion that sensible qualities exist but without a subject or substance in which they exist.

Article 8
Hume's idealism refuted

609. Let us suppose that Hume's thesis is true, that sensible qualities can be conceived alone, without a subject. What is the result?

If we thought sensible qualities alone existed in the universe, we would certainly conceive (according to the hypothesis) that something exists; these sensible qualities, existing alone, would be the object of our understanding.

A Humist could however come into conflict with a follower of the old philosophers. Tasting victory right from the start, he would probably conclude: 'It is not true therefore that sensible qualities, in order to exist, need a subject in which to exist. That is a prejudice of the ancient philosophers. This subject, this substance is simply a product of their imagination. Why can't sensible qualities exist by themselves, having their existence in themselves and not in something else?' The dialogue might continue as follows:

Follower of ancient philosophers: I grant that once you have boastfully rid yourself of old prejudices, you have formed the idea of sensible qualities existing by themselves and making up the whole universe. I presume that I may analyse this new and wonderful idea of sensible qualities in order to understand it better. You agree, I am sure, that analysis, or the breaking-down of our ideas, is the process by which we gain deep knowledge of them. Is it true therefore that these sensible qualities, which you conceive as unattached to any hint of substance, exist?

Humist: Yes. They are in fact the only things that exist in the universe.

Follower of ancient philosophers: That means they exist in themselves, because you have excluded any kind of subject, any kind of substance in which they might exist.

Humist: Yes. This is precisely the discovery of the new philosophy, Hume's discovery.

Follower of ancient philosophers: Before we go any further, I must recall what the ancients understood by substance. Do you know the definition of this entity, which is perhaps, as you say, a product of their uneducated imagination, but necessary if our reasoning is to progress.

Humist: The scholastics defined it as 'that which subsists *per se*'[81] (*ens quod per se subsistit*), that is, not through something else, like accidents, which subsist (according to their expression) in substance and therefore through substance.

Follower of ancient philosophers: If that is the case, you yourself grant substance.

Humist: How?

Follower of ancient philosophers: Although you claim to have removed all substance from sensible qualities, you have yourself made these qualities subsist in and through themselves, which is precisely the definition of substance. You have changed them into substances because you supposed them to exist in and through themselves, independently of everything else. You have got yourself in a tangle and it is difficult to get out. You don't deny sensible qualities. You acknowledge their existence, and then say they exist by themselves. Any addition, you say, would be the result of arbitrary imagination. In other words, you are saying that sensible qualities are substances because substance is that which exists in itself and through itself without need to think it in and through something else. Consequently it is clearly impossible to grant the existence of anything whatsoever and at the same time deny substance. The proposition, 'Sensible qualities alone exist; substance does not exist', is a clear contradiction in terms; it means, 'Sensible qualities are existing substances, and substance does not exist.' This is the great thought of your master, Hume, fully exposed and stripped of its multiple, over-expressive words which often hide

---

[81] Subsistence *per se* must be understood as subject. The definition will be discussed later in clearer and more precise terms.

the contradictions inherent in arguments. I really do not see any way of escape. Your argument leads you in a direction totally contrary to the one you wished to take at the start. You declared yourself an enemy of substance — an obsolete, useless word devoid of meaning —and a supporter of sensible qualities alone, or accidents (as the ancients normally call them). But the result is the opposite of what you intended. You have, as it were, enthroned sensible qualities and wished them alone to rule the world, yet unawares have found them changed into substances. Only substances exist now; you have destroyed all the sensible qualities you held so dear, by changing their nature and, as it were, annihilating them through the honour you gave them. In fact, if sensible qualities are substances, as you come to claim in your philosophy, you have posited a thesis directly opposite to the one you intended to defend. Your thesis is: 'Only sensible qualities exist', but the thesis you have demonstrated is: 'Only substances exist'. If in reality sensible qualities exist in and through themselves, only substances are present in the universe.

In conclusion, I think I see the origin of your error. Instead of upholding the ancients' definition of substance, you have contested an imperfect, gross idea of substance conceived by you. In order to constitute a substance, you have required something solid and material, that is, more than what is really required; in short, you have turned some supposed nature into an idea by giving to certain normal words a different, metaphorical sense to be understood with great caution. For example, the words 'foundation', 'substrate' and 'substance' itself, understood etymologically, mean something located under something else, as if what forms substance lay in a place more internal and intimate than the place of the accidents. These are all dangerous ideas and expressions, capable of confusing minds when ideas and expressions are not explained and understood.

Article 9

Origin of the idea of accident

610. I am not sure how a Humist would reply to this argument. In my opinion, it proves rigorously that if something

exists, a substance must necessarily exist, and that if we think the existence of something, we necessarily think a substance.

Let us suppose however that our Humist is a reasonable, discerning person, and has accepted the observations made by the follower of the ancient philosophers. Let us also suppose that after solving the apparently insoluble opinions that divided them prior to their discussion, they have overcome their original mutual antipathy and are ready to continue their dialogue.

What still remains to be said to the Humist? How could both of them, now bound together by feelings of esteem and friendship, gradually be guided to the same doctrine by evidence of the truth which is sparked off, as it always is, by friendly arguments?

This, I think, is how the discussion could develop and how they could finally reach full agreement. To make the presentation simpler, I will use 'H' for the Humist and 'F' for the follower of the ancient philosophers.

H: I'm grateful for your observations about Hume's philosophy which I had chosen as my guide. I have no reply. However, I think we are still a long way from the core of the problem. I grant that we cannot deny the existence of substances, in the sense that we have defined and explained them. Nevertheless, I do deny the distinction between substances and so-called accidents. It may be impossible to deny substances but you have not shown that it is impossible to deny accidents. In fact, accidents could themselves be substances, which would mean that the ancient schools' distinction between substance and accident does not exist. They defined substance as 'that which exists through itself', and then added 'and supports the accidents' (*ens quod per subsistit, et sustinet accidentia*). In short, sensible qualities are all that exists, whether they are called substances or something else. This is the core of Hume's philosophy.

F: Your difficulty will be solved by the analysis we began, and interrupted, of your concept of sensible qualities according to Hume's system. In your concept, sensible qualities are like substances: they exist independent of everything else. Now, do all the qualities exist in this way, or only one?

H: All of them. If I said a few, I would be accepting the distinction between substance and accidents, which I want to eliminate from philosophy as troublesome.

F: But when we say 'sensible qualities of a body', are these qualities grouped together to form a single ens, the body, or do they exist in different places without a bond to unite them?

H: They are united and cannot be divided. A body cannot be broken up in such a way that the quality of whiteness is in one place, the weight in another, the sound elsewhere, etc. If the qualities are not united, they cannot even be conceived as subsistent.

F: Right. Consequently all the sensible qualities noted in a body have something in common, that is, the energy which makes them subsist, and subsist joined together, in such a way that once separated they can no longer be thought as retaining the energy by which they exist.

H: I agree.

F: Now, note carefully whether the following inference is correct: the common energy making these qualities subsist is neither any one of these qualities, nor all the qualities together.

H: Yes, that's true.

F: In fact it is so true that the energy, if it were one of the qualities, would make all the others subsist, that is, this quality would contain them all, which is absurd. Alternatively, the quality would at least have to be distinguished from all the others because it alone, not the others, would be the energy.

H: That's correct.

F: Again, all the qualities are not the energy because they are multiple and the energy is one. This has to be the case if it has to join all the qualities into one.

H: I fully agree.

F: All your sensible qualities therefore have a common element which is not one of the qualities nor all of them; it is the energy which makes them subsist, makes them exist in and through themselves; in a word, it is substance.

H: Yes, all right.

F: But are they distinct from each other?

H: Certainly. The characteristics proper to each sensible quality are the distinguishing elements.

F: What do you mean?

H: Well, red is different from yellow; it's another colour. Sound differs from colour, and similarly for all the other qualities of things. These differences are clear, and they are best explained simply by indicating them to the imagination.

[610]

F: Very good. Do you agree then that in the qualities which, according to you, existed alone in the universe, there is something in common and something proper, and that the common element is the energy which unites them and makes them subsist?

H: Yes.

F: I repeat therefore: we agree that red, yellow, etc., different sounds, odours, etc., and all other qualities have this in common: they have in them an energy, a force, through which they exist. Indeed, when we say a thing exists, we are expressing an act, an action, a force, while non-existence expresses the absence of every action, of every force whatsoever.

H: But I wish to make an observation here. 'To exist' expresses an energy or, better still, existence is synonymous with a certain energy. But I would presume you do not consider the existence and the energy as two different things. The energy we are discussing is existence; it is one, individual, identical thing, an act itself. This is important.

F: I agree entirely, and the explanation is as follows: saying that all the qualities equally have the energy which constitutes their existence, and that only the characteristics you have indicated distinguishes them, is exactly the same as saying that the proper, different characteristics which distinguish the qualities from each other exist through the energy all equally have in common, as you yourself have admitted.

H: But aren't you really saying that the characteristics exist because they exist, because they have the energy called existence? You're not really saying anything.

F: I may not be saying anything new but what I am saying is clear. If our discussion begins by saying they *do* exist, we cannot later deny, as the argument develops, that they exist. If we did, all reasoning would be impossible; we would not be reasoning but simply uttering sounds at random without any meaning; we would play at building up and knocking down. But if it is true that the sensible qualities all exist together, it is also true that they have an energy through which they exist; possession of this energy is, as I have observed, synonymous with existence. I ask you therefore, can what is proper be simultaneously common, and what is common, simultaneously proper?

H: Not at all.

F: Do you know then what the ancient philosophers meant by 'accident'?

H: Well, they defined substance as 'that which subsists through itself and supports the accidents', and accident as 'that which subsists in or through another' (*quod in alio subsistit tamquam in subjecto*).

F: Haven't we also seen that the proper characteristics distinguishing the sensible qualities from each other exist through one single energy which makes them exist together and constitutes their existence?

H: Yes.

F: What prevents us therefore calling 'substance' the energy through which the characteristics, or rather the qualities we are discussing, exist, and what prevents us calling 'accidents' sensible qualities in so far as they clearly differ from one another and have another mode of existence?

H: If that is all you mean by the distinction between substance and accidents, I have no objection, but who on earth understands this distinction simply as an abstraction?

F: Any good philosopher. Take any of the ancients you like. All I have done is to remind you of the old definitions you yourself have indicated. Keeping strictly to these, I think I can now conclude as follows.

We have to acknowledge two things in the qualities of a body, which you have imagined as existing through themselves: 1. a force constituting their existence, which must be a single force common to them all, and 2. the qualities which exist, each with its own characteristic, through the force. This is exactly the distinction made by the ancients. They distinguished two elements: the first they called 'substance', the second 'accidents'. If you want to be coherent with yourself, you must confess that although you express yourself differently from them, your teaching is the same. Consequently, your proposition, 'Only sensible qualities exist', necessarily implies a contradiction. Although we pretended that the proposition was true, and that only sensible qualities existed, we found, after analysing these imaginary sensible qualities, that they necessarily resulted from two elements: something which makes them exist (imparts the act of existence to them, united as they are) and something which exists (receives existence). In other words we found something which is existence itself, the very energy of existence, that which exists in and through itself (substance); we also found something which this thing has, something which is not existence, and therefore exists through the energy which makes it exist, that is, something that exists through and in this energy (accidents). Hence, your proposition ('Only qualities exist') is just as absurd as the other proposition, 'Qualities exist but do not have existence'.

Look at it another way. We are talking about ideas. Analyse the words of your proposition. When you say 'qualities', you do not know whether they exist or not, but when you say 'exist', you express and bestow energy upon them and make them exist. These two things are therefore distinct from each other even in the words you use.

You could in fact think and name the *qualities* without thinking that they exist in reality. In this case you would not be thinking of the substance. On the other hand, if you thought of the existing qualities and of the energy through which they exist, that is, through which they become capable of existing, you would also think of their substance, through which alone they exist.

I think I can now explain why modern philosophy has arrived at the extraordinarily bizarre opinion that there is no distinction between substance and accidents.

611. *H*: Tell me, just as you have explained how Hume wanted to annihilate substances.

F: The cause, I think, was an erroneous understanding of the ancient teaching. We must admit that in recent times scholasticism has taught ancient philosophy very materialistically. The Schools have presented the language, or jargon if you prefer, of ancient philosophy rather than the philosophy itself. In addition, the world was for many reasons ill-disposed towards ancient philosophy. As a result, new philosophers mocked and mangled it for the sake of *bon ton*, as the French say, without any attempt to understand it. If some silly, ridiculous meaning suggested itself to their mind, even when they first heard the scholastic dicta and axioms, they avidly accepted and granted it, without any investigation, as the most suitable for their intention. They were happy to have found an opportunity to devour and ridicule such arid teaching; in place of ancient authority, they could now triumphantly proclaim their new discoveries. They could boast about a new light, and with one fine, authoritative leap change their lowly position as disciples to that of ambitious masters of the universe.

Apply the general practice to those who tried to do away with the ancient distinction between substance and accidents, and you will find that they were battling against a distinction drawn from their own head rather than a true distinction. They imagined that substance and accident meant things totally separate from each other, like two real, equal elements which make up a third thing. These two elements were taken as two things and therefore as two substances. They were unaware that this contradicted the scholastic definition of these two elements. If I think some existent thing, I have the idea of something indivisible. I can however mentally analyse my concept of this thing, and thus break it down. In other words, I turn my attention to a part of it and ignore the rest. This certainly does not mean that any parts I discover in the concept are separable *in se*, or that as parts they have the same nature; they may simply be aspects, or internal or external relationships present in the concept of the thing. Thus, the distinction between substance and accident is made solely by mental abstraction; the mind sometimes considers a thing under the aspect of energy of existence, sometimes under the other respect of the mode of existence, prescinding from the energy through and in which the mode exists.

I conclude. It is impossible to think an actual ens[82] without distinguishing in it 1. the energy of existence, and 2. the mode of existence, that is, accidents. To think an actual ens means to have the concept of an actual ens. In that concept the mind can always distinguish, if it wishes, the activity causing existence, and the mode of existence. Hence, we form two elementary concepts of 1. substance, and 2. accidents or, more generally, mode of existence. This distinction, made by the mind, is really contained in the idea of the thing itself and is therefore true and real.

[82] I am speaking only of limited entia.

Article 10

An observation on the invariability of substance

612. As far as I can see, this argument renders undeniable the distinction between what exists relatively in and through itself and what exists relatively through and in something else, in other words, substance and accidents. The whole force of the argument consists in a simple explanation of the notions of these two things, accompanied by a determination not to introduce into the discussion about them any imaginary, foreign element which serves only to distort them.

If the ideas of substance and of accident are considered as two abstracts in which the thing itself is thought at one moment as the *force* that makes the thing exist and at another as the *mode* in which it exists (prescinding from the force), the distinction under discussion is no longer difficult, mysterious or repugnant.

Our imagination however, which acts on and, as it were, plays with our ideas, easily adds something extra to the simplicity of our ideas. In this case, our first, clear ideas of substance and accident become confused. We mix with them properties which may indeed follow but are not the ideas themselves. One of these properties is the *invariability* of substance and the variability of accident. These two, unnecessary additions must be understood with great care and discernment because the clarity and simplicity of our notions depend on how, at the start of our reasonings, we strip them precisely of all that is unnecessary.

613. Let us suppose that the discussion we described earlier now turns on this secondary property, so to speak, of substance and accidents. Beginning with the Humist, the dialogue would, I think, proceed more or less as follows.

A: According to ancient teaching, substance is something invariable; accidents, variable. If, according to the hypothesis, the sensible qualities existed through themselves, they would not be variable. Red could not change into yellow without being destroyed, and the same would be true for all the other qualities. We cannot say therefore that, in Hume's hypothesis, these sensible qualities are accidents; they might cease to exist, but could never change.

[612–613]

B: Before I reply, you must recall the definition of substance and accident.

A: Substance is that which exists through itself; accident, that which exists in and through something else.

B: Note, the definition says no more than that, so do not add to these notions anything not contained in their definition. We must remember that the first characteristic of substance, which forms the essence of substance, is existence through itself *relative* to the accidents. This means that we ourselves think some existent thing without a subject other than itself, because substance is the activity of its existence.[83] On the other hand the essence of an accident consists in its existing in something else as in a subject. This means that an accident is an abstract concept in which we think the mode of a thing's existence and prescind from the activity which makes it exist. Hence we can think the accident really exists only when we think of this mode of existence joined with the activity that makes it exist, that is, with its substance or (if we prefer) with the substance in which it exists. Now, I have shown that a sensible quality, as imagined by Hume, can be only a thing in which we think 1. an activity constituting an actual existence, and 2. a particular mode of existing, a mode which exists only through the activity. Consequently I have shown that when analysed, Hume's idea consists of a substance and an accident, that is, of the activity of existence itself and the term of this activity, and that the term exists only through and in the activity. After this, if we allot other properties to substance and accident, we have to speak of them separately and see whether they derived from that property or not, that is, from the essential, primal characteristic. And if these properties which are attributed to substance and accident are implicitly contained in the primal, essential property, they also must be essential to substance and accident. If however they do

---

[83] I define substance as 'the activity of existence of an ens', or 'a thing of which we can form the first concept without having to think of something different from the thing'. I say 'first concept' because if we thoroughly examine any created substance we will find that we cannot think it independently of a primal cause. But in the *first concept* we form of things, we think only of their *essence*, not of the *conditions* through which they exist. In the *first concept*, which is as it were outline knowledge of things, we do not expressly conceive their necessary bond with the first cause.

not derive from the primal property, they cannot be absolutely necessary to the notion of substance and accident. For example, in the case of *variability*, is what exists in something else as in a subject necessarily *variable*? If so, there is no problem; you have discovered a necessary property of accident, *variability*. If however it is unnecessary, you cannot conclude that *variability* is necessary to the concept of accident. And if through experience you know that accidents do in fact vary, you will say that this happens through some particular circumstance, not because it must always happen like this. But to analyse Hume's concept of qualities which exist through themselves, and to show how that analysis provided a concept composed of the idea of substance and the idea of accident, I only needed to show that the two elements into which that idea breaks down present the notion of substance and accident respectively, according to the definition of these notions. My task therefore is complete.

Article 11

Sensible qualities do not exist through themselves, that is, they are not substances

614. One question remains: despite everything we have so far said, do Hume's speculations improve the ancient notions of substance and accident? On the one hand, the ancients supposed that a totally invisible force underlay the sensible qualities which it maintained and supported. On the other, according to Hume's analysis, the opposite has to be said: the sensible qualities exist through themselves. In this case, although the concept of sensible qualities provides something existing in itself (the energy of existence, substance) and something existing in something else (mode of existence, accidents), there is nothing hidden or mysterious about this. Everything is clear and visible, just as the sensible qualities themselves are clear and visible.

The question vanishes if we note that the energy through which sensible qualities exist is not visible and cannot fall under our senses. It is seen and abstracted only by the power of our

[614]

mind. In fact the Humist could be convinced by the following argument:

B: We agree then that sensible qualities have properties by means of which, aided by our senses, we distinguish and know them?

A: Yes.

B: We also said that these properties, through which we distinguish sensible qualities from each other and which constitute the sensible qualities themselves, are accidents because they need some energy to exist, energy which is not present in their concept?

A: Correct.

B: Now, when I asked you to list these proper characteristics, do you remember what you replied?

A: I appealed to the senses. I said that by means of our senses we clearly saw that yellow was not green, etc., that colour was not sound, and sound not taste.

B: Good. Well, aren't yellow, green, red, sounds, tastes, odours, etc., truly sensible qualities? Or are sensible qualities something other than these?

A: They are definitely sensible qualities.

B: And can we call what does not fall under the senses a sensible quality?

A: Certainly not.

B: Now remember: characteristics by which sensible qualities are distinguished from each other are accidents, but these proper characteristics are everything that in the sensible qualities falls under our senses. Conversely, everything that falls under our senses is called sensible quality, and cannot be called this unless it falls under our senses. 'Accidents' therefore is a correct designation for sensible qualities; calling them 'substances' would be nonsense. We also saw that they truly exist and have a force which makes them exist. Hence in addition to sensible qualities (accidents) there is a substance, which does not fall under our senses, but is the energy producing sensations in us and our perceptions of sensible qualities. This substance is known only by the mind, which analyses the concept of 'existent sensible qualities'; only the mind, not the senses, has the aptitude to perceive *ens*. It is the concept therefore which, when analysed, gives us some *sensible*, *existent* thing. If we then divide the force of existence from what is sensible and think of it alone, we call it 'substance'.

Because this force is an abstraction, it clearly cannot fall under our senses. I have demonstrated this by abstracting from it everything that falls under the senses. If I were to say that the substance, after the abstraction, is still sensible, I would be contradicting myself; I would destroy the thought I had first formed of it and would no longer be thinking. To form a thought and immediately cancel it is not thought; it is, as I have constantly stated, nothing. But when I turn my attention to sensible qualities, prescinding from the force that makes them exist, I think of things essentially sensible, that is, of accidents, not substance.

CHAPTER 4
Origin of the ideas of cause and effect

Article 1
Purpose of this chapter

615. The idea of cause, taken with the idea of substance, forms the basis of human cognitions. We shall not be wasting time, therefore, if we try to clarify its origin and show its validity clearly enough to prevent foolish attempts to overthrow the foundation of knowledge, the source of human dignity.

Common sense asserts: 'That which happens must have a cause.'

Our aim is to discover why human beings agree about this; why they accept it as evident; why they use it as a rule from the moment they begin to reason, although they form it much later as an abstract proposition worthy of philosophical attention. The origin assigned to the idea of cause must show how it comes to exist in the mind and explain the facts we have indicated. How is this idea conceived so easily? How can the uneducated, and even children, employ it as soon as they begin to chatter? How can we explain children's fascination with the *why?* of things, and their determination to know the cause of what affects their senses so wonderfully?

To answer these questions, let us: 1. express as clearly as possible the proposition we want to demonstrate; 2. analyse it in order to pinpoint its difficulty; 3. explain the difficulty.

Article 2
Proposition

616. We have to demonstrate the following proposition: 'Every fact (change) necessarily requires a cause capable of producing it.'

By *fact* I mean any *action* whatsoever, whether its effect is found externally or internally, provided it indicates some change or, in the most general sense, some movement.

It is not necessary for me to describe the various kinds of possible *actions* because my intention is to include in this word every type of action.

The proposition effectively states: every time we perceive an *action*, we perceive an agent or cause of this action. Explaining this fact, describing how it comes about in us, or showing the way in which we come to the idea of cause from the idea of some fact (happening, action), is to indicate the origin of the idea of cause.

Article 3
The proposition analysed, and the difficulty uncovered

617. The proposition we have undertaken to analyse is a judgment made up of three parts: 1. a fact, a happening or an action that we must have conceived mentally; 2. the connection between this action and the unknown agent or cause; 3. the idea of this agent or cause.

To explain how we mentally conceive such a judgment, we have to show how we come to conceive each of the three parts of which it is composed.

618. We first perceive the *action*, or happening, with the help of our internal and external sensibility.

Our consciousness assures us of our passivity when real, corporeal things impinge upon the nerves of our body,[84] and of our activity when we will to do something and, through the stimulus of our will, go on to think, move, etc.

Through the idea of being we proceed to form the idea of *action*, both that produced by us and that which happens in us without our positive intervention.

---

[84] I express myself like this to determine the action in some way. In fact, knowledge that our body has been touched by real things comes after awareness of our passivity so that the expression used is posterior to our experience.

When we have acquired the concept of action and mentally conceived different kinds of action, we also learn of the existence of other real actions either through what others[85] tell us, or by imagining them for ourselves.

It is not difficult, therefore, to explain how we perceive *action* and form various concepts of it. We know it primarily through what takes place in us (given the idea of being), and through similar things which we can imagine happening to us.

Moreover, our consciousness provides awareness of all the actions of which we ourselves are the authors and causes.

We realise that it is we ourselves who desire, think, and so on. The cause of all these kinds of actions, therefore, is known to us, by *perception*; we know that we ourselves are doing these things. Analysing them, we distinguish *myself*, as responsible for them (their cause), from the actions caused. In this way, we form the idea of *cause* relative to actions done by us.

Once more, there is no difficulty, although here we already have an idea of *cause*.

619. We now have to show that the idea of cause contains something clearly seen as necessary to every happening or action. Our proposition ran as follows: 'Every new fact demands a cause.' In this proposition, one finds a necessary connection between what is produced and what produces, between action and agent. But a necessary connection between two ideas must come from the nature itself of the ideas which, like relative terms, cannot be thought separately. One of them is entailed in the thought and definition of the other in such a way that an analysis of either concept inevitably shows that the other is contained in it.

The whole difficulty lies here. We have to submit the two terms of the proposition to a rigorous analysis and show that: 1. *action*, and 2. *cause*, (that which produces action), cannot be thought except together.

If we succeed in doing this, we shall also have shown that: 1. a

---

[85] Language would be of no use to us unless we already possessed the ideas signified by language, or had the capacity for forming them on the occasion of sounds that we hear. St. Augustine acutely notes: 'We can all move a finger to indicate something but we cannot confer the faculty of sight. Similarly we can speak words externally, which are signs of truth, but we cannot bestow the power of understanding, which belongs to God alone.'

fact or *happening* cannot be thought without a cause; 2. no *cause* can be conceived mentally without thought of at least a possible effect.

After this, it will only be necessary to indicate the way in which we acquire one or other of these ideas. Analysis showing that one is in the other will also demonstrate that the presence of one accounts for the presence of the other.

The idea of action and the pure and simple idea of a cause present no difficulty. These ideas are given by experience and interior awareness. We are conscious of our actions, and of being their cause, as we have seen (cf. 618).

The difficulty lies in showing that when we think of action, we also think implicitly of cause, and vice versa. Let us examine the problem.

Article 4
Explanation of the difficulty in uncovering
the origin of the idea of cause

620. All things, including actions, can be objects of the understanding (cf. 603).

But according to the principle of knowledge (cf. 564–565), every intellectual operation has being or ens as its object.

Everything, therefore, that pertains to or determines being or ens is not thought *per se* by the understanding but only as a determination of being or ens.

In order to think that which pertains to ens, but is not itself ens, the understanding must first think ens, and through it (not without it) conceive and understand these determinations.[86] We have seen all this in the course of our work, and I have to say that the argument, if considered in itself independently of the

---

[86] It is easy to see that this necessity arises from the nature of what is thought. The necessity is therefore an *objective*, not a *subjective* law of the intellectual faculty. The determination of ens exists only through ens. But because the determination can be mentally conceived only in so far as it exists, it would be absurd to say that it could be conceived before or independently of the ens to which it belongs, and through which it is something.

rather abstract expressions used, should not raise any difficulties. However, in order to facilitate understanding, I shall present the teaching as smoothly and familiarly as I can.

First, in everything we think, we must think one of the following kinds of things: 1. an ens; and 2. some quality or attribute belonging to an ens.

I believe there is no middle term between these two. If we examine all the possible objects of our thought, we will see that everything we understand is ultimately classed either as an ens, or as something necessarily pertaining or related to an ens.

It is important, however, to understand the word *ens* correctly, and not to restrict its meaning unduly.

By *ens*, I mean that which *is*; that which is not, is nothing. Consequently, that which is not an ens, nor even something included in ens, is nothing. The word *ens*, therefore, embraces everything; nothing is excluded; nor can we say that there is something outside the 'all'. If we conceive something, therefore, either we conceive ens, or something contained in ens. Affirming the contrary would be an obvious contradiction. We would both affirm and eliminate the affirmation. In other words, we would not be speaking, but 'sounding off' unintelligibly.

It is true, of course, that through abstraction we can consider the appurtenances of ens separately from ens but in carrying out this operation, by which we mentally separate from ens something which belongs to it, we do not form, from what has been separated, an ens on its own. And we must have already thought ens in its entirety because it is on the idea of ens that we have carried out our abstraction. Abstracting, or taking something from a whole is impossible if we do not already possess the whole from which we separate and rescind the required part.

Things which in themselves are not entia or being, but pertain to some ens in which they are perceived, are intellectual abstractions and as such presuppose the total idea of the thing of which they are considered as a part. Consequently 'ens is thought *per se*. By means of ens and using our faculty of abstraction, we think the things contained in or pertaining to ens or in any way related to it'.

The truth of this principle can also be understood if we consider carefully the nature of abstract ideas.

When we separate a quality or relationship or any of the parts from an ens, we have indeed separated and mentally cut the thing off from the whole. However, we are not deceived because we can view the part only as pertaining to its ens as a whole. It is impossible for the understanding to think of anything pertaining to an ens without first thinking the ens itself. If afterwards the understanding fixes its attention willingly upon a part of the ens (which is what abstraction means), it never forgets (unless it deceives itself) that the part is inseparable from the ens in which it is seen to exist.

621. If these very simple principles are kept in mind, it is no longer difficult to see how the understanding forms the idea of cause.

In our perceptions, as I have said, we are conscious of an *action* done in us of which we are not the authors.

If we ourselves initiated the action, we would perceive it as something pertaining to us, that is, we would perceive it (something pertaining to an ens) in our own ens. In this case our intellective perception would have all the conditions necessary to take place. But if our consciousness provides an *action* for our understanding without also proffering an author of the action, could it perceive and understand the action?

An *action* is not an ens, nor does it make an ens subsist (substance); it merely pertains to an ens.[87]

Moreover, we have seen that the understanding cannot conceive anything except through the conception of an ens in which it conceives the thing.

The understanding therefore conceives the *action* only by referring it to an ens which, although unknown to the understanding, is necessarily felt by the understanding as that to which the action pertains or by which it is produced. This ens we call *cause*.

These are all undeniable propositions, comprising an irrefutable demonstration that our understanding must think, together with the idea of *action* of which we are not the authors, an ens different from ourselves as the author. In other words, it must think a cause.

---

[87] We prove this proposition from the definition of the action of which we are speaking. We are not considering *first, immanent* act, which is existence itself, but an action following upon first, immanent act.

All that remains to explain is how the understanding can think this ens (cause) which is presented neither by consciousness nor by internal feeling. I have shown that it must do this but not *how* it must do it.

This will become clear however if I sum up all that has been said in this Section.

The idea of a cause is the idea of an ens that produces an action. Analysing this idea, we find it is composed of three parts: 1. action; 2. ens, and 3. their connection.

But the *action* is given by feeling; *being* is innate [*App.*, no. 20]; their *connection* arises from the *necessity* already indicated as inherent to the nature of the understanding, or more properly to the nature of its objects which cannot be conceived mentally without being. Ens is the first thing conceived by the intellect because it is the first thing to exist, and that through which all other things are conceived, since everything else exists through ens.

Article 5

Distinction between substance and cause

622. When, as intelligent natures, we supply being to our *sense perception*, we form for ourselves the idea of *substance*, that is, of an ens which we conceive as existing in itself and not in something else.

When we supply ens in the *intellective perception* of an *action*, we form for ourselves the idea of *cause*, that is, a substance that carries out an action.[88]

Our act of understanding is the same in the formation of the idea of substance and of the idea of cause; both operations consist in supplying ens[89] to what is provided by feeling or

---

[88] We could imagine something operating differently from substances: for example, one thought producing another. This takes place, however, through abstraction. The true cause of all our thoughts is the substance of the spirit.

[89] 'Supplying this ens' does not mean that we create it or produce it as something immanent to ourselves; it is the object of our intuition from the first moment of our existence.

perception. This is possible through the identity of the subject (MYSELF) which feels, perceives intellectually, and reflects. In addition to enjoying external and internal sense, we possess the idea of being which constitutes our intellect [*App.*, no. 21]. *What is felt* is perceived by our senses, and we refer it to being, of which we consider it a determination. We think a determined ens, and with it the idea of substance. When we perceive an action, we refer it to an ens and consider it as an act of the ens. In this way, we come to perceive the ens as operative, and along with it the idea of cause. Substance is an ens producing an act which we consider immanent to the substance itself (accidents);[90] cause is an ens which produces an action outside itself (effect).

The idea of substance is generated by the need for an ens antecedent to accidents; the idea of another ens, or cause properly so called, is generated by the need for an ens antecedent to the coming into existence of contingent ens.

Article 6

The understanding completes sense perceptions

623. A *sensible quality* cannot exist without a substance; an *action* cannot exist without a cause.

The understanding adds being to the *sensible qualities* (the terms of sensations) and forms a determined ens. To the *action* it adds the ens which produces the *action*. In this way, by completing sensation, the understanding arrives at *substance*; by completing perception, it arrives at *cause*.

From the instant that being is present in the closest way to the intellect, which it constitutes, the intellect must perceive ens, nothing else.

In intellective perception, therefore, the intellect can first see

---

[90] Although substance is therefore 'cause' relative to accidents, it is called 'substance' when considered under the concept of *act of being* relative to its terms, which exist through and in this act. It is not called 'substance' when considered as producing something. We need to remember that all these concepts are abstraction.

[623]

only ens; secondly, in seeing ens, it must see that in which ens is grounded (*de ratione entis*). If it did not see everything in which ens is grounded, it would not see ens. But if we grant that it does see ens, and at the same time deny that it sees that in which ens is grounded, we affirm and deny the same thing.

This is not difficult to understand if we grasp that ens, and 'that which is grounded' in ens, are the same thing. It is confirmed to the highest degree once we know that the idea of being is the most universal of all ideas, as we have seen, and consequently the simplest.

Hence, perceiving with our sense some appurtenance of ens, something which is grounded in ens (such as sensations or action that renders us passive), and seeing being, as we already do in a continual, fundamental, natural vision, we immediately perceive *substance* and argue to *cause*.

Our perception of substance and our conception of cause is simply 'perception of an ens to which pertain sensible qualities, and to which we attribute the action that we experience or perceive.'

Once a philosopher has demonstrated his teaching, he may use images. We could say therefore that undetermined ens, continually and unmovably present to us, is like a sheet of white paper. The determinations of the object are accidental additions, like writing on the paper. The writing, or determinations of the object to which our intellect continually directs its watchful, interior gaze, are sensations or feelings referred to being as terms to their principle.

Thus, with the same act with which we see being, we also see in it the determinations of being, determinations which we never see without being. We are like people looking at a screen: with one and the same gaze we see both the screen and all that is happening on it.

624. Our understanding, therefore, is governed inexorably by the following law which it receives from the nature of its object: it must complete feeling and perception. The nature of the understanding consists in a continual gaze directed to being and ens, a gaze which beholds everything in which ens is grounded, such as the determinations and conditions of ens itself. When the particular power of internal or external sense provides determinations of ens, the understanding naturally integrates

and completes them. With our internal vision we inevitably add being to what we sense and from being form a determined ens, to which we again add all that necessarily belongs to ens. This intellective aptitude can be called 'integrative faculty of the understanding.'

Article 7
Application of the teaching on substance to internal feeling

625. I have shown that the understanding cannot conceive sensible qualities without thinking a substance. This argument is universally applicable, valid for both external qualities of bodies and facts connected with internal feeling.

As I have said, human beings when thinking of sensible qualities, think them in a subject and thus form the idea of substance in the way I have explained.

Let us apply the same argument to facts connected with internal sense, that is, to feelings.

Human beings have interior feelings and are aware of possessing ideas, along with spiritual pains and pleasures. We conceive these feelings of ours intellectually as well, and refer these modifications to an existing ens (ourselves). In this way, we can form the idea of our own substance.

626. But the reality of our own substance is presented to our understanding in another, more immediate way, prior to what we have described. The feeling of OURSELVES is a substantial feeling. Our understanding, therefore, does not *supply* but *perceives* our own substance immediately in the feeling which proffers it to us. Perception of our own substance enables the intellect to acquire from the beginning the positive idea of substance by abstracting from the judgment invariably united to intellective perception.

627. There is a very noticeable difference, therefore, between perceiving the substance of *external bodies* and the substance of *our spirit*. In the perception of external bodies, our feeling receives only 1. a force, 2. to which we refer sensations as effects, considering them as *sensible qualities* determining the *force*. This force is indeed a substantial *action*, but because it

lacks *subjective existence* it is not an ens. Nevertheless because
we have to consider it as an *ens* (this is a necessary condition of
our perceiving it intellectually), we attribute to it a mode of subjective existence which makes it exist in itself as well as relative
to us. In this way, we assign to the force the support or *substance* without which it would not be an ens. However, because
we experience this substance only in its action upon us, we conceive an ens to which this action belongs, without defining what
the ens is. For us the ens remains defined as the *proximate cause
of the action*.

For this reason, some philosophers have considered the substance of bodies as hidden. We are in fact obliged to consider the
actual agent as substance and give it the substantive name
'body'. This agent is therefore a substance determined by a relationship, although a *real relationship*. I call 'extrasubjective'
everything mentioned here concerning bodies, because in such
an idea of the substance of bodies we do not think any subject in
a positive way, but solely something foreign to ourselves, foreign to our own subject.

In the perception of our own substantial feeling, however, a
substantial subject is present. Here only the idea of being need
be applied; we have no need to supply this substance with a concept of relationship.

628. Finally, we can perceive our own body in the way we
perceive any foreign body, that is, *extrasubjectively;* we can also
perceive it as the term of our internal feeling, *subjectively*. But I
shall have to deal with this subjective perception of our body at
greater length later.

CHAPTER 5

Observation on the origin of the ideas of truth, justice and beauty

629. Among pure ideas, in addition to those I have dealt with, are the very important ideas of *truth*, *justice* and *beauty*. They should really be discussed here, but in this treatise on ideology it is sufficient for me to indicate their source, which is always being.

For me, these three ideas constitute the supreme principle of three extremely important sciences: the idea of *truth* constitutes the principle of logic, the idea of *justice* the principle of moral science, and the idea of *beauty* the principle of callology. However, not wishing to repeat the same things in many places, I leave to each science the analysis of the principal idea which forms its base, and the demonstration that the idea of being is called, under different relationships, either 'truth', 'justice' or 'beauty' and thus becomes the supreme criterion, or first and certain rule, for judging all *truths*, all *actions* and every kind of *beauty*.

Moreover, because on occasion I have had to discuss these sciences, I have not neglected to analyse and deduce these three ideas. The reader who wishes to know how I assign their origin can easily consult the places and treatises where I have discussed them.[91]

---

[91] I speak about TRUTH as the basis of logic in Section 6 of this work. I have dealt with JUSTICE as the basis of moral science in *Principles of Ethics*, and the idea of BEAUTY as principle of callology in *Saggio sull'Idillio e sulla nuova letteratura italiana*, vol. 1, *Opuscoli Filosofici*, Milan, 1827.

PART FIVE

Origin of *Non-Pure* Ideas, which derive Something from Feeling

630. So far we have spoken about ideas that come from deep within *being* and are obtained either through analysis of this form-idea or by considering its relationships; no determination of it by feeling has been suggested to our mind. We have called them *pure* ideas because they involve only being in all its universality, the simplest of all principles.

We must now gradually apply this pure part of our knowledge to *feelings*, to explain the origin of non-pure ideas. Non-pure ideas proceed not only from the formal principle but also from a principle of spiritual and animal feeling associated with it in our subjective unity.

631. We will first deal with the pure idea of substance and then see how feeling makes it a *specific* idea, changing it into the idea of the substance of spirit by means of the spiritual feeling, and into the idea of the substance of matter and body by means of the material, corporeal feeling.

CHAPTER 1

Origin of the difference between the ideas of corporeal substance and spiritual substance

Article 1

The opinion already expressed about substance and cause

632. We have shown how, on the occasion of external and

internal sensations, the understanding naturally conceives the ideas of substance and cause. This refuted Hume's system which affirmed that in the whole universe nothing existed except pure ideas, pure accidents, pure facts, without subject or cause.

Hume, applying all the force of his genius to creating a totally empty doctrine, an idol in which he can worship himself, bequeaths to the world one of the best known sophisms.

His genius and his profound, zealous meditations produced a monster, 'a wonder for every well-grounded heart'. Standing at the height of a culture proudly proclaimed by the century, he reveals his ignorance of what is known even to the most humble, uneducated person, and clearly understood by the most uncivilised of people. Ideas, which to the minds of others are extremely simple, elementary and clear, go awry in the mind of Hume; they become blurred and lose all the light which enables them, like most faithful stars, to shine before the human family. Dazzled and blind to these ideas, Hume gropes about for them; unable to find them, he imagines and falsifies them, recreating them without any exemplar. In the end, even someone who had lost all common sense would be a better judge of the matter.

633. From what has been said, we can conclude:

1. Hume does not know what substance and cause are, nor what accident and effect are. Although he speaks about these things, he makes no attempt to investigate what the world understands by 'accidents', 'substance', 'causes' and 'effects'. He gives the words an arbitrary meaning. For him they are contemptible —woe to anything that is contemptible for a philosopher! But he is in fact attacking his own creations, not ideas expressed by words.

2. He groups into one idea the three distinct ideas of sensible quality, sensation and intellective conception.

3. With this one idea (a monster with three heads) he has limited the number of things that make up the universe: he has made one species out of three.

4. Nevertheless, sensible qualities, sensations and ideas, reduced to a single thing (a pure idea), left two elements in the universe: ideas and their subject. So, because the world still lacked sufficient philosophical regularity, Hume ingeniously decreed that the world was one, single thing, and that subject

and idea were identical, that is, he destroyed the subject, leaving only pure idea. Thus, the universe, through Hume's decree, was reduced to perfect simplicity; there was no longer anything decorative in it. At last, human artistry had remedied the imperfections of the Creator!

634. Now, I have shown how absurd it is to grant the existence of sensible qualities without a substance or act through which they exist. I have also shown that our concept of the universe is neither of accidents alone nor of substances alone but of accidents *and* substances. However I have not investigated the nature of the substance through which sensible qualities exist; I have not answered Berkeley who maintains that the subject of sensible qualities is not something different from us, but ourselves. According to him, the substance of our spirit is the sole subject of sensible qualities and of our internal feelings. It is also certain that common sense censures this system and that the idea people form of the subject of corporeal, sensible qualities is different from the idea of the subject of their internal feelings. This is a fact to be explained; we must therefore examine the origin of the difference between the idea of corporeal substance and the idea of spiritual substance.

Article 2

The subject of the following investigation

635. Berkeley, unlike Hume, does not deny a subject to sensible qualities. He simply says that we ourselves are the subject and that there is nothing outside us. Common sense accepts, with Berkeley, that we are subject to sensations but adds that *sensations* come from an external cause in which there must be different energies corresponding to and producing the different kinds of sensations we experience. We can call these energies *sensible qualities*. Common sense also affirms that this cause is a substance and the necessary subject of these qualities or powers. Berkeley's idealism distinguishes only two things in the fact of sensations: 1. sensations and 2. their subject (*myself*), nothing more. The realism of common sense distinguishes four things in the same fact: 1. sensations; 2. their subject (ourselves); 3. the

sensible qualities, what is felt; and 4. the subject of the sensible qualities, *body*: two subjects with their qualities instead of one. We must see which of the two systems is more true to nature. Does Berkeley's idealism omit real facts, which should be noted or, in the system of common sense, does popular imagination introduce non-existent facts?

636. Before I begin this investigation however, I will clarify further the notions of *subject* and *cause*. Only a proper understanding of these notions will enable us to see things clearly and find firm ground as we discuss such obscure matters.

Article 3

The difference between the idea of cause and
the idea of subject

637. One thing that produces another is its *cause* but not always its subject. The thing produced can have its own existence, that is, an existence seen mentally by us as separate from what produces it. It can also be without an existence of its own so that we can conceive it only as united with the same existence as the cause. In the first case, that which produces is only cause of the thing produced; in the second, it is both cause and subject. Granted that a son is an ens with his own separate existence, a father is only the cause of his son.[92] But the intelligent spirit is not only the cause of our thoughts, it is also their subject; our thoughts have the same existence as the spirit and can be conceived only as existing in our spirit that produces and holds them in being. In this case the spirit is at the same time subject.

When a cause therefore produces something remaining within it, it is said to be also subject of the thing produced. This is the case with our thoughts; they all remain within the spirit, of which they are inseparable modifications. On the other hand, a cause can act externally by detaching from itself the thing

[92] There is no need to point out that the father is not the full cause of his son, because a human being cannot make matter exist nor create the human spirit. But the example helps.

produced, which then acquires its own existence. That thing is now conceived in itself without need of the cause which, in this case, is only the cause not the subject of the thing produced.

638. This difference is true and important. Only one observation needs to be made: we must not misunderstand the statement 'When the *thing* produced remains within the cause, the cause is also subject.'

The word 'thing' in this proposition can give rise to misunderstanding.

It is generally used to mean that which exists in itself, while what is produced in a *thing* is a modification or something similar, of a thing, not a thing itself. So we must note that in our proposition the word 'thing' has a very wide meaning; it indicates everything we think in any mental conception, whether such an object has its own existence or not.

If what has been produced has no existence of its own, its conception is a pure abstraction which we could not arrive at without first thinking of that which produces it (subject). We do this later through abstraction by which we break down our first concept. We separate the accident from the subject and give it a name as if it were a *thing per se*, thus making it finally a mental object of our exclusive attention (a dialectic ens).

Article 4

A further analysis of sensations

§1. *The purpose of this analysis*

639. Having distinguished *subject* from *cause* we must now approach step by step the truth we are investigating.

To do this accurately, we will first limit ourselves to proving that in both subjects (spirit and body), about which common sense and the philosophy of Berkeley disagree, we can and must distinguish by mental abstraction a third thing between sensations with their sensible qualities and the pure act by which they exist. It is in fact impossible and contradictory to imagine that the act by which sensations or sensible qualities exist, extends to them only, irrespective of their union with anything else. This implies demonstrating that the subject we have proved to be joined to *sensations* and *sensible qualities* (whether there is one spirit, as Berkeley holds, or two, that is, there is also a body, subject of *sensible qualities,* in addition to the spirit, subject of *sensations*) cannot be simply and solely the act by which we understand sensations and sensible qualities to exist. Such an act presupposes an entity that, in addition to supporting sensations and sensible qualities, is also something in itself, that is, has an absolute property unrelated to things outside it.

I shall first speak about the subject of sensations, granted by both systems, and then about the subject 'body', granted only by realists and denied by Berkeley's idealist disciples.

§2. *There is in the sentient subject something other than the act by which sensations exist*

640. I have distinguished sensations from that through which they exist, that is, their substance; I will now analyse this idea of substance.

When I analyse the energy by which sensations exist, its concept includes something more than the act of their existence. Careful consideration of the supposition about which the whole argument turns, shows the truth of my affirmation. We have supposed that we are ignorant of the existence of substance; all we know is that sensations exist. Given only this fact, I have demonstrated by analysis that the idea of a *substance* is contained necessarily and implicitly in this fact.

The second step of the argument is this: if we proceed to analyse *substance* found in this way, we encounter in its concept something more than an energy capable of making sensations subsist. The proof is as follows.

Sensations exist; therefore there is an energy making them exist. But what are these sensations, of colour, sound, taste, smell, etc. and how do they come about? Observation first shows that sensations happen in me (attention confirms this): colours, sounds, etc. are so much my own sensations that if I did not exist or could not feel, I would not only be deprived of them

— they would not even exist. I am speaking about all the sensations I experience, which are quite different from those experienced by someone else. The sensations that I have when smelling an onion, listening to a violin or tasting an orange would not exist at all if I did not feel them. But what I say about my own sensations can be said equally about anyone's sensations: if they are sensations like those from which I draw the concept and understand the word 'sensations', then certainly they would not exist if there were no one to experience them or the person were deprived of feeling or were not actually experiencing them at the present moment. There is no sensation, colour, taste, etc. that is not found in human beings, since every colour, odour, taste etc. is a modification of the feeling of a sensitive ens.

Once this nature of sensations has been observed, it is clear that, in addition to sensations and the act of their existence, the sentient subject must contain something which is the foundation of their act of existence. This is so evident that it hardly needs proof.

When I say 'I smell odours, I see colours, etc.', I posit *myself* as the subject of the sensations perceived. *Myself*, however, is not simply the act by which they exist, because I do not find *myself* in the pure idea of existing sensation. On the contrary, without *myself*, I would have to think of as many things existing *per se* as there are sensations. But as I think of the existence of the sensations in the way I experience them, I am convinced that many of them are referred equally to just one *myself*. Hence *myself* that experiences many sensations is one, while the sensations are many; *myself* is different from the sensations just as the subject is different from the modifications it undergoes.

641. Furthermore, *myself* can experience many present sensations, which then give way to others. While this is happening, *myself*, despite the different sensations, remains itself. Thus it has the power to feel and to be modified, although the power to feel many sensations is totally different from each actual sensation.

642. Finally, sensations are felt by *myself*, while *myself* is that which feels. These two characteristics are not only different but opposite and as such clearly demonstrate that sensations and their act of existence cannot be conceived without the presence

of a subject, that is, without their act of existence first terminating in something other than themselves, something from which they receive and have existence.

643. It must be noted in everything said so far that the sentient subject is not deduced by reasoning but by simple analysis of the idea, 'existing sensation'. Earlier I showed, against Hume, that to conceive an 'existing sensation' (Hume grants sensation) means to conceive a substance, and that we do this by analysing the idea of *existing sensation*. In the same way, I show here that to conceive a *substance* is to conceive something that exists different from sensations (their subject): this is the result of our analysis of the idea of substance.

§3. *The subject of sensible qualities must be an act involving more than these qualities*

644. A similar argument is used in the system of the realists to prove that it is impossible to think sensible qualities existing through an act that terminates in them alone. The act enabling these qualities to exist has to make something else exist, different from them.

In fact, for realists, sensible qualities are powers producing sensations in a sentient subject (cf. 635).

But it is absurd to imagine that these powers exist and that nothing exists which can be mentally distinguished from them.

Let us analyse the idea of existing *sensible qualities*, that is, of powers that excite sensations in us.

As realists understand them, all sensible qualities emanate from a sort of centre called 'body', assumed to be their subject. If these qualities are united in this way and refer to an ens from which they originate, this ens which potentially unites them, whatever it may be, must be implicit in their idea. In this case, in addition to qualities, this idea includes the existence of some other thing necessary for the existence of the qualities in the way we think of them.

645. It may be argued that this approach is not founded on the pure concept of *sensible qualities* but on the concept obtained from experience, and that the centre, the connection uniting

these powers, has nothing to do with the pure concept. But if we examine just one sensible quality, we are still thinking of something in addition to the quality.

I define a sensible quality as a power which can produce a certain kind of sensation.

If this power really exists, we must think, and do in fact think of it as something in itself, other than in its relationship with us. This subsistence of the quality in itself is different from its relationship with us or its action on us because it is impossible to think of a pure relationship or action of an ens without thinking of the ens itself. It is impossible to have relationship and action between two entia, unless there are two entia. If, therefore, in conceiving a potency to modify me, I conceive the real relationship of something with me, we must say that something exists capable of modifying me. This potency is: 1. something existing independently of me; 2. a relationship and action that this something exhibits in me.

Thus the analysis of the concept 'existing sensible qualities or potency to produce sensations in me' results in two ideas: 1. the idea of an ens really existing in itself; and 2. the idea of a relationship with us or of an action producing sensations.

However, before continuing the demonstration of the existence of these two subjects, one spiritual, the other corporeal, we must say something about essence.

Article 5

The difference between the ideas of *substance* and of *essence*

§1. *Definition of essence*

646. I define *essence* as that which is understood in any idea. An idea is the thing thought by me as simply possible. But this possible thing, considered in itself and independently of the mind that thinks it, is the essence. Essence therefore is everything I think in any idea whatsoever.

§2. *Specific, generic and most universal essence*

647. Determined ideas are of two kinds, *specific* and *generic*.
To these correspond two kinds of *essences* in our minds: *specific
essence*, that is, what I think in the specific idea of a thing, and
generic essence, that is, what I think in the *generic* idea.

Besides these two classes of more or less determined ideas,
there is *idea* in all its universality, the idea of *being*; what I think
in the idea of being can be called most *universal essence* or simply *essence* (*essentia* from *esse*), as Plato often calls it.

§3. *Specific essence*

648. I have already indicated that a thing can be considered in
a perfect and complete state, or in more or less imperfect states.
Imperfection is only a lack or privation; everybody accepts the
truth that evil is simply the lack of good.

So the only idea we can have of something complete, free
from every defect and imperfection, is the fully positive one. All
the other ideas of inferior states are simply the first idea, the real
type and exemplar of something, from which some perfection
has been removed; they are *modes* of the idea (cf. 500–503
[500–509]). *Specific essence*, properly speaking, is what is
thought in the complete, perfect idea; to this idea are reduced all
other ideas of the thing in its various states of imperfection.

649. But another consideration is necessary to understand
clearly what a *specific idea* is.

The various *modes* we have mentioned come from defects and
imperfections, but in addition to these *modes* there are *modes* of
the idea itself which originate, not from its defects, but from its
manner of being. These modes are as follows.

The pure object of our mind in any perception is a determined
ens (the possibility of something real) (cf. 491). The determined
ens has within itself something by which it is what it is and
without which it would not be: this is its *first act* (cf. 587),
immutable and immanent.

This first act produces other acts which are the *activities* and
various *actuations* of the ens; these can be called *second acts*
because they follow on the first.

These activities and actuations together with their effects and terms remaining in the ens[93] and following on the first act, are not always necessarily joined to the first act; sometimes they can be absent. If they are necessary, they do not have to be of any particular type. For instance, although a body must have a colour (as a quality), the colour is not necessarily blue or red or yellow.

Now, as long as I am thinking of the *first act* and all it involves as its term, I am still thinking of the ens, because I am thinking of that through which the ens is what it is.

But the *first act* is not necessarily connected with the many activities and actuations following it, or with their terms, as I have said. Hence, because the act does not involve these, they can be absent or vary, while the ens can continue to be thought.

For example, to be able to think of a human being nothing more is required than what is contained in the definition 'rational animal',[94] because the definition involves the first act by which a human being is a human being, without consideration of any further determinations. Some determinations, such as a particular amount of knowledge, a body of a particular weight and size, are not necessary at all; but if they are necessary in a general way — for example, in the present order of things a human being has weight or extension — then they are already virtually contained in the definition.

If therefore I am thinking of everything included in the first act, I am thinking of the ens; if I am not, then some other ens is the object of my thoughts.

These observations on the nature of many entia suggest the following conclusions: 1. there is something *necessary* in an ens for it to be what it is, and therefore thinkable; 2. there is something *not necessary* for it to be thought; and 3. the necessity comes from the *intrinsic order* of the ens itself.

Let us imagine an ens that has things not necessary for its *constitution* and existence but necessary for its *perfection*.

Moreover the things necessary for its perfection are not necessary for my *conception* of it — for this, it is sufficient to think

---

[93] For example, inclinations, habits, ideas, objects and terms of thought.

[94] I am not concerned here with judging the merits of this definition; as the one commonly held it is sufficient to illustrate my concept.

the act by which it can subsist, since ens is the object of knowledge. If, in my idea, I think of the ens equipped with everything necessary for its possible subsistence but not for its perfection, I have those *modes* of the idea mentioned above, which derive from its defects.

If I am not thinking of that through which the whole ens exists, I am not thinking that ens.

However, there is another case. I can think of that element in an ens by which it exists, without thinking expressly of the things necessary for its perfection. I do not deny or exclude them. On the contrary I consider them virtually included in the thought of the ens' existence. In this case, I have *modes* of the *specific idea* not dependent on defects of the thing but on the particular way I have conceived it and on the ens itself. The ens is such that thinking its root act is sufficient for thinking the ens. These *modes* therefore of the *specific* idea are formed by a kind of *abstraction*. I am not thinking of the *defective ens*, as in the first *modes*, nor of the *perfect* ens, as in the complete idea — I prescind from everything belonging to the ens' *perfection* and concentrate solely on what makes or can make it subsist.

650. We must also note that because of the imperfection of understanding, human beings can rarely form that full and complete idea of things of which the *mode*, as we have just described it, is a kind of outline or seed. Thus when they lack the *complete specific* idea (the *type* or rather the *archetype*), they make the *abstract idea* the foundation of species, an idea which, properly speaking, is only a *mode* of the full and absolute idea.[95]

---

[95] The *chronological* order in which we receive the *specific ideas* mentioned above, is as follows:

1. First we acquire the *full idea* of a particular imperfect ens, which is the state of all entia in nature; in fact they are not only imperfect but sometimes *damaged* — it is rare to find in nature an ens without some degree of *damage*.

2. From this full idea of an *imperfect ens* we form the *abstract specific idea* by abstracting whatever is damaged and imperfect and without adding perfections; in short, we abstract everything that is not needed to conceive the ens mentally. This abstraction gives us the *specific essence* in outline, so to speak; it gives us the idea commonly used by human beings.

3. Finally we try to ascend from this to the *full specific idea* (the archetype). But we do so with difficulty because it is beyond our ability to know everything composing the ultimate natural and supernatural

651. It is this *abstract specific* idea that contains what is simply called essence, since the *essence* of things is only what is thought and presented to our spirit in such an idea.

652. We see that, in the formation of this specific idea, we make use of a kind of *abstraction* as well as *universalisation*. However this process does not form *species* strictly speaking, but only *abstract species* because the abstract is already understood in the *full species*. To obtain the *full species*, we need the *integration* as well as the *universalisation* of the imperfect idea we first receive of the thing, although this depends not on the nature of the idea but on the accidental defect of the entia we perceive. This perception gives us our first idea of these entia, an idea we form for ourselves by detaching it from the judgment on their subsistence.

§4. *Generic essences*

653. Generic ideas are formed by *abstraction* (cf. 490–503), specific ideas by *universalisation* alone.[96] *Abstraction* is a multiple operation; it takes place in different ways and at different levels, and thus provides different types of genera. We must now list these.

654. There are three forms of *abstraction*, which give us three kinds of generic ideas and generic essences; they can be called *real, mental* and *nominal* genera.

655. The origin and distinction of these three kinds of genera begins with the fact that there are two ways in which I can carry out an *abstraction* on the *abstract specific essence*. I can abstract something from the essence in such a way that, in the resulting abstract idea, I still think an ens that can be realised;

perfection of an ens. However, we continually try to come close to this noble idea by using that power of our spirit we have called the *integrative faculty of human intelligence*. Even when we cannot do this, we know it must exist and that we could reach it if we were capable; therefore we direct our thoughts to it as to their possible term at least.

[96] I have called *specific ideas* (formed only by universalisation), *full* but *imperfect, specific ideas*. From them we form, by *abstraction*, *abstract specific* ideas, and by *integration*, *complete* or *perfect specific* ideas.

alternatively I can abstract in such a way that I remove everything that constitutes an ens and think only of some *mental*
characteristic, like an accident or a quality, or anything at all
that, by itself, does not make an ens known. If the idea still contains an *ens*, then relative to the specific idea on which I carried
out the abstraction, it is a *real generic* idea. If the idea contains
only a *mental entity*, then it is a *mental generic* idea. It expresses
and presents only an abstract that does not exist outside of
thought — at least it does not exist as an ens in the way our mind
conceives it.

Take, for example, the idea of *human being*. This is an abstract
specific idea and I can exercise abstraction on it in the two ways
indicated.

First, when I abstract the specific difference of *reason*, the idea
is now one of *animal*. Relative to the species *human being*,[97] this
idea of *animal* is a *real generic* idea and includes a *real generic*
essence.

Secondly, I abstract everything constituting an ens and retain
only an accident, for example, a colour. Here, the idea of
colours is a *mental generic* idea and, because the abstracted colour is simply an entity of the mind, the *essence of colour* can be
called *mental*.

We must also note in this case what I have often pointed out:
when I am thinking only of abstract *accidents*, the law of my
intelligence, according to which I must think ens, makes me
consider those accidents as entia, although I know they are not.
Because they are not entia but only a form of the mind, I call
them *mental* or *dialectical entia*.

656. Finally, in addition to these two ways of abstraction,
there is a third way: I can abstract and prescind from both the
ens and the *accidental qualities*, retaining only a *relationship*, for
instance, a sign. Consequently I can arbitrarily impose names
and consider them as the foundation of genera. For example, if I
were speaking about the genus Smith or the genus Brown, I
would call them nominal genera, and their corresponding
essence, *nominal generic essence*.

[97] Relative to *brute animal*, the same idea is *specific*.

§5. *A more perfect definition of substance*

657. From what has been said, we can gain a more perfect definition of substance in general.

Having examined the difference between *abstract specific essence* and *full specific essence*, we said that the first, present to the mind, makes known everything unchangeable in a given *determined ens*. Any change would mean the loss of the ens' identity; it would either cease to exist, or become another ens to the mind.

When, in a *determined ens*, we think this unchangeable element that constitutes its abstract specific essence, and consider it in relationship to the changeable element united to it in the *full specific essence*, the *abstract specific essence* is called substance. It is regarded as the element necessary for the ens to exist, the act by which it subsists and which, as a base, supports the changeable element.

Substance, then, can be defined as 'That by which a determined ens is what it is', or 'Substance is the abstract specific essence considered in a determined ens', or 'considered in relationship to the full specific essences of the ens'.

658. If an ens lacked *abstract specific essence* and had nothing changeable that could be abstracted, any change we might make in it mentally would immediately entail the loss of its identity. If this were the case, the word 'substance' could not be strictly applied to it. We would have to say the whole ens was substance or that its substance was everything found in its *full specific essence*. This is the case in the divine Being.

659. To conclude: the variety of *abstract specific essences* is the reason for the variety of substances. Therefore to make the general formula express special substances, we must replace the words 'abstract specific essence in general' with the particular *essence* that represents the desired substance.[98]

---

[98] The error of Spinoza's followers consists in taking *being* for *substance*. They concluded that because being, as ens, is one, substance must also be one.

Article 6

Resumption of the question under discussion

660. Let us return to our argument.

So far we have analysed the concept of substance in order to make it sufficiently clear and distinct, and inconfusable with any other element.

We have seen that if a subject of sensations exists (and its existence was proved in the preceding chapter), it cannot have an existence purely relative to sensations. There has to be something subsisting beforehand, capable of receiving and supporting external sensations (cf. 639–645).

Likewise, if a subject of sensible qualities exists different from the subject of sensations (as the realists claim), it must be an activity that extends not only to providing subsistence for the sensible qualities but is itself something antecedently, and possesses the dispositions called sensible qualities as its own potencies rooted in its being.

After demonstrating that substance or the subject of the accidents, is something existing in itself, an act by which a determined ens is what it is, I then examined how different substances are specified and distinguished, and found that this was due to the different terms in which the act of being constituting a determined ens terminates.

I was thus able to perfect the definition of substance further, reducing it to the following general formula: 'Substance is the abstract specific essence considered in a determined ens.' Then, in order to remove any misunderstanding, I explained *essence* and its various meanings, amongst which is found *abstract*, *specific essence*, the foundation of the substance of an ens.

With the way now clear, I can return to the argument about special substances, and refute Berkeley, as I refuted Hume.

The argument is based on the demonstration, already given, that a substance as subject of sensations (MYSELF) exists. I must still show: 1. that the subject of this substance contains nothing found in the concept of corporeal substance; and 2. that a corporeal substance exists. This latter point, however, will be discussed in the following chapter.

[660]

Article 7

A perceiving subject, MYSELF, exists

661. There are internal and external sensations. They have a subject, and my consciousness tells me that MYSELF is that subject. We have already seen this in previous discussions.

Article 8

The concept of MYSELF, a perceiving subject, is entirely different from the concept of corporeal substance

§1. *There are two series of facts in us, in one of which we are active, in the other passive*

662. We can all observe this for ourselves. Some effects take place in us without any effort on our part, others take place because we cause them. When I deliberately want something and use my will to obtain it, I feel I am moving myself by my own force, internal to my nature. I am the cause of the actions; I act, I am not passive. When something happens to me without my willing it and even against my will, then I am passive and do not act.

663. It is not a question of whether it is I who am passive when something happens to me nor whether there is any co-operation on my part. What is certain is that, although the action is done in me and I am responsible for the state in which I have to receive it, the activity producing the action is not mine, and I cannot reasonably say that I myself am acting at all. This is not the place to investigate more deeply the nature of passive experience. It is sufficient to indicate the undoubted fact that *passive experience* exists and is different from the *action* of our spontaneous will. What has been said is sufficient for my purpose, namely, the necessity of recognising in ourselves two series of events, one in which we justifiably say we are active and another in which we are passive.

664. Among passive occurrences we find sensations that come

from outside ourselves; it is these that principally concern us at the moment. We have to recognise sensations as facts taking place in our spirit, which is mainly passive in their regard; it suffers but does not produce an action. Thus, with my eyes fixed on the sun, it is impossible for me not to see its dazzling light and feel its rays on my eyes. If I have not stopped my ears, I hear, even unwillingly, the drums and trumpets of a military band. I feel pain when pricked by a needle, although I prefer not to suffer pain — no one likes pain. In short, if I were not passive to sensations aroused in my body, I could get rid of all harmful ones, have only pleasant ones, and never suffer or die.

665. I mention these particular examples, although more general ones would do, to refute the objection that a person could avoid pain and unwanted sensations by concentrating his attention elsewhere. Objectors claim that even unwanted sensations are due to human action in so far as human beings willingly dispose themselves to receive sense-modifications.

I first reply that human beings cannot avoid all pain because, if that were so, they would be capable of making themselves immortal, or at least of dying without the slightest pain even when a bullet had passed through the heart — which is quite contrary to experience! Second, concentrating our thoughts elsewhere requires great effort on our part and is sometimes so demanding that it is impossible to sustain. The only reason for such a great effort is to avoid pain or any unwanted sensation; in our effort we are using our activity to avoid a hostile force that makes us suffer. But if force is needed to prevent an effect, there must also be an opposing force trying to produce the effect: reaction supposes action, and the force that dominates supposes the force that is dominated. Thus the action we sometimes take to avoid being passive is proof of our passivity.

Finally, we must see if the effort we make to free ourselves of sense-impressions does in fact prevent sensation. Perhaps all we are doing is simply turning our intellective attention from what we are suffering. We can be suffering in our sense-faculty without being conscious of it (we do not perceive our suffering intellectively) and therefore we cannot speak about it. With our attention thus suspended, we no longer think or pass judgment on what we feel.

[665]

666. Every fact taking place in us is a modification of our spirit. Thus our spirit is the *subject* of every fact, as consciousness attests when I say to myself 'I am the one who feels, thinks, decides, is happy or sad', that is, I affirm that I am the subject of all these facts.

However, if we are the *subject* of *passive facts*, we are not their cause. As we have said, they do not happen through our action; we suffer and receive them. Anything at all can produce them, against our will or at least without our co-operation.

This distinction between the two series of facts, of one of which we are cause and subject, of the other only subject, is the same as the distinction made above between the series of active and passive facts. The analysis of what is active and of what is passive in us shows that the idea of activity contains the idea of cause and subject, but the idea of passivity only the idea of subject, not that of cause.

Hence the proposition above is contained in the first proposition, which is a fact.

§3. *What we call 'body' is the proximate cause of
our external sensations*

667. At this stage we do not need a complete, final definition of body; it is sufficient to know some of its essential properties to avoid confusing it with anything else. For this purpose the definition we can obtain from what has already been said will suffice.

I use the word 'body' to mean 'the subject of qualities', that is, the subject of those powers that produce sensations in us. Body therefore is the subject of extension, shape, solidity, colour, taste, etc. in so far as these qualities are powers in bodies producing corresponding sensations in us [*App.*, no. 22]. These powers or sensible qualities are the proximate cause of our sensations. So we can define body as 'the proximate cause of sensations and the subject of sensible qualities.' Even if bodies did not exist, it is still true that the definition contains the idea people have of body, and this is what we were seeking.

§4. *Our spirit is not body*

668. This is a corollary of the preceding propositions. If 'body' is the proximate cause of our external sensations (cf. 667), and if these are facts taking place in us and independently of us, then we are only their passive subject (cf. 666). We have to conclude therefore that MYSELF is not a body. The word MYSELF expresses a feeling, thinking subject; hence this subject is a substance entirely different from corporeal substance.

669. This reasoning enables us to form a distinct *idea* of the subject MYSELF. This subject, completely different from body, we call *spirit*.

Article 9
Simplicity of the spirit

670. By indicating the difference and even the opposition between an ens that experiences and an ens that causes experience, I have shown that spirit is something totally different from body. To have shown this is to have demonstrated that spirit is incorporeal.

671. As further proof of the same truth, I will present the arguments of a contemporary Italian philosopher.

> I feel *what is outside me* as multiple.[99] I feel each part of this multiple as distinct from the other parts; in my feeling, the modifications of one part are not those of the others. The trunk of a tree is distinct from its branches, and each branch differs from the others; one branch can move

[99] It is indeed a fact that I feel many things outside me, although the nature of body does not consist in *multiplicity*. I have not yet investigated or discovered what body consists of.

without another moving or without the whole tree moving. This is what is meant by *feeling something outside me*.

But we must investigate the nature of this feeling of myself which perceives *what is outside me*. Consciousness of reasoning is perception of *myself* who reasons.[100] Perception of *myself* who reasons is perception of *myself* who says 'therefore', which in turn is perception of *myself* who judges the inference and the premises. *Myself* perceived or felt by consciousness of reasoning is the same *myself* in each of the three judgments that compose the reasoning. In feeling, therefore, *myself* that reasons is the same *myself* that judges, but *myself* that judges is *myself* that says 'is' or 'is not'. Consequently, it is *myself* that perceives the subject and predicate of the judgment. *Myself* is therefore one in notion, judgment and reasoning.

The subject of a judgment can have both a physical composition and a logical unity. For example, when I say, 'A circle has equal radii', the subject has a physical composition because a circle is *multiple*;[101] it also has a logical unity because the subject of the judgment is one, and the thought that judges must include the whole circle. Thought therefore makes a circle one; I call this unity of thought 'synthetical unity', that is, unity of synthesis. But to perceive synthetical unity is to perceive *myself* who *synthesises*,[102] and to perceive *myself* who *synthesises* means to perceive *myself* who unites the truth of the perceptions of the logical subject.[103] Hence *myself*, felt by the perception in the synthetical unity, is *one* despite the variety of perceptions it unites. *Myself* therefore which begins a reasoning, a demonstration or any science whatever is the same *myself* that terminates it.

---

[100] Strictly speaking, *consciousness of reasoning* is not *perception of* myself *who reasons*. Perception of *myself* who reasons contains awareness of reasoning as one of its parts.

[101] It is multiple in potency, that is, it can be distinguished into parts. But if we understand it as a *physical* not *mathematical* circle, the reasoning is rigorously correct.

[102] Cf. footnote 99.

[103] It is true that the subject *unifies* multiple things, but not through its own nature. It does this through the unity of the logical object in which it contemplates these things. From this unity of the *logical object* (ens), however, the unity of the subject is necessarily induced.

I will try to throw more light on this important truth. Bayle says, 'If a substance which thinks were one only as a globe is one, it would never see a whole tree, never feel pain when beaten by a stick. The following will convince us of this.

'Look at the shapes on a globe of the world. You see nothing on it that contains the whole of Asia or even a whole river or the part representing the kingdom of Siam; the Euphrates is seen to have a left and a right side. Consequently, if the globe were capable of knowing the shapes upon it, nothing on it could say, "I know the whole of Europe, all France, all Amsterdam, the whole Vistula"; each area could know only that part of the shape which falls upon it. Because this part would be so small that it would not represent any place in its entirety, the capacity to know would be absolutely useless to the globe and would not result in any act of knowledge, unless such acts differed vastly from those we experience. Because our acts represent to us a whole tree, a complete horse, it is obvious that the subject acted upon by the full image of these objects is not divisible into many parts. Consequently a human being, as a thinking being, is neither corporeal nor material, or composed of many beings' (*Dict.*, art. *Leucippe*).

Consciousness of the synthetical unity of perception encompasses therefore the perception of *unity* or of the *simplicity* of *myself* which *synthesises*. If we think about the comparison that we make between the objects which act on our senses and the judgments caused by their impressions, the feeling of the simple, indivisible, immaterial unity of the thinking being would be obvious. For example, when our hand is warm, we certainly experience one kind of pleasure, but if at the same time our nose smells a pleasant odour, we feel another kind of pleasure. If we are asked which of these two pleasures we like most, the answer is one or the other. We compare them and simultaneously judge them. If, after the warmth and the odour, we taste some food, we can certainly say which of the three pleasures is the greatest; the thing in us that judges must therefore have felt all three objects. *Myself* that judges knows whether a pleasure of the senses is greater than the pleasure of the discovery of a truth or the pleasure arising from the exercise of virtue, and chooses between them. The same subject which experiences sensible pleasures, also experiences spiritual pleasures, and judges and wills. This is proof that consciousness of *myself* which feels affected by all these sensations and acts as a result, is by no means consciousness of our nose which senses odours, nor of our hand which feels heat. The hand and nose are two absolutely distinct things; it is just as impossible for one to sense what the other senses as it is for us to sense in this room the pleasure felt by the audience in a theatre. The consciousness I have of *myself* who simultaneously senses odour and heat includes not only the perception of my nose and hand but also the perception of a single, simple subject that has no parts. If the subject had parts, one part would sense the odour, another the heat; there would never be the feeling of a thing which could simultaneously sense odour and heat, compare them and judge that one is more pleasant than the other.

The feeling of the body is then the feeling of a multiple, of something composed.[104] The feeling of *myself* is the feeling of what is *one*, *simple* and *indivisible*. One feeling is therefore distinct from the other.

— A science is a sequence of reasonings intended to give us the clearest knowledge possible of any object whatsoever, and reasonings are a series of judgments. No human science would be possible without the direct synthesis of judgment and the indirect synthesis of reasoning. Synthetical unity in reasoning is necessary: there would be no reasoning without 'therefore' just as there would be no judgment without 'is' or 'is not'. In reasoning, 'therefore' binds into a unity of thought the different parts of the reasoning; the 'is' or 'is not' of a judgment binds its different parts into a unity of thought. As I have explained, consciousness of the synthetical unity of thought encompasses consciousness of the unity of the thinking subject. I call this unity of the thinking subject (*myself*) the *metaphysical unity of myself*. In other words, the synthetical unity of thought necessarily presupposes the metaphysical unity of *myself*; they cannot exist without each other. The metaphysical unity of *myself* is the simplicity or spirituality of the thinking principle. Without it knowledge would be impossible because knowledge presupposes the union of all thoughts composing it. If one thought differed from another, how could their union be effected without

---

[104] Or at least we certainly perceive many bodies. This is sufficient to demonstrate the unity of the spirit perceiving them.

a centre of union?[105] How could we become acquainted with the different branches of knowledge without a centre uniting them? A builder must have all the materials necessary for building. Newton's *myself* which discovers noble calculus is the same *myself* that learnt arithmetical numeration. *Without the metaphysical unity of myself the synthetical unity of thought would be impossible, and without the synthetical unity of thought all human knowledge would be impossible.*[106]

[105] This centre of union is also a *logical object*, the foundation and cause of the simplicity of *myself* that intuits it.

[106] Galluppi, *Elementi di filosofia*, vol. 3, c. 3, §24–25.

CHAPTER 2

Origin of our idea of corporeal substance

Article 1

The way to demonstrate the existence of bodies

672. Having shown that the sentient subject (the spirit, MYSELF) cannot be what is understood in the word 'body' we must now see if what we mean by 'body' really exists, or indicates an imaginary concept without content. Our aim is to discover if there is such a thing as corporeal substance, as common sense affirms, and if so how we attain our idea of it.

When we have found the way in which we form our idea of body and persuade ourselves, as we form this idea, that bodies really exist, we shall also have demonstrated the existence of bodies. Such a demonstration, taking its origin from the persuasion of the existence of bodies, is valid provided that reasoning, dependent upon perception for its first link, is capable of finding or proving the truth. Most people do, in fact, take the existence of bodies as the most certain of all things, but modern sceptics have tried to throw doubt upon ordinary reasoning. In the next Section of the work, we shall refute the objections against the validity of reasoning, and thus reinforce what we intend to say here about the existence of bodies.

673. We have said that the concept underlying the word 'body' is that of 'a proximate cause of our sensations' and that 'this cause is the subject of qualities' (cf. 667). We have to show, therefore, how we obtain a reasonable persuasion of the existence of 'a cause of our sensations different from ourselves', and that this cause is 'the subject of qualities'.[107] This will not be difficult if we remember what we have said.

---

[107] As we said, these definitions depend upon the meaning given to the word 'body' by common usage.

Article 2

The existence of a proximate cause of our sensations

674. Sensations presuppose a cause different from ourselves.

External sensations are facts towards which we are passive (cf. 661–666).

Passive facts are actions done in us of which we are not the cause (*ibid.*).

Such actions suppose a cause different from ourselves because of the principle of cause (cf. 567–569).

Consequently, sensations suppose a cause different from us. And this was what we had to show.

Article 3

Any cause different from ourselves is a substance

675. We have seen that sensations suppose a cause different from ourselves (cf. 674).

It was shown that a cause is always a substance (cf. 620 ss.).

The cause of our sensations, therefore, is a substance.

Article 4

The substance causing our sensations is immediately joined to them

676. Because our sensations are actions done in us of which we are not the cause (cf. 662–666), we experience energy capable of changing us. This energy is a substance working upon us and we call it 'body' (cf. 667). The action of a body upon us is, therefore, the effect not of any particular power of the body, but of the body itself. In our definition of *body*, we do in fact call it that which modifies us in this way. Moreover, we recognise no other co-ordinated powers in the agent indicated by the word 'body'.

But the action of an operating substance is always intimately joined to the substance itself, because the force or energy of an ens is inseparable and indivisible from the ens itself. The substance which causes our sensations is therefore joined to them immediately.[108]

Article 5

The cause of our sensations is a limited ens

677. The energy or force which we experience as producing our sensations is limited because its action within us, of which we are not the cause, is limited.

But this is the energy which gives us the idea of substance or, as we could say in equivalent terms, we perceive in that energy or force an ens, the cause of our sensations, which is distinct from ourselves. But the ens in which we mentally conceive this energy is as limited as the energy we experience because this ens is for us only the energy itself considered as existing.

Hence the ens we think of as the substance and proximate cause of our sensations is limited.

Article 6

We name things as we conceive them intellectually

678. This proposition is evident.

We cannot name anything unless we know it and according to the way in which we know it.

Hence we cannot name it except in so far as we know it.

Article 7

How to use words without making mistakes

679. Words express entia in so far as we know them intellectually.

---

[108] This is explained more clearly in *App.*, no. 22.

The meaning of words is limited, therefore, by our knowledge.

It is an abuse of language, leading to equivocation and sophisms in our reasoning, to use a word with a wider sense than the concept of the ens it names; we are using it for what it could mean, although we have no idea or perception of what this may be. Words used like this have neither the meaning nor the purpose given them by the human race.

Article 8

Bodies are limited entia

680. Defining a body is equivalent to stating the use made of the word 'body'.

If we wish to define this word, therefore, we can do it either by analysing all the ideas which form its meaning, or by indicating some characteristic idea, wholly proper to the ens under review, which will lead us to the ens named by the word in question.

For the present, we need to clarify the word 'body' only in the second way. Later on, we shall define it more fully and closely.

We have seen that we form the idea of body from that which acts in us, that is, from the force or energy we experience in sensation (cf. 640–643).

Because this energy is limited, we can draw from it only the concept of a limited ens (cf. 677).

All our knowledge of bodies is therefore that of limited entia.

But words express entia in the way in which we perceive and know entia (cf. 678).

The word 'body' was therefore invented to signify a limited ens. Using it in some other sense would be to abuse it (cf. 679).

Article 9

God is not the proximate cause of our sensations

681. Bodies are the proximate cause of our sensations (cf. 667). Bodies are limited entia (cf. 680).

God is not a limited ens.

Therefore God is not the proximate cause of our sensations.

Article 10

Bodies exist, and cannot be confused with God

682. The proximate cause of our sensations is an existing substance.

This substance is called 'body'; it is not God (cf. 681).

Hence bodies exist, and cannot be confused with God.

Article 11

Berekeley's idealism refuted

683. This demonstration of the existence of bodies refutes Berkeley.

His sophism began by falsifying the idea indicated by the word 'body'.

If this idea is correctly understood, it is impossible to confuse it with God. It is the idea of something completely limited, that is, of the energy we feel acting on us and underlying sensations, something thought in itself.

Our understanding, thinking about this force we experience, supplies only *existence*, and has no right or reason to add anything else. Hence the force remains limited in the way it is.

684. The demonstration can be expressed and summarised as a sufficient refutation of Berkeley's idealism in the following propositions.

    1. Everything that occurs in our feeling is a fact.

2. In sensations and *corporeal* feelings (*corporeal* is used to determine the feelings, and may be taken here as an arbitrary sign), we experience in our feeling an action of which we are not the cause; we experience an energy, a force different from ourselves, at work in us.

3. This energy, or felt force, conceived intellectually, is the idea of an ens. Our understanding, through the necessary principle of substance (cf. 583 ss.), conceives this energy as really existing.

4. Such energy is real and limited; consequently, because the conceived ens is only the same energy considered in its existence which we conceive as precise and isolated, it too is real and limited.

5. This limited ens which we call 'body' is not the sentient subject (MYSELF), nor can it in any way be God, whose idea embraces that of an infinite being.

6. Body, therefore, a limited substance and proximate cause of our sensations, exists.

As far as I can see, all these propositions are irrefutable and form part of human common sense.

685. I think it will be helpful if I further explain how Berkeley's individual sense failed to follow the wide road of common sense and fell into error.

Before Berkeley, Locke had placed the source of ideas in *sensation* and *reflection*. But his ignorance of the nature of reflection led him to describe it in such a way that it could be easily confused with sensation [*App.*, no. 23]. According to him, reflection could not furnish us with the idea of substance.

As a result, the first step taken by Locke's philosophy in England and France was to suppress *reflection* and reduce all ideas to one single origin, sense [*App.*, no. 24]. When this is done, substance is an illusion; Hume drew the general conclusion; Berkeley restricted his attention to corporeal substances.

But if Berkeley considered only senses, what was his idea of bodies? His definition is: 'Sensible things therefore are nothing else than so many sensible qualities or combinations of sensible qualities'.[109] He confused *sensible qualities* with *sensations*. Granted this, it was easy to show that 'sensible things are in us

---

[109] Dial. 1. — Condillac gives the same definition.

as modifications of ourselves' because sensations certainly have this condition.

Berkeley's idealism denied corporeal substances because its starting point was a philosophy which had removed intelligence from human beings. Leaving them with the senses only, it banished the very faculty with which substances are perceived. It was not idealism therefore that caused scepticism but the principle on which Berkeley's idealism rested and which contemporaneously produced Hume's scepticism. Berkeley's acceptance of these substances was dependent on his remnant of age-old good sense, which is not completely destroyed in a moment.

Substances and *causes* must be seen as separate things in Berkeley's mind, like our own prejudgments made without proof or unconnected with our other principles. Substances and causes cannot be explained in any way by his philosophy.

Whatever the truth of this, Berkeley denied the substance of bodies. Nevertheless, he knew through the principle of cause that sensations must be given a cause, which for him was God. In philosophy *substance* and *cause* enjoy the same state and, as I said, Berkeley's approach was incoherent.

686. He erred therefore in removing the *proximate cause* of sensations and turning to the *ultimate cause*. God is indeed the ultimate cause of all that is and happens, and in this sense God is also the cause of sensations. But the word 'body' was not coined to mean the ultimate cause, and philosophers want to know the proximate not the ultimate cause of sensations.

If our investigation is restricted to this particular philosophical problem, we come to the two results mentioned above: 1. bodies exist, and 2. they are the proximate cause of our sensations. This will receive greater light from the following considerations.

Article 12

Reflections on the demonstration of the existence of bodies

687. In order to know if corporeal substances exist, we must first recall the definition of substance. As we have said,

substance is 'something capable of being conceived intellectually with some first conception of ours.'[110] Note that the definition contains the following implications.

1. In order that something be a substance, it does not have to exist independently of every other thing. If that were the case, there would be no created substances because they exist only in dependence on the first cause. For something to be worthy of the name 'substance', it is sufficient for us to be able to conceive it by itself, separate from its first cause. Although it cannot exist totally of itself, it has its own proper existence which enables it to be thought by us in isolation from everything else; its *first concept* contains no extraneous element.

2. Consequently, a thing can be called 'substance' even if we have to rely on knowledge of something else, such as its cause, in reasoning to its existence or in understanding it completely. As we have said, although nothing can be understood without knowledge of its ultimate cause, this does not prevent us from calling it *substance*. A *first mental conception* can be formed of the thing without further need of anything; it can be seen of itself with our first intuition and thought. In a word, its first concept is independent of every other concept; it presents itself as an incommunicable essence, so to speak, mentally distinct from other essences.

We have already noted that if we give to the word 'substance' a more extensive meaning than that granted by common usage, we open the way to false reasoning and countless errors.

688. Bodies, therefore, are substances from the moment they can be conceived by us with our first mental conception as separate and isolated things that cannot be confused with our spirit, with God or with anything else. Accidents, on the other hand, are such that they cannot be conceived with our first intellectual conception as isolated, but only in dependence upon some other ens in which they exist or to which they

---

[110] This characteristic is relative to our mind, but founded in the nature of the thing. The other definition I have given regards the thing itself: 'Substance is that through which an ens is what it is', or 'Substance is the abstract, specific essence of an ens considered in relationship to its full, specific essence'.

belong. This is not the case with bodies whose perception, as we have seen, terminates in them without need of anything further (cf. 515–516).

689. This was Berkeley's mistake. He did not analyse sensation carefully. As a result he did not distinguish its two elements: 1. the force acting in us (relative to which we are passive), common to all species of sensation; 2. the various terms and effects of this force, that is, the various sensations. We experience both the *force* and its *different effects*, but while we feel the former equally in all sensations, the effects are felt differently according to the variety of means and bodily organs in and through which the force acts upon us. But if the variety of terms and effects of this force (the sensations in so far as they vary amongst themselves) cannot be conceived without the force that produces them, this in its turn cannot be thought without the ens which operates (through the *principle of knowledge*) (cf. 536, 483–485). Thus we arrive at substance, because that which constitutes an ens is called a substance.

690. We can now sum up all that we have said about the origin of our ideas of bodies.

1. We attain the perception of bodies with the act by which we judge that bodies exist (cf. 528).

2. Analysing this *perception*, we find it made up of two elements:

    a) judgment on the subsistence of a body, and
    b) the idea of the same body.

3. Analysing the *idea* of body, we find it made up of three elements:

    a) the *idea of existence* — we cannot conceive anything, including bodies, without thinking their existence;

    b) the *primary determination* of the idea of existence — this is the *essence* (the abstract, specific essence) of the thing; in the idea of body it is necessary to think, besides the idea of existence, the term in which the act of existence necessarily terminates, that is, the force or energy at work in all our sensations;

    c) the *secondary determinations*, or sensible qualities — these are the various capacities into which the single force is resolved for producing different sensations.

4. We conceive the three elements of the idea of body in the following way:

a) The *idea of being* is present naturally in our spirit.

b) When considered in isolation from the variety of sensations we experience, the *energy* at work in us producing sensations is a mental abstraction (an abstract, specific essence); but, in so far as it acts on us, is known through our interior consciousness — in this respect, consciousness, because it reveals its own passivity equally in every kind of sensation, could be called a 'common sense'.

c) Finally, sensations are provided for me by the exterior sensories.

I have within me, therefore, all the faculties necessary to explain the origin of the perception and idea of body. I have: 1. the faculty that continually beholds being (the intellect), the first element of the idea of body; 2. the faculty (a 'common sense') that perceives a *force* at work on me which is not myself, and which therefore forms the essence of body, the second element in the idea of body; 3. the five exterior sensories that perceive sensations, the third element in the idea of body; and finally, 4. the faculty of *primal synthesis*, or judgment, with which I judge as subsistent what I think in the idea of body.

691. Having established the faculties enabling us to perceive the individual elements composing our intellectual perception of bodies, we now have to explain how we unite these elements.

First of all, our various sensations and the energy at work on us are bound together naturally in such a way that we have to make use of abstraction if we wish to have and to think this energy separate from its particular term, that is, from one or other of the sensations. Because energy is the sensation itself considered in its general concept of action done on us and not by us, it cannot be perceived without sensation. Sensation itself, taken whole and entire as it exists in our feeling, that is, as the feeling of a *determined action*, is what we have called elsewhere *corporeal sense perception*.

We now unite corporeal sense perception with the idea of ens in all its universality through the principle of knowledge, which includes the principle of substance. We do this for the first time through the act with which we judge that a body subsists, that is, the intellective perception of body. This act may be described briefly as follows: we are intelligent; as such, we perceive all things as they are, as entia, when they act on us; the bodily force corresponding to the essence of bodies acts on us[111] so that we perceive it as subsisting; this is the perception of bodies.

We have given a general description of the formation of ideas of body. We still have to describe how we perceive our own and other bodies.

---

[111] As a result, the feeling we experience of bodies is a substantial feeling, an immediate action of bodies upon us, which allows us to use the word *perception* for the first knowledge we acquire of bodies.

CHAPTER 3

Origin of the idea of our own body, as distinct from exterior bodies, through the fundamental feeling

692. Bodies exist as substances different from God and ourselves.

As the proximate cause of our sensations their essence consists in a certain *energy* acting upon us, relative to which we are passive. And any activity, different from our own, constitutes a different existence. Hence Berkeley's error: he denied corporeal substances (cf. 672-686).

But we do not think of body only as a substance causing corporeal sensations. We bestow upon this substance other qualities such as extension, shape, solidity, mobility and divisibility, and generally speaking all the physical and chemical properties that bodies manifest in their relationship to one another and to us. The principal property with which we endow body is its aptitude for life when it correctly unites with spirit (cf. 668–669). We also endow it with the aptitude for modifications which cause it to lose life by separating it from spirit, and for modifications which cause pleasure and pain, sensations of colours, sounds, tastes, and so on.

We have yet to show however how body is known by us as the *subject* of these properties and capacities. If we succeed in doing this, we shall also be able to explain the ideas of the various qualities attributed to body.

It is clear that, in order to complete our study of the ideas of matter and of body, we are about to enter the wide field of physical nature where we have to deal with life, feeling, and different kinds of sensations.

Article 1

First classification of the qualities observed in bodies

693. Bodies possess a physical relationship amongst themselves, and a relationship with our spirit. Observation enables

us to know the facts constituting and determining these two relationships.

In the physical relationship between bodies observation shows that, when bodies are related to one another locally, various changes take place, according to stable laws. This capacity for receiving modifications or alterations corresponding to their respective positions results in the *mechanical, physical* and *chemical* properties of bodies.

But are these properties, such as propulsion, attraction, affinity and so on, true powers of the body in such a way that bodies are the true causes of all the modifications to which bodies are subject?

This question has nothing to do with my argument. I mention it in order that it may not distract the reader if it should occur to him. We are not asking if propulsion, attraction, cohesion, and affinity are true forces; we merely want to know exactly the simple facts presented by attentive observation.[112]

694. All these facts can be reduced to the following formula: 'When bodies are placed in certain positions relative to one another, *alterations* occur which are constantly the same, given the same bodies and the same positions.'[113] We now ask how we form the ideas of these *alterations*, ideas presented to our spirit by the *alterations*.

We conceive mechanical, physical or chemical alteration or change in bodies through their presence in certain positions only in so far as: 1. the modified body acquires a different capacity for acting upon us by causing internal or external sensations different from those caused previously; 2. the modified body acquires a different capacity for modifying another body — in the last analysis, this modification is reduced to the different capacity that the modified body possesses for acting upon us. When a body changes colour, taste, hardness, extension, force, or any of the sensible qualities resulting from a new state, it has changed only its capacity for producing sensations in us.

[112] Nevertheless what we shall say will throw light on the question.

[113] Any new condition changing the results would be reduced to a *body's* approaching or distancing itself, which is excluded by the formula. It is understood that no account is taken of the action of spirits; bodies alone are considered in their mutual relationships.

Only through our senses can we come to know when a body receives or loses some property or power without changing its sensible qualities. If the change were of such a nature that it presented no direct or indirect sign to our senses, we would not perceive it in our feeling, nor could we think, imagine or assert it.[114] If we adhere to pure observation, we have to say that any change in a body must be sensible to our senses in order to be something for us. It must finally produce some effect or action on our senses. Any difference found through such changes on the part of bodies can be reduced to a change only shown directly or indirectly to our senses. If one body changes colour in the presence of another, as grass and leaves become green on contact with the light, that body has suffered a change shown immediately to our senses.

If I magnetize a needle, the change in the needle is not immediately obvious to my senses; neither touch nor sight present any change. Its new properties are shown only by its power to attract other ferrous metal, or to point towards the pole when set on a balance. But seeing the needle act in this way means that I now receive a certain series of sensations I did not possess while the needle remained unmagnetized. As far as I am concerned, the new power acquired by the needle is reduced to certain new capacities for producing different sensations in me. And this is true whenever we examine the effect of one body's action upon another; any changes mentally conceived in a series of bodies acting upon one another effect only their capacities for acting upon us.

Let us imagine that the last of these bodies acts upon us. Through it, and only through it, we know the changes which have taken place in the others. If the series of bodies is called *A, B, C, D, E, F, Z,* we find that the change suffered by *Z,* which has affected us, can be defined as follows: 'The change in *Z* consists in its losing the capacity for producing one series of sensations in us, and acquiring the capacity to produce another

---

[114] If we were told about it, we would either have already experienced it with our senses, or not. In the first case, we would have some positive knowledge of the fact, together with belief in what we have been told; in the second case, we would only believe in such a *change,* our knowledge of which would be merely negative.

series.' I go on to define the change experienced by F as follows: 'The change in F consists in acquiring the capacity for bringing about the change described in Z.' I have experienced the alteration in Z through my senses, but the change in F is known only through that in Z. If I now wish to substitute the known value of Z in the definition of the change in F, I produce an awkward definition, but nevertheless the only one possible: 'The change in F consists in its capacity for producing the change in Z through which Z loses its capacity for producing one series of sensations in me and acquires the capacity for producing another.' In the same way, the change in E can be defined only in relationship to the change in F, and so on, back to A.

Amongst the alterations in all these bodies, only that of Z is known to me of itself. The rest are known as first, second, or third, etc., causes of Z. Everything I know about the properties of bodies to modify one another is reduced to the acquired capacity to modify me. Knowing the modification I experience, I know the capacity producing it in me. Knowing this, I know relatively the causes more or less remote to it.[115]

Our observations show clearly that all mechanical, physical and chemical qualities or properties constituting the relationship of bodies to one another are (when we limit ourselves to observation alone) simply powers capable of modifying us and producing sensations within us.[116] Hence, all the ideas that we have or can have of these properties are reduced to the different impressions the bodies make upon us, and to the different feelings they cause in us. We can mentally conceive only those mechanical, physical and chemical powers of bodies that either modify us, or modify and change the powers to modify us.

Our question, therefore, has been reduced to a careful examination of the relationship of bodies to us as we explain the

[115] My knowledge of corporeal capacities or forces, derived from their activity upon me, is the *first* knowledge I can possess about them. This must not be taken to imply that I cannot deduce other truths about bodies from my *first* knowledge. I simply affirm that my *first* experimental knowledge is the *basis* of all my other reasoning about corporeal qualities.

[116] This does not remove from sensation the *extrasubjectivity* I have spoken about, and which I intend to explain more fully later in this work.

origin of their sensible qualities, to which all other qualities are finally referred.

Article 2

Classification of the corporeal qualities which immediately constitute the relationship of bodies with our spirit

695. In speaking of the mutual connection of bodies, I have kept to pure fact and avoided difficult questions. I intend to follow the same method in indicating the connection of bodies with ourselves, and I ask readers to remember that I am confining myself to the limits placed by observation. I mention this to prevent a fruitless search for something not contained in the work.

Observation does, however, take us further in this field than it did when we examined the connection of bodies amongst themselves. We ourselves are one of the terms of the present relationship, and it is obvious that we can observe ourselves more intimately because our consciousness shows us the facts taking place in our spirit. While observation cannot tell us if bodies are the true causes of the modifications discerned in them, we can, given certain relative positions of the bodies in question, distinguish our own actions from other actions by simple observation on ourselves.

696. Observation of the connection of bodies with ourselves offers three distinct relationships which can usefully be indicated here.

The first relationship: an intimate bond between our sense-principle and a body that becomes its term (matter). This I call *life*.[117]

The second relationship: a *fundamental feeling*[118] proceeding from life, that is, from the first bond. Through this feeling, we habitually feel all the material, sensitive parts of our body.[119]

---

[117] That is, *animal life*.

[118] Proofs of these assertions will be given later.

[119] We all know that our bodies are composed of sensitive and insensitive parts. The sensitive parts, we say, are the nerves. Albert Haller's experiments on the sensitive and insensitive parts are well known and have been repeated

The third relationship: the capacity possessed by the sensitive parts of our body for being modified in certain ways. Various species of external sensations correspond in us to these modifications, and in them the perception of bodies external to our body.

697. The connecting bond between external bodies and ourselves consists, according to the idea we have formed of it, in considering these external bodies as capable of modifying the sensitive parts of our body and providing our spirit with varied sensations.

Article 3

The distinction between life and the fundamental feeling

698. First, I have to clarify the opinions I have proposed, then prove them. To clarify them, I begin by establishing clearly the distinction between *life* and the habitual, fundamental *feeling* caused by life.

I said that life was a certain intimate, unique bond of spirit with matter. In this bond, matter becomes the constant term of the sense-principle in such a way that the two things form a single, underlying factor.[120]

Life is not feeling, or at least not feeling as observable by us;

and confirmed in Italy by Leopoldo Caldani. These gentlemen had the patience and courage to experiment with a great number of dogs and other animals to test every part of the body and discover which parts were endowed with feeling and which not. It was love of humanity that made them cause pain to so many sentient beings. Later, other scientists introduced the expressions, 'vital contractility', 'vital force', etc., and claimed that in addition to life a certain *latent* sensitivity was present in all parts of the body. But Michele Araldi, speaking about Haller's distinction between the sensitive parts, says: 'Anyone who is not firmly convinced of this distinction and instead listens to futile systems is inevitably plunged into darkness where a single step irreparably ensnares him in errors.' Cf. *Saggio di un' errata di cui sembrano bisognosi alcuni libri elementari delle naturali scienze*, etc., Milan, Royal Typographer, 1812, p. 53.

I cannot discuss this question now. It is sufficient that the nerves, but not other parts, definitely demonstrate signs of sensitivity when appropriately stimulated.

[120] We do not want to describe the union here, but simply indicate it under its own name to avoid confusion with any other kind of union.

feeling is an effect of life. We can see this if we realise that all the parts of our body, provided we are alive and healthy, enjoy a life of their own and are joined to us according to their condition in such a way that this bond is called *life*. Thus all the animated parts in us carry out the vital acts proper to them, the principal of which are nutrition, heat, and vital movement, which result in incorruption and the capacity of each of the various parts of the body for different functions. But the seat of feeling, as we have seen, is not every part of the body, but only those parts we call *nerves*. We say this without wishing to enter the physiological field, foreign to our argument.[121]

699. We can usefully employ our imagination to form a clear concept of the sensitive body. Let us picture the human body present to us simply as a network of nerves and bereft of all parts that have no feeling. This is the sensitive body which, when joined to us vitally, enables us to feel. In my opinion, we perceive this body habitually and uniformly with an innate, fundamental feeling which, however, we do not advert to easily because of its continual sameness, although we are aware of the changes that take place as one or other of our nerves is touched. Stimulation of the nerves produces a more marked sensation, easily adverted to because it is unusual, temporary and incomplete, not universal and constant like the first, stable feeling which, diffused throughout the nervous system, often goes unobserved, even by philosophers, because it is connatural and permanent.

700. We now have to examine in detail: 1. how we feel our sensitive body in which the fundamental feeling is present; and 2. how we perceive external bodies which only touch and stimulate our sensitive body.

Because bodies, as we have said, are perceived by us as substances causing sensations, and as subjects of corporeal qualities, it will help us if we apply what we have noted about the perception of bodies in general, first in a special way to sensitive bodies, and then to sensible, non-sensitive bodies. We can then discuss both kinds considered as subjects of the qualities

---

[121] Some physiologists have pointed to apparent anomalies in this law. For our purposes, it is sufficient that sensitive and non-sensitive parts are present in the human body, given certain circumstances and moments.

indicated in them, qualities which are either sensible or reduced to sensible qualities (cf. 693–694).

Article 4

Two ways of perceiving our body: subjective and extrasubjective

701. First, I note that our body (and when I speak of our body I always mean the part where we are sensitive) is perceived in two ways.

1. Like every other external body it is perceived by touch and sight or, in a word, by all five sensories. When I perceive my sensitive body as *acting* on my five organs, I do not perceive it as sharing in sensitivity (this must be clearly understood because of its supreme importance), but as any other external body which, falling under my senses, produces sensations. In this case, one organ of my body perceives another. It is as if someone were to anatomise and perceive the nerves of another living, sensitive ens whose nerves are not sentient to the person anatomizing them, but only to the person to whom they belong.

2. We also perceive our body through the universal, *fundamental feeling* by which we feel life in us (a feeling witnessed by our consciousness, as we shall see later), and through the modifications experienced by the fundamental feeling itself by means of adventitious, particular sensations.

These two ways of perceiving our sensitive body can be distinguished appropriately enough by the words 'extrasubjective' and 'subjective.' When we perceive our body subjectively, through the fundamental feeling given to us with life itself, we perceive our body as one thing with us. Hence, through its individual union with our spirit, it too becomes part of the sentient subject, and we can truly say that it is *felt* as *co-sentient* by us. On the contrary, when we feel our body extrasubjectively, in the way we feel external bodies through our five senses, it is outside the subject, like other bodies, and different from our sensitive powers. We do not feel it as co-sentient, but merely in its external data, in so far as it is capable of being felt. We must

[701]

take great care to distinguish the *subjective* from the *extrasubjective* way of perceiving our body. A great part of what we have to say depends upon this distinction.

Article 5

The *subjective* way of perceiving our body is twofold: the *fundamental feeling* and *modifications* of this *feeling*

702. The *subjective* way of perceiving our body is twofold. We perceive the sensitive parts of our body subjectively with both the *fundamental feeling*, of which we have spoken, and with the *modifications* experienced by this feeling when impressions are made on the nerves.

703. The *second, subjective mode* of perceiving our body is shown by an accurate analysis of external sensations which reveals two things in every sensation:

1. The change arising in the sensitive, bodily organ which, as a result of the change, is felt differently, that is, the fundamental feeling suffers modification.

2. The sense perception of the external body that has acted upon us.

Let us take the sense of touch as our example. When we rub some rough surface against the back of our hand, we feel two things: the hand and the surface rubbing against the hand. The first is what I have called a *modification of the feeling* of our body; the second is the *sense perception* of the rough surface.

704. This *twofold quality of sensation* must be noted with extreme care. But here it is sufficient to indicate the connection between these inseparable, simultaneous feelings included in the single fact of sensation. What I am saying is this: on the one hand, the feeling that we experience through the simple change[122] occurring in our bodily organ is a modification of our fundamental feeling; on the other, we have a sense perception of

---

[122] The change in our sensitive organ is still not feeling. Nevertheless, given that change, we feel because of our habitual feeling of the organ, whatever its state. Hence its changes are also felt. But we must not confuse: 1. the physical impression on the organ, with 2. our first feeling of the same impression.

an external body accompanying this modification, but altogether different from it. This fact occurs in us on the occasion of
the first change and feeling, although we are unable to find a necessary connection of cause and effect between these two
things. Nevertheless, as we shall see, we can note the presence of
a single cause of both the *subjective feeling* and the *extrasubjective perception* experienced in the senses.

Article 6

Explanation of sensation in so far as it is a modification of
the fundamental feeling of our body

705. What do we mean when we say that our first feeling of
change in a bodily organ is simply a mode of the fundamental
feeling of life through which we feel all the sensitive parts of our
body? This feeling begins when life begins and ends with life
itself, but what does it enable us to feel? As we have said, the
matter of this feeling are the sensitive parts of our body. But
when we feel them, it is natural for us to feel them *as they are*;
and if we feel these parts *as they are*, it follows that we feel them
differently when they change their state. The matter of feeling
has changed because the state of these sensitive parts has
changed.

706. The activity of the fundamental feeling, therefore, is
always the same in so far as it is alert to feel the *state*, whatever it
may be, of our sensitive body. Consequently all the changes
taking place in our bodily organs must be perceived by us
through the act of the primal, fundamental feeling. The act by
which the feeling is modified as changes take place in the body
constitutes the first of the two elements forming our adventitious sensations which arise when foreign bodies influence our
body (here I follow common opinion).

Our body is perceived by one and the same act in two ways,
substantially and accidentally. The primal feeling and the
change it suffers are two facts from which I conclude that the
spirit, on first uniting itself individually with an animal body,
must direct its activity in such a way that it mingles, as it were,
with the body which it embraces and unceasingly perceives. As

long as this vital union endures, the spirit perceives the body *in the act and state* in which it finds itself. When the body changes through external influence, the sense-activity of the spirit united with the body also undergoes a change of form. The spirit's activity experiences inevitable modification because its matter changes, although without deliberate intervention on its part. It is as though a person finds a scene changing before his eyes not because his glance varies, but because the object of his vision changes. In our case, the act of feeling is the same whether we are dealing with the body's first state, or with all the other acts and states and partial modifications of the sensories that follow the first state.

Article 7

Explanation of sensation in so far as it perceives external bodies

707. If the nerves possess all the necessary conditions[123] for sensitivity, they feel when suitably touched and affected by external bodies. If we then go on to say that the sensitive faculty of the soul is spread throughout the sensitive body, and that the soul with its power of feeling is therefore present to every part of the body, we are not offering a theory[124] but merely affirming what observation tells us. Because our power of feeling possesses a primal, essential act (the fundamental feeling), extending to all sensitive parts of our body, it is inevitable that this power, or rather the ever-present soul, experiences a disturbance (I mean, undergoes some passive experience) when the sensitive parts of the body are changed through the action of

[123] For example, communication with the brain. Without this, the organ feels nothing.

[124] Galluppi also describes this fact: 'I say that the spirit is intimately united and present to the whole body' (*Saggio filos. sulla critica della conoscenza*, etc., bk. 2, c. 6, §112). He adds that the mode of this union is *incomprehensible*. Relative to Galluppi's statement, note that exact knowledge of the fact equates to a sufficient knowledge of the union itself, as we shall see when I explain the fact, that is, when I explain its origin, which is all that is needed.

[707]

some external body. Perception of this passivity, experienced in a determined way according to the quality of the sensation, is what I call *sense perception* of bodies, as I said above (cf. 674).

Article 8
The difference between our own and external bodies

708. If our previous observations are correct, they show that two different forces affect our spirit. One causes our vital, fundamental feeling; the other modifies and changes the matter of this feeling, producing simultaneously both subjective sensation and bodily perception. According to our definition, the essence of body consists of an action done in us *in such a way* that we feel ourselves passive relative to the energy perceived intellectually as an ens at work in us but different from us (cf. 674, 684). Experiencing two species of feeling, undergoing two kinds of action, and feeling two sorts of energy, we realise that there are two species of body, our own and external bodies.

The existence of these two kinds of body is proved by the fact of our consciousness, and is as certain as that fact [*App.*, no. 25]. Not even sceptics deny the fact of consciousness. The existence of these two bodies, therefore, is proved by observation, not by reasoning. In the same way, their definition does not exceed the limits of observation because we make it consist in a *certain* energy[125] which we feel working in us and of which we are conscious that we are not the authors.

709. But because it is difficult to reflect upon the fundamental feeling of our sensitive body, we need some suggestions to help us observe what takes place within us and become aware of this feeling which has escaped observation by so many thinkers. What follows, therefore, is not a proof from principle, but an attempt to make observation easier.

---

[125] I say a *certain* energy, not any kind of energy, because this energy has its own characteristics, as I have already noted. These determine and specify it, and I will deal with them later.

Article 9
Description of the fundamental feeling

710. First, it is necessary (and we cannot insist sufficiently on this) to distinguish the existence of a feeling within us from our awareness of it. We can indeed experience a sensation or a feeling without reflecting upon it, or being conscious of it, although without reflection and the consciousness resulting from it, we could not affirm, even to ourselves, that we have and experience such a feeling. Indeed, if we did not know how to advert to it, we could happily deny its existence. Leibniz saw this. Locke and many others did not (cf. 288–292). In order to conclude that a feeling was not present in the first moments of my existence it is not sufficient therefore to say: 'I did not notice then, and do not notice now, the universal feeling of my body that you posit.' You could have experienced it, and could be experiencing it now, without paying sufficient attention to advert to it.

Thinkers accustomed to concentrating on what takes place in their consciousness notice matters connected with the human soul that totally escape ordinary, unreflective people. 'Know yourself' is a much-needed reminder of where we normally stand with regard to self-knowledge. It is extremely difficult to discern what really takes place at the source of our passions, where our affections, habitual tendencies, and intentions are rooted. Only those generous enough to pursue virtue with all their mind and heart attain to adequate self-knowledge.

We must insist, therefore, that those who have not yet recognised in themselves the feeling of which we are speaking should focus their attention more carefully and delicately upon themselves rather than reject blindly any notion of the feeling.

But if people have not been able to distinguish between *feeling* and *noticing feeling*, they are certainly ignorant of the essential difference between *sensation* and *idea*. Sensation can never be aware of itself; the understanding alone is aware of sensation because such awareness is either intellective perception of sensation, or reflection upon intellective perception. The act by which we understand sensation is altogether different from the act of sensation itself, that is, from the act with which we feel. Consequently, if an ens undergoing sensations does not

[710]

perceive them intellectively, and remains unaware of possessing them, it can never indicate them to others or to itself. This explains why beasts lack the power of speech: they lack reason.

711. On the other hand, it may appear easy to advert to the existence of the fundamental feeling. In this case, there could be danger of mistaking the nature of the feeling. We need to remember that it always remains in us, even after the elimination of all acquired, external sensations. If I sit in a totally dark room, and stay perfectly still for some time while trying to disengage my phantasy from every image I have ever received, I will eventually arrive at a point where I seem to have lost all knowledge of the limits of my body. My hands and feet, and other parts of my body, will no longer be located in any discernible place. When I carry out this experiment as perfectly as possible, or try to arrive by abstraction at a moment anterior to all acquired sensations, I maintain that I still have a vital feeling of the whole of my body. It is easy to see, therefore, that if this feeling exists it must be very difficult to recognise and indicate because we do not normally pay attention to what is in us unless we experience change, without which we lack awareness, reflection and a means of comparison. Change is necessary for awareness; it is not necessary in order to have *feeling*.

Let us imagine that we move from a cold to an oppressively warm room. Obviously we notice the higher temperature immediately. But this is not the case with people who are accustomed to such warmth. For them it is tolerable and perhaps natural. Because they are used to it and experience it stably, they feel the warmth of the room without adverting to it. Hence, if we are going to believe we feel something, it must be enough simply to know that it acts upon our senses. We have to reason in this way: because the heat acts upon my senses, it is felt, although it may not be adverted to.

712. It may be objected that the feeling of life, or of being alive, which only death can obliterate, extends to all the sensitive parts of my body. In that case, it would seem that my feeling necessarily puts me in touch with the size and shape of my body without the intervention of sight and the other senses.

The objection is based upon a misunderstanding of the point at issue. The size and shape of our body are not comprised in the vital feeling of which we are speaking. This feeling alone would never enable us to form visible or tactile images of our body which depend upon the use of sight and touch. The phantasy simply imitates what our eyes and hands have presented to us. But the primal feeling contains nothing like this. What we see and what we touch is not the matter of this fundamental feeling. Indeed, we have already noted the difference between perceiving bodies through the (supposed) *representations* coming from our external senses, and perceiving our own body through the *fundamental feeling*. The two, or rather three kinds of perception of our own body, are to be kept separate and distinct (cf. 701–707). I cannot say: 'Perceiving my body in the first way (with the fundamental feeling), I do not perceive it in the third way (through sense-representations); therefore I do not perceive it at all.' This kind of argument is mistaken because it implies that the first kind of perception has to possess the characteristics of the third.

The real difficulty consists in forming a precise, clear-cut concept of the fundamental feeling. If more is demanded of the fundamental feeling than it actually possesses, it immediately appears absurd and pointless. But its denial in these circumstances is nevertheless unreasonable.

713. There is another difficulty to overcome. Attention is normally given to *sensible representation* of bodies, the third kind of perception which naturally holds our attention for several reasons. First, because exterior sensations are more vivid and impressionable than the other two kinds of bodily perception. Second, because sensations continually change and, as we have said, *change* draws the attention to differences and comparisons in such a way that we think we understand things only through this attention. Third, the *direct* act of understanding, through which our intelligence perceives exterior bodies, is our first, easiest and most *natural* intellection. On the other hand, in order to perceive intellectually our *subjective* body, we have to turn back and reflect upon ourselves. This is not easy. Drawn outside ourselves almost naturally, reflection is our last act and seems to lack light when compared with our vision of exterior things.[126]

---

[126] The *chronological* order of feelings, therefore, is the inverse of the order of *advertence* to them. First, we have our interior and fundamental feeling;

714. Our primal feeling, therefore, does not make us know the shape or the visible size of our body; it makes us perceive our body in a totally different way, which can be grasped only by intense concentration upon ourselves and the vital feeling quickening us. As we turn our attention and observation to this feeling, we must be careful to become aware of it as it is, without speculating about its nature or adding to it products of our imagination and reason.

Article 10
Existence of the fundamental feeling

715. This feeling must also extend to all the sensitive parts of our body. To recognise this, it is sufficient to note the movements continually occurring inside the body, such as the circulation of the blood, the constant movement of liquid substances, the various kinds of assimilation, and the general vegetable life, which inevitably act on the sensitive parts of the body through the pressure they exercise. These facts also help to remove vestiges of doubt about the existence of the great number of small, habitual, unadverted sensations which take place in us unceasingly. It is clear that when a nerve is touched and modified some sensation must be present, even though our capacity for adverting to it distinctly has been obliterated by its constant recurrence.

second, our exterior sensations. But we advert to our exterior sensations first, and then to our feeling. Moreover, in order to advert to our feeling, we need to have acquired control over our will, because we are free to reflect on and advert to our internal feeling. I have already shown, however, that we acquire this control over our thoughts only after having formulated abstract ideas (cf. 525–526). In order to *advert* to our interior feeling, therefore, we must have: 1. *adverted* with our understanding to our external sensations, and *perceived* bodies; 2. obtained *ideas* from these *perceptions*; 3. obtained (generic) *abstract concepts* from these ideas. When our spirit has developed to these three levels, and by means of the last of them, acquired dominion over our thought (which is done only with the help of language) (cf. 521–522), we are in a position finally to direct our thought to our interior, fundamental *feeling*. We see therefore that *chronologically* this thought is last and must be preceded by all the mental work on *external* sensations [*App.*, no. 26].

I have no wish to investigate here the mysteries of the origin and continuity of life, but I must note that our habitual, fundamental sensation would be easier to understand if some interior movement amongst the components of the body were considered essential to life (and certainly here on earth such movement is a necessary condition for life). It is not difficult to conceive the existence of sensation where the sensitive parts of the body undergo change.

716. Some detailed observations may help us to understand that we feel our body continually.

1. We are unaware of the constant atmospheric pressure on all the parts of our body, even the most sensitive parts, although granted the surface of the human body (13,500 cm^2.), this pressure (12,922 kg.) produces a worse effect than if we were encased in a leaden suit. Uneducated people, who may claim that such a weight must be felt, can scarcely be convinced of its existence. Nevertheless, we do unconsciously feel the pressure because it is equally diffused over the surface of our body and is continually and habitually present. It is, as it were, something of ourselves, of our own substance (fish are in the same situation relative to the pressure of the water around them and would, if they could speak, deny any sensation). However, were we to change the air about us, we would soon be aware of our feeling. For example, climbing a very high mountain[127] where the air is rarer and lighter can produce vomiting, nausea, dizziness; the loss of pressure on our blood vessels can produce bleeding because the blood pressure itself is no longer held in check.

2. The same observation is applicable to the circulation of the blood itself which, coursing through the veins in so many intricate channels and impelled by a marvellous force, will certainly produce some habitual sensation. Nevertheless, despite the obvious pressure on the sides of the veins, it seems that this movement is either not felt at all, or hardly felt. Then, suddenly perhaps, a change takes place: the blood flows more rapidly or more slowly than usual as a result of inflammation or fright. Then the heart beats more rapidly, while veins and

[127] A rise of one degree in a barometer means a reduction of 61 kg. of atmospheric pressure.

pulse tremble — or we faint. It was not the case that we felt nothing before the change; rather, we were unable to pay attention to the sensation because there was nothing new to attract our attention.

3. Our body has a certain temperature which we feel because we feel heat. Nevertheless, we scarcely notice it unless some change takes place. Let us imagine that different degrees of temperature, from freezing to very hot, are applied successively to a part of our body. We feel them all, and we notice that we feel them. Amongst these changes in temperature is the degree of heat normally experienced by our body which, however, we normally do *not* notice. We do notice it, however, amongst other variations in temperature because we compare various feelings produced by the different temperatures. Nevertheless, the comparisons we make do not produce the sensations. Comparisons are possible because we feel each sensation independently of any other, and independently of any comparison, although the comparison is necessary if we are to advert to the sensations which, however, exist even when there is no comparison and no passage from one sensation to another. We have to say, therefore, that we feel habitually the natural temperature of our body, although we do not notice this habitual sensation.

4. All the particles forming our body are attracted to the earth by the force of gravity. There is continual action on every molecule of our body and although we do not advert to it, some sensation must result from it. This is more noticeable in overweight people, but it also causes tiredness when people walk a lot. Nevertheless, we are naturally accustomed to a uniform feeling from the first moments of our existence, and normally are unaware of it. If, however, the attraction of gravity were to cease, or fall appreciably, we would experience a new kind of general sensation which would attract our attention by its novelty. We would notice in ourselves a sense of lightness, agility and mobility never before experienced. If the attraction increased suddenly, we would be overburdened by the weight of our body and immediately notice the change even in the shape of our body. On the other hand, without gravity our body would at least lengthen (there may be other difficulties as well) because all its particles, instead of pressing

on one another, would tend to expand rather than move downwards. If these changes in the force of gravity caused a feeling in our body, this would take place because the attraction does indeed exercise an effect on our sensitive body and excite a feeling. This would also happen relative to the force actually exercised in normal circumstances, although the evenness of such a force would provide no stimulus for attention.

The same argument could be used about the cohesion present in the body, about the continual movements and alterations caused by breathing, digestion, growth and the infinite chemical changes taking place in us. Everything leads us to think that our body must be felt by us with a feeling of its own, made up of many tiny, particular feelings habitual in us from the first moments in which we are joined to our body.

But besides this complex of innumerable, particular feelings which fuse into a universal, constant feeling in the human being (as I have said, I do not wish to say whether they form part of life, although they are certainly necessary conditions for it in our present state), I believe that there is in the spirit itself, joined to matter and to being, a single, fundamental feeling that mingles with all other feelings, forming them into an undifferentiated, unknown something through which we feel our spirit with its body. It is a pure, very simple feeling, not an idea, from which it differs according to the distinction already established between ideas and feelings. According to this distinction, feelings are the realisation of ideas.

Article 11

The origin of sensations confirms the existence of the fundamental feeling

717. Feeling, therefore, is an original datum. Consequently, we are not investigating its origin, but discussing its modifications and the genesis of sensations.

718. Those philosophers who imagine that human beings begin to exist without feeling truly make statues of them, and then go on to claim that sensations arise in these statues when

they are touched by external bodies. Such a sequence of events, however, only creates inexplicable difficulties at odds with nature's normal way of acting. That feeling should suddenly arise where no feeling had previously existed would be as difficult to understand as creation from nothing. According to this hypothesis, sensation, which comes about in the statue when exterior bodies act upon it, informs us of our own existence. In this case, we feel something different from ourselves without being able to feel ourselves!

But the hypothesis (and it is nothing more than an hypothesis) is also contrary to the constant order of nature, which never works by leaps. There certainly would be a leap if we passed, when touched by an external body, from not feeling ourselves to feeling both ourselves and something outside. The external movement, which has nothing in common with sensation, would be accompanied by the creation of a spirit within us. How could we form the idea of a spirit totally devoid of any feeling and thought? Spirit has no extension, nor any other bodily qualities. Deprived of spiritual qualities such as feeling and understanding it is annihilated, or rather its idea is abolished from the mind even though imagination may pretend to fill its place with a spirit not attested by observation and consciousness.

719. All these reflections confirm the existence within us of a fundamental feeling. Serious attention to the nature of *myself* would indicate the existence of this feeling because *myself*, reflecting upon itself, in the last analysis discovers itself to be a feeling constituting the sentient and intelligent subject.

Article 12

Explanation of St. Thomas' teaching that the body is in the soul

720. What we have said explains the classical teaching, repeated by St. Thomas, that 'the soul is in the body by containing it rather than by being contained'.[128]

[128] *S.T.*, I, q. 52, art. 1.

The word 'body' indicates something known, as we noted earlier; we give names only to what we know (cf. 678). In order to know the meaning of body, therefore, we have to rely on experience (cf. 672–673), not on speculative reasoning or *a priori* deduction. Experience indicates as fact a certain action done in us of which we are not the cause. The essence of body was found consequently to be a certain[129] force modifying us (cf. 676). We feel this force from the first moments of our existence, although we do not advert to it; we feel it (cf. 715–716) in a constant, uniform way in a determined mode; and this is what we call 'our body'. This force, although essentially different from *myself* (cf. 668–669), nevertheless acts in *myself*, in our spirit. We can rightly say, therefore, 'Our body is in our spirit' rather than 'Our spirit is in our body'. Later, we shall explain why common usage prefers the second to the first way of speaking.

Article 13

Physical relationship between soul and body

721. This also explains why long arguments about the question of harmony between soul and body are unnecessary. We have to find the answer to this celebrated question in the fact provided by consciousness. Examining this fact, I find that which is passive to action and that which acts, that is, spirit and body. My body, therefore, is in *fact* and by *definition* a substance acting in a special way in my spirit. The physical influence needs no proof because it is already contained in the notion of body.

---

[129] Later, when we perfect the definition of body, we shall specify the precise meaning of 'certain'.

CHAPTER 4

Origin of the idea of our body
by means of modifications of the fundamental feeling

Article 1

The analysis of sensation (contd.)

722. To form an exact idea of sensation,[130] we must set aside completely the idea of external bodies, which we always imagine as something striking our organs and producing sensations there. This cause must be considered as if it did not exist. Sensation is the only fact provided by consciousness and we must confine ourselves strictly to it.

723. The analysis of a particular sensation results in two elements: 1. a feeling which, as we have seen, is a modification of the fundamental feeling (cf. 705–706) (its matter is the modified organ); and 2. a believed representation or, as we call it, a *perception* of something different from us and our body (cf. 708–709). The first of these elements is *subjective*, a modification of the subject; the second, which I have called *extrasubjective*, is a perception of something different from the subject.

A correct understanding about the nature of bodies and the way we perceive them depends on an accurate distinction between these two elements, which are never found separated. Time spent on the distinction will not be time lost. We should also note that the first of these elements, the partial modification of our feeling, is the weaker of the two and therefore usually escapes our observation, which generally notes only the second to the exclusion of everything else.

---

[130] The word 'sensation' is generally taken to mean an *acquired, particular* sensation.

Article 2

Definition of the fundamental feeling; how it is distinguished from the sense perception of bodies

724. In every corporeal sensation, we perceive our sensitive organ in a new way. Moreover, in every modification experienced by our sensitive organ there arises a perception of an agent different from us. The particular perception we have of our organ as *perceiving* is the modification of the fundamental feeling. As I have said, the fundamental feeling is a constant perception of the sensitive parts of our body in their first, natural state. The modified fundamental feeling is the perception of some part of our body modified and violently changed from its first, uniform, natural state.[131]

In order, therefore, to know a particular perception of our modified organ and distinguish it from the perception of an agent that accompanies the perception but is different from it, we must consider the nature of the fundamental feeling, of which the particular perception is only a new mode.

725. The fundamental feeling that comes from life is a feeling of *pleasure*, granted life in its natural, unspoilt state. It is uniformly and pleasantly diffused in all the sensitive parts of the body, without distinctive features. Thus, it would be impossible for anyone who has experienced only the fundamental feeling without ever experiencing particular sensations, to form the image or representation of our body (shape, size, etc.) which our sight and external senses offer. The fundamental feeling, then, is only pleasure diffused in a determined way,[132] and its

---

[131] When I describe a particular perception of our sensitive organs in this way, I am not taking anything for granted. Certainly *modification of the organ* is part of the definition; but the modification is not gratuitous from the moment the organ itself is a body and therefore part of the energy acting in us and simultaneously producing the fundamental feeling.

[132] Although the pleasure of life is truly diffused throughout all the parts of our body that have feeling, we cannot use the expression 'We refer the primal feeling to different points of our body's *extension*' with the same meaning without putting the reader on his guard. This way of speaking could be confusing because it is not the way we know the body in the primal feeling, nor therefore see or touch its *extrasubjective* extension or, *a fortiori*, its parts. When we speak about the feeling of the whole of our sensitive body, we

modifications are only a particular *kind* of *sensible pleasure* and *pain*.

726. These considerations give us a more complete definition of the fundamental feeling as 'a fundamental action that we feel done directly and necessarily in us by an energy that is not ours; the action is naturally pleasant but can vary according to certain laws, being in turn more or less pleasant, or even unpleasant.'

Article 3

Origin and nature of corporeal pleasure and pain

727. The action we experience of the fundamental feeling is the very essence of corporeal pleasure and pain. The particular modifications the action undergoes (according to a law we need not investigate at the moment) are particular perceptions of our organs felt more pleasantly or painfully. Pleasure and pain are thus feelings which must be distinguished from what, in a sensation, is external and has shape. We shall go on to describe this second element of sensations when our idea of the first is so accurate (if that is possible) that we can no longer confuse it with any other.

Corporeal pleasure and pain are simply a change experienced in our spirit; they represent nothing and have no shape. They are a fact; they are what they are, and cannot be understood by anyone without experience of them. Because such a change has nothing in common with anything outside it, it is undefinable and unintelligible to anyone who has not experienced it.

728. However, *corporeal*[133] pleasure and pain: 1. terminates in the *subjective extension* of the body (I call this extension therefore *matter* of the corporeal feeling); and 2. has different levels of intensity.

should always remember it means nothing more than a *mode* of that pleasure. This mode becomes clothed, so to speak, with external, figured extension at the time we obtain the perception of our body with our external senses. But more of this in a later chapter.

[133] I use the word 'corporeal' as a simple sign to indicate the difference from any other feeling, without going more deeply into the difference and discovering a third element of sensation.

Article 4

Relationship of corporeal pleasure and pain with extension

729. There is no difficulty in proving that corporeal pleasure and pain terminate in corporeal *subjective extension*.[134] For example, a square piece of metal placed on the hand is felt at every point it touches the skin; if the metal were a disc or some other shape, the points of contact with the skin would correspond to each shape.

730. In the same way, the fundamental feeling is present in all the sensitive parts of the body and therefore must extend and be referred to them; this is its *mode* of being. However this does not mean that just by looking we know the shape and size of the parts occupied by our pleasure or pain. The imagination is no suitable guide in these matters. Pure feeling, not the images seen by our eyes, makes us perceive the extension. Thus I call this extension *subjective*[135] to distinguish it from the extension presented by our sight or other senses relative to external bodies.

731. This should cause no difficulty if we reflect that this extension can be understood only as a *mode* of the feeling, as I have already said; the extension can change but never be separated from the mode of feeling.

We must not think that feeling and subjective extension are two entirely separate things, nor that feeling is first centralised and then spreads through the extension already felt as through something different from itself. This imaginary explanation, which is not given by careful observation, contains images

---

[134] Corporeal pleasure and pain are *experienced* passively in the spirit but at the same time are accompanied by some *activity* of the spirit. I cannot stop at this point to describe how these two conditions are united — I have touched on this elsewhere. It is enough to note that in so far as pleasure and pain are acts of the spirit, it can be said they terminate in extension; but in so far as they are *experienced*, it is more accurate to say that corporeal extension terminates in them with its *action*. The reason for the truth of these two seemingly contradictory ways of speaking must be found in that strange but true and perfect *unity* between what is *subjective* and what is *extrasubjective*, between what is active and what is passive at the time of the action.

[135] This name does not indicate its nature because all extension is *extrasubjective*; it indicates its intimate union with sensation which is itself subjective and takes its mode from this extension.

taken from the sense of sight. All such images, however, must be excluded; we must restrict ourselves to the pure subjective feeling we are discussing. If we concentrate carefully on ourselves and observe our own feeling, refusing to be distracted by these images, we will easily recognise in our own subjective feeling that it is impossible for the soul to perceive an extension different from the same feeling with which it perceives that extension.[136]

Anyone wishing to observe the nature and modifications of the fundamental feeling we are discussing, must set aside every *shape* presented by sense; he must get rid of the idea of external extension given by the sense of sight or any other sense. He must turn in on himself attentively and reflect on the pains and pleasures he may be experiencing uniformly or variably in the different parts of his body. He will then find that these feelings have no *shaped* extension comparable to the extension we perceive with our eyes and other external senses in external bodies. However, he will find that they have a certain limitation, a *mode*. Now if we abstract this mode from the sensations and compare it with the extension perceived through our eyes or other external senses, we find that it harmonises with *extension*, and is called *extension*.

Article 5

Confutation of the opinion: 'We feel everything in our brain and then refer the sensation to the relevant parts of our body'

732. The following argument will be enough to show that the feeling of our own body must extend to all its sensitive parts. I agree with those who say: 'It is by touch that you project outside yourself the objects you see; otherwise they would be attached to your eye like a veil' [*App.*, no. 27].

733. But they go on to say: 'In the same way sensation takes place in the brain. If communication between an organ and the brain is interrupted, you feel nothing; you locate the sensations

---

[136] Extension is therefore the *matter* of the feeling, since matter and form are one thing.

at the affected organ by means of habitual judgments.' Here I part company with them altogether. In my opinion it would be impossible for bodies that I see to be projected outside myself by touching them if I referred the sensation only to some centre in my brain rather than to the extremity of my hand.

734. If by touching an object I see that I locate it outside myself, how do I locate my hand outside myself? For example, if I believe that the response of the sensitive nerve is in my head, why do I do not feel in my head the sensation I feel in the touch of my finger-tips? Why do I not feel the response in my spirit or along my arm or in some other part of my hand instead of only at my fingers-tips? In my opinion, this cannot be explained by acquired habit. If it could, we would have to demonstrate that there was first a time in our life when all sensations were not located at different points of our body, and later there were some *means* by which we learnt to locate them at the outside points; but no one has ever indicated this *means* nor can they.

If our eyes need touch to project things seen externally to the correct distance, and we conclude that the same must be true for the parts of our body felt by touch, then we must invent another sense of touch in the soul that would move the parts of the body outside the brain. This is absurd and denied by experience.

There is therefore in the soul a power that immediately, and not by acquired habit, refers sensations at various parts of the body and feels them there.

Article 6

Comparison of the two subjective modes in which we feel and perceive the extension[137] of our own body

735. The extension of our own body is a *mode* of the fundamental feeling. But this *fundamental* feeling is either in its *first*, natural state or in its state of accidental, adventitious

---

[137] We should not forget that this *subjective extension* is known to us only as a *mode* of the fundamental feeling without any *shape*, unlike the extension of external bodies.

modification. Whatever its state however it always has the *mode* of extension. Hence we feel our body's extension *subjectively* in two modes: 1. by means of the fundamental feeling; and 2. by means of the modifications of this feeling, or the partial sensations we receive through our organs.

736. The difference between these two ways of feeling our body *subjectively* must be noted:

1. The whole extension of our sensitive body is perceived by the fundamental feeling. But when the fundamental feeling is modified by some external sensation, only the *part* of the extension affected by the sensation is felt.

2. The extension of the body is felt in a *constant* mode by the fundamental feeling. The part affected by a sensation is felt in a *new* mode, more vividly than the other parts, or at least in a different mode; it stands out from the other parts, and presents itself alone and isolated from them all in the feeling experienced by our spirit.

3. If life is present, the fundamental feeling produces a *necessary* mode of feeling; in a sensation the affected organ is felt in an *accidental*, adventitious mode.

4. The extension is felt *equally* with almost no variation by the fundamental feeling; at least we are certainly not conscious of any inequalities. In a sensation the organ is felt in very *different* modes, according to the different levels of pleasure or pain and the phenomena of colours, sounds, tastes, smells.

737. These four differences are sufficient to show clearly how unsuitable the fundamental feeling is for attracting our attention and coming to notice. It is connatural to us, one with and part of our nature. Hence there is nothing extraordinary or curious about it to engage our attention; it is in us as ourselves. On the other hand, no sensation of our own organ is essential. It is *partial, new* and *vivid, accidental* and *changeable*; it is equipped in every way for exciting our curiosity and attention; it attracts us to itself and makes us aware that we perceive the individual parts of our body with a subjective perception.

We can therefore conclude that, relative to the two subjective ways of feeling our body and its extension, the first (the fundamental feeling) easily escapes our observation, whilst the second makes itself known without any difficulty. It is not surprising that few people know they have this fundamental feeling, when the sensation of our own organs is so blatantly evident to all.

Article 7
Further proof of the existence of the fundamental feeling

738. When one of our own sense organs is stimulated, the sensation we experience is a fresh confirmation of the existence of the fundamental feeling, which precedes the sensation. For how could we locate the sensation at a certain part of our body if we had no feeling in it? Note carefully: to say we feel the part at precisely the same time as we have the sensation is not sufficient. To feel the part means to locate the sensation at the part; this would mean we locate the sensation at the part without having any feeling there. Such a fact would be inexplicable.

739. The same can be said about the capacity for moving our limbs. If these were not naturally felt by us, they would be extraneous to us, and our will would not be able to move the limbs it wished with its internal act.

Without the fundamental feeling, therefore, two kinds of acts of our spirit would remain inexplicable and even absurd: the act by which our spirit locates a sensation it experiences at different parts of the body; and the act that imparts movement to them as it pleases. We must understand that it is *myself* which locates sensation and produces movement as an effect of its own very activity.

Article 8
All our sensations are simultaneously subjective and extrasubjective

740. I call sensation *subjective* in so far as I feel my co-sentient organ in it; I call it *extrasubjective* in so far as I simultaneously feel an *agent* outside my organ. If we observe the fact of sensation attentively, we find there is no sensation in which we do not

feel our sentient organ. Likewise, when we feel a modification of our organ, a perception of something outside the organ takes place in our spirit. We call this *corporeal sense perception*; it is very often so strong and vivid that it engages all our attention, so that we forget the organ completely and are unaware that we sense it.

741. The difference between *corporeal sense perception* and the *sensation* we have of the sentient organ is so important that we cannot be too careful in identifying it. The solution of a great number of psychological problems depends on the clear recognition and demonstration of this difference.

To indicate the co-existence of these two perceptions, I will begin with the sense of sight. We all accept that feeling our own eye, the organ of vision, is different from seeing bodies with our eyes. Anything perceived by our eyes has such a vivid, attractive presence that it draws all our interest, especially when our eyes have been conditioned and taught, so to speak, by touch. When our gaze is captured by a panorama or a beautiful work of art, we pay no attention to our eyes themselves where we are experiencing a weak sensation caused by the light striking them and passing through unnoticed. But this sensation, although unnoticed, is very real. Imagine a beam of strong light suddenly striking our eyes so that it is too intense for the pupils. At once we will feel and be conscious of an unpleasant sensation in our eyes which smart from a light too strong for them. In situations like this, we fix our attention on the organ affected by pain. We may conclude that, to be aware of feeling our perceiving organ, there must be a level of unusual, vivid pleasure or pain drawing our attention away from the exterior agent perceived by the organ.

What I have said about the eyes clearly demonstrates the elusive but true fact that granted a suitable modification of a sense-organ, we experience the two things I have mentioned, that is: 1. we feel the modified sense-organ; and 2. we perceive the exterior *agent* in a way compatible with our feeling. This *perception* has nothing to do with the *sensation* we have of the organ; but the perception is so indivisibly joined to the sensation that it forms one thing with it; one cannot exist without the other.

742. The same can be said of hearing, smell and taste. Hearing gives us sound, but sound is not the sensation we have of the

acoustic organ with which we perceive sound, nor is it the exterior body. Sound, which arises when our organ is modified, has no similarity with the feeling we have of our organ; the stimulating action we feel is different from the action produced in us by our modified organ. The stimulating action accompanied by the phenomenon of sound is more assertive than the feeling we have of our organ and is able to attract our attention, especially when the action has special qualities. Thus, if I hear a flute or harp, I am attracted by the pleasant sounds and pay no attention to my ear, which would need to be modified in a painful way, for example, by a deafening explosion, to turn my attention from the sounds to the feeling of my ear. When such a thing happens, we usually cover our ears to protect them, which is a clear sign that we perceive the organ.

743. The same is also true for the senses of smell and taste: these are the phenomenal part of the sensation experienced when the organs are modified by their corresponding agents. For example, when we smell a carnation or taste honey, we can note the same two things. In the first place, my olfactory nerves are stimulated by particles from the carnation; it does not matter whether the stimulation is a slight vibration of the nerves, or s small mark or impression made on them. The question is: what do we perceive by smell? We certainly do not perceive the vibration or impression to which smell bears no resemblance. Nor does smell suggest any movement of, or form received by the olfactory nerves. Smell is a particular feeling arising in our spirit on the occasion of those minute and perhaps imperceptible movements of our nostrils. It is this feeling I call the phenomenon of smell. On the other hand the odorous particles striking our nostrils could be of sufficient force and intensity to cause us pain, and make us aware of the feeling of our nose, as happens when an offensive smell makes us wrinkle it with displeasure. Although the weakness of the impression may prevent this, we cannot say that the phenomenon of smell (in which we have the term of an external action) is not completely different from the feeling we have of the organ itself.

The same can be said about taste. The different form that our taste buds assume on contact with honey is not what we feel in the taste. The *taste* is the phenomenal part of the sensation and is completely independent of the perception of our palate.

[743]

Article 9

Touch as a universal sense

744. Touch is a universal sense; it is equally present in all the sensitive parts of our body.[138]

745. The other four senses are themselves touch, from which they are distinguished only by the phenomenal part of sensation. When they are stimulated, these senses are subject to touch-perception and to this extent are the same as touch.[139] But certain kinds of touch affect our spirit with four kinds of phenomena: colour, sound, smell and taste. These phenomena distinguish the organs and, as a group, are different from touch which is common to them all and diffused through the rest of the body.

Article 10

The origin of touch

746. The sense of touch in its *subjective* element is only the receptivity of the fundamental feeling for experiencing a modification. But because the fundamental feeling is extended to all the sensitive parts of the body (in other words, this extension is only the *mode of being* of that feeling), the feeling changes when this mode of being changes. This is why we experience sensations of touch when some suitable motion takes place in our body.

The four specifically different phenomena of which we have

[138] The ancients also noted that all the senses are ultimately touch. St. Thomas says: *omnes autem alii sensus fundantur supra tactum* (*S.T.*, 1, q. 76, art. 5).

[139] We have seen that *touch* has a *double* nature: it is simultaneously *subjective* and *extrasubjective* in so far as we perceive 1. the sentient organ (the subjective part) and 2. the touching, external agent (extrasubjective part). From what I will say later, it will be more evident how the *twofold sensation* and the four *phenomena* are present in the particular senses we are discussing.

spoken, and others which need not be listed here, are united to some of these sensations.

Article 11

The relationship between the two subjective ways of perceiving our body

747. Because the sense of touch is the foundation of all the different kinds of sensations, we also feel a modification of the sentient organ although we do not always advert to it. In fact we rarely advert to a modification of those senses in which the four sensible phenomena are found. The intensity and singularity of these phenomena, like their usefulness and necessity, attract all our attention away from the unassertive sensation of the organ itself. But this does not happen so noticeably in the sense of touch which, phenomenally weaker, concentrates our attention more on the organ itself.

The second way of perceiving our body (by means of particular sensations) is not, therefore, essentially different from the first. It is *subjective* in so far as, together with it, we sense our organs as *co-sentient*, not just as *felt*; in short, we feel them as forming one thing with the sentient subject, *myself*.

748. But in these two ways of feeling and perceiving our body, the matter of feeling and of sensation (the body itself) is always the same. Hence there can be no contradiction between them. What makes these two ways of feeling coherent and equal is the fact that we locate feeling and sensation at the same points in space.

CHAPTER 5
Criterion for the existence of bodies

Article 1
A more perfect definition of bodies

749. After our analysis of the fundamental feeling and acquired sensations (in their subjective part), we can offer a more perfect definition of bodies.

First, however, the most famous definitions given by modern thinkers:

I. Berkeley and Condillac defined body as a complex of sensations. But as we have seen, *sensation* can be an effect only of a body's action on the spirit. The definition, therefore, lacks an *agent*, that is, the substance of a body, and retains only the accidental effect. But the substance of a body is body. The definition therefore excluded body and contained idealism, that is, the negation of bodies.

750. II. Descartes and Malebranche posited the essence of body in extension. The concept of extension however does not present any activity or force. On the contrary, it is the term of an action. Observation informs us that the first thing we experience of bodies is the feeling they produce in us by a certain action. Analysing this feeling, we find it refers to certain points in extension and spreads through and terminates in an extended element. Initially, therefore, we find extension to be like a *mode* of the feeling produced in us by bodies. It is true that if we analyse this *mode* of feeling (an effect of the action of bodies), as we will do in a moment, we also find that it must indeed be real in the cause that has produced it. Bodies must therefore be extended. This discovery is however a secondary discovery. According to Descartes the *essence* of a thing is that which we first conceive in the thing thought. But extension could not be thought unless we first thought of an *action* which, when done on us, reveals extension.

751. III. Leibniz saw that the essence of body had to be

posited in some *force*. However, his argument did not begin from observation, which is the only starting point for a well-founded argument. Instead of being satisfied with the idea of a force acting on us and making us passive at the moment of corporeal sensation (a fact of consciousness), he imagined that body had to be a force acting not on us but only on itself through an internal energy, like all his other monads; body was a force acting in harmony with, but not on us. In this way, he removed the sole means for knowing the force, which is known only through observation of what is happening in us. The hypothesis that we ourselves form and develop within us some knowledge of the force is a gratuitous phantasy totally unsupported by observation, analogy or true intrinsic arguments. If bodies are to be conceived by imagination, not by observation, the forces we call bodies could indeed be fashioned in any way we like; we could suppose them to be simple[140] and endowed with *perception*. In this case, they would not be substances causing feeling but substances that feel. Leibniz's idea of body is therefore completely different from the idea I am presenting.

752. I start from observation because the description I give is intended to depend on this. Whether bodies have something that is outside our experience or our intellective conception of them is irrelevant.

Observation confirms that we are passive in sensations, that is, we experience an action of which we are not the authors. Consciousness of such an action is consciousness of a certain energy acting on us; and knowledge of such energy is knowledge of an ens, a substance. Hence the first but still imperfect definition we gave of body: 'a substance acting on us in a *certain mode*.'

To perfect this definition, we had to discover the meaning of 'in a certain mode', which we then inserted into the definition. We went on to analyse sensation because sensation or corporeal feeling is the action of this kind of substance.

The analysis showed a constant, uniform feeling[141] and an action partially modifying this fundamental feeling, that is, two actions, two energies, two substances, two bodies. Our own

---

[140] Later I shall directly refute the simple points of Leibniz and Boscovich.

[141] The fundamental feeling is modified as the human body grows.

body produces the fundamental feeling and an external body modifies our body; we experience a body that is co-sentient as well as felt, and a body that is only felt.

The fundamental feeling, the action of our body, is not only a pleasant feeling, but is a pleasure with its own mode and limitation called *extension*, which does not derive from the simple notion of pleasure.

All acquired sensations are a species of touch.

Touch is both a *subjective* and an *extrasubjective* sensation because in it two things are felt: the sentient *organ* (the *subjective* part) and the *external agent* touching us and producing a sensation of touch (the *extrasubjective* part).

The *subjective* part is a modification of the fundamental feeling and makes us feel in a new, more intense way whatever part of our body is affected, while locating it at the same points as the fundamental feeling.

Furthermore, there are four classes or species of sensation particular to four organs of our body. They have four kinds of phenomena attached to them, *colours, sounds, tastes* and *smells*.

This analysis of the action of corporeal substance on us indicates that the essence of bodies must consist in: 1. pleasure and pain; and 2. extension, in which pleasure and pain are experienced. These are the two common, variable elements of the action. We can therefore improve our definition by saying: 'Body is a substance producing an action on us felt by us as pleasure or pain and having a constant mode called *extension*.'

To which we may now add: 'It can be accompanied by four kinds of phenomena called colour, sound, smell and taste'; but we should note that this addition does not mean these phenomena must be present. They are only an *aptitude* of a body to arouse them, given the necessary conditions.

753. Thus, such a substance, if firmly joined to us in the bond we call *life* (I am not investigating this here, whatever it may be), is a subjective body, exercising in our spirit a constant, uniform action called *fundamental feeling*. If this bond is absent, the substance is a foreign body, able to produce only partial, transient sensations.

Article 2

The general criterion for judgments
about the existence of bodies

754. With the establishment of the definition of body (cf. 752), we have also established the criterion for judging about its existence: 'I can say I am certain of the existence of a body when I am certain of the existence of that which, forming its *essence*, is expressed in its definition.'

Article 3

Application of the general criterion

755. In the first perception of our body we experience the feeling of life as pleasure or as the pleasant, individual union of a body with us.

This feeling, endowed with extension as one of its modes, is located at different points of space.[142] Thus by means of extension we perceive a body.

756. The existence of external bodies is proved in the same way. We perceive the two elements found in the definition of body.

The primal extension in which we locate our feeling undergoes some modifications from a cause different from us. In this modification we find

1. a partial, adventitious sensation of pain or pleasure which

2. is diffused in an extension more limited than, but not exceeding, the first extension.

Sometimes the phenomena of the four organs, eyes, nose, ears and palate are also present, if the organs are stimulated.

These conditions once more confirm our perceptions of an external body.

757. A sensation of pleasure or pain by itself does not indicate

[142] To say the feeling is located at different points of space is the simple way of indicating space perceived in a *shaped* way. But calling extension simply a *mode* of feeling keeps us within the subjective sensation of extension.

the presence of a body. It tells us that an action is being done in us and that the action must have a cause different from us, but of itself it would never tell us that this cause is a body, because the essential element of extension would be missing. The sensation must be capable of making us perceive an extension if we are to have a corporeal sensation. Extension determines our sensation, making it a *corporeal* or *material* sensation.

And vice-versa: extension by itself is not body, since the first essential element of body is the *energy* for producing a feeling in us.

To avoid making a mistake about the existence of a body, we must verify for ourselves the two following conditions or elements that form its essence: 1. a feeling (our passivity, external action); 2. an extension to which the feeling is referred (*mode* of the feeling).

758. There is an *action* done in us that constitutes the fundamental feeling; joined to this feeling is the *mode of extension.*

Thus a body exists permanently united to us. Its existence is no longer subject to doubt because we cannot be deceived as to whether we are alive or dead; the two elements constituting our body in this case are two facts of consciousness.

In adventitious sensations we distinguish:

1. a modification of the fundamental feeling, that is, a new, more intense sensation of some part of our body; and

2. a perception of an agent outside the extension in which our fundamental feeling is diffused.

The modification is the second *subjective* way of perceiving our body; the perception is the *extrasubjective* perception of external bodies.

The existence of our body therefore is always founded on the evidence of the fundamental feeling.

759. The certainty of the existence of external bodies is also founded on the fundamental feeling, because their action on us is indivisibly joined to the modifications of the feeling, while their extension is measured by the extension first occupied by the fundamental feeling.

Article 4

The certainty of our own body is the criterion for the existence of other bodies

760. Our body, therefore, perceived in the first mode, becomes a *criterion* for the existence of all other bodies.

The other modes of perceiving a body must be reduced to this first mode, that is, perception by the fundamental feeling. Thus, the second *subjective* mode is reduced to the first because it is a modification of the fundamental feeling, and the third *extra-subjective* mode (for external bodies) is reduced to the first because the extrasubjective extension becomes known through a comparison with the subjective extension.

Article 5

Application of the criterion to possible errors about the existence of some part of our body

761. We cannot err about the existence of our own body perceived in the first mode, that is, with the fundamental feeling (cf. 755–759).

We can be misled about the existence of some part of our body when it is perceived by acquired sensations. A perception of this kind includes the other two modes, the *subjective* and the *extrasubjective* (cf. 760).

762. For the moment I am not concerned with possible error in the third mode, that is, in perceiving our body as an external agent rather than as a subject. This error, common to the perception of all external bodies, will be dealt with later.

For the moment I want to examine possible error concerning the existence of some part of our body perceived in the second subjective mode. For example, an amputee acutely feels the pain of a lost hand or foot, not in the stump but in the limb that still seems to be there. In this case the person locates the pain deceptively and wrongly at the extension.

[760–762]

The error can be discovered by applying the criterion.[143]

The amputated limb is not felt by the fundamental feeling but by the adventitious sensation of the pain. To know whether such a sensation is misleading, it must be reduced, as we have said, to the fundamental feeling as its criterion and proof.

This is done when we verify that the acquired sensation is a modification of the fundamental feeling.

In the case of the amputee, the sensation of pain in the arm or leg is certainly a modification of the fundamental feeling but this fact does not prove the existence of our body (cf. 757); the extension felt by the sensation must be capable of being reduced to the extension of the fundamental feeling.

Now we have noted that there are two characteristics of the fundamental feeling: 1. its constant, uniform existence; and 2. its aptitude to be modified. By applying this second characteristic, let us see if the extension of the amputated limb is felt in reality.

If the limb we perceive is the same limb felt by the fundamental feeling, it must be subject to modifications, because the fundamental extension (our hand perceived by the fundamental feeling) is essentially modifiable. If then the hand exists, it can be touched, seen, moved, etc. because these are modifications of the fundamental extension. But this cannot happen with the amputated hand — it is felt, but not by the fundamental feeling. It is a misleading phenomenon since it cannot be reduced to the fundamental extension nor shown to be a modification of it. Indeed when I feel my hand through the pain I experience in it, the mode of this sensation, that is, extension, must be identical with the extension of the fundamental feeling; the only other possible difference is that the sensation in the fundamental feeling endures and is less vivid, while the acquired or adventitious sensation is more intense, partial and transient.

---

[143] The cause of this error lies not in the sensation but in an *habitual judgment*. When we still had our hand or foot, the pain we felt was referred to them by a necessity of nature because that was where we felt the pain. This necessity then became a *habit* which remained even when the necessity had disappeared. And because we now feel a pain that is no different from the previous pain in our hand or foot, we think it is the same and assign it to the same place without adverting to the real place.

Article 6

Response to the idealists' argument based on dreams

763. The idealists' argument, drawn from what we see in dreams, is clearly without foundation. They ask: could life not be one long dream?

They do not observe that the images in dreams may mislead us about the existence of external bodies but not about the existence of our own body; in fact, they contest this.

The illusions of dreams are the result of the body's being stimulated in a certain way and would therefore be impossible if we did not have a body. They do not cast doubt on the existence of bodies in general; on the contrary, they prove and confirm their existence. Later we will see how to distinguish between what is false and true in external phenomena.

CHAPTER 6
Origin of the idea of time

Article 1
The connection between what has already been said and what follows

764. We have seen how we perceive our body in the first two *subjective* ways. We must now speak about the third, the *extrasubjective* way, which is valid for all bodies as external agents applied to our corporeal sensories. Even our own body can be perceived, not only as ours, but as any external body.

However, before examining this third way, we must mention some *abstract ideas* that can be obtained, at least in part, from the body perceived subjectively.[144] They are the ideas of *time, movement* and *space*.

765. In fact, *time* is connected with all the actions and experiences we are aware of; *movement* does not require our exterior senses for its perception, because *our locomotive faculty* is an *internal*, subjective faculty whose existence is confirmed by our consciousness; lastly *space* or *extension* also is a mode of our corporeal, subjective feeling[145] from which it cannot be separated, although we can distinguish it mentally in our own feeling just as we can note its *mode* of being in any other ens, even if the mode is *per se* inseparably united to *being*.

The starting point for these three ideas of *time, movement* and *space* is found in the ideas we have so far discussed. However, it will help if we make use also of our exterior senses and *extrasubjective* perception of bodies, so as not to separate what our mind customarily sees as united.

---

[144] Our mind makes this abstraction only when it is sufficiently developed. This happens only through the use of our exterior senses. But this does not prevent the body, subjectively perceived, from being the foundation of the abstractions we are discussing.

[145] This is all we have discovered so far about extension; later we shall understand its nature better and see that it exists not only in the subject but also in the agent.

Article 2

The idea of time derived from consciousness of our own actions

766. When we perform an action we are limited in two ways.[146] The immediate, interior feeling by which we are conscious of performing the action informs us of this double limitation.

The first limitation is the *level of intensity* in the action; the second is its *duration*. The words 'intensity' and 'duration' indicate the *limitations* in their abstract state, after they have been mentally separated by us from the internal and external actions they are limiting and made into two mental entia.

767. We can increase the *intensity* and *duration* of our actions up to a certain point, and we can imagine them increasing indefinitely. *Successive duration* is the idea of *time*.

768. Just as my present action has *successive duration*, so has every other action done by myself or others.

Comparison of the duration of one action with that of other actions gives a certain relationship, called the *measure of time*.

769. The measure of time is generally based on an important, uniform, constant and easily noticed action, such as the movement of the earth on its axis around the sun. The parts of this movement form the parts of common measures of time: years, months, days, etc. Any action at all could have been chosen, provided the duration of all other actions was related to it.

770. I can increase or decrease the duration of my own actions. But if I want to retain the same *quantity* of action in a shortened duration, I must compensate with greater intensity; and if I increase the duration, I must reduce the intensity. There is therefore an invariable relationship between the *duration* and *intensity* of the action.

In motion, *intensity* is *velocity*, which is greater in direct proportion to the distance covered and in indirect proportion to

---

[146] Life, which also has the limitation of *duration*, is the first action we feel ourselves doing. Hence the feeling of *time* is included in the *fundamental feeling*. But the analysis of this feeling is difficult, and here I need only mention what is necessary for my purpose.

the time taken to cover the distance; hence we have the formula $V = \frac{S}{T}$ or $T = \frac{S}{V}$.

771. The constancy of this relationship is founded on two constant data: 1. the constant quantity of the desired effect or action; and 2. the limited quantity of forces involved, which is also constant and given.

Thus, a law founded in the nature of things establishes that within a certain duration, only a particular, fixed *intensity* can produce a determined *quantity of action*.

772. Let us now suppose that the duration of a desired action is fixed but not its quantity and intensity. By applying various levels of intensity to the duration, we have various quantities of actions or effects proportionate to the levels of intensity. The general result is that for any duration, the quantity of action will be exactly proportionate to the intensity of the action; this gives us the idea of the *uniformity of time*. No matter what is done within a fixed duration, there is a constant relationship between the intensity of the action and its quantity; where little has been done, more can be achieved, provided the intensity is heightened. In short, I can think the possibility of doing something within a certain duration by means of a determined intensity of action; the same applies to any similar duration.

773. We can express the relationship between quantity, intensity and duration of action by the formula: $T = \frac{Q}{S}$, where $T =$ duration, S intensity, and Q quantity. This is valid where there is only one agent; if in Q there are several agents, then the formula is $T = \frac{Q}{SM}$, where M is the number of agents.

Article 3

The idea of time indicated by the actions of others

774. What has been said about actions attested as our own by consciousness can also be said about actions we perceive, but of which we are not the authors.

In this case, time is a *limitation* not only of actions but also of passive experiences. *Passive experience* and *action* are very often the same fact considered from opposite points of view.

Article 4

Pure idea of time

775. The limitation we have called 'successive duration' can be abstracted from all the actions and passive experiences of finite beings. If we then add the *idea of possibility* (of a possible action, that is) which, as we have said, is innate in us, we have the pure idea of time, that is, of time in a possible, but not real action.

Article 5

Idea of pure, indefinitely long time

776. We perceive successive duration as 'a possibility that a certain quantity of action can be obtained by means of a certain level of intensity.' This is the idea of time in general, the pure idea, given by observation.

777. Granted constant intensity, *quantity of action* is the *measure of time*, while *uniformity of time* means simply 'the same quantity obtained by a constant level of intensity.'

778. This quantity of action, obtained by a constant level of intensity, can be conceived as repeated an indefinite number of times, if we use the idea of *possibility*. Hence the idea of *pure, indefinitely long time* composed of: 1. the idea of *possibility*, which is *per se* indefinite; and 2. the (abstract) idea of one of the two limitations to which successive actions are subject.

Article 6

Continuity in time

§1. *Everything that happens, happens by instants*

779. Anything subject to succession begins, grows, comes to perfection and then deteriorates and perishes. But at whatever

moment we observe this process, we find a determined state. Indeed, according to the principle of contradiction, there cannot be a part or perfection that is and is not at the same time. Let us take for example a baby cutting a tooth, or an adolescent's facial hair changing into a beard. In answer to the question 'Has the tooth come or the beard grown?' we can indeed reply 'Not yet, but it is *beginning*.' Nevertheless, although the word 'beginning' involves a mental relationship with the future state of the thing, that is, when the tooth is formed or the beard grown, the early form of the tooth and the first growth of hair already exist as such. Their state is not something between being and not-being.

780. This simple observation of fact leads us to the remarkable but true conclusion that all that happens, happens in an instant — provided we understand 'all that happens' to mean not something composite, that is, an already formed nature (which always attracts our attention), but that thing whatever it may be (a part of nature or an element) which is at each instant. This thing, whatever it may be, which finds itself in being in a given instant is perfect relative to itself, relative to its own existence, although it may be imperfect considered as part of something greater of which it is an element or outline or beginning.

781. However a serious difficulty now presents itself. If all that happens, happens in an instant, what is the origin of continuous time? Is this idea of time obtained by abstraction from what happens, from actions? When we think a series of things which happen, each one of which happens in an instant, we perceive a series of points, a succession of instants, but never continuous time.

§2. *The difficulty is not solved by the idea of time obtained by observation alone*

782. Let us return to the example of the growth of hair and see whether observation alone offers us an idea of time containing the characteristic of true continuity.

Suppose one hair has taken two months to grow ten centimetres.

This growth is an *action* which we call *composite* because it consists of many little actions of shorter duration.

The same would be true for the production of any other kind of thing: the unfolding of a flower, the sculpting of a bas-relief; any event whatever that gave or changed the being of anything, would be called a *composite action* because it could always be mentally subdivided into many parts which would be so many lesser actions or events.

We must first note carefully that the time taken by the hair to grow maintains a constant proportion to all the other actions done within the two months, as we mentioned above (cf. 764–765 [766–773]), that is, taking into account the intensity of the action.

With the intensity of the action fixed for two months, any entity acting within this period can give only one *quantity of action* or determined effect.

Let us see how this composite, successive action, or total effect, can be thought as divided into instants during the two month period.

Suppose we distribute the instants in such a way that the hair has grown 10 cm. in 5,184,000 instants. In each of these instants it will have acquired its corresponding tiny increase. Now, if at the end of two months the hair's length must not exceed 10 cm., the interval between the instants of its growth must be determined. If we presume the interval is uniform, it will be exactly one second.

Intervals as small as these (or smaller) would completely escape our observation and could not be measured. They can be measured only by reasoning, that is, by knowledge of the total effect or quantity of action taking place in a any fixed, observable length of time, like the two months. The measure of the quantity of action is the comparison with the other quantities of action within the same length of time.

Let us return to the little intervals we suppose exist. In themselves they are not observable, because as such they are a negation, a cessation of action. They are observable only through the relationship between the different frequency of instants in different actions. If we could observe the successive, instantaneous growth we have supposed takes place every second in the hair, we would not be able to measure each of the seconds by observation of the action alone, unless we compared them with the intervals of something happening in us, like our heart beat or a degree of tiredness. On the other hand, if we compared different actions, like the growth of an old man's hair and a young boy's, we would notice that while the old man's grows a certain amount, the boy's grows two or three times that amount. This would give us a measure of the interval: it would be the quantity of action (the intensity being uniform) taking place in the course of two instants. The measure of the intervals, granted it is observable, would simply be the relationship between the quantity or total effect of different causes acting within two instants. It would not differ in any way, therefore, from the measure of a noticeable duration or series of instants, at the end of which we compare greater quantities of actions or total effects large enough to be observed.

So far we have shown: 1. everything happens by instants; 2. the idea of time given by observation is an interconnection of these events, that is, of the quantities of actions within the instants. We can therefore conclude that 'any observation, even an observation so acute and penetrating as to be beyond our capabilities, could never directly offer our mind the idea of a *continuous* time, that is, of a continuous succession. It would supply only the idea of a series of instants of greater or less proximity to each other and their relationship'.

Nevertheless, we do have the idea of a *continuous* time, although *observation* has not explained it. We must therefore look elsewhere for it.

§3. *We need to consider the simple possibilities of things, which must not be confused with real things*

783. We now separate our conceptions of time given directly by observation from those we form by abstract reasoning, which itself starts from observation.

Observation presents *matters of fact* to our understanding, that is, to our faculty of judgment. *Ideas* express *pure possibilities*, not matters of fact. We must not arrogantly disdain pure ideas that express simple possibilities as the custom was in the last century, although *possibilities* must be kept distinct from cognitions of *real* things and facts.

Ideas or possibilities are important for two reasons: 1. we cannot reason without them, even about things of fact, as we learn from the theory of the origin of ideas, which shows how possibility is necessarily mingled in every idea (cf. 470); 2. reason can sometimes establish which element in possible contradictions is true.

The greatest mistake, however, is to combine what is possible in a thing with what is fact; this falsifies method itself that is the means of finding the truth.

In our case, therefore, we must carefully distinguish ideas of time obtained directly by observation and presenting us with facts,[147] from ideas that express only simple *possibilities*.

§4. *Granted the same intensity of action, observation presents time simply as a relationship of the quantity of different actions*

784. Only *large actions* are observable because any action, divided and reduced below a certain minimum, escapes observation.

The relationship of the quantity of these large actions (with due regard for the intensity involved) can be observed.[148]

Granted the same intensity, the different quantity is followed by a circumstance enabling observation to provide us with the knowledge of time.

An action of smaller quantity (the intensity still being uniform) is finished and observable at an instant in which we cannot observe the action of larger quantity, that is, the total effect, because it is not yet finished.

This explains the aptitude of the smaller action, part of the large action, to be observed at the time when the large action,

---

[147] These cognitions are perceptions of things composed of *ideas* and *judgments*. *Ideas* separated from *judgments*, and not subject to any other action, express *possibilities*, some of which have been actuated in reality.

[148] Previously conceived, of course, by our intelligence because only intelligence observes *relationships*, as I demonstrated in vol. 1, 180–187.

composed of a more or less long succession, is not yet fully present to us. We call this aptitude the *successive duration of an action*. It is the same as the idea of time offered by observation.

§5. *The idea of pure time and of its indefinite length and divisibility are mere possibilities or concepts of the mind*

785. Up till now we have dealt only with the *fact*. So, granted the fact, what are the *possibilities* that present themselves to our mind? We must remember that, in deducing *possibilities*, our mind goes as far as it can, right to the point where it sees contradiction.

I. First, our mind observes many real actions happening between any two given instants. These actions, although differing in quantity, maintain a certain relationship. By abstraction the mind thinks these real actions as simply possible and thus forms the *pure idea of time* (cf. 775); it thinks that between two given instants[149] certain quantities of action can take place having a certain relationship with their respective intensities and amongst themselves.

786. II. Next, the mind considers that the various large actions it observes are longer and shorter, that is, between two given instants, an action is sometimes repeated twice, three times or even a thousand times. Mentally therefore, we think the *possibility* of *indefinite* repetition of the action, even beyond the two instants, and see the action no longer as real but as a never-ending possibility. Hence we have the *indefinite length of pure time*, which is only a mental *possibility*. The mind sees no contradiction in the indefinite repetition of any action no matter how many times it has been performed in the past.

787. III. Noticing longer and shorter actions amongst those we can observe, we realise that while one action is being done, another is repeated many times. Our mind then reasons as follows: the shorter is repeated twice, three times, a thousand times, while the longer action is performed only once, but at the

[149] These instants are only the *beginning* and *term* of a possible composite action taken as a norm.

instant when the shorter action is completed for the first time, only a part of the longer action is done. Hence our mind thinks an action to be the result of many parts or else a composite of many smaller actions. It is true that a very short action escapes our observation but we then think of the *possibility* of a powerful observation, beyond human capacity. Such a thought, which contains no contradiction, enables us to see the possibility of an action shorter than the minimum we can observe. We recognise the *possibility* of indefinitely shorter actions because our mind finds no contradiction in any action, however short. This is the source of our idea of the *indefinite divisibility of time*.

788. IV. The *indefinite divisibility of time* is only the mental possibility of identifying a series of ever-closer instants and thinking of ever-shorter actions, whose beginning and end are precisely the instants of the sequence, just as the ends of a line are its points. But we are still without the idea of *continuity* which we are seeking. We must therefore consider how this idea also is a mental possibility to be identified carefully because of its importance and difficulty.

§6. *The phenomenal idea of the continuity of time is illusory*

789. We have seen that *large actions* producing something have to be subdivided into smaller actions, and that the minute intervals separating these little actions from each other completely escape our observation. Thus new existences, that is, the total effect of countless tiny actions, are presented to us as a product of a single, truly *continuous* action (cf. 784–788). But this is only what appears, and consequently observation offers us a *phenomenal* idea *of the continuity of time*. That the idea is purely phenomenal and apparent is shown by our proof that everything necessarily happens by instants (cf. 779–781). A series of instants can never be identified in a continuous time, no matter how close to each other they are.

790. Because this truth is so important, I want to reinforce it with another proof which, leading us to the principle of contradiction, shows that the idea of a perfect *continuity* of time or the

continuous production of a large observable effect contains an immanent contradiction. As we said, the mind moves freely in its world of possibility until it encounters something contradictory, about which it cannot think because a contradiction is impossibility itself. I now add that *continuity in succession* is a contradiction, and therefore impossible to be thought. The proof is as follows.

First proposition: 'To think the existence of an undetermined number is a contradiction.'

An idea of an existing number means the number must be determined. The fact that I think of a number means the number itself is determined; if it were not, I could not think of it as a number. It would no longer be a particular number but number in general, a purely mental being. For instance, if I write the series of cardinal numbers 1, 2, 3, 4, 5, etc. and suppose it continued, this series is the formula expressing and including all possible particular numbers. If I then think of a particular number, I must necessarily think a number contained in the formula. But all the numbers of the series are determined; each number is itself: 3 is 3, not 2 or 4. The specific essence of number is such that it must be determined, and therefore an undetermined number does not and cannot exist.

Second proposition: 'For a number of things to exist, the number has to be *determined*. Therefore it must be *finite*.'

If a number is *determined*, it must include the idea of *finite* being, because to be determined, as I have said, means that the number is itself, neither more nor less; its existence must not be confused with the number preceding or following it in the series. No number can be chosen outside the series, since the series contains all particular numbers, and any number chosen from the series will always be the preceding number increased by one unit. But the preceding number is also finite, which is true for all the preceding numbers right back to the beginning: every number equals its preceding number plus one, and the whole series is a sum of finite numbers. Thus every particular number must be finite in such a way that the idea of particular number includes the idea of finite number. The existence therefore of an infinite number of things is an absurdity.

Third proposition: 'A succession of things infinite in number is a contradiction.'

The explanation of this proposition is found in the two preceding propositions.

A succession of things infinite in number cannot be thought because to think an infinite number involves contradiction.

What cannot be thought because of the contradiction involved is not possible.

Therefore a succession of things infinite in number is impossible, that is, it involves contradiction.

Fourth proposition: 'The production of an entity by means of a continuous, successive action gives a succession of things infinite in number.'

I can assign an indefinite number of instants in a continuous succession but I fully understand that this number of instants, no matter how large, can never form or diminish a continuum in any way. An instant has no length; it is a perfect point without any continuous length whatsoever. Mentally I can assign and abstract any number of instants in a continuous time but I do not diminish the length of time by the smallest fraction; I have not abstracted any length from it but assigned a number of points in it that have no length at all. Thinking like this, I conclude that, although the same continuous length still remains (divided into parts maybe, but with each part continuous), I could never finally exhaust this length even if I multiplied the instants to infinity: an infinite number of non-lengths can never make a length. However, this nature of the *continuum* does not involve contradiction because it does not contain an infinite number of points which I only imagine or make myself imagine in it.[150] Such a nature may be mysterious but it contains no intrinsic repugnance or contradiction.

On the other hand, I maintain that, granted a *continuous succession* (which is our case), there would be no question of being able to note mentally an indefinite number of instants but of having to distinguish in reality a *truly infinite number* of instants in this succession.

In fact, the instant in which a thing is, is distinguished in reality from the preceding instant when the thing is not.

Let us suppose that the hair in our previous example has

---

[150] Later, when I speak about the *continuum* in space, it will be more clearly seen that the concept of a *continuum* is not repugnant in itself.

grown 10 cm. with a continuous movement. The time required to do this can be divided by me into any number of instants. No matter how many points I freely imagine present in a continuum, there is also a corresponding real division in fact. Let us take the second, third and fourth instants of the series I have imagined; the hair is longer in the fourth than it is in the third, and longer in the third than in the second, if the growth is continuous. No matter how small, this difference is real, so that the growth in the third instant did not exist in the second instant, and the growth in the fourth did not exist in the third. So these little growths or differences exist at different instants and are therefore really distinct from each other. Now if the growth is continuous I am able not only to increase the number of instants indefinitely but also to see that they would not exhaust the continuum even when increased *ad infinitum*.

But what proves my thesis is this: granted a *continuous, successive increase*, the division into an infinite number of instants, which I am not able to make, would be made by nature herself, which would be absurd. In fact, we have seen that, when I assign a large number of instants in the continuous growth of the hair, they presuppose a real division in nature and an equal number of differences in the hair, and therefore a real number of different states and lengths. It is not I who have divided the hair into a fixed number of instants and created the differences; the differences exist independently of my mind. I see I can multiply the number of instants at will and find differences really distinct from each other. The number of instants, even if infinite, does not equal the continuum; for this reason I also see that an infinite number of really distinct differences should correspond to this infinite number, and each of these would have its own continuous length. If then a successive, continuous growth takes place, an infinite number of differences or lengths have to be distinguished in time in an infinite number of instants through which the hair has successively passed. We note that, if this result involves contradiction, the contradiction comes only from the *infinite number*, such that, granted the premises, the infinite number is *necessary*; and if the *infinite number* is absurd, as it in fact is, we must say that the premises contain absurdity.

Fifth proposition: 'The production of an ens with continuous succession is absurd.'

This is a corollary of the third and fourth propositions and is therefore demonstrated.

Our final conclusion, then, is that the continuity of time as given by observation is purely *phenomenal* and illusory because reason proves it to be impossible.

§7. *The continuity of time is a mere possibility, that is, a concept of the mind*

791. Although we have no idea of the real continuity of time by observation, we do have an idea of its abstract continuity; a confused idea obtained by considering the *possibilities* of things.

While one observable action is taking place between any two instants, that is, within the space of time in which an observable action takes place, we can also see a large number of other shorter or longer actions happening or at least beginning. Now let us consider the beginning of these other actions: the instant in which they start is not determined by their nature. We think therefore of the *possibility* of their commencement at any instant within the space of time of the initial observable action. Thus the whole of this space of time has no particle of time relative to the commencement of another action, which is different from any another particle; it has no interval of any sort. Rather, we can fix a point anywhere for this other action to start. This aptitude possessed by the initial space of time — its perfect equality and indifference to any starting point within it, its absence of interval and exclusion at any instant — is precisely that which provides us with the abstract idea we have of the continuity of time. In effect, the idea is reduced to the *possibility* of assigning the beginning or end of an action indifferently to all the thinkable points in a certain space of time.

792. But we said that this *abstract* idea of continuity is *confused* because, although we find on analysis that an action can begin at any instant we choose, the instants cannot be totalled together or result in any continuity of time.

§8. *Distinction between what is absurd and what is mysterious*

793. Absurdity is that which involves contradiction; mystery is that which is inexplicable.

No matter how often sophists confuse the two concepts, they remain distinct. What is absurd must be rejected as false; what is mysterious, far from having to be rejected, frequently cannot be rejected at all. Very often, what is mysterious is a fact, and facts cannot be denied.

If physical nature itself is so full of mysterious facts, how can anyone claim there is no mystery in spiritual nature, which is far more sublime, active, immense, and profound?

794. Although I have shown that a *continuum in succession* is absurd, I believe that the concept of a *simple continuum*, which is mysterious but not absurd, definitely exists in reality. So, while I have rejected a *continuum in succession*, I have neither the right nor power to reject the *continuum* in nature, because its concept implies no evident contradiction. And just as I have proved that a continuum in *time* is absurd, I shall also prove the non-absurdity of a continuum in *space* and of *duration* without succession.

§9. *There is no succession in the duration of complete actions and therefore no idea of time, only of continuum, is present*

795. An action, an ens, the essence of an ens endures, and sometimes changelessly.

In the existence of an unchanging essence there is *duration*, but not the *succession* assignable to actions and entia which have been produced and generated but not yet perfected.

Although there is no succession in the duration of a completed ens, there can still be a *continuum*. The possibility of a continuum in a succession is excluded in only one case, that is, when its presence would mean, as we have seen, an infinite number of things really distinct from each other, which implies an absurdity.

796. The existence of God, of our soul, and of all things that endure, is *continuous*.

On the other hand succession, as found in what is generated, is not continuous, and it is this that gives the idea and measure of time.

However, it is difficult for us to think *duration* without *succession* because, as I have said so often, we are accustomed to seeking enlightenment for our thoughts from change and limitation.

§10. *The idea of being constituting our intellect is not subject to time*

797. The idea of time is the idea of a succession related to duration.

Succession is found only in passing, transient actions, that is, in the production, generation and change in things.

The idea of being that constitutes our intellect, is unchangeable, simple, and always the same. It is not subject in any way therefore to time.

798. Consequently the idea of time is not obtained *a priori*, as Kant thought, but only *a posteriori*, from finite things perceived as changeable, that is, by the use of reason.

799. This clarifies even more the ancient truth that the intellect in its superior part is outside time[151] and, when reasoning *a priori*, abstracts from time, which it does not find within itself. I mean that it does not find time in its first constitutive idea, in the analysis of which alone consists the matter of its *a priori* reasoning.[152]

[151] Properly speaking the intellect is the superior part. St. Thomas says: *Supremum in nostra cognitione non est ratio, sed intellectus, qui est rationis origo* [Intellect is the highest part in our knowledge, not reasoning; the intellect is the origin of reasoning] (*C. Gent.* I, 57).

[152] St. Thomas, too, deduces the idea of time *a posteriori*, from phantasms: *Ex ea parte qua se (intellectus) ad phantasmata convertit, compositioni et divisioni intellectus adjungitur tempus* [By turning to phantasms the intellect adds time to composition and division]. This explains why the Fathers of

CHAPTER 7

Origin of the idea of movement

Article 1

We perceive movement in three ways

800. One of the great actions carried out successively that form and measure time[153] is movement, which we now have to examine.

Relative to us, movement is *active* and *passive*.

I call it *active* when we ourselves cause it by using in any way the locomotive faculty with which we are endowed. Thus we may walk or otherwise dispose the position of our body.

Movement is *passive* when it is produced by an exterior force causing our body to change place.

801. Besides our own movement, there is also movement in bodies surrounding us, which however we experience neither actively nor passively.

802. Because movement is something affecting both our own and external bodies, we perceive it along with our perception of bodies in a kind of *co-perception*. Hence, we apprehend it in as many ways as there are perceptions of bodies. As we have seen, we perceive bodies in three ways:

1. *Subjectively*, through the fundamental feeling. This applies to *active movement*, where consciousness indicates that we are its cause.

2. *Subjectively* once more, through acquired sensations

the Church speak so eloquently about the noblest part of the human mind; century by century they all repeat those expressions, consecrated by a constant tradition, which assert that our mind is *joined to eternal and immutable things* and enjoys the vision of an *unchangeable truth*. As St. Bonaventure says, it sees *sempiternalia, et sempiternaliter* [eternal things eternally] (*Itin. mentis*, etc.).

[153] *Succession* in general forms time, but each particular *succession* is called a measure of time when it is taken as a norm with which to compare other successions.

which cause us to feel movement in the parts of our affected sensitive organs; in this way we perceive subjectively some kind of *passive* movement.

3. *Extrasubjectively*, through the senses which, in enabling us to perceive our own and external bodies, also make us perceive the movements, active or passive relative to us, taking place in all bodies. These variations of *activity* or *passivity* of movement can be distinguished and perceived only *subjectively*, not *extrasubjectively*.

Strictly speaking, I should confine my attention to the *subjective* ways of perceiving movement because so far I have only dealt with subjective, not *extrasubjective* ways of perceiving bodies. This, however, would leave our work very lop-sided, and I think it better consequently not to separate totally the *extrasubjective* from the *subjective* way of perceiving the movement of bodies.

Article 2
Active movement described

803. I have no wish to go too deeply into an examination of the nature of movement. My sole aim is to indicate the origin of the ideas of movement.

Here, too, observation and especially the facts presented to us by consciousness must be our guide.

I shall speak first about active then about passive movement.

We have the faculty to move our body.[154] What is this faculty? What does observation tells us about it?

The fundamental feeling causing us to perceive our body directly is furnished with a *mode* we call extension.

The faculty for moving our body as presented to us directly through observation is a power of our spirit over the fundamental feeling consisting in a faculty for changing the *mode* of the feeling in a given way.

The new *mode* taken by the feeling is a new space in which it

---

[154] We could not begin to move any part of our body spontaneously if we lacked the feeling that we could do so. The power that we have over our body, therefore, must be included in the fundamental feeling.

is diffused, enabling us to say that changing the mode of the fundamental feeling indicates a change of *space* or *place*.

Because the soul has the power to change the mode of the fundamental feeling, it is also said to have power of movement over its own body.

In fact, if the body is the agent producing in the soul the fundamental feeling which has extension as its term, the soul must be acting on the agent if facts show that it can change its action in a given way.

Article 3

Passive movement described

804. Not only do we possess the energy to move ourselves; we can also be moved.

When we move ourselves, the *quantity of effort* we make gives us some perception of movement and a way of measuring it.

When we are moved by some external force, however, we do not always perceive our movement.

If the force moving us produces change in our sensitive organs — for example, when we are pushed or dragged from one place to another — we experience an action upon us and perceive our movement. This movement, however, is not seconded by the other inert parts of our body outside the immediate effect of the moving force. If we are moved by an external force making us change the position of the whole of our body simultaneously, the force changes nothing in the body because it does not disturb any individual particle relative to the whole body. In this case, our interior feeling provides no perception of the quantity of movement, or of the movement itself.

This explains why we have no perception of the movement with which we are involved by living on a planet revolving on its axis at a speed of thousands of miles an hour. We are not aware of being moved because we do not move ourselves, but depend upon a uniform force without experiencing any internal or external sensation in our vision or touch, or in any other senses indicating our movement.

[804]

805. While our active movement is perceived in two ways, through the interior feeling of consciousness and our external sensations, our passive movement is perceived through external sensations alone.

Article 4

Of itself, our movement is not sensible

806. A corollary of this observation is that our movement is not *per se* sensible to us.

Observation shows that we can be moved, and not feel movement in any way.

As we have said, we know movement subjectively through its *cause*, and extrasubjectively through its *effects*, but if our position is changed not by ourselves but through an external force producing no change in our sensitive organs we cannot know this *movement* because there is no change in our feeling [*App.*, no. 28].

Article 5

Movement in our sense organs is sensible

807. It is true that when a movement of any sort is produced in our sensitive organs, we feel the sensitive particles composing those organs in a shape different from that to which we previously referred the fundamental feeling. Consequently, the feeling itself is moved and heightened in such a way that, along with its modification, we perceive a movement in so far as the *matter* which is felt stimulates our fundamental feeling by changing its form. Nevertheless, the movement is not felt through itself but through the particular circumstance by which it changes the *state* of the sensitive organ that is always felt by us in its actual *state*.

Such movement, therefore, is change of the respective position of the molecules composing the sensitive organ that is felt by us according to a law determining the position of the molecules making up the organ. If the position required for one *state* of the organ (relative to feeling) is altered, the organ takes on another *sensible state*, and is felt in a new mode and place according to the nature of the change it has experienced.

The sensitive organ could, therefore, be transported vast distances (and this actually happens relative to the daily motion of the earth) without our feeling movement in any way.

We have to conclude that we feel not the movement of the organ, properly speaking, but its *sensible state*.

We affirm that the feeling and sensible particles making up the organ give the *whole* organ another form when they are compressed or separated in different ways, proportions and relative positions. In this new form the organ is felt in another way, with varying pleasure or pain, while the change itself is also felt. The new pleasure or pain, that is, the new sensation, is referred to all the sensible points within the new form where the force has acted. Because the previous form was different, the different pleasure or pain with which the organ was felt was referred to different points. We do not feel the change of place undergone by each individual sensitive molecule (the absolute movement of the molecules), but only the change in the total form of the organ, that is, the change of place of several molecules at a time (the relative movement of the molecules), which causes the various parts of the organ to be felt in different places.

808. If we analyse this subjective feeling with which we perceive the sensitive parts of our body when a sensible movement takes place, we see that:

1. this feeling is of variable, corporeal pleasure or pain diffused in an extension of given limits and shape;

2. the *shape* of this felt extension can change through a relative movement of its parts, and that the feeling is, nevertheless, always diffused, in the extension of all the shapes it assumes;

3. consequently our *subjective feeling* perceives the particular *movement* taking place when the *shape* of the organ changes, but only in that part where the force applied operates in the way necessary to produce a sensation.

Our subjective feeling perceives movement, therefore, in so far as it is a change undergone by its matter.

Article 6

Relationship between movement and sensation

809. Absolute movement in all its universality is therefore altogether different from sensation.

Relative movement, which takes place in parts of the sensory organ as it changes shape is 'a change in the matter of sensation', and is felt along with the affected matter.

Article 7

Movement relative to touch-perception[155]

810. Touch perceives the hardness and surface of bodies. But do we perceive movement with touch when the tip of a body, a pencil, for example, is drawn along the length of our stationary arm? At first sight, it seems we do; certainly we perceive something similar to movement.

Nevertheless, we are faced with a difficulty. Although we feel a sensation moving, as it were, along our arm, and through the sensation perceive the body producing it, it would seem that we cannot be sure of the identity of the body producing the sensations. Instead of a single body running along the arm, we could posit a multiplicity of bodies substituting one another in rapid succession and without a noticeable interval [*App.*, no. 29].

Article 8

Movement relative to sight-perception

811. When we move, what we see around us changes. The changes themselves become signs by which we learn about our own movement and that of others. How this comes about, I

[155] I have distinguished in external sensations: 1. the *sensation* in the organ; 2. the *perception* of something different from the organ. I have dealt with movement relative to sensation (cf. 806); I am now speaking about movement relative to corporeal perception.

shall explain when we deal with the third way of perceiving bodies.

In the meantime, we ask whether we can perceive movement through vision when with motionless eyes we see something which itself moves.

A black dot moving across a white surface gives us the concept of movement, and although we cannot be sure about the movement of the external thing because of the existence of apparent, illusory movements, the concept itself is present to us.

But while the difficulty about the identity of a body relative to sight-sensation is similar to that caused by touch-sensation, it is also less than it. The characteristics of bodies we see are greater in number than those of bodies we touch, so that the union of the former characteristics in different bodies is very difficult. In the case of touch, however, the same sensation can easily be produced by various bodies.

Article 9

Movement relative to aural-, smell- and taste-perceptions

812. In so far as these senses have something in common with touch, perception of movement is the same for them as it is for touch (cf. 810); in so far as they are distinguished from touch by their own special phenomena they do not perceive movement although they can, like all the other senses, measure it by means of time. The time needed for a body to come within range of our touch, sight, smell, taste or hearing is an indication of the length of its movement towards us or our movement towards it.

This measure of movement is possible for those born blind, and for those lacking some, but not all senses.

Article 10

The continuity of movement

§1. Observation cannot perceive minute extensions

813. It is a fact that minute extensions escape our observation.

[812–813]

Although the invention of the microscope has revealed a world hidden to observation, nature will always provide subtleties beyond the range of the most developed instruments. The intimate texture of bodies is such as to make me believe that it will always remain veiled to our senses; if an extension is continuously reduced, we must come to a level so minute that it is entirely beyond our advertence.

§2. *Observation provides only phenomenal continuity of movement*

814. Whatever observation tells us about the continuity of movement, therefore, can only witness to an *apparent or phenomenal continuity*. Unable to tell us anything about the minute, possible intervals that escape our observation, it cannot provide any certain proof about the real continuity of movement.

§3. *Real continuity of movement is absurd*

815. Although observation fails to provide us with anything certain about the real continuity of movement, we can try to reason about it.

It is true, of course, that reason cannot provide us with facts, but because possibility is the object of the mind alone, it can as such allow us to say something about their possibility or impossibility.

We have already shown that *continuity of succession* is absurd (cf. 779–799).

But succession is present in movement, as in every action subject to increase and decease.

In movement, therefore, true, real continuity is absurd.

In this way, reason is sometimes able to pass from an argument about mere *possibility* to conclusions about facts. It can *deny them* when they are seen to contain an intrinsic repugnance. If this repugnance is absent, however, it cannot affirm their existence; it can only declare them *possible*.

[814–815]

§4. *Solution to the objection drawn from leaps in nature*

816. If no true continuity is possible in movement, movement must come about by leaps. But in human thought, leaps have always been excluded from nature.

And indeed a *leap* in nature is absurd.

817. However, lack of true continuity in movement does not imply the introduction of *leaps* in nature.

The idea of a *leap* is not and cannot be present in what occurs in an instant.

A *leap* supposes two points, and a *passage* from one to the other without touching what is in between. When we think of *passage*, on the other hand, we have to include the notion of *touching* what is between the two points; passing from one place to another without touching what is in between means passing without passing. In this sense, the concept of a leap in nature is absurd because it implies putting links in the middle (the necessary steps) and at the same time mentally jumping over them, an obvious contradiction.

Real movement on the other hand only offers successive existence of a body in several places without our having to think of it as leaping from one to another, provided our imagination does not add anything to the concept of real movement. Such a concept does not imply a leap because it does not entail a necessary passage from one place to the nearest place. Our imagination renders this passage necessary because we are accustomed to the presence of phenomenal continuity of movement in which we think we observe continual passage. But what we see is the simple, successive existence of a body in several places so close together that it is impossible to advert to the distance between them.

We will understand this better if we remember that extension is simply the term of a force, according to our explanation of the concept of force. Force, however, can vary its term and extend itself in one space rather than another without our needing to suppose a true continuous passage between the spaces. It can withdraw itself at immense speed from one place while simultaneously diffusing itself in another. Certainly there is no contradiction in such a concept.

818. I realise that this will be difficult to grasp; our understanding is constantly complicated and confused by the use of our imagination. And it has to be admitted that we have no experience of the fact. The different spaces in which the corporeal force gradually diffuses itself are (according to a law established by the author of nature) so close that separation between them is imperceptible. Hence, our apparent vision of continuity, and our difficulty in thinking that movement could come about in some other way. But let us consider carefully and philosophically the reasoning which leads me to deny perfect, true continuity in local movement.

§5. *Mental continuity of movement*

819. The difficulty present in understanding the truth of what we have said is aggravated by the presence in our mind of the idea of a certain *mental continuity* of movement, as well as of *time*.

This abstract, *mental continuity* consists in the possibility (which we conceive as equal and indifferent) that movement may begin or end in any point whatsoever of time and space.

Because no point of time or space is more apt than another for receiving the beginning or the term of movement, the equal *possibility* of all points produces, or rather is, the confused idea of *abstract continuity* in movement of a body between any two moments or points whatever. I call this a 'confused' idea because analysis immediately shows that no continuity can ever be formed by a number of neighbouring points.

CHAPTER 8

Origin of the idea of space

Article 1

Distinction between the ideas of space and of body

820. I have defined body as 'a substance capable of producing in us an action which is a feeling of pleasure or pain having a constant mode we call extension' (cf. 749–753).

Extension, therefore, when derived from body, is a mental abstraction, like pure *time* and *movement*. It is the particular mode of the feeling which body causes in our spirit. Once this abstraction has been formed, it can exist independently of bodies, like all abstract ideas.

Article 2

Extension, or space, is limitless

821. Extension, or space, taken in this abstract way, or in any other, is *limitless, immeasurable and continuous.*

We must now examine how our concept of space, taken only from bodies, acquires these undeniable characteristics. We shall begin with limitlessness and immeasurability.

The potency for moving our body (cf. 672–692 [800–802]) means simply changing or reproducing the *mode* of feeling of our body. In other words, we reproduce the extension our body occupies.

But we can reproduce acts of our potencies indefinitely; and even when our limited energies prevent our reproducing them any further, we can still imagine ourselves reproducing them indefinitely. This capacity is given us by the idea of possibility, continually present to our mind, which we can join to anything we mentally conceive (cf. 403).

We have already explained, through the idea of being, how

our spirit can add the idea of what is possible to any event or object it conceives and, with the help of this idea, imagine the indefinite reproduction of the event or object (cf. 469 ss.).

Thus our capacity for imagining or thinking of the indefinite reproduction of our body's extension enables us to acquire the idea of *limitless extension*. This idea is, in fact, only 'the possibility of reproducing indefinitely the mode of our feeling that we call our body's extension by abstracting in thought and imagination from the body itself.'

822. In this way we draw the idea of limitlessness of extension from extension perceived subjectively.[156] At the same time, extension perceived subjectively can also be perceived extrasubjectively, that is to say, in external bodies, because the exteriority of a body is only the extrasubjective mode with which we perceive bodies.

Granted this perception of bodies, we have by abstraction the perception of their extension.

Hence the limitlessness and immeasurability of extension conceived in this way, which can in general be defined as 'the possibility of thinking the indefinite reproduction of the extension of bodies.'

Article 3

Space or extension is continuous

823. As we have seen, the idea of unending space which first lends itself to analysis is an abstract idea, expressing the possibility of limitless, successive change to the extension of a body.

It is true that in dealing with this we have been paying more attention to our own body than to that of external bodies, because until now we have spoken intentionally only of subjective perception. However, what we shall say about space

---

[156] Extension is something in exterior objects. It is also something in the *fundamental feeling* in which, and related to which, it has the nature of *matter* and term. Moreover, extension is common to our sensations and to external bodies. In our sensations we call it their *matter*; in external bodies we call it the *external term*.

perceived subjectively, the reader will be able to apply for himself to external bodies, that is, to bodies which we perceive extrasubjectively.

Dealing with our present question, 'Does the concept of space contain perfect *continuity*?', we must be careful not to confuse feeling as it actually exists with the possibility of its other states. We could indeed raise an extremely difficult problem connected with the fact of feeling: does the actual feeling of our body include the feeling of the perfect continuity belonging to our body?

To answer this question through experience would not only require very accurate and extremely shrewd observation and insight; it would in the end be impossible. Only conjecture or very acute philosophical reasoning would perhaps provide a solution. What we are asking is whether sensation could be stimulated along the nerves in such a way that sensitive parts are mathematically contiguous. Now observation can tell us nothing about such a problem because it cannot attain such depth.[157]

However, this kind of research is not necessary for our present question.

An explanation of the *continuity* of extension is not furthered by knowing whether all the mathematical points encountered in a nerve passage are truly sensitive. We are not dealing with a factual truth, but with an abstraction or idea resulting from the clear possibility of locating the sensation we experience at any of the points along the nerve. If the nerve we feel has pores and gaps in its delicate texture, it is entirely accidental whether these gaps come in one place rather than another. We can think of a nerve full of them, although it may in fact be devoid of them; mentally we can change the place of any of the sensitive particles of the nerve, just as we can for the empty spaces found along it. This power of the *intellective imagination* is sufficient to explain how we can fully conceive 'the possibility of locating a feeling at any assignable point whatsoever', that is, how we are able to conceive the idea of continuity.

This *possibility* for locating a feeling at any assignable point in a space arises from the neutral disposition of the nature of space

---

[157] However, there is no absolute repugnance, rationally speaking, in the thought of such observation.

which receives feeling indifferently at any point. Because of this indifference, a sensation may terminate in any point within the confines of the body. The possibility of locating the feeling indifferently at any point or place includes, and is, the idea of the continuum in abstract space.

Our potency for movement facilitates the attainment of this idea because it indicates in fact the indifference of every part of space relative to the diffusion of our feeling. Let us imagine that we have a microscope powerful enough to show us the nerves in our hand. Such an instrument would reveal how the molecules composing them cling together, and how there are tiny spaces between the molecules where the nerve lacks feeling because it is insensitive. But now we move our hand slightly, and find that the spaces previously occupied by the molecules have been left empty while empty spaces have been filled. In the new position of the hand, feeling is now located at places which were empty. Movement, therefore, enables us to dispose our feeling in any mathematical point of space, and such a possibility makes us conceive space as an absolute and perfect *continuity*.

It is true, of course, that the feeling of the organ acquired through movement remains unchanged (granted that movement is *per se* unfeelable, cf. 806). This, however, does not prevent the mind, assisted especially by the external sensation of bodies, from arriving at the idea of the continuity of extension in the way described.

Article 4

The real continuum

824. So far, by mentally placing together various possibilities we have arrived at the idea of a continuum. But does the continuum really exist in corporeal extension?

I shall have to answer this question later, when I deal with the extrasubjective perception of bodies; this provides an easier approach to the problem and throws greater light on it. In the meantime, it is enough to know that continuity of bodies and of space is not repugnant.

[824]

Article 5

The continuum has no parts

825. Continuum means that which has no gap or division or split.

The continuum, therefore, cannot have parts, because parts presuppose separation amongst themselves.

Article 6

The continuum can have limits

826. So far, we have defined the *continuum* as 'the possibility of a body's terminating simultaneously in any assignable point of a given extension.'

The idea of *limitless continuous space* has been defined as 'the possibility of a body's reproducing indefinitely its continuous extension.'

But we can also restrict our thought to the possibility of some, rather than all, possible changes.

In this way, there arises within us the idea of something *continuous, yet limited*, for example, an area measuring a thousand square metres, or something similar.

Because it has no parts in itself, this area although limited is also continuous.

While I can imagine as many of these areas as I please, each of them, whatever its size, remains continuous, that is, without parts.

827. All these ideas of continuous limitations are, therefore, potentially comprised in the idea of what is unlimitedly continuous, that is, unending space.[158] Each one, moreover, has a relationship of size with every other (one may be twice, or three

---

[158] That which is in potency cannot truly be said to be. In what is continuous, therefore, we find only the limitations we ourselves put there, and nothing more. The infinite number of ideas imagined by Malebranche as possessed by our mind in the conception of space and shapes — his infinite number of infinites (Book 3) — is fallacious. The idea of the continuum is a single idea which, when limited by us, produces other ideas but always in a limited number because our mental effort finally comes to an end without ever arriving at an infinite number of limitations.

times the size of another, and so on). In other words, it has yet another of the characteristics assigned by mathematicians, whether this characteristic is actually measurable or not.

828. In this way, we come to consider lesser continuous things as parts of those which are greater, although this depends on various acts of our mind and its capacity for limiting in different ways its conception of the continuum. Lesser things, as parts of larger, are only mental, not actual things.

829. Consequently, these mental parts do not form one continuous thing while they are conceived as parts; they are lesser continuous things and nothing more. When we want to consider them altogether as a single continuous thing, we have to remove the idea of parts and division completely, running them together with our imagination so as to eliminate even mental confines. The concept of continuum is clean contrary to the concept of part.

Article 7

How the continuum can be said to be infinitely divisible

830. The continuum can be said to be infinitely divisible only in the sense that we can limit it indefinitely.[159]

This indefinite reduction arises from the nature both of the continuum and of our faculties, which can always repeat what they have done previously. This is especially the case with our power of thought which, by means of the concept of possibility, can imagine and think as possible all that is not contradictory.

Infinite divisibility, therefore, is only the possibility of repeating indefinitely the limitation of the space we think of. Hence St. Thomas' teaching: 'The continuum has infinite possible parts (in potency), but none in reality.'

---

[159] The continuum is improperly said to be *divisible* because what is *divided* is no longer *continuous*.

CHAPTER 9

Origin of the idea of bodies
by means of the extrasubjective perception of touch

Article 1

Analysis of the extrasubjective perception of bodies in general

831. We have indicated two elements in acquired sensations:

1. A modification of the fundamental feeling, by which the affected part of our sense-organ is felt in a new way.

2. A sense perception of an external body.

Subsequent analysis of this extrasubjective perception also results in two elements:

a) A feeling of the action done in us.

b) Extension, in which we locate this feeling and which includes some extended thing outside us.

832. We can therefore conclude that when we have perceived something different from us, something extended, we have the perception of a body through acquired sensations. I must now explain how our exterior senses furnish us with a subject of these three qualities. I shall begin with touch.

Article 2

All our senses give us a perception of something
different from us

833. Each of our senses receives an action.

An action done in us, of which we are not the author, indicates something different from us.[160] Therefore each sense perceives something different from ourselves.

[160] Cf. 672–691. The distinction which Royer-Collard attempted to establish between the senses cannot be accepted. He considered some senses merely as instruments of sensations, others as instruments of both sensations and perceptions (cf. parts of *Lezioni del Royer-Collard* printed by Jouffroy). All senses however perceive and all have their *extrasubjective* part which is more distinct in some, less distinct in others, as we shall see.

Article 3
All our senses give us a perception
of something outside us

834. In order to ensure clarity in our ideas, we must first note the distinction between what is *different* from us and what is *outside* us.

Something *different* from me means simply something different from *myself*.

Difference as a concept does not include any idea of extension nor any relationship with extension. On the other hand, the word 'outside' in its proper sense has a relationship with extension: one thing outside another does not occupy the *place* of the other. Thus, outside ME means outside the parts and sentient organs of my body,[161] and only by transference is applied to our spirit.

While therefore 'different from me' indicates a relationship of difference from my spirit, 'outside me' correctly indicates a difference from my *body* in so far as my body is co-sentient through its intimate union with my spirit.

In order, then, to show that each of our senses perceives what is outside us, we must demonstrate that each sense perceives something different from our body perceived subjectively.

835. That this is the case results from what was said, when we showed that the fundamental feeling is produced by an activity different from the activity that changes it. Hence two kinds of activity: 1. my body which acts directly in my spirit; 2. external bodies which act on my body.

Thus in every sensation we perceive an active principle or body different from our body; every sensation is an experience we receive from something other than our body. Therefore each sense gives us something outside us.

836. The following observation will help to remove all doubt on the matter.

---

[161] Every part of my body, whether sentient or not, can be said to be *outside me* in so far as it is perceived *extrasubjectively*. In such a perception we consider what the part has in common with all external bodies; as such, it is outside the *subject*, that is, the *perceived part* is perceived as outside the *perceiving part*.

My body is felt in the fundamental feeling; what is felt outside this feeling is not my body.

Let us fix our attention on the four phenomena, colours, sounds, smells and tastes, and also on the various qualities of touch, like hardness. If we ask ourselves whether all these things are perhaps nothing more than our sense organs, we will see that the term of these sensations possesses something different from our organs. Smell, for example, does not have the slightest similarity to our nose, nor taste to the tongue or palate, nor sound to our ears, and so on for all other qualities. The sensations, therefore, cannot have only our body as their matter. Even if the *sensation* of our own body is included in them, our body is certainly not everything we perceive with them. They therefore indicate a principle external to our body, a term different from the term of the fundamental feeling.

Article 4

Touch perceives only corporeal surfaces

837. When we are touched on a sensitive part of our body, we feel our body, that is, a certain pleasure or pain.[162] We also feel an action done in us by something foreign, that is, we perceive an agent outside us (cf. 834–836).

The action, different from a sensation in an affected part, is a feeling with an extended *term* and is diffused in a surface extension.

For instance, if a sharp point touches us we locate the discomfort at a point, at a very small surface; but if we are touched by a bigger surface, a coin for example, we locate the discomfort at points enclosed within that surface and feel nothing outside it.

[162] There are feelings essentially different from pleasure and pain. For example, the sensation of tickling seems to be wholly *sui generis*, and the same can be said of many other feelings. It is not my intention to investigate this matter but it seems to me beyond doubt that all the feelings we experience are accompanied by some level of pleasure or pain, or are themselves *modes* of pleasure or pain. So I say 'a certain pleasure and pain' or else 'corporeal pleasure and pain' where 'corporeal' indicates the differences not investigated in this work.

Suppose a piece of metal in the form of a cross is pressed to our arm. The sensation we have terminates in that particular shape, and is diffused throughout the whole area covered by the metal, to which it corresponds exactly.[163]

Article 5

Touch together with movement gives the idea of three dimensional space

838. When we are touched on the surface of our body, we receive a sensation confined within a surface space.[164]

If we add the faculty of movement, we have the power to repeat at will the space in which the fundamental feeling terminates (cf. 803).

The same faculty enables us to repeat at will the surface felt by touch.

Thus, a surface moved by a motion outside the plane of the surface itself traces a solid space having three dimensions, length, height and depth.

The power to move ourselves, and other things with us, makes touch-sensation possible at any surface of solid space;[165] hence the idea we have of this possibility.

The idea of the possibility of indefinitely changing and repeating the surfaces which are the term of our sensations of touch is the idea of solid, indefinite space acquired by means of the sense of touch joined to movement.[166]

[163] It is really the ends of the nerves that are touched and hence the contact takes place at the surface, which is true for external touch.

[164] I am speaking of adventitious sensations, not the fundamental feeling of which, I am convinced, there is a continuum in the parts where it terminates.

[165] This solidity need not be known to our senses. Of itself, motion is not sensible, as we have observed, but is a means for us to form the *thought* of sensible solidity.

[166] Spontaneous movement is the principal cause of the information we acquire about distances and measured spaces. Touch (by means of time) and sight do nothing more than make us perceive exactly the *termination* of the distance. A delicate sense of touch, therefore, is not necessary for measuring great distances. Birds are an example: they fly and measure immense

Article 6

A review of the ways we perceive solid space

839. What we have said shows that the idea of extension or space is formed in two modes: 1. by means of the fundamental feeling accompanied by the faculty of spontaneous movement of our body; 2. by means of the sensations of touch aided by the same faculty.

The indefinite space in the first mode is produced by a movement in all directions of a solid space felt by us, that is, of our body; this movement is mentally conceived as indefinitely possible.

The indefinite space in the second mode is produced by the possible movement of a surface that is felt — a movement in all directions outside the plane of the surface itself.

This explains how people born blind perceive indefinite space and are able to understand mathematics.

Article 7

It is easier for us to think about the idea of space acquired by touch and movement than by the fundamental feeling and movement

840. We have seen, on the one hand, how hard it is to think about and be aware of the fundamental feeling and, on the other, how easy to be aware of acquired sensations (cf. 710–721).

For the same reason, indefinite space perceived by the possibility of the movements of our body easily escapes our reflection. On the other hand, because sensations of touch are acquired, they and their movement attract our attention more easily.

distances, having only the weak sense of touch of their claws. The vulture, for instance, measures the *space, time* and the *speed* necessary to catch its prey. But all it needs for this is its weak sense of touch and its powerful eye-sight together with its great power of movement.

Article 8
Space perceived by the movement of touch-sensation is identical with space perceived by the movement of the fundamental feeling

841. The term of the external sensation of touch is a more or less extended surface (cf. 837).

This surface is identical with the external surface of our body because the sensation is felt only in the nerve endings where we are touched.[167]

The same surface[168] is also the term of both the *subjective sensation* we feel in our organ and the action done in us from outside. Consciousness of this action constitutes what we have called the *extrasubjective perception* of the senses. Because the external agent is called an external body, the surface, when touched, is not only the term of our body but also of the external body. Now if we think of this surface (felt and perceived by us and common both to our body and the external body) as being moved in all directions (cf. 839), we arrive at the origin of the concept of indefinite space.

Indefinite space is therefore perceived by us in two ways: either by moving the organ felt by us through a modification of the fundamental feeling or by moving the surface perceived in the external agent. In both cases it is always one and the same surface.

Space, therefore, whether perceived in the two *subjective* modes or the *extrasubjective* mode, is one and the same, because any modification of the fundamental feeling (an acquired sensation of our organ) has the same extension as the fundamental feeling.

[167] The sensation of our body must always be distinguished from the perception of an external thing in the same surface. Although we feel the same surface, we feel two things: 1. our body, a subject that feels and is felt; 2. an external agent that is felt but does not feel.

[168] The unity of this surface determines the nature of touch, and of the mysterious unity of agent and recipient in every kind of action, as we have already pointed out. [Cf. *App.*, no. 22]

[841]

Article 9

Identity between the extension of our body and of an external
body is the basis of the communication
between the idea we have of each of them

842. Our body, when considered in association with its
sentient *subject*, shares the same extension with the external
body, which is simply the agent we feel.

The communion of these two bodies in the same extension
provides the step from the idea of one to the idea of the other; it
is the *communicating bridge* we were looking for. The very act
by which we perceive the mode of our body's existence is the
same act by which we perceive the mode of existence of an
external body.

Article 10

Continuation

843. This consequence (cf. 842) is of the greatest importance.

We have established two elements necessary for the essence of
a body: 1. an action done on us; 2. an extension in which that
action is diffused and terminates.

Our own body exercises a continuous, internal action on us,
occasioning the fundamental feeling, and this effect of the agent
spreads throughout an extension. Here we have therefore the
two elements forming the essence of body. Hence the perception of our body is undeniable, and its essence is as certain as the
fact of consciousness.

844. The perception of an external body is brought about
when we first feel an action done on us, although the immediate
effect of this action is simply a modification of our fundamental
feeling.

This effect alone does not draw us out of ourselves. We still
feel our body as we did before, but in a new way (with an accidental sensation).

But we are then easily led to argue to a cause, which is
unknown because the action is still undetermined. This alone

would not suffice to make us perceive a *body* outside us. For this, the action has also to be *extended*. We would perceive an *agent in extension*, which is the notion of a body.

But how are we able to perceive the extension of an agent? The author of nature, in his wisdom, provides the answer: we feel extension habitually, that is, the diffusion of the fundamental feeling. Consequently, we are able to feel the extension of the external agent when it diffuses its action in the *same extension* as our fundamental feeling.

This explains why the surface of the extension of our fundamental feeling and the surface of the extension of an external body should unite to form a single surface in which we experience two feelings. Hence the action of an external body takes place in and extends over the very same surface in which the fundamental feeling is diffused and terminates. Consciousness itself tells us that the action comes from outside and takes place in an extension already felt by us naturally.

We perceive: 1. an external action; and 2. the surface in which this external action functions or terminates. Thus we perceive the two essential properties of body, common to our own and external bodies, and confirm for ourselves the existence of two bodies, each having the same corporeal nature, although their effects upon us are quite different.

Article 11

The subjective sensation of our body is the means of corporeal, extrasubjective perception

845. What we have said explains how the extrasubjective perception of bodies is founded on the subjective perception.

The first element in extrasubjective perception is a force modifying us. We perceive this force in its action according to the kind of impact it has on us, and with it perceive a subjective modification of our fundamental feeling.

The second element is extension, and in particular the extension of the fundamental feeling, which we feel naturally. But because the fundamental feeling is changed in extension by an external force applied to each part of the extension, we perceive this force as extended in its term. This explains why the criterion for the perception of an exterior body is ultimately the perception of our own body (cf. 843–844).

Article 12
The extension of bodies

846. Before continuing, I must give some attention to the real extension I have sometimes attributed to a body; it is a very important matter, discussed by others at various times. I will show that the *extension* we perceive in a body is real, not apparent and illusory [*App.*, no. 30].

§1. *Multiplicity is not essential to corporeal nature*

847. Many thinkers have considered multiplicity essential to corporeal nature.

But it is easy to see, as Leibniz pointed out, that the concept of multiplicity cannot be the concept of an individual nature but of the coexistence of several natures. It is a relative concept, presupposing and based on an absolute concept. In short, where the many is, there must be the one; multiplicity is merely the aggregate of many unities. Thus the nature of things must be sought in unity[169] and not in a multitude, which is only several natures joined together.

848. The essence, therefore, of a body or of anything else will never be *multiplicity*, which is purely a mental entity. Only idealists, especially transcendentalists, who suppose that bodies are an emanation of our mind,[170] are content to posit corporeal nature in multiplicity.

---

[169] If corporeal nature is to be found in the elements from which composite bodies result, such elements cannot be thought of as unextended. Continuous extension is sufficient because the continuum is one, as we saw (cf. 825).

[170] I mean *actual multiplicity*, although the nature of what is extended always involves the idea of a *potential multiplicity*, which however is not yet multiplicity.

§2. *The composite unity of our sensitive body*

849. Certain conditions are required for our organs to feel, one of which is communication with the brain.

We may conclude from this that the sensitivity of each part of our sensitive organ depends on the form of the whole sentient system, that is, on a division and organisation of parts whose harmonious result is a single whole, sensitive in all its parts. Thus the parts composing the organ are sensitive because of this single whole, or rather because of a unity rooted in the whole.

We can say that our body, in so far as it is sensitive, enjoys a certain composite unity which makes it one because it has in itself an order or harmony of parts.

850. This truth remains valid even if we cannot say whether there is a centre in the brain, and if there is, whether it consists of a single particle or several in which all the nerves end. For even independently of the intelligent spirit, the unity of the human body is sufficiently established by its need of a certain disposition if it is to be vivified and inhabited by the spirit, and its different powers be, as Dante says, 'organated.'

§3. *We cannot err about the unicity of our body*

851. Let us imagine we possess two bodies. In this case we would then have two fundamental feelings and extensions, because these are the two essential elements of our body. Our consciousness, therefore, which indicates one fundamental feeling only, diffused in a definite extension, indicates the unicity of our body.

Let us imagine that we feel we have two bodies. In this case we could not have one only because in our sensation the two constitutive elements of our body would be perceived as doubled. Thus we still could not err in judging whether our body is one or two [*App.*, no. 31].

§4. *The multiplicity of the feeling of our body*

852. Because our body is *one* through the harmony of its

parts, we perceive its *unicity*. Anything outside this harmony and foreign to us is not felt. However such unity and unicity does not exclude multiplicity from our body, as I must now explain.

Through the organisation of the body, my spirit feels all its sensitive parts by means of the fundamental feeling and of the adventitious sensations in its sensitive parts. This makes it possible at least to conceive multiplicity.

853. If we keep to sensation, because the same reasoning can easily be applied to the fundamental feeling, we have to ask what can and cannot be affirmed about the multiplicity of sensation?

Let us suppose that we experience a sensation of touch and that its impression has a certain extension. If the extension is sufficient, we feel it and generally advert to it. But if the extension is small, it escapes our attention.

The smallest extension we can be aware of may be called the *minimum* extension.

Now if this *minimum* is regarded as the basic element of an extended sensation, it is certain that one element is not another because in each we find two separate things: 1. sensation; and 2. extension, which are the two constitutives of body.

Thus we can consider these *elements* as tiny bodies, subsisting separately and outside each other, which cannot be confused nor take one another's place. In our body therefore we perceive with equal certainty both *multiplicity* and *unity*.

§5. *Our perception of multiplicity in external bodies*

854. A similar argument can be applied to external bodies. When an external body is so minute that its extension is less than a certain limit, it entirely escapes our attention.

If we take this *minimum* (that is, the smallest noticeable body) as the basic element, it can safely be said that in the perception of a larger body we can mentally distinguish and separate *minimum* perceptions as possible, and even as really distinct when considered individually.

Furthermore, because the two constitutive elements of body

are present in each of these *minimum perceptions*, we can mentally distinguish minute *bodies*, whether they are divided or not.

They can also have an independent subsistence because they have separate and incommunicable action. As we have seen, in each of these minimum spaces that we have distinguished, there is an extension outside every other extension. Thus each agent is outside every other agent and is a substance that, while it can be contiguous with another substance, appears separate and isolated in its own existence. In this way we perceive *multiplicity* in external bodies also.

§6. *The distinction between a body and a corporeal principle*

855. We 'name things according to the way we intellectually perceive them' (cf. 647 [678]).

To investigate what a *body* is, is to investigate the notion given by the human race to the word 'body' (cf. 653–656).

We found this notion was the result of two elements, an *agent* acting on us and an *extension* in which this action and our own experience of it were diffused.

However if the *agent* effected nothing in us, we could neither know it nor name it, since we know it and name it in so far as it acts on us. So the word 'body' is determined by the *immediate effects* of the agent on us and by the laws governing its action.

But the *agent* could have powers and laws unknown to us, different from but not contrary to those we experience. If all possible or unknown effects and their laws were like this, they would be neither known nor named by us. The name 'body' therefore cannot be applied to these qualities as long as they remain unknown: 'Words may not be used with a sense wider than that for which they were devised' (cf. 648–652 [679]).

Suppose however that the order of things were changed. We might discover new effects with new laws dependent on the same principle as the effects now determining the meaning of the word 'body'. In this case the common use of the word would change.

But while we continue to use the *word* in the present condition of things, it has a meaning limited by its immediate effects or actions and by the laws according to which bodies present themselves to us.

856. For this reason I prefer to distinguish *corporeal principle* from *body* and include the former in the definition of body only in so far as body is accompanied by effects and laws enabling us to know the principle. But I would also grant to the corporeal principle all that it has in addition to and different from what its nature reveals to us.

857. Speaking therefore about *body* in this sense, I have no hesitation in affirming that we know with certainty the *multiplicity of bodies*.[171]

§7. Granted that corporeal sensation terminates in a continuous extension, a continuous real extension must also be present in the bodies producing it

858. Let us suppose that the surface of our body where sensations take place is continuous, or at least that there is in it some continuous space.

It seems to me that a body producing an extended, continuous sensation must also be extended and continuous.[172] This is a corollary of what has already been said.

I have said that 'bodies are the *proximate* cause of our sensations' (cf. 639–645 [667]). I have explained that 'proximate cause' means an ens receiving its name only from the immediate effect it constantly produces. I concluded that the constant sensations (the fundamental feeling and its modifications) are not produced by a *power* of a body but by a body's *substance*, by a body itself; the word 'body' indicates only those immediate effects which are its total meaning.

The result of these findings was the recognition that in each space where we experience a sensation diffused in extension, we

---

[171] No new properties would falsify former properties, whatever might be discovered in bodies or whatever change they might undergo from a force above nature. Hence the extrasubjective qualities we now perceive in bodies are not deceptive; they are true even if they were to be changed.

[172] The same would be true if the fundamental feeling were diffused in a surface or solid continuum, that is, without any interruption.

must acknowledge an agent possessing all the characteristics required for what we call 'body'. Hence we must acknowledge a *multiplicity* of bodies obtained from a multiplicity of sensations in a multiplicity of spaces. I can always imagine a sensation ending in one space while continuing in another, or beginning here while ending there, so that all I know about sensations in different spaces indicates their mutual independence.

This essential difference of effects compels the acceptance of a substantial difference of causes, and therefore a multiplicity of causes. This in turn shows that, granted a continuous sensation, there must be a continuity of extension in the body producing it.

859. We have imagined various small spaces as divisions of a larger space in which sensation is diffused. We saw how a force or a minute body is present, producing a sensation in each small space.

Now if we fuse all these small spaces together, they become one large, continuous space. But this fusion does not affect our argument; nothing is altered. Provided the spaces are distinct, a corresponding minute body is necessary for each of them whether the spaces are distant, near or even contiguous with one another. However, their continuous contiguity, resulting in one large, continuous sensation, must also give one continuous body.

The whole force of the argument lies in this one principle: wherever there is sensation, there is also an acting force. So if a sensation is continuous and equal in every assignable point of a space, an acting cause, the body, is present throughout the same space. Hence if there is no interval in the sensation, there is no interval in the body. Granted a continuous sensation, the body producing it is continuous.

The need for such a conclusion is found in the wonderful, mysterious but undeniable nature of continuous extension. No space, however small or wherever present, can be assigned in continuous extension unless it has its own entity outside and fully independent of other spaces. Every smaller space can be at least mentally separated from the whole, giving us the *indefinite limitability* of the continuum we have noted. The fact that each space is outside every other means that the action confined to one space cannot operate within any other; the smallest space presupposes an agent outside the agent acting in the next space. In the external body therefore we must be able to identify as many contiguous parts acting on our body as there are identifiable contiguous spaces in our own body felt by us.

860. Someone might object: when an external body wounds some part of our feeling faculty, it produces pain more extensive than itself, as the pain spreads, by sympathy, to other parts. There is no necessity therefore for the extension of a sensation to correspond exactly to the sensation of the body causing the sensation.

I reply as follows:

1. I note that in all the places where the pain extends by sympathy there must be sensitive parts. The argument given above must be applied to these parts; if the pain extends in a continuous space, the injured parts producing it must be continuous.[173] Now if the parts of our body are continuous, there is a continuum in bodies, which was to be proved.

2. Diffused sensation, propagated sympathetically, follows the same law as all other sensations: 'A force is felt at the spot where it is applied.' A sensation spreads precisely because the force changing the state of the parts in the sensitive organ spreads. Let us suppose that the movement of the organ which gives rise to the pain (it does not matter whether the pain is produced by a mechanical, physical or chemical force) spreads from one part to another part of the limb, let us say from one layer to another. The third layer receives the movement from the second. It feels only the pressure or action of the second layer, not the external body. The pain present by sympathy or communication in the sensitive material does not indicate an *external body*. Only the limb is perceived more acutely, that is, those parts of it causing the pain actively and immediately. But in this case, the sensation produced directly by the external body is indeed detected and indicates the existence of the body; we are conscious of feeling a disturbance at the place where the body is acting. Thus the principle I began with, to demonstrate the continuity of bodies, is valid also for sensations diffused

---

[173] We can sometimes wrongly locate a sensation, as in the pain of an amputated limb; but here our habitual *judgment* is deceived, not our feeling (cf. 762).

sympathetically. It is always true that 'in every place where we feel a sensation, there is a force in act, a body acting.'

§8. *The sensitive parts of our body*
do not produce a feeling extending beyond themselves

861. This truth has been demonstrated in the preceding paragraph. It is also proved by the definition of the sensitive parts of our body.

Because we feel a sensitive part only where we feel and confirm a sensation, sensations therefore do not extend outside the sensitive parts, and vice versa.

§9. *The extension of external bodies is neither greater nor*
smaller than the sensations they produce in us

862. This follows from the preceding proposition.

The size of an external body is measured by sensations, especially touch. We have already seen that the extension of our body, perceived subjectively, is the measure of the extra-subjective extension of external bodies.

Therefore the extension of external bodies is neither greater nor less than the extension of the sensations produced in us by the contact of external bodies.

§10. *Phenomenal continuity is present in our touch-sensations*

863. When we touch a very smooth surface with a part of our body, we are unable to notice any break in the sensation we experience.

The sensation, spread throughout the surface, seems to be continuous, that is, the continuity is phenomenal.

However if we look at the surface through a microscope, it is seen to be uneven and rutted. This would seem to contradict what we have just established, that a sensation of touch

produced by an external body does not extend outside the size
of the body itself. But we must always bear in mind the real, necessary distinction between a *sensation* and our *awareness* of
that sensation.[174] We must convince ourselves by observation
that there are very minute sensations which entirely escape our
awareness. This explains why we think a surface is even and
smooth, because in the sensation of the surface we do not advert
to the tiny corruscations and intervals. Hence a large sensation
is not in fact continuous; we think it is because we do not advert
to its very minute intervals.

§11. *Elementary sensations are continuous*

864. There is no perfect continuity, therefore, in a notably
extended sensation (like the surface we have discussed); there
are intervals and irregularities in its parts.

The large sensation is broken up by intervals, so to speak, into
small, elementary sensations, next to each other but not contiguous on every side.

It is my opinion that these tiny, elementary sensations are diffused in a truly continuous extension, as I will now show.

We begin by supposing the opposite, that is, they have no
continuity and are therefore merely mathematical points.

865. Mathematical points would necessarily have between
them spaces of various minute sizes which would always be
continuous, and also contiguous because a mathematical point
does not break contiguity.

But here we must note a law governing sensations: 'If our
body has two or more sensations located in quite different
places, we notice the space separating them', because we refer the sensations to different points. When these spaces are

[174] On many occasions I have distinguished between *feeling* and *awareness*
of feeling. I am certain and will show that, although a corporeal stimulus
acting on our spirit may produce a sensation, the stimulus needs to be quite
intense for it to produce a sensation capable of drawing our attention with
relative ease. The weaker the sensation, the more difficult is it to advert to it,
even if it exists. Hence, a very weak sensation must be totally unsuited to
making us aware of itself or of its extension.

noticeably extended, we feel them, especially by comparing the places affected and unaffected by sensation.

Now if we were to feel the sensation only in many un-extended points, would it be possible for such a sensation to be phenomenally continuous, as it is in fact? It would not, as the following reasons will show:

I. If we were capable of adverting to sensations that have no extension, we would be much more capable of adverting to the tiny spaces separating them, for these have an extension infinitely greater than mathematical points. Thus the total sensation could never seem continuous. If it were continuous, we would have to advert to it as something composed of unextended points, distantly separated from each other. In such a case it would be impossible to explain the phenomenon of continuity in sensations.

866. II. An infinite number of mathematical points placed together could not cover a surface or even a line. They cannot give the extension they do not possess. Thus, if we were to join together all the supposed unextended points we feel, the size of the surface in which they are spread would not be covered in any way. We would have to feel on the one hand the sensation of the unextended points, and on the other, the surface exactly as it was previously felt by our fundamental feeling, or indeed feel no continuum at all. All the tiny spaces that as a result had no sensation would, taken together, form an extension as large as the extension existing prior to the sensation of the points. If therefore the whole extension we felt in the points were non-existent, we would have to be aware of the extension remaining between the points. This extension would be exactly the same as it was before we received the impression that has only unextended points but no extension. In this case we could never have a perception or idea of any continuum.

867. III. Again, if we felt simple points, we would feel a composite of non-corporeal sensations because such sensations would not terminate in extension (cf. 754 [755]), which is of the essence of corporeal sensations; nor would sensation of this kind supply matter for the idea of a body.

868. IV. Finally, let us suppose we feel only unextended points. It would be possible to locate them at different places in the body's periphery. This can be done only by measuring in

some way the distance between one point and another. Now either we feel these distances, or we do not. If we do, we will feel a *continuum*; if we do not, we will have no means of locating the points at the places we do locate them. In this case, they would be sensations, foreign to every place, located perhaps in the simplicity of our spirit but nowhere else. There is no doubt that only the *continuum* can be a measure of distance; a simple point is no measure because entirely devoid of extension. But granted we perceive a *continuum*, we can measure the interval between one point and another. The size of these intervals is only a projection we make of their ability to repeat a certain number of times the *continuum* we use as a unit of measure.

We have to recognise therefore that small, elementary sensations, whether acquired or forming the fundamental feeling, are extended, that is, terminate in a continuous extension.

§12. *Elementary bodies have a continuous extension*

869. We cannot affirm or deny the simplicity of the *corporeal principle* because the principle may (cf. 855–857) in part be unknown.

But it is clearly false that *bodies* can be a composite of simple points, as Leibniz maintained.[175]

We have seen that: 1. elementary sensations are extended and continuous; 2. the size of bodies, which are the *proximate causes* of sensations, is equal to the size of the sensations.

We therefore conclude that elementary bodies have a continuous extension.[176]

[175] Leibniz's error seems to consist precisely in his desire to speak about the *corporeal principle* rather than *bodies*; in other words, about the unknown rather than the known. But who can speak clearly and accurately about something he does not know?

[176] Besides having a certain continuous extension, elementary bodies must have certain regular forms, like crystals, and must be perfectly hard and unchangeable.

§13. *Argument against simple points*

870. Points escape our senses. We can never perceive un-extended points which, therefore, cannot be *bodies*. We cannot give a name to what we do not know; names indicate things only in so far as things are known.[177] Thus the word 'body' must indicate things known, things falling under our senses that we touch, see and perceive with our other organs. The word does not mean unextended points, of which we have no experience at all.

Wherever there is a sensation, there is an experience relative to ourselves, and an action relative to the agent, a *force in act* that we call body. Now if there are continuous sensations in some of the little spaces, the force must be diffused in the whole space, be present in every point, and be extended and continu-ous. Hence elementary bodies must possess real continuity and cannot be simple points, if we use reason, not imagination, as our guide for the data provided by observation.[178]

[177] Cf. 647–652. However we must always remember that words indicate the *real thing*, although only in the limited way we know it.

[178] If the action of simple points terminated in one point only, these agents would pass from one part of our body to another without causing the least disturbance. But if they are granted a tiny sphere by which they are surrounded and into which their force extends, they are no longer simple forces; on the contrary, this tiny sphere of force is precisely the extended body. To verify that the points were of this form, we would need to show that the force of elementary bodies acts like rays emitted from a centre. This research, which has not yet been made, may need to be carried out. If it is not proved, there would be no difference between the centre and the sphere because the force is in every point of the sphere without exception. If the *centre* is something ideal in the extended part, we have a mental postulate, which constitutes no nature. Again, the forms of primal bodies would have to be spherical if we suppose that the centre emits a force, but this cannot be the case for all bodies. On the other hand, if they are not spherical, the law of the centre of gravity is at odds with the centre of the force. But whatever the case, the only meaning possible for *body* is that of a force endowed with some extension.

[870]

Article 13

The definition of bodies completed

871. Having established that continuous extension is real in bodies, we can now perfect the definition of body[179] by adding to it this quality of extension: 'A body is a single substance[180] endowed with extension, and producing in us a pleasant or painful feeling terminating in the same extension.'[181]

Article 14

We perceive external bodies by touch and movement

872. If a body is a force whose act terminates in a solid, continuous extension, we must investigate how we perceive a body by touch.

Extension has three dimensions, length, breadth and height, which we first perceive in our body through the fundamental feeling (cf. 692 *ss.*).

In the action of external bodies on the surface of our body, we cannot feel and perceive more than a surface, that is, two dimensions, length and breadth. Our body alone does not allow us to perceive the dimension of depth in an external body.[182]

---

[179] I first defined bodies imperfectly, basing the definition on common sense (cf. 635). I say 'imperfectly' not 'falsely' because it contained the entire essence of bodies without analysis of their elements. Analysis of the definition has allowed me to perfect it (cf. 749–753), especially here. The progress of knowledge, I believe, must be something like this, and begin with natural, composite ideas (popular understanding), which are analysed and then scientifically synthesised to form knowledge. Hence those who deny the necessity of starting from definitions, fall into the opposite error. If anyone wishes to be understood, he has to begin with definitions; but there are scientific definitions and popular definitions, and both are true. We must begin with the popular to finish with the scientific.

[180] It is *single* because it is *continuous*, nothing more.

[181] This was demonstrated earlier.

[182] Sometimes an external body seems to act simultaneously in all the points of a solid space of our body, for example, a penetrating, acidic substance. Granted this, we would indeed perceive our own body's solidity

But if we consider the external surface, perceived by our touch, in relationship with the faculty we have of moving the surface, we obtain the idea of a solid body.

Just as we obtain the idea of solid space by conceiving a body movable in all directions outside its plane, so the idea of a solid body comes from the movement we partly experience and partly expect or think as possible, of a corporeal surface moving outside its own plane.

873. As we consider this movement, we conceive as possible that all the surfaces imaginable within a solid space can be felt, that is, they can be terms of the action done in us by a body.

To help us understand this, let us imagine a body formed as a perfectly hard cube. If I touch all six faces of the cube of very hard material, pressing as firmly as I like, I perceive simply the limits of a solid space shaped like a cube, that is, corporeal surfaces. This gives me only an imperfect idea of body because all I have perceived are surfaces enclosing and terminating a solid space; I have perceived only the body's limits, not its solid extension.

Next I take a cube of soft material, such that I can change its form or break it into parts. If I shape or divide it, there is only one result: more and more surfaces are revealed, which I did not feel before because they were not uncovered from within the cube and were certainly not surfaces.

As I continue to divide it up, I have to conclude that the solid cube presents not only a corporeal surface externally, but has the ability to present more and more surfaces internally. Experiments and thoughts like this lead me to the concept of corporeal solidity, completing my idea of solid body, that is, of a substance diffusing its activity in solid extension according to certain laws.

but not the solidity of the external body. This observation can help us to distinguish our body's extension from the extension of the external body; the two bodies can easily be confused because we perceive them united in our sensation of touch. A relationship that distinguishes two agents differs relative to each agent.

[873]

Article 15

Origin of the idea of mathematical body

874. The previous experiment taught me that, by applying force to the cube sufficient to change its form or divide it, I can obtain more surfaces from within the space enclosed by the corporeal surfaces of the cube.

Examining this fact, I cannot find any reason why the exposed surfaces should be in one particular part of the cube and not in another.

There is no repugnance in thinking that these corporeal surfaces are equally present in all parts, that is, in every plane assignable within the cube. Now the possibility of thinking of the corporeal surfaces dividing the volume of the cube in any plane, is the idea of mathematical body, which is always conceived as perfectly continuous.

Article 16

Origin of the idea of physical body

875. As long as I think the *possibility* of finding a corporeal surface in any imaginary plane within a cube, I have the idea of a *mathematical body* (cf. 874). But if, instead of this simple possibility, I try as well as I can to determine the forms of a particular, real body with my touch or other senses (even with the use of instruments), I become aware of irregularities, ridges and spaces between one section and another. In this case I form the idea of a composite of tiny parts, not in perfect contact, differently shaped and interspersed with intervals and links so strongly bonded together in some places that they cannot be forced apart. I call this *physical body.*

All this explains how people born blind can form the idea of both mathematical and physical bodies by means of touch, movement and intellect.

CHAPTER 10

The particular criterion for the existence of external bodies

Article 1

The criterion for external bodies is an application
of the general criterion for the existence of bodies

876. We have dealt with the general criterion (cf. 749 ss.) and seen that, applied to the external bodies we know, it gives us the criterion for their existence. In other words, to be certain of the perception of an external body, we must perceive:

1. A force modifying us.

2. Its action communicated to us in a feeling endowed with extension.

3. An extension that is stable, that is, able to repeat the sensation (otherwise we could not speak about a substance acting).

4. An extension endowed with three dimensions.

Thus it is not sufficient to perceive corporeal surfaces. We must perceive a solid space which, when divided, reveals new surfaces to our senses.

Article 2

Applications of the criterion for the existence
of external bodies

877. I. Wet a coin and press it against a child's forehead, pretending to make it stick. It is now possible to remove it without the child's noticing. In fact he will think the coin is still there and bend his head to make it fall. But if he touches his forehead, he finds nothing and is aware that: 1. he experienced something there; 2. the substance producing the experience is no longer present, because the substance's presence involves a constant

experience and the possibility that the feeling can be repeated and reinforced, granted the necessary conditions (cf. 876, no. 3).[183]

II. We could touch what looks like a rod of solid silver and be deceived about its solidity; we might look inside and find another substance, or a hollow.[184]

[183] Sensation in the nerves lasts some time even when the cause has been removed, as in the case of red streaks left in the eye caused by gyrating fireworks. The pure sensation indicates itself, and consciousness of the experience indicates a cause but not the actual presence of the cause. This must be due to a judgment, which, if all its necessary conditions are not present, is misleading. Sensation, however, does not deceive us as regards the existence of the part affected in our body; sensation is the result of a modification of the fundamental feeling and of a cause producing the modification.

[184] Here too it is our judgment, not the sensation, that misleads us, because it includes more than the sensation; in the example, it includes the inside of the rod.

CHAPTER 11

The subjective and the extrasubjective content in external sensations

Article 1

The necessity of this distinction

878. After observing and describing *extrasubjective* perception of bodies by touch, we should follow with observations on the other four senses to see what perception reveals for each one. But before doing so, we must carefully distinguish the *extrasubjective* and *subjective* elements present in every sensation, so that nothing subjective remains in the extrasubjective element. When this has been done, the extrasubjective perception will stand out clearly and indicate for us the extrasubjective value of each sense.

Article 2

Some truths recalled

879. I have demonstrated two things:

1. Sensation is in us, not in external agents (cf. 632 ss. and 672 ss. [652]). The idealists misused this fact. I grant them its truth, but they should not have neglected other facts while acknowledging it. Their error was the result of insufficient observation, not of defective observation.

2. Sensations are in us as the term of actions done by something other than ourselves (*ibid.*).

This was the other fact neglected by the idealists, although no less clear than the first. In every sensation we experience a passive modification or disturbance within us, of which we are directly conscious, which expresses the term of an external action. By their nature, therefore, sensations, although in us, inform us of something outside ourselves. We must either deny the difference between activity and passivity, or accept that to be conscious of an experience in us is to be conscious of an action done in us, but not by us.

Article 3

The understanding analyses sensations

880. Consciousness tells us that: 1. we are modified; 2. this modification is an action done in us, not by us. It tells us these two things simultaneously, with a single voice, as it were.

Reflection then analyses this united evidence of consciousness, recognising the two things and considering each one separately.

Next, the understanding applies the concept of substance to our consciousness of the action done in us, not by us. In this way it isolates and makes its object the external things on which it then meditates and reasons.

Article 4

The general principle for discerning what is subjective and what is extrasubjective in sensations

881. The principle for accurately distinguishing the subjective and extrasubjective elements in sensations is: 'Everything contained in sensations considered in themselves (and not according to the way they are produced) is subjective; everything contained in the concept of our passivity, a passivity attested by consciousness, is extrasubjective.'

Article 5

Application of the general principle
to determine the extrasubjective part of sensations

882. Applying the principle, we discover the following extra-subjective parts in sensations:

1. Consciousness tells us we are passive in sensations, that is, we perceive a *force in act*. Our understanding then sees in this action an *ens different from itself*, that is, a body. *Force* then is the first part of the extrasubjective perception of bodies.

2. Consciousness attests that the disturbances and forces we feel are multiple. *Multiplicity of bodies* therefore is the second part of our extrasubjective perception of bodies.

3. Consciousness again, and reason, tell us that a *force* is actively present in every point of an extension without exception. We are thus led to the conviction that there is a *continuous extension*. This is the third part of the extrasubjective perception of bodies.

883. Analysis of these first three extrasubjective properties of bodies shows many others. I only make the following observation:

The *force* which is a property of bodies, is not any force capable of acting on our spirit. It acts in a particular way, determined by the subjective effects it produces in us, that is, by the subjective part of sensations such as pleasure, pain, heat, light, colours, etc. Now, corresponding to all the different kinds of sensations and effects of this force, there must be, in bodies, *aptitudes* or potencies for producing them. These potencies proceed from the *force* which is the essence of body, and is the body itself. The first quality of bodies, therefore, generates many other qualities, that is, causes all those aptitudes in which it expresses itself in its different effects (determinations of the force).[185]

884. *Multiplicity* is not a real property of corporeal nature except in so far as it is *possible* to imagine it in the continuous extension with which bodies are endowed. In fact, real

---

[185] These determinations explain the element we have so far ignored in order not to complicate the argument. It has been included in the word 'corporeal', used to qualify 'force'.

multiplicity is accidental, a relationship of many mentally conceived bodies.

885. Finally, *extension*, especially when united to *force*, is the source of a great amount of information about corporeal properties. Because extension includes *mobility, shape, divisibility, impenetrability*, etc., all these properties are both real and extrasubjective, that is, in bodies themselves, not simply in us.[186]

Article 6
The difference between
primary and secondary properties of bodies

886. The famous distinction between *primary* and *secondary* properties of bodies has its foundation in nature.

But it would be better to call the former *extrasubjective* and the latter *subjective*, although *primary* and *secondary* are not out of place because we form the idea of body with the extrasubjective properties and apply the subjective properties as accidents of bodies.

Article 7
Application of the general principle
to determine the subjective part of sensations

887. All that forms a sensation considered in itself is subjective (cf. 881).

Hence if we remove from sensations multiplicity, extension, and the *force* producing them and making them subsist (and anything else discovered through analysis of these three parts), anything left that we can observe is subjective.

---

[186] The true part of the ancient opinion that phantasms are *likenesses* or images of external bodies is therefore the *extrasubjective* part with which external bodies are perceived, not the *subjective* part. Hence the *multiplicity* and *continuity* of phantasms are *similar* to those of external bodies. The *force* proper to external bodies is, however, experienced by us passively in phantasms although it is active in bodies. Nevertheless, it is the same force in act in us and in bodies because sensations are its term and direct effect.

We may note that feeling in the human being has a unity, that is, the unity of the sentient principle that gathers and unites its various modifications. Moreover, it is reasonable to believe that the nature of this sentient principle, and of the animal fundamental feeling, generates the different feelings, establishing and determining the characteristics of each. Nevertheless, we do not know sufficiently the nature of the principle and the feeling to understand this connection. The many, various changes undergone by feeling seem to us arbitrary and independent of each other; we cannot deduce them *a priori*.

888. I do not know whether this is due to my ignorance or whether, in this case, something lies hidden and mysterious to the human race. I have to be satisfied with indicating the many, varied kinds of sensations as basic facts without explaining them. I do not need to explain the laws that govern the generation of such different, unpredictable feelings from a single first feeling.

But it does seem to me that something is in fact hidden from us, because our imagination cannot pass from one kind of sensation to another which we have never experienced. A person born blind never gains an image of colours with the help of the other senses. Generally speaking, it is impossible for anyone born without one of his senses to use the sensations of the other senses, even if they are particularly powerful in him, to form an image of the sensations he has never experienced. It appears undeniable therefore that at least external, acquired sensations have something incommunicable, and are completely separate from each other. Their noticeable simplicity would lead to the same conclusion.

889. On this basis, it seems to me that the first subjective element is the pleasure diffused in the sensitive parts of a body animated by the fundamental feeling. The nature of this pleasure, produced by our body, is determined by the *state* of our body itself, granted the presence of life.

The *modifications* of the fundamental feeling are certainly determined by the *state* of our body but, as I have said, to investigate the laws governing this fact is beyond my powers.

890. Because the various parts of the body have a different *state*, they receive impressions in a different way, and modify the fundamental feeling differently. This varying *state* of the

parts of the body was wisely ordained by the Creator in such a way that different organs were fittingly designed to determine various kinds of sensations. Hence the wonderful structure of the eye is designed to receive certain modifications of feeling different from those received in the ears, nose and palate.

891. Besides the *modifications* of the fundamental feeling presented by these sensories, modifications also take place in different parts of the body, according to their constitution and composition, or according to some particular organisation. The sense of hunger, of thirst and of sleep, of the sexual drive, are all different in kind. But they are not considered as senses because the particular name of sense is reserved for what helps our understanding in a very special way to acquire cognitions of external things.

892. The special condition and organisation of each sense-organ makes it capable of receiving the particular kind of *modification* of the fundamental feeling for which it was designed. However, the modification does not take place unless, in addition to a good organic system, a stimulus acts in the appropriate way. Light is needed if the eye is to give colour-sensations; hearing needs air, the nose needs odour-particles and the palate taste-particles. There has to be an appropriate, suitable cause relevant to both the matter and form of the organ, so that the organ can undergo the change necessary for bringing about a particular kind of sensation in the fundamental feeling.

893. A simple *cause* however is not enough; it must also act in the *particular way* necessary for stimulating each of the four senses.[187]

894. Thus, to produce special sensations, three things are necessary, in addition to life: 1. the quality of suitable organisation, and the condition of the organ; 2. the right kind of *agent*; 3. an appropriate manner of action by the agent.

895. Consequently the effect, or subjective sensation, produced simultaneously by these three principles, is certainly not an indication of the condition of one of them only. It is a

---

[187] In the sense of touch there are a great variety of sensations according to the type of touch. Without previous experience, no one could imagine the peculiar sensation of tickling, a sensation that makes us laugh even against our will and has no connection with any other sensation.

mistake to think we can establish the quality of the external cause from the subjective sensation.

For example, the sensation of heat is subjective; it is in us, not in the external body producing it [*App*., no. 32]. It is not therefore a suitable measure of the quantity of heat. We can be persuaded of this if we put a very cold hand into water that is not so cold; the water will seem warm. The same will happen when a hand that feels very hot is immersed in lukewarm water; the water seems cold. The reason is the different state of the hand due to the necessary change in the fundamental feeling.

Article 8
Resistant extension felt by touch

896. Although we have seen that the elementary sensations of touch and the particles corresponding to them are extended and continuous, we cannot conclude with certainty that touch can perceive every minute extension.

It is true that every space assignable in an elementary, continuous sensation must be felt; but we cannot attribute to each tiny space considered in itself what is said about it considered as an ideal part of the continuum.

There could be a law stating that sensation never takes place below a certain minimum extension. If so, observation in this case is powerless to affirm anything with certainty except about possibilities or probabilities. For instance, there is no contradiction in affirming on the one hand that we can think of an indefinitely small sensation and on the other that such a sensation must necessarily have some extension. Because we cannot reasonably exclude either of them, their possibility must be granted.

897. However, whether sensation is of such a nature that its extension can be reduced indefinitely, or whether it has a *minimum* extension, there seems no doubt at all that it is usually much more acute than our *awareness* of it. As a result, sensation feels spaces so minute that we are not aware of feeling them.[188]

---

[188] This further emphasises the distance between *sensation* and *understanding*; *awareness* is an act of understanding, not of feeling. *Awareness* is

The fact that the *sensation* of touch is far more refined than our *awareness* of the sensation is evident in those born blind. It is commonly said that their sense of touch is *more acute*. It is known that they can distinguish coins, playing cards, the quality of cloth and even colours by touch alone; they can sense the breathing or movement of anyone silently approaching them, even at a distance. They can indeed do wonderful things with their sense of touch, but not, I think, because it is *more acute* in them or because nature has endowed them better. What has been developed is their *awareness* about sensations. Their sense of touch is the same as that of others, who may or may not be blind.[189] But blind people, not having the distractions of sight, need to profit from their sensations of touch. They acquire very sensitive attention and concentration relative to all the different impressions on their touch, including delicate impressions which escape other people. It is not exaggerated, therefore, to believe that if awareness could make even further progress, human beings would realise that their touch, although limited, is a sense of unbelievable delicacy [*App.*, no. 33].

898. As we have observed, it is more difficult to be *aware* of sensations when they are motionless and hardly change. When we wish to note the unevenness of a surface with our hand, it is not sufficient to press our finger on one spot only. We may feel the minute differences in the surface but not be *aware* of *feeling* them. To be aware of them we move our finger firmly over the surface. Because this action affords us sharper sensations of the uneven surface, it is easy to be aware of them and, through them, of the unevenness.

899. Hence a solid body, in so far as we are *aware* of feeling it, is different from one we actually *feel* by touch. The body we are

only intellective attention given to what we feel or understand. Because the ancients had clearly seen that *reflection* is an act of understanding, not of feeling, they sometimes characterised the intellective faculty by reflection. We see this in Dante, where he mentions the three powers of living, feeling and understanding:

> ... a single soul
> which lives, feels and *continually turns upon itself.*

[189] We must also note that animals have a certain power over their nerves. With this power they extend and apply their nerves to receive sensations better. Its use can be perfected by skill and by habit.

aware of may perhaps be perfectly continuous and smooth on the surface, while the body we touch is possibly uneven, with high and low points, as any powerful microscope will reveal. As I have said, it seems we cannot put a limit to the acuteness of our touch. The microscope, while revealing the high and low points of the surface, also reveals the body as joined at several places and composed, too, of small, apparently continuous spaces. This is not the continuity of elementary bodies we have spoken about, a continuity which we believe escapes the most acute attention. Nor can we call it true continuity, because elementary bodies can be so close to each other that we cannot observe any interval between them. Nevertheless, the perfect adhesion of elementary bodies is not impossible or absurd, in my opinion, for there is nothing impossible about a true contact.

900. But let us leave this dangerous, unobservable world. A solid body perceived by touch and *adverted to*, has a shape we can distinguish fairly well. We ignore the unevenness of the surface and use our imagination to shape the body in the way we find most convenient for mentally conceiving it. This explains the regularity of shapes offered by touch. We perceive them easily because of their simplicity, which presents enough distinction and information for our purposes; we are quite satisfied.[190]

Article 9

The extrasubjective sensation of the four sense organs

901. Our eye perceives light directly and light informs us

[190] The mind has no difficulty in grasping regular shapes, like triangles, squares and any figure with a perceptible number of sides, because their component elements are few. On the other hand, if we greatly increase the number of sides, we can no longer *advert* to them, although we perceive them all equally with our *sense*. If the sides are of varying length, it is even more difficult to have a *distinct idea*. Imagine that the surfaces of a solid are all different from each other. The differences and multiplicity are beyond the power of our attention. The shape is too complex for our mind because it is conceived only by means of conceiving the unity of the parts. These, however, are so many and different that we are unable to keep them simultaneously before our mind, or to give them the amount of attention we could pay to a smaller number.

about external things [*App.*, no. 34]. I am concerned with the eye only in so far as it perceives light, its immediate agent, not as it indicates distant bodies that do not touch it. We have seen that the three parts of the extrasubjectivity of our senses are force, multiplicity and extension.

Force is felt equally by all the senses, has the general concept of agent only and in itself presents nothing determined. We must now see how we perceive, with the other four senses, multiplicity and extension, the parts that in some way determine the agent's nature.

902. As regards extension, we note that the four senses are touched and affected by bodies so minute that if one alone were to strike our senses, it would be impossible to isolate and observe it. No one can see or touch particles of light or fire or air or smell or molecules of food stimulating our sense of taste, because they are so tiny that we cannot note or advert to them.

As regards multiplicity, we find particles crowding in on our organs in such numbers that even if we could identify their size, we could never determine their number clearly.

These two circumstances, that is, the size, shape, movement and changes that cannot be observed in the particles, and their uncountable number must cause a vivid but *confused* perception in us of the mass of particles. The extrasubjective part of the four organs under discussion must be, as it were, blind, and lacking in *differentiation* [*App.*, no. 35]. Hence, although the extrasubjective part of these sensations is vivid, they offer to our understanding little that is clear about their immediate agents, and seem to present something more mysterious than what is offered by the sense of touch. In fact, when the understanding receives only a few clear perceptions, mystery seems inevitable. We should also note that the understanding takes its perceptions from the extrasubjective part of sensations which, confused at its origin, renders our intellections confused and vague.

903. The difference of these four organs from touch should be carefully noted. Touch perceives larger solid bodies;[191] the

---

[191] Even liquids, in so far as they act on the sense of touch, occupy a definite solid space, and present precise, determined shapes to our observation because, although mobile, they are nevertheless stable, large and regular.

particles of such bodies adhere to each other either through real contact or very close proximity (I believe both cases are true). They therefore present to touch a large, single *shape*, with the intervening spaces and high and low points escaping observation. Thus the extension of large agents acting on the sense of touch is easily identified and their regular shape easily conceived. On the other hand, the particles that impinge on and stimulate the four senses, are scattered, indefinable, moving at great speed, never remaining in the same place or state or maintaining the same shape. They move about haphazardly in all directions, disappearing in the air on which they arrived. In short, even if they were only small in quantity and of a size we could advert to, they would still escape observation because of the tremendous speed and instability of their continual movements.

904. Another comment must be made which will clearly demonstrate that the immediate agents of the four organs are of such a kind that their size and shape cannot be observed[192] nor present us with a distinct perception. Without this perception, all the sensations of the four organs will necessarily be confused, and therefore, mysterious, although pleasant and vivid.[193]

We have distinguished two parts, subjective and extrasubjective, in adventitious sensations, and have seen that an external body can make an impression and stimulate a sensation on any sensitive part of our body. We have also seen that the affected part must be distinguished from its surrounding parts into

[192] It is *size* and *shape* that give us a distinct perception of an agent, as we have already said, because they are the *extrasubjective* parts of sensation.

[193] How vivid they are depends on the particles producing a strong impression in the organ through their vast number, speed and perhaps, in the case of light, their elasticity, for light impinges and rebounds in the briefest of time without a very strong impression. The result of any strong impression must be a pronounced movement or perhaps a vibration of the nerves causing a large *subjective* sensation, as the soul feels the effect of the quivering nerve. In general we can establish the following fact given by observation: 'A very pleasant sensation is produced in a nerve when it is stimulated by rapid, frequent vibrations which do not damage or sever the nerve.' Now every time the stimuli are very small and many, they can do this, provided their number is not excessive and their impact moderate. Thus a carpet of roses or any soft material is very pleasant to lie on, and every soft surface is pleasant to our touch, in the same way that gentle colours can please our eyes and faint sounds our ears.

[904]

which the movement, together with the sensation, sometimes spreads in sympathy. But this kind of sensation, spreading from the touched parts, contains nothing *extrasubjective*, because the spread and communication of the movement experienced by the sensitive nerve differs from the impulse or kind of disturbance initially experienced by the nerve. The disturbance causes the nerve to pass from rest to excitation. This first impression or disturbance indicates that a force has been applied, while on the other hand the communication and continuation of the movement present no new disturbance or force, except that of the parts themselves of the nerve. These parts pass the movement to each other through the force they have received proper to them. But because this force passes from one part of the nerve to the other, it follows, as I have already said, that the whole sensation propagated by sympathy can be referred only to that feeling part of our body which allows movement of the parts and feeling to pass through it. The increase of the sympathetic sensation is subjective only, or at least certainly not united with the perception of an external body; it remains in the stimulated nerve as in its source and matter.

905. The special nature of the four organs must be now noted. A single particle of air vibrating in the ear could definitely not produce a sensation of sound; only the entire body of undulating air causes this sensation. In the same way, although I do not know if a single unit of light could move the visual organ, I do believe that, in order to have a sensation of colour, a certain quantity of light must act upon our eyes.

Similarly it seems to me that a sensation of taste or smell is not aroused by virtue of small, flavoured or odorous bodies but by great numbers of particles striking the taste buds and nostrils and causing such a movement that they produce a frequent, general vibration which alone occasions the sensations. If this is the case, and it seems probable to me, we can no longer say that each one of the minute acting particles must have produced some sensation of taste, smell, etc. All we can say is that each tiny body, despite its minute size, has made its impact. But this is not yet sensation. Taste, smell and other sensations begin only when the vibration along the length of the nervous membrane or cartilage has been propagated and reached the level of agitation required for the sensation to take place.

[905]

If this is the case (and it cannot be doubted relative to hearing), I believe that the four kinds of sensations would generally take place through sympathy among the parts, that is, through communication of movement. This would make the *extrasubjective* part of the sensations still more hidden and confused. We would be dealing with unobservable parts, and the sensation would be stimulated not so much by the impulse they imparted, as by the agitation following in the affected part of our body. If both impulse and consequent agitation together gave sensation, one mixed with the other would be almost indiscernible.

CHAPTER 12

Origin of the idea of bodies
through the extrasubjective perception of sight

Article 1

The eye perceives a coloured surface

906. Let us imagine a human being standing still with eyes open. Vision in this person is limited to a variously-coloured surface adhering to his eyes, without background or perspective.

Article 2

The coloured surface is a corporeal surface

907. Because body is an agent producing feeling with an extension mode, feelings located at points in space are corporeal actions. But our coloured surface is a feeling extending over a surface. It is therefore corporeal.

Article 3

The coloured surface is identical with
the light-affected surface of the retina of the eye

908. All senses are touch (cf. 744–745) and as such are subject to the laws governing touch; they differ amongst themselves only through their accidental phenomena. Our study of these phenomena showed that the sensations of our four organs possess, as a general characteristic, highly developed subjectivity with limited, confused extrasubjectivity (cf. 887–895). Such phenomena, therefore, are simply the mode of these four species of sensation; and indeed touch itself furnishes similar

phenomena (*ibid.*), although not so distinctly. Phenomena of this kind add nothing that is capable of altering the common laws to which touch in general is subject.

In touch, however, the touching surface of the external body forms a unity with the touched surface of our body. As a result, the same surface is felt simultaneously in two ways: in our body, subjectively, and as the term of perception of the external agent, extrasubjectively (cf. 841).

It is clear, therefore, that 'the coloured surface perceived by the eye is identical with the surface of the retina touched by the light.'

We have to consider carefully the fact that the eye perceives the coloured surface in the same way as touch perceives hardness and resistance in an extended body.

In corporeal vision, therefore, we must distinguish: 1. the sensation of the retina; 2. the entire confused perception of the innumerable particles of light which fill the retina in which they are spread.

Article 4

The coloured surface we perceive is as big as the retina
touched by light; but the colours are distributed
in that surface in fixed proportions

909. This extraordinary, but irrefutable truth is a corollary of the preceding affirmation.

Nevertheless, it is sometimes called in doubt as a result of inadequate observation, because of our habit of attributing to bodies perceived visually the same size that we perceive in them through touch and movement. Later I shall explain how this habit arises and show that it depends upon the judgment we add to the sensation of sight, and not upon the sensation itself.

910. For the time being, we first notice that, whatever the size of the agents perceived by the eye, the eye indubitably perceives them in a definite proportion relative to one another. For example, while my eye receives all the colours of the agents in its view, it can also receive those of another person's eye. But his pupil is perceived as considerably smaller than his body, which

in its turn is perceived as smaller than the room in which he is standing. The reason is that his pupil occupies less of my retina than his body, and his body less than the light-filled room.

The eye, therefore, perceives the *relative sizes* of bodies that are equidistant from it, although it does not perceive their absolute size.

People born blind who later gain sight can confirm these observations. In the first moments of their use of sight, they experience a sensation adhering to the retina of their eye, but no distance or real distinction of external bodies. What they perceive is a painted canvas, that is, the surface of their retina covered with varying light (cf. 811).

Article 5

The coloured surface cannot furnish the idea of solid space, even through the movement of colours taking place in space

911. We have already seen that the eye perceives movement. But any change whatsoever, taking place in the coloured surface we perceive, is reduced to change in the surface itself. The succession of coloured surfaces provides no idea of distance or depth; pictures succeed one another in the eye like the scenes offered by a magic lantern. By itself, therefore, the eye cannot form an idea of three-dimensional space.

Article 6

Colour sensations are signs of the size of things

912. So far we have supposed that only the eyes have been used, but not touch or movement, to discover what the eyes contain and what occurs in them. We have tried to find what term the eye can achieve when left to itself. We saw that, without movement or touch, a person would perceive a coloured surface adhering to his eye; it would be no larger than the retina affected by light, and would stimulate sensation (cf. 909). We also observed that in this tiny surface colours are spread out and

divided in a certain order, not haphazardly; the same can be said about the movements taking place in them. The colours are in certain proportions, corresponding precisely to the proportions in the sizes of the external things furnished by touch (*ibid.*).

The constancy of these proportions and the order maintained in the movements of the perceived colours is of great benefit in permitting the colours to act as signs by which we may learn the true sizes[194] of things, and the distances and quantities of movement in our own body.

913. Let us examine what takes place relative first to the size of external things, and then to distances and quantities of movement. External things transmit light to our eye from every point of their surface. Larger things transmit a greater number of rays which, when the things are equidistant from the pupil, cover a greater area of the pupil. Things seen at the same distance, therefore, are indicated and depicted by sizes proportionate to that which they possess in themselves.[195] The pattern of things imprinted by the light on our retina, resembles a map; its scale, although less than the reality, perfectly preserves the proportions between the parts found in reality. In the same way, external bodies are depicted in a smaller scale on our retina without changing the proportions in any way. The eye and light cooperate so well in drawing visible things on a lesser scale but in constantly equal proportion that the instruments used to reduce a larger to a smaller scale are only an imitation of what is done more perfectly by nature.

914. This example of the map is very helpful for our present purposes. When we look at a map, we pay immediate attention not to the colours or other qualities reproduced there, but to the

---

[194] That is, those provided by touch, as we have seen, and will explain more fully in the next chapter.

[195] If this theory is clearly understood, we have an answer to Molineux's question 'whether a sphere, already distinguished from a cube by touch, can be distinguished solely by sight'. The eye itself is also touch; it perceives shape just as well as touch does by hand, although with one less dimension. Thus, in the case of the sphere and cube, one of the signs impressed by the light on the retina is circular, the other rectangular. The difference between the signs is *like* the difference found by touching with the hand. Hence Leibniz's affirmative answer to the question is certain.

scale of what we see, which indicates the real size of the area depicted. In the same way, it is not the quality of the colours that provides true, immediate knowledge of what we see in the variety of colours perceived by the eye in any sensation; colour, as such, is the subjective part of sensation,[196] as we have seen. The size and proportion of the different coloured spaces is the extrasubjective part, which indicates the size of exterior things. It offers a *true likeness* of them: a small triangle or square truly resembles a large triangle or square; the proportion between a city and a house is equal to that between the two symbols, which stand for the relationship between the city and the house.[197] In the same way, the eye indicates the size of things through a *likeness* of the sensation to them, and not through their other properties.

Now, if we wish to see how we come to know the size of things from the colour sensations experienced in our eyes, we have to begin by employing our touch. Here we suppose that, with this sense and with movement, we have already perceived external bodies along with their absolute extensions and their proportions. Using touch and sight simultaneously, anyone can notice an extraordinary relationship between the parts of bodies

---

[196] Colours also indicate the qualities of things, although as the subjective part of sensation they have no *likeness* to things. But on the basis of our experience, they do serve as *signs*. The written word, for instance, is a sign of the spoken word to which it bears no resemblance, although a *portrait* is the sign of the person whom it resembles. Colours thus enable us to know innumerable things — whether fruit is ripe, whether a human being is healthy or sick, what kind of mood another person is in, to mention only a few. Yet colour bears no resemblance to ripeness, health, depression or other qualities which it indicates through an association of ideas. Experience has shown us that the colour of a particular thing is joined to its qualities, so that whenever we see the colour we immediately understand the qualities. Sensation, therefore, as *subjective* can be a sign, but not a likeness of external things; as *extrasubjective*, it is a *sign bearing a resemblance* to things.

[197] I would like to state categorically, once and for all, that I am speaking metaphorically in referring here and elsewhere to the marks formed on the eye by colours. There is no question of impressing on the eye real marks serving as objects to be seen by others, but of subjective sensations, indicated by those marks. If I want to speak of a yellow sensation of a certain size, I speak of a yellow mark —and so on for other colours. I do not want my use of figurative language, intended to facilitate the argument, to be a cause of equivocation.

perceived by touch, and the colours perceived by sight. My hand, held out to touch a body, removes a colour from my sight; every point that it touches is a spot hidden from me because my hand covers it. By repeating these experiences, I finally learn that the sensations of touch and sight are stably related to one another, and realise that a touch-sensation outside myself corresponds to every coloured point in my eye. If one of the light- marks affecting my retina is larger, my hand can move further with its touch to cover it. Touches like this are continuing perceptions of external bodies, and serve, as we have seen, as a measure of their size. Because every coloured point of the eye corresponds to the touch-perception of a body, and every more or less large light-mark corresponds constantly and proportionately with the touch-perception of different sized bodies, it must and does occur that the marks on the eye from different rays of light are sure indications and signs of external bodies and their size, which only touch perceives immediately. We thus form a habit of passing with extreme rapidity of thought from sight-sensations to persuasion about external, touchable bodies. This habit, which never ceases in us, is strengthened and developed to such an extent that we confuse and exchange the signs with what they signify and say as soon as we perceive a light-mark with the eye: 'I see a body, a touchable object,' instead of: 'I perceive a light-mark, which assures me of a touchable body outside me.'[198]

When we look at a map, we know the size of the places indicated provided we have a clear idea of the scale on which they are depicted. However, it is much easier to measure the size of things on the 'map' supplied by the eye than to recognise almost

---

[198] Notice that we never stop to consider *signs* once they are well-known and their use habitual. We go directly to the things signified which we appear to see and perceive in the signs themselves. Signs seem so identified with the things they indicate that it becomes very difficult to distinguish one from the other. Hence we say, for example, that 'we have heard some truth or other from so-and-so, an expert in his field', as though we had heard the truths themselves and not simply the words alone, which bear no resemblance whatsoever to the truths we have heard. We speak of a portrait as though the person herself had been depicted, and give it her own name, because we no longer confine our attention to the portrait. *We think the thing in its sign*; and this occurs universally in all our operations as intelligent beings.

intuitively from a topographical map the size of the area under examination. The reason is clear: our visual map is always before us and, with the help of touch to correct and test the sizes it shows, is being continually applied to various situations.

915. There is another difference between seeing a country on a map and perceiving external bodies through the perception of the retina invaded by varying colours of light-marks from the light refracted by bodies and reflected to the pupil. The map is totally separate from the country shown on it, without any lines, so to speak, tying it to the country. On the other hand, the picture in the eye has an admirable, physical connection with bodies perceived by touch: rays of light emanating from bodies join them to the impressions experienced by the eye. It is not a question, of course, of the eye being drawn outside itself by these rays of light passing from the bodies to itself, nor of its perceiving anything other than the extremities of the rays. The extremities are changed with lightning speed and accuracy by every movement in the bodies that communicate them to the eye, especially by hands touching the bodies. Because experience teaches children that they have a light-sensation for every point touched by their hands, the points of light felt by their eyes are commensurate with those touched by their hands. They are thus led to identify visual measure with that of touch by superimposing one on the other, point by point, as it were, line by line, surface by surface. Experiences of this kind, provided by nature herself, allow us to find without difficulty in the coloured light-marks of the eye, the measure itself of bodies as given through touch-perception.

916. Yet another difference between a map and its countries, and between tactile bodies and the retina speckled with colour, will help to explain the fact under consideration. The countries as such and the map are both terms of sight, one larger than the other. An external body and colours, on the other hand, are both terms of touch, but of touch in two different parts of our body. One of these parts, the pupil, is extremely delicate and far more complex than the part connected with ordinary touch. This difference has given to sight its own particular name, separating it from touch. Now as long as we are dealing with two terms of sight such as two triangles, one much larger than the other, their likeness enables one to be a sign of the other.

Nevertheless, their unequal sizes cannot be easily disregarded; there is an obvious difference between the triangles. This is not the case with the coloured surfaces perceived by the eye and the surfaces perceived by touch, both of which manifest extremely different sensible qualities. Their likeness in form and their diversity in size cannot be easily noticed without, so to speak, superimposing one on top of the other. But nature prevents this and provides instead a kind of special, deceptive superimposition so that, when our hands touch visible bodies, we seem to superimpose the apex of pyramids of light in our eye on the objects we touch. In fact, however, we superimpose the base of the pyramid which we do not perceive. What happens is that we mentally connect the apex we perceive with the base we do not perceive.

This explains why it is more difficult for us to recognise the difference in size between what is seen and touched than to believe in their equality.

Article 7

Our sight, associated with touch and movement, perceives the distances and qualities of movement of our body

917. Let us now imagine we are in motion with our eyes open.[199] The changes caused in our sight sensations by this movement consist in a constant change of colour, and change from obscurity to clarity and vice-versa. If you look from a distance at the colour and form of a great building, it will perhaps appear as an indistinguishable whitish point against the blue of a high mountain behind it. As you move towards it, the white point grows bigger and gradually takes shape as its outline becomes sharper. As you get near it, you see it in all its size. Your movement causes the points or marks of the coloured surface (the only thing your eye sees) to expand, become distinct and take shape. But these changes are in constant relationship with the different movements you make, as we have seen.

---

[199] It is the task of anthropology to explain how an animal can move in space before it has perceived space by means of its external senses.

Movement has no likeness to colour; the two are as different as taste and sound. Nevertheless, the constant relationship of colours, especially of light and shade, with movement, allows the variation of colour to present a clear sign for knowing and measuring movement itself.

918. Colours thus become a kind of language used by nature to speak to us of distance and size. This natural language is taught in the same way as the language we learn from one another.

In artificial language we use words to express ideas, although words are material sounds without any likeness to ideas, which are thoughts belonging to the spirit. Words are functional *signs* of our ideas. As soon as we hear them, force of habit brings to mind the ideas they represent. We form a single object of thought from ideas and words. This comes about because of the constant, analogical relationship we have created between things which differ as greatly as ideas and articulate sounds; it is this relationship which enables words to function as we have described. The same thing takes place with colours as a result of light and shade. They become quasi-words indicating the distance of things from us, and the movement carried out or required to approach things; they are analogous to what they signify.

Another likeness will help to explain more easily the perception of distance by the eye, or rather by animal perspicacity. Colours impressed upon our retina can be considered equivalent to letters of the alphabet which I write on paper but have no similarity, or even material resemblance, with the sounds called words caused by use of my speech organ as it sends out variations in air-waves. Nevertheless, despite the lack of similarity, the written curves and strokes and dots and crosses call forth words and ideas for the reader through the constant relationship, partly arbitrary and partly analogous, between the ink marks and the sounds indicating ideas. This relationship is a rule according to which thought passes with extreme rapidity from the perception of writing on paper to what the writer wished to convey.

The same is true of colours and movement. Although they have no natural resemblance, their analogous relationship enables us to use colours as signs for knowing and measuring movement, as an animal does with its natural instinct.

919. Just as we have to learn from society how to speak and write, so we have to learn from nature how to discern distance and movement with the eye.[200] After learning the art of reading distance with the eye, and the use of colours as signs of movement, we gradually perfect our habit of interpreting the signs until we think that with sight we see distance immediately and measure the movement needed to travel it. The truth is, however, that we never see anything with our eye except a surface, although the speed with which we unite the idea of extension in depth to the various colours of this surface is such that the surface finally escapes our attention. We then believe we see depth immediately, just as a reader thinks he perceives the words immediately, or a listener thinks he receives images and ideas with ears that perceive only words.

Article 8

Smell, hearing and taste compared with sight

920. These three species of sensation cannot be signs as precise and general as colours enabling us to know the presence and distance of bodies, because smells, tastes and sounds do not mark off for us a corporeal surface as distinct and as continuous as that provided by the eye. Instead, they offer indistinct, changeable, perfectly homogeneous and uniform corporeal

---

[200] Accurate observation is needed of the time required by children to learn the connection of the size furnished by the eyes and that coming from touch and distance. It should be noted that such a connection can be obtained in two ways, instinctively and intellectually. Hence, perceiving the proportions between these sizes depends upon educating: 1. the *sensitivity*, which takes place in animals also; and 2. the *understanding*, which is proper to human beings. Sensitivity learns about the connection practically through associations of *sensations, phantasms, feelings, instincts and habits*, all of which in human beings are accompanied by judgments. Experiments with children should help to distinguish the progress of each of these faculties, but this is extremely difficult. Cabanis claims to have seen a deranged boy totally incapable of knowing distances by his sight alone, although his eyes were perfectly healthy (*Rapports du physique et du moral de l'homme, etc.*, Mem. 2). If this is true, the boy must have been defective in his animal instinct as well as in intellect.

points. Moreover, because the normal objects of touch do not have the same relationship with the ears, palate and nostrils as with the eye, these sensations cannot be authenticated, as it were, by touch.

921. However, hearing does furnish a variety of sensations which, although without the intimate connection of colours to touch, are governed by fixed, simple laws which enable such sensations to be available for the formation of language. As the eye becomes a natural, although limited, language through touch (things seem to speak to us directly through ordered colours), so hearing offers a means for the discovery of a universal language.

CHAPTER 13

The criterion of bodily size and shape

Article 1

The criterion of the size of bodies
is the size perceived by touch

922. When we wish to know if a thing is true or false, we have to compare it with the genuine, certain notion of the same thing. The power we possess of perceiving a thing immediately, rather than its sign or image, is that which gives us this genuine, certain notion or essence.

We have already seen that extension is a mode of the fundamental feeling.[201] Hence the fundamental feeling is a power whose immediate term is not only matter, but also extension. It is the fundamental feeling, therefore, that gives genuine, certain extension, and with it the first measure of every size.

923. But the extension of the fundamental feeling is partly commensurate with extension (cf. 841).

As a result, touch also furnishes the genuine, certain size of bodies and, because of the impossibility of an immediate application of the measure provided by the fundamental feeling, becomes in fact the measure used.

924. On the contrary, the eye and other senses, in so far as they differ from touch: 1. do not perceive immediately the size of distant things; 2. do not perceive their distance, but only signs of distance. The size of things presented by the eye has to be compared and rectified with that given by touch. If sight is not to be the source of error for us, we must continually relate the size we see to that offered by touch. This is the fixed measure provided by nature for comparison and emendation of visual size.

---

[201] The philosopher who declared our body to be the measure of all things would have made a truly remarkable affirmation if he had confined his assertion to the size of spaces and bodies.

[922–924]

Article 2

Application of our criterion to illusions about the visible size of things

925. We are used to making very rapid judgments as soon as we receive sight-sensations. We take these sensations as signs, but because they allow us to discern almost automatically the size of bodies, we also seem to perceive size itself through sight.

This false judgment is made by practically everyone, and it would not be out of place to call it a common-sense error [*App.*, no. 36].

Errors of this kind lead to research which becomes entirely superfluous once the error has been dissipated. Let me give an example of such a pointless inquiry. With my eyes open, I can behold immense vistas. Amongst many other things making up the panorama, I catch sight of another person, dwarfed in comparison with the rest of the scene. His two eyes are tinier members of a tiny body. In each of them I notice a little black hole behind which is stretched a small, delicate and extremely sensitive background, called a retina, where light carries out its marvellous task of stimulation. On this very restricted backdrop which forms the final clothing of his eye, the other person sees me and everything else, just as I, in a similar, small, nerve-sensitive space, see him and everything else — earth, sky and immense universe. Nevertheless my eye, which sees the other person's eye, or itself in a mirror, tells me that the screen receiving the colours of so many things is no broader than a tiny line, although the things depicted in it appear immensely greater than it. How can it receive such vision? Does it deceive me by showing me objects of an immense size, when the impression it receives is so small?

The difficulty vanishes totally if we keep in mind that, as we have shown above, the eye perceives neither size nor distance, but only their signs from which the mind with a rapid judgment passes to conceive distance, while the animal acts with the shrewdness of habitual instinct as though it had conceived distance.

Signs do not have to be of the same nature and measure as the things they indicate. They enable us to know size provided we know the proportion between the size of the signs and that of the things. In the case of the eye, we know this proportion habitually because through touch we grasp the real size of things and form a habit of comparing them with the apparent size administered by the eye.

926. Another possible difficulty merits every attention. The eye is also an organ of touch, and light really touches it. Why can we not apply the law of touch to the eye? This law states that when we size up a body with our hand, which is a very suitable instrument of touch-sensations, we measure the body with the hand itself, using it as a basic unit superimposed upon the body to make the comparison. In this superimposed touch we have distinguished the sensation in the hand from the perception of the external body, and have already seen that the extension of the sensation in the hand is the measure of the extension of the body that has contact with the hand. Hence the *subjective* sensation of our own body is the measure of *extrasubjective* perception, that is, of the external agent compared in such an operation with our body. We apply this law to our eye touched by particles of light. In this case, our eye will have: 1. a *subjective* sensation of different parts of the retina as touched by light rays of varying breadth; 2. an *extrasubjective* perception of the particles of light. It will measure what acts upon it with the extension of *subjective* sensation, that is, the thinnest rays of light, or at least the extension of the bundles of rays that work like artists' brushes upon the screen of the eye. If we now confine our attention to the sensation of sight considered as touch, we cannot avoid noting the smallness of the depicted images and realising that they are smaller than the small aperture of the eye which is, as it were, the general scene or picture whose various parts are obviously smaller than the whole. Noting, as we must, the smallness of the images received in the eye, we must also feel the proportion they have with the eye itself. It is true that these tiny images can be signs of the true, tactile size of things, after we have learned to use our touch, just as the marks on a map are signs of the size of a territory when we know the scale of the map, but this does not weaken the validity of our first knowledge, through which we compared the little images in the eye with the eye itself and, like every other object of touch, measured them with the eye

[926]

according to their own, real size. Nevertheless, we have no inkling of this in our experience.

927. The difficulty may be solved as follows. The marks in the eye should not be called *images* until we have noted, through touch, that the colours impressed upon the eye are signs of external bodies. Only touch can tell us this. Because the colours tinting the eye form only light-marks which do not of themselves signify or represent anything, they are neither images nor signs for us prior to the use of touch. But the simultaneous use of touch and sight enables us to discover the constant relationship between the size furnished by touch and that provided by the marks in the eye. Because these marks vary as bodies vary to the touch, they become signs for us, and appear true images of bodies.[202]

Although the eye, of itself, perceives only sensations or, as I have called them, certain colour-marks felt only in the retina, the use of touch allows these marks or sensations to function as signs of distant things and to acquire a new state or, better, relationship with us through which we consider them totally different from what they were previously. In fact they seem to take on another nature.

The *marks* or sensations on the retina, therefore, and the visual *images* are the same thing, as far as their own being is concerned, but two things as seen by us. In other words, when we consider the sensation as a mark felt in the eye, and as an image of something external, our attention is brought to bear on two entirely opposite terms: first, upon the *mark* we feel, that is, the sensation in the retina; second, upon the mark as *image*, when we move on directly to the thing represented and consider it as the only term of attention, without resting in the sign. Thus when a person sees a portrait of a friend, he thinks immediately of his friend without stopping to examine the picture in its own being. He ignores the canvas, types of paint, and other elements that compose it. This is possible because the mark felt in the eye is changed into an image through the intervention of touch and, as an image, immediately stimulates our attention to move well away from the portrait in its search for the object of which the

---

[202] I say *appear*, because their only likeness with external things lies in their *extrasubjective* element.

mark is an image. But we cannot understand this most important fact without practical conviction of the supremely important distinction between *sensation* and *advertence* to sensation
upon which we could say the whole of philosophical knowledge rests.[203]

928. The law governing advertence is as follows: 'That which
we advert to is the term of our intellective attention.'
Advertence of something arises in us when our attention moves
towards and terminates in the thing in such a way that it
becomes the final object of our attention. The intermediate
links through which our attention and thought pass without
making the links their *term*, are perceived fleetingly, but not
adverted to. If we want to advert to them, we have to turn back
and pass rapidly over the road we have taken so that the links
we have previously ignored may become terms of our attention.
We *advert*, therefore, to that which involves and terminates our
act of attention; the many other things we feel and perceive
remain outside our attention and inadverted.

In our present case, when the sensations experienced in the
retina of the eye have acquired the quality and state of images,
they cannot of themselves be terms of our attention because, as
we have said above, images of their nature draw us outside
themselves by becoming guides directing our attention to what
they represent. An image provides a special relationship between two things, one of which serves as a scale or means for
directing our thought to the other; an image, as such, moves our
attention from the nature of the thing acting as image towards
the object represented, which then becomes the term of attention. The sensation on our eye, once it has become a sign and
quasi-image of external things, no longer holds our attention
and advertence, but directs it to another term. Thus the sensation itself remains unobserved and inadverted.

[203] Depending upon circumstances, I call advertence: *observation, attention, consideration* and *awareness*. All these words express an intellective act,
fixed upon a sensation, which forms an idea and adverts to the sensation.
Galluppi states correctly that ideas are formed by *meditation* on sensations,
but does not tell us the nature of this meditation, reflection, or action of the
understanding. It can only be the application of a universal idea to sensations
(cf. 482–489); without this, *meditation* has no meaning and *reflection* is
inexplicable.

929. Another consideration may be added: 'Our advertence is attracted more easily by distinct than by confused perceptions.' If we now ask what makes sense perception distinct or confused, we find three obvious reasons for its heightened clarity. Our sense perception is more distinct when bodies perceived by sense are: 1. fewer in number; 2. of sufficient size to be grasped in their entirety; 3. more stable in the forms they present to sense. But particles of light are innumerable, incalculably small, perpetually mobile, and as such capable of providing only a vivid, but altogether confused perception as they simultaneously strike the retina. Moreover, when we perceive a body in a confused manner, we seem scarcely to perceive it at all, and often say, for example, that we perceive nothing if all that we see are spaces of air illuminated by uniform light.

On the other hand, our touch-perception is by nature extremely distinct, a characteristic it shares with the vivid signs of perception furnished by the eye. These signs are quite different amongst themselves, and possess extraordinary definition in their minuteness. Consequently, while we advert scarcely, if at all,[204] to the immediate perception of particles of light and their variety in the sensations on our eye, we pay great attention to observing the bodies furnished by touch in so far as the sight-sensations signify them to us. Observing bodies in this way is immensely useful in life's daily contingencies and far removed from pointless consideration of light-marks in our eyes.

Article 3

Application of the criterion to visual illusion about the distance of things

930. If objects delineated by light in the pupil are at different

---

[204] I say 'scarcely, if at all', rather than 'not at all', because everyone can notice some sensation in the eyes. We feel light falling upon our eyes, and find quite a difference in our pupils when we close our eyes. But, as I said, we do not advert to what takes place in our eyes when we have so many beautiful things to look at.

distances, they do not maintain their proportional size; more distant objects send a smaller image to the eye, and closer objects a larger image. This is due to the converging rays of light; the more distant their point of departure, the more acute the angle at which they strike the eye and arouse a sensation. The result is a smaller vestige of the object on the eye than there should be. This kind of delusion must not, however, be attributed to the sensation which, as such, tells us nothing of the object. It is the judgment made by our mind that deceives us as we infer the size of exterior bodies from the sensation of light taken as a sign.

931. But this error also is soon corrected. The images coming to us from various distances follow another kind of proportion which serves to distinguish the distances themselves. Apparent size now becomes a sure sign and measure of the distances of bodies in so far as the image in the eye increases in size as the distance diminishes, and vice-versa. Apparent sizes and their distances bear a constant inverse proportion to one another. The constancy of this proportion is the foundation of the art of perspective.

Spontaneous movement and touch indicate true distances. Habitual observation enables us to know the relationship between the apparent size of bodies, and their distance measured by touch and movement. We then learn to pass with great speed from one to the other, and to note immediately, from the apparent size, the distances of bodies from one another, at least approximately.

If we stand at the end of a long drive of trees, we see an apparent decrease in the size of the trees on both sides. It is this which makes us aware of the ever-greater distance of the trees from one another, and finally of the distance between the last and the first trees.

Once I have become used to relating the height of the trees to their distance I no longer err. Decreasing size becomes for me the effect of distance and nothing else. I amend the disproportion of apparent height, and by mentally positioning the trees at the same distance, I know that they are of the same height (granted they are in fact equal).

[931]

Article 4

Application of the criterion to illusions
about the position of things

932. Although light imprints bodies on our eyes upside down, we see them right way up because this reversal of the seen bodies is not and cannot be in contradiction with the various parts of the images themselves, nor with touch-perceptions. It contradicts only the fundamental feeling by which we feel the eye, and the modification of the fundamental feeling by which we feel our eye subjectively.

933. First of all, I note that if I perceive a bodily image upside down, the different parts of the image do not contradict the perception. The eye, by fixing its attention only on the image, cannot perceive that it is upside down.

In fact, when I turn a vase, for example, upside down, I notice its new position only through the relationship it has with the surrounding bodies which remain right way up. But let us assume that all the surrounding bodies, and we ourselves, are turned upside down in the whole image without any relative change of parts. In this case, it would be impossible for us to become aware of the new position of the vase and ourselves. No other body would remain to serve as a sign with which we could compare the change in our body. As we have seen, movement cannot be felt of itself, but only through the relationship between bodies which have been moved and perceived by us. The rotation of the earth, inverting us each day, proves the point. We have to discover this inversion through reason rather than through feeling because of the fixed position of our bodies relative to other things. The same is true about our eye. Whatever position images take in our eye, whether they are the right way up or upside down, it could never be recognised by the sense of sight alone. The images revolve together and retain their natural proportions while we ourselves, as seen, revolve with everything else. In our eye the whole world revolves, and because there is no change or contradiction between the different parts of the visual image, it is impossible to notice the inversion of particular bodies through the upside down position of their images; if the eye changes the images, everything changes together. It is like our incapacity for feeling or noticing the inversion resulting from the daily rotation of the world.

934. All the eye can do is to notice things upright, that is, in their true, natural positions relative to one another; even touch itself cannot give us any indication of the eye's upside down view of things. The position of the images on the eye, whatever it may be, cannot be in contradiction with the position of bodies felt by touch. The eye sees the relative position of bodies as it is; touch also senses the same relative position, and nothing else. For example, what is positioned above my head (this relationship establishes the position of things) is there whether I perceive it by sight or by touch. This is true whether I am standing upright, lying down, or standing on my head: the things around me remain in the same position relative to my eyes and hands. There can be no contradiction, therefore, between the position indicated by sight and by touch whatever direction may be proffered by the images traced on the sensitive 'screen' of the eye.

935. This is not the case relative to the fundamental feeling and the acquired sensation which makes us perceive the sensitive 'screen' of the eye. Here the images do contradict the position of bodies as it is given by touch. Let us suppose that an image is felt adhering to our eye so that we have an image-perception joined to the sensation of the whole eye and superimposed upon the retina. This is what takes place in touch-sensation, which is always twofold because it is superimposed upon the felt surface of the hand that touches the surface of the exterior body so that one measures the other. In our supposition, I would feel the image upside down in my eye, which simply means that its position is opposite to the position of my eye. If I were now to have in my eye the image of another eye, the latter would be upside down with the eyebrows underneath, relative to my eyebrows which hold the opposite position, that is, above. If then the tiny eye depicted in my pupil were perceived by me immediately by touch, it would be an *extrasubjective* perception opposed, as far as position was concerned, to the *subjective* perception of my eye. Why, therefore, do I not notice this contradiction between the *subjective* and *extrasubjective* parts in sight-sensation?

936. The difficulty is completely resolved by my observations

[934–936]

on sight-sensation in the preceding Article. I observed that
when the eye is considered as touch, that is, as a sense that perceives colours immediately, we can no longer rightly speak of it
as perceiving *images* but only colour-*marks*. Now as long as we
consider colours perceived by the eye in themselves, without
reference to their nature as *signs*, their position upon our eye
means nothing to us. Consequently, reflecting on them relative
to the position of the eye itself must be extremely difficult, if not
impossible.

Moreover, when the colour-marks have changed into images,
we no longer give them any attention, as we said. We use our
eyes continually for the sole purpose of knowing exterior bodies, not for knowing what happens in our eyes. As a result of
this continual attention to external objects that we see, we are
incapable of concentrating our attention on the eye and on the
change that it undergoes.

937. In the second place, although the extrasubjective light-
sensation is strong, it is still not easy for us to measure the size
of the very restricted subjective sensation. Furthermore, it is
impossible to advert to its position relative to our sentient eye.
In fact, to know and advert to one position of the image relative
to my eye rather than another, I must: 1. note the position of the
colour-mark; 2. note and advert to the position of my eye; 3.
compare these positions; 4. note which parts of the mark represent to me the extremities of the external thing; 5. note and
advert that the part of the mark representing the top extremity
of the external thing corresponds to the low part of the eye, and
vice-versa. All these operations are extremely difficult, and
probably impossible. To avoid an endless task, it would be well
for me to comment only on the difficulty of the third step,
where the position of the colour-mark is compared with the
position of my eye. I feel this position with my fundamental
feeling alone, and feel the position of the mark with the acquired
sensation. We have already seen how difficult it is to advert to
the fundamental feeling, and this difficulty would be compounded if we had to advert to the relative position of the parts
felt in the fundamental feeling with the clarity, distinction[205] and

[205] I also think it altogether impossible to advert distinctly in the
fundamental feeling to the *relative* position of its parts without the help of

[937]

firmness needed to compare it with the position of adventitious sensations or of the colour-marks we are discussing.

938. Everything I have said explains why I cannot agree with those ideologists who say we first see things upside down and then turn them the right way up. On the contrary, we always see things the right way up and cannot see them any other way. As far as I can understand, it is impossible, even with the most acute advertence, to succeed in noting through sight alone the following extraordinary fact: 'When we take the shape of the sensation as a sign of the external body, the lowest point of the sensation in our eye indicates the highest point of the external thing, and vice-versa' [*App.*, no. 37].

Article 5

The criterion of the shape of bodies is their shape
as perceived by touch

939. Touch, united with spontaneous movement, perceives extension immediately (cf. 837–875).

Hence it is this sense that perceives the limits of extension, size, shape.[206]

It follows that the shape of things perceived by touch and movement is the criterion against which to compare the shape ministered by sight.

acquired sensations. Can one say, in fact, that the fundamental feeling has clearly distinguishable parts?

[206] Space does not change shape for the same reason that it does not change size. Two different shapes are only two independent pieces of space. One space, therefore, can never be transformed into another. A shape in space cannot rightly be said to change into another. If succeeded by another, it is not what it was. The second is an altogether new shape, not the first transformed.

Article 6

Errors about the shape and size of bodies occasioned by sight

940. Light enables us to perceive distant bodies because they refract and reflect it to us in such a way that its modifications are proportioned to the size, shape, distance and other qualities or conditions of the bodies themselves.

But rays of light can be deviated or altered as they pass from bodies to ourselves if they meet something on the way, or can become accidentally united. In these cases, the impression they give does not correspond to the shape we already know and use as a faithful guide to judge the bodies, which we now judge falsely because the light does not faithfully present them. Hence such optical illusions as branches bent in water, or pebbles appearing as rocks in very cold climates where the condensed air acts as a magnifying glass, and other mistakes discovered and corrected by touch.

CHAPTER 14

The extrasubjective perception of bodies by means of the five senses considered in their mutual relationship

Article 1

The identity of space unites different sensations, so that one body is perceived

941. Sensations of smell and taste have a very confused extra-subjective perception and consequently cannot serve as signs indicating distant bodies. The distinct perception of distant bodies comes from the differences we perceive in their size and shape. Smell and taste particles striking the relevant organs do not follow any law of proportion to the size and shape of external things. However they do help in some way. We habitually note, for example, that the scent of a flower disappears when the flower is taken away. The scent becomes for us an *indication* of the fragrant object which it recalls because the scent-sensation is associated with the idea of the body also known through touch and sight. Although taste and smell are not by nature signs indicating bodies present to our touch, artificially they can become signs indicating anything or any thought.

942. The same can be said about sounds which, however, lend themselves far more effectively to intelligent use in the formation of languages.

943. Sight-sensations on the other hand are arranged and ordered harmoniously by nature itself, as we have seen. Consequently they become signs, not of anything whatsoever or any thought, which demands ingenuity,[207] but of external bodies perceived by touch.

This occurs because of the relationship of the different sizes and shapes of sight-sensations with tactile bodies and their

---

[207] By means of writing, human ingenuity indicates all human thoughts through sensations of sight and in this way gives hearing to the deaf, so to speak, and speech to the dumb.

distances. The proportional sizes and shapes of sight-sensations represent perfectly the size and shape of bodies we can touch but, through long habit, are no longer considered as signs of the sizes and shapes presented by touch. Instead, they become one with them and take their place. In this way the sizes and shapes given by sight become the space itself occupied by distant, external things. But various colours depict these signs and shapes which, if considered as external bodies, necessitate the projection also of the colours to outside objects. In a word, the coloured signs of the sizes and shapes received in our eye are taken as the sizes and shapes of the external things themselves, so that we consider as coloured the sizes and shapes of the external things we touch.

944. As a result we are not satisfied with calling the impressions on our eye signs of external things or signs indicating something. We prefer to call them *images*, as if the light, on bringing colours into our eye, first looked at the bodies and then, like a painter making a portrait, chose from them various tints, shadings and outlines to make its own creation.

Article 2

Our attention is chiefly engaged
by the visual perception of bodies

945. After we have formed the habit of judging distant bodies by their colours so that bodies and colours can be reduced to the same space to form one thing (as far as we are concerned) (cf. 941–943), visual perception becomes attractive, pleasant, rapid, helpful, clear,[208] precise. It also attracts our attention much more than the immediate perception of bodies by feeling or touch and movement. We are so occupied with our visual perception that we no longer think about other ways of perceiving bodies, persuading ourselves that we know everything by our sight alone.

---

[208] Sometimes it provides us with a sensation that we notice and distinguish more easily than touch. Touching a delicate rose petal can give us such a weak sensation that we do not distinguish it from the feeling in our fingers, although our eye notices the petal straightaway.

What we cannot see, we do not know, and even touch-perception becomes blind and cumbersome for us.

946. Not only the mass of people but thinkers are subject to this error. Philosophers, who do not suddenly cease being ordinary people, allow themselves to be so charmed by the clarity and attraction of sight that they reduce all their arguments about perception and cognition of bodies to this single sense.

This is not my observation; it is Stewart's. He says:

> In considering the phenomena of perception, it is natural to suppose that the attention of philosophers would be directed, in the first instance, to the sense of seeing. The variety of information and of enjoyment we receive by it; the rapidity with which this information and enjoyment are conveyed to us; and above all, the intercourse it enables us to maintain with the more distant part of the universe, cannot fail to give it, even in the apprehension of the most careless observer, a pre-eminence over all our other perceptive faculties. Hence it is, that the various theories which have been formed to explain the operations of our senses, have a more immediate reference to that of seeing; and that the great part of metaphysical language, concerning perception in general, appears evidently, from its etymology, to have been suggested by the phenomena of vision. This kind of language, even when applied to this sense, indeed, can at most amuse the fancy, without conveying any precise knowledge; but, when applied to the other senses, it is altogether absurd and unintelligible.[209]

947. By describing our perceptions of bodies through the sense of sight, we are using *metaphorical*, not proper language.[210] The result is infinite errors and any number of useless,

[209] *Éléments de la Philosophie de l'Esprit humain*, c. 1, sect. 1.

[210] Because metaphysical expressions taken from the sense of sight and applied to the other senses are used universally, the difficulty of guarding against this common vice of philosophical language is so great that I would be afraid of asserting that I myself have not sometimes made similar inexact statements. I will simply note an expression of Galluppi who was certainly not ignorant of the danger and falsity of expressions taken from sight and applied to the action of the other senses. He calls 'intuition' the perception of bodies carried out equally by all the senses (*Critica della conoscenza etc.*, vol. 2, §71). The use of the word 'intuition' to explain the immediate perception

inexplicable problems which, when the language is corrected, disappear as rapidly as empty superstitions in the minds of people who are receiving religious instruction [*App.*, no. 38].

Article 3

Whether sensation gives us the species of corporeal things, or we perceive things themselves

948. Aristotle and the scholastics said that we do not perceive things themselves but their likenesses, stamped on our organs and then received into our spirit by means of the organs.

I believe that these likenesses or sensible species originate from the above-mentioned errors, that is, from applying to sensitivity in general what happens solely in our sense of sight.

If these philosophers had carefully analysed the action of each sense, they would not have made common to all the other senses, what is proper to the most noble and beautiful sense. Each sense would have been described by words proper and adapted to it.

According to their analysis, only touch, out of the five senses,[211] perceives bodies immediately.

But we have also seen that the senses of sight, hearing, smell and taste manifest two very different functions. The first is that they are all touch: they make us perceive immediately the bodies touching them. These bodies, although minute and innumerable, leave a lively but confused perception of themselves. The second function of these particular senses is totally different: it arises because we use the sensations brought to us by the touch-function of these senses as *signs* to know other external bodies situated at a distance from these organs. The sense of sight by its nature performs this function much better than the other senses.

of bodies by all our senses seems just as inappropriate as saying that our eye perceives bodies by means of rays of light.

[211] I say 'five senses' because the first perception of a body is made with our fundamental feeling. This perception is not only immediate but makes us perceive corporeal nature at a deeper level than any other perception, as I have explained.

Sensations of sight, as signs indicating distant bodies, can be very suitably called *species* or *visual species* so as not to confuse them with ideas. The word itself, *species*, means in Latin *sight, look, aspect.*

949. However, as I said, these *species* of bodies furnished by the eye are not full likenesses of bodies. They present an element of a body (surfaces), not the body itself (solidity).[212] Relative to colour, they are a cause of deception because they make non-existent surfaces appear as coloured, and thus are commonly called *images*, as I have said.

950. Although the surface of bodies is not the full likeness of the bodies themselves, it is more than a purely arbitrary sign, as I said. It contains a vestige and even a true but partial likeness of external bodies 1. in the perception of a corporeal *force* (the first element of body); 2. in the proportional *extension* (the second element of body); 3. in the *shape* similar to the surface of external bodies; and 4. in other tactile qualities, such as *hardness, roughness, smoothness, softness*, etc., which are the effect of the force distributed differently in the extension.

Furthermore, a very close bond between similar species and the external body is given by nature and formed by the continuous rays of light, which I have already explained.

[212] The perception of bodies by sight is always completed by *habitual judgments* or *associations of ideas*. When I see a portrait, I see only a surface, but this surface not only recalls the surface of the person in the portrait; I also seem to see the person herself alive and complete. I immediately recall in the likeness the full idea of the person; I seem to be talking with her here and now. All the solidity, as it were, of the person (body, soul, learning, habits, virtues) is recalled by a single act. I inadvertently add everything, as soon as I see the outline, with which I have always associated many ideas. These associations accompany the use of touch as well as use of the eye, because a single touch often makes me think of the whole of a solid together with the qualities I know it has.

Article 4
Reid mistakenly denies all sensible species in the perception of bodies

951. Aristotle erred when he made *sensible species*, which are proper only to the sense of sight, the same for all the senses.[213]

Reid denied all *sensible species* and fell into the opposite error. Aristotle made what is proper to sight alone common to all the senses: bodies were known through species. Reid made what is proper to touch alone common to all the senses: bodies are perceived directly, without *species* or likenesses.

Article 5
Reid's distinction between sensation and perception

952. Reid removed all *sensible species* from the perception of bodies and in their place analysed the way we arrive at the sensible knowledge of bodies. The apparent result was his distinction between *sensation* and *perception*. Although I have already

---

[213] The impropriety of applying the words 'sensible species' to sensations different from sight seems to me inexcusable. However if the im- propriety is removed, the two apparently contradictory propositions, 'Touch perceives bodies directly' and 'We perceive bodies by touch through likenesses' can be true. The first is true in the sense that bodies act directly on our organs. We therefore perceive their direct action, which is the essence through which we know them (bodies are known only through their action). Hence we perceive directly the essence we call body. The second is true in the following sense: the action of external bodies is a modification of our own body. This modification gives a sensation which terminates in an extension. In this extended sensation we perceive the external body in its likeness. These two ways of speaking, which can be used in a discussion on touch- perception, is founded on the double nature (subjective-extrasubjective) of sensation, which I have already explained. The double nature does not exclude a constant, necessary union between the two elements which give rise to sensation. However, although both propositions have their truth, the second could not be applied to the perception we have of our body through the fundamental feeling. This feeling is not known to us by any kind of likeness, although it can make itself a likeness of external bodies in the way I have explained.

dealt with this distinction of Reid's, I will examine it more closely. He describes it in the following passage:

> When I smell a rose, there is in this operation both *sensation* and *perception*. The agreeable odour I feel, considered by itself, without relation to any external object, is merely a *sensation*. It affects the mind in a certain way and this affection of the mind may be conceived, without a thought of the rose, or any other object. This sensation can be nothing else than it is meant to be. Its very essence consists in being felt; and when it is not felt, it is not... It is for this reason that we before observed that, in sensation, there is no object distinct from that act of the mind by which it is felt.[214]

He also tells us that whenever he considers sensation in this way, that is, separately from *perception* of the external object, he considers it abstractly.[215]

This way of speaking could make us believe that *sensation* is not really separate from Reid's *perception*. In abstraction, we mentally separate in some way things which cannot be thought as separate without contradiction [*App.*, no. 39].

But this is not the case. According to Reid, the power governing *perception*, a mysterious potency totally different from *sensitivity*, differs from the potency governing *sensation*. It is a kind of natural *suggestion* (as he calls it when describing perception) which posits the existence of the external object we sense. It seems certain therefore that he is speaking of a real distinction between *sensation* and *perception*.

Article 6

Galluppi improves Scottish philosophy

953. Galluppi noted a defect in Reid's distinction. If it were true, as Reid thought, that we *perceive* bodies with a potency different from that by which we receive *sensations* and without

---

[214] *Essay on the Powers of the Human Mind, etc.*, Essay 2, c. 14.
[215] *Recherches sur l'Entendement humain, etc.*, c. 2, sect. 1.

any knowable bond with *sensation*, scepticism about our cognitions of bodies would be inevitable. If, when we receive sensations, a law of nature forced upon us the persuasion of the existence of bodies without any other reason, the persuasion would be blind. This unique, arbitrary belief would be a pure fact justified by nothing.

Galluppi therefore rejected Reid's real distinction between *sensation* and *perception*, regarding it as a pure abstraction.[216] For him, the perception of bodies was included in sensation. He granted the direct connection of our spirit with external bodies but considered this connection *essential*, not *arbitrary*, as Reid claimed.

In Galluppi's system the objective and subjective elements are, in his own words, two relatives forming one single thing in sensation:

> The object of perception is a necessary condition for perception. The objects of our primal perceptions are concrete things, that is, modified subjects. Every sensation is by its nature the perception of an external subject. The connection between sensation and an external object is not that of causality; it is also the essential connection of perception and its object. Moreover, this connection is not that between a representation and the thing represented. According to me therefore sensation is *intuition*[217] of the object.[218]

---

[216] He says: 'In sensation, our act of consciousness distinguishes the internal modification from the subject felt as something outside us. Many subjects outside us are therefore *objective*. Consciousness isolates and distinguishes these from what is *subjective*, but does not isolate the modifications of external realities from sensation. This gives rise to *appearances*' (*Saggio filosofico sulla critica della Conoscenza*, vol. 2, c. 6, §114).

[217] Cf. *intuition* in footnote 210.

[218] *Saggio filosofico sulla critica della Coscienza* [*Conoscenza*], vol. 2, §71.

Article 7

The contribution to Galluppi's theory
of the foregoing analysis of sensation

954. Although Reid affirmed the direct communication of our spirit with external bodies,[219] he found it inexplicable.

Galluppi, who made a better analysis of sensation, found that the perception of bodies was already contained in sensation. This was his solution to Reid's difficulty concerning the connection or communication between sensation and the perception of bodies.

My analysis of sensation shows that if Reid had exaggerated the separation between perception of bodies and sensation, Galluppi had exaggerated their union by maintaining that the perception of an external body was included in the intimate nature itself of sensation.

955. It is true that a close bond exists between sensation and the perception of an external body. But the connection does not come from the nature of sensation or from feeling in general; it comes from the special nature of acquired sensations.

We have shown that the fundamental feeling[220] exists before all acquired sensations. The soul is united to the body by means of a wonderful bond, an intermingling, so to speak, called *life*, and it diffuses the feeling of life into the extension of the whole sensitive body, called its matter. Because an external sensation is a modification of this first feeling and cannot be thought without it, the contrary claim that *myself* and its animal feeling depend for their existence upon an external sensation, is not true.

---

[219] A serious defect of Reid is his failure to see in what this direct communication consists. I said it was in *sensations*, but he talks about intellective acts which apprehend bodies directly. Not even Galluppi is entirely free from this error, an error which reveals his sensism.

[220] It might be asked whether *myself*, considered alone, contains passivity, and therefore perception. The answer to this question would necessitate analysis of *myself*, which is outside the purpose of this work. If, however, such an analysis were to reveal passivity and perception, it would not concern the perception of external bodies we are discussing. The present argument does not seek to establish generally 'that sensation can be deprived of all perception', but 'that sensation or feeling can exist without the perception of external bodies'.

956. We can now indicate how, and with what limitations, external sensations are joined to the perception of bodies.

Touch gives an immediate communication with external bodies. The four senses of sight, hearing, smell and taste, in so far as they are touch, give an immediate communication with their own stimuli, that is, with the minute particles affecting them. The sense of sight (and proportionately the other three senses, as we have explained) indicates distant bodies that do not touch it. It has no immediate communication with them but makes them known by means of signs or *sensible species*.

957. We cannot say that the senses, even as touch and proffering an immediate communication with bodies, fully perceive bodies themselves. They perceive only certain corporeal elements, two of which are force and surface extension.[221] To complete the perception of a body, *solidity* or extension in three dimensions must be added, or at least the possibility or expectation of finding new tangible surfaces, according to a fixed law. Touch itself, joined to movement, discovers and perceives new surfaces within the given space and thus an *expectation* arises in us of being able to discover new surfaces according to the same law. In this way the sense perception of external bodies is completed.

958. Of itself, therefore, the sensation of touch does not give a full, complete perception of bodies. It perceives some corporeal elements and should more correctly be called, as we have said, *corporeal perception* rather than perception of bodies. But it is completed through an association of many touch-sensations.

959. In this sense, it would not be out of place to say that we perceive bodies by means of certain traces or impressions that they leave in us as the inchoate perception we have of bodies.

960. Although this *corporeal perception* comes immediately from bodies, it is nevertheless in us, in our sensation, an effect of bodies upon us. Because our sensation is characterised by a *passivity* which extends to the whole *surface* encompassed by the immediate sensation, it makes us aware of this passivity, that is, indicates something outside us. To be aware of the surface in

---

[221] The *fundamental feeling* of our body is the only way we feel a solid body completely, that is, our own; in itself, no external sensation does the same.

344 A New Essay concerning the Origin of Ideas

which the passivity is diffused is to be aware that whatever is outside us is *extended*. In fact, as long as we are thinking of the external body acting on us, its extension and that of our sensation are identical; thus there is an immediate communication between the body and us. But once the body has been removed (even by abstraction), it is the extension of the sensation that gives us the extension of the body. Considered separately, then, the sensation becomes a *likeness* of the body because it has an equal extension. In this sense we can say that we know bodies by means of *likenesses* that they leave in our senses or in our imagination. This proposition can thus be reconciled with that which says we communicate immediately with the external world through the senses, although it is dangerous to use it without some kind of explanation.

CHAPTER 15

The relationship between intellective and sense perceptions of bodies

Article 1

The distinction between intellective perceptions and sense perceptions

961. I know of no modern philosopher who has not confused, at least occasionally, *sense perception* and intellective *perception*. This leads me to believe that it is very difficult to grasp the distinction, and that it would be helpful to focus carefully upon it. I shall attempt this in the present chapter and take the opportunity also of indicating the useless disputes generated by the confusion and eliminated when the confusion is removed.

962. First, we must pay careful attention to the fact that the term of feeling is always something particular. With this principle in mind, we can discover the properties of both sense perception and intellective perception, since one of the consequences of the principle is: 'Whatever is universal in the perception of bodies, must be attributed to the intellect, not to feeling.'[222]

When I mentally perceive a body, that is, when I judge that an *object* having the nature of body exists, I have an intellective perception of body. But I could not think it like this unless I had the universal notion of *existence*.

963. What is involved in sense perception? With the fundamental feeling we feel our body as something that is one with us. This perception, although complete, is difficult to observe and analyse. So let us turn to touch, which is the second way by

---

[222] This truth was known and affirmed by the whole of antiquity. Thirteen centuries ago, Boethius correctly stated: *Universale est dum intelligitur, singulare dum sentitur* [What is understood is universal; what is felt is particular] (*Sup. Porphir. Proem. In Praedic.*). This was a repetition of Aristotle's opinion nine centuries earlier.

which we attain sense perception of bodies. The sensation of touch, in itself subjective, is also *corporeal perception*: 1. in so far as it is a term of the action of something outside us and 2. presents this term as an extended surface.

Repeated, varying sensations of touch, promptly helped by those of sight, unite to give our sensitivity the expectation of finding, by the use of movement and force, new surfaces under any perceived surface. Sense is also subject to this law of the *instinctive expectation* of similar feelings, as experience shows us. It is due to a habit or inclination formed in sense, a kind of instinct to repeat acts similar to those that have been done many times and expect similar results. This instinctive *expectation* of new corporeal surfaces, after the first surface has been removed, perfects sense perception.

964. Let us now see what the understanding does to complete its perception of bodies. When, through the senses, our spirit has received the corporeal elements so far described, the understanding completes the perception in the following way.

The experience we undergo in a sensation has two aspects: from the point of view of its term, ourselves, it is *experience*; from the point of view of its origin, it is *action*. Action and experience indicate the same thing under two different, opposite aspects. *Sense* perceives what we are talking about simply as *experience* and the *expectation* of new experiences; only the understanding is able to perceive it as *action*, while adding nothing to it. The understanding considers the thing *absolutely*; sense perceives it in a particular *respect*, that is, *relatively*. Understanding originates in us, particular entia, but directs its attention to things in themselves; sense never moves from the particular subject, ourselves, to which it belongs.

It is, therefore, the work of the understanding to conceive the action of something 'other'. But to conceive an action means to conceive a *principle in act*. Thus, when the intellect perceives an action, it always perceives an *agent* as such, that is, an *ens in act*. But it does this by means of the idea of being that it possesses. When it perceives the *agent* as an ens different from ourselves and *endowed with extension*, it has *perception of bodies*.

We see that to perceive a body the understanding does nothing more than consider what the senses present. But it does not do this relatively to ourselves as sense does; setting us aside and ignoring us, it adds the universal concept of being. The intellective perception of bodies is, therefore, the union between the intuition of an ens (agent) and sense perception (experience); it is a judgment, a primal synthesis.

965. But if we set aside the judgment about the actual presence of bodies, we are left with their simple possibility. This is their *pure idea* or *simple apprehension*.

Article 2

Locke confuses sense perception of bodies with intellective perception. Criticisms levelled against Locke

966. When Locke says that the soul receives simple ideas *passively* from the impressions of external things,[223] he is confusing both *sense perception* and *sensation* with *ideas*.

The whole of antiquity had recognised the truth that passive sensations are not *ideas*, and that some activity of the understanding is required if ideas are to be acquired from sensations [*App.*, no. 40].

967. Eventually Locke's error was seen. Thinkers recognised the necessity of some action of our understanding on sensations if we were to have ideas. But modern philosophers are divided in their opinions on the nature of this intellective operation.

Laromiguière recognised the necessity of an intellective operation. According to him, ideas are produced by the understanding's meditation on sensations. This was a step forward, but his *meditation* needed to be defined. He reduced it to a simple *analysis*, defining idea as 'a distinct feeling, a feeling resulting from other feelings'[224]

Galluppi also held that ideas are a product of *meditation* on feelings but thought that Laromiguière, by restricting *meditation* to analysis, had not defined it accurately enough. He

---

[223] 'We have hitherto considered those ideas, in the reception whereof the mind is only passive, which are those simple ones received from sensation and reflection before mentioned, whereof the mind cannot make one to itself, nor have any idea which does not wholly consist of them' (bk. 2, c. 1).

[224] Vol. 2, c. 1.

pointed out that analysis could not form ideas of *relationship* because, as Laromiguière himself agreed, these ideas demand a comparison and hence a *synthesis*. Nor do they have any external reality from which the feeling of the ideas could come. Galluppi added *synthesis* to Laromiguière's *analysis*. He says:

> Some simple ideas are produced by an analysis of sensible objects, others by a synthesis. — Some simple ideas are objective and correspond to realities; others are subjective and do not correspond to any object outside the spirit; they are simple views of the spirit which derive from its faculty of synthesis.[225]

968. This was another step forward by the new philosophy, but I do not think that Galluppi carefully examined the conditions required for intellective *analysis* and *synthesis*. This omission prevented him from finding the truth.

I have pointed out that reflection or meditation, synthesis or analysis which adds nothing to feelings, can never produce an idea. They never get beyond feelings themselves in which they end and rest and by which they are individualised. The intellective operation necessary for forming ideas must therefore *add* to feelings the *universality* feelings lack. Attention which adds nothing to feelings ends in them, and does not produce anything further. Adding universality to a feeling means simply seeing it with a universal view, that is, seeing it not only in its individual entity but even before that in its possible entity. If we consider a feeling not in so far as we experience it here and now but in so far as it is and could be anywhere, we are considering it outside its actual perception and in its essence, that is, in its idea. Meditation which forms ideas from feelings must therefore be an intellective activity which can consider things not as actually existent but in themselves and as possible to exist in any place whatsoever. This activity or abstraction, a species of analysis, presupposes the idea of *thing* in all its universality; it presupposes antecedent thought through which we know 'that every feeling or sense perception, every felt thing has essence or possible existence in addition to individual existence.' In short, *possible being* present to the mind is the condition without which

---

[225] *Saggio filosofico sulla critica della Conoscenza*, vol. 3, c. 1.

the understanding's meditation on its feelings cannot be conceived as apt to produce ideas.

The same conclusion results when we take particular note of what *synthesis* requires. I have shown how the comparison of two or more things needs a preceding *idea* to which the two things may be compared. Synthesis therefore presupposes universal ideas already formed in us (cf. vol. 1, 180–187). If Galluppi had asked himself, 'What conditions are necessary if the intellective meditation on feelings that forms ideas is to appear possible?', he might have seen with his usual insight that a previous universal idea is required for this meditation. If he had seen this, he would not have denied every primal, innate idea in human understanding, nor have attributed the cause of ideas to some inexplicable, inept and undetermined intellectual activity; he would thus have escaped being numbered among the sensists.

Article 3

Reid recognised better than others the activity of the spirit in the formation of ideas, but fell into the same error

969. Reid recognised better than others the nature of the internal *activity* of the spirit through which, on the occasion of sensations, ideas are formed.

He could see that Locke contradicted himself by saying that sensitivity is a purely passive power and, in the case of the source of ideas, by associating a judgment with it, unaware that judgment, according to his own teaching, must be an operation posterior to ideas, not prior to them or their cause.

Reid distinguished perception from sensation: sensation was passive and furnished no ideas at all; perception on the other hand was active and consisted in a natural, spontaneous judgment through which persuasion of the existence of external bodies was acquired.

He claimed that sensation was in no way similar to perception but was always united to it, that is, perception followed immediately upon sensation by means of an inexplicable law of nature. As a result of this proximity, judgment was attributed to sense in everyday speech (which he praised and defended).[226] He says:

> I cannot pretend to assign the reason why a word, which is no term of art, which is familiar to common conversation, should have so different a meaning in philosophical writings.[227] I shall only observe, that the philosophical meaning corresponds perfectly with the account which Mr. Locke and other modern philosophers give of judgment. For, if the sole province of the senses, external and internal, be to furnish the mind with the ideas about which we judge and reason, it seems to be a natural consequence, that the sole province of judgment should be to compare these ideas and to perceive their necessary relations.
>
> These two opinions seem to be so connected, that one may have been the cause of the other. I apprehend, however, that, if both be true, there is no room left for any knowledge of judgment, either of the real existences of contingent things, or of their contingent relations.[228]

970. Granted this observation and the discovery of the *necessity of judgment* for forming ideas, Reid should have investigated the *conditions* necessary for making judgment possible.

[226] Nevertheless, according to his principles, Reid should have recognised a common error in this mode of speech when it says 'Sense judges', and thus confuses sensation with perception. Reid had in fact made great efforts to distinguish the two and affirmed in many places that perception did not in any way resemble sensation; the two facts depended on principles which observation could not reduce to unity in any way. But the example he gives of ordinary speech attributes the two operations of feeling and perception (judgment) to a single power, sense. In the other words, the evidence he adduces in favour of his opinion is ranged entirely against him. Indeed, it is often very difficult to know what the mass of people think, to know whether they think correctly, and even whether they have an opinion about certain matters!

[227] According to Reid, philosophers use the word 'sense' to mean 'a power that gives ideas without judgments', but ordinary people use it to mean 'a power which gives us ideas together with a judgment'. His observation indicates that the fundamental proposition of the whole of this work is confirmed by the authority of the human race whose manner of speaking shows mankind's belief that 'a judgment by the mind is necessary for forming ideas'.

[228] *Essays on the Powers of the Human Mind, etc.*, vol. 2, p. 76.

[970]

An analysis of judgment would have shown the absolute necessity of a pre-existent *universal idea*.

But he lacked either the courage or the energy to take this step, or possibly he drew back because of the horror (drawn from the education of his time) of the smallest intellective element connatural to the human being, to which the analysis would have inevitably led him. He was content to say that the judgment was made through some *unknown* law of human nature itself.

Galluppi considered this language very vague: the perception of bodies could not be something totally different from sensation. He meditated on the relationship between sensation and perception in order to re-unite them, if possible. He concluded that every sensation by its nature was a perception and that the essence of perception consisted in perceiving something, that is, in having an object. Hence, he ended by confusing what Reid had so strenuously tried to distinguish.

But careful investigation will show that the difference of opinion between these two men arose from their failure to distinguish between *sense perception* and *intellective perception*.

Reid was aware of intellective perception, and saw that it had to be something entirely different from sensation. It required a *judgment*, an essentially active faculty; sense however considered in itself is a passive power.

Galluppi concentrated on *sense perception* and saw that it was joined to sensation — it was in sensation itself. He therefore denied Reid's separation of sensation from perception. Because he went no further than this kind of perception, Galluppi was unable to calculate the full measure of intellectual activity necessary for the formation of ideas. He certainly saw that ideas were formed by the understanding's meditation on feelings. He also knew, better than Laromiguière, the nature of this meditation which Laromiguière limited to analysis. Galluppi proved the necessity of a synthesis, but stopped there.

If Galluppi had continued and analysed the *synthesis*, he would have discovered that it could not take place without a *judgment*. He would have known therefore, like Reid, all the force of the intellectual activity necessary for the generation of ideas. And after discovering the need for a *primal judgment*, it would have been easy for him to recognise the necessity of a universal idea antecedent to the judgment. In this way, he would have discovered both the nature of the *intellective perception* of bodies and the sole source of this perception.

971. The natural steps taken by philosophy to discover the *idea of being present naturally to the human spirit* are therefore (in the order of theories, not of time):

1. First, sensations are considered substantially the same as ideas (Locke).

2. Next, *meditation* on sensations is recognised as necessary for ideas.

3. This meditation is analysed and is thought to consist in pure *analysis* (Laromiguière).

4. Meditation is investigated more deeply and is seen to require *synthesis* (Galluppi).

5. But synthesis cannot be made without a judgment. This meditation of the understanding must therefore be an act of the faculty of *judgment* (Reid).

6. Analysis of this faculty of judgment shows the necessity of previous universal ideas.

7. Universal ideas are classified and their connection investigated, resulting in a series of universal ideas, some of which cover a wider sphere than others. Narrower ideas are seen to be deduced from more extensive ideas.

8. Finally, the most universal idea cannot be deduced from any other, because there cannot be a more universal idea above it. It is the primal idea, and with its discovery we can now see the possibility of the judgments necessary for the formation of all other ideas.

Article 4

Continuation

972. I have shown that Reid was aware of the distinction between sensation and the intellective perception of bodies but failed to consider the middle term, *sense perception*. Consequently he found the two terms so far apart that, although he united them in time, he separated them totally in nature.

However, in several places we can see that he did not have a clear and distinct concept of intellective perception and of the idea of bodies. The blame lies with the prejudices of the education given at the time: it held in contempt any claim that there can be something outside the limits of acquired sensation.[229]

973. We can see this particularly where he refers to Aristotle's teaching and confuses the latter's *sensible species* with *ideas.* Sensible species have nothing to do with ideas. When I have a sensation in my eye, I have a sensible species of the distant body. This body which I perceive by means of the sensation has not touched me; I am touched only by the light emitting from the body. The species is obviously different from the touchable body to which through habit I refer it.

The *visual species* of a body differs totally from the *idea* I have of a perceived body.

The *idea* is essentially universal; the *species* is essentially particular.

In the *idea* I find the definition of body; the *visual species* is simply a *sign* of it.

To have both the *idea* and the *intellective perception* of a body, I must judge that 1. an ens *exists*; 2. this ens has modified me and *acted on me* in a way determined by its extension and other sensible qualities. To make these judgments, I must 1. perceive the sensible qualities; 2. perceive, by means of touch and loco-motive force, the felt term in its action (sense perception); and 3. form the act of judgment about this felt term, by which I

---

[229] The degree of confusion among minds after Locke's time and the loss of the distinction between sensation and idea can be seen in the way 'idealist' is generally applied to Berkeley, Hume and their followers. These authors wanted to reduce all human cognitions to *sensation* alone. They supported their systems with the following argument: 'If sensations are in us, the external world is in us.' Thus, because they called sensations *ideas,* they called themselves *idealists,* a name used by everyone. But their correct name should have been simply *sensists.* This observation removes any wonder that may arise from seeing how close *idealists* and *materialists* are. All wonder ceases if we bear in mind that the title 'idealists' was incorrectly given them and means simply 'sensists', because the gap between *sensists* and *materialists* is clearly not great. However, the wonder universally experienced when philosophers called 'idealists' are seen to associate so easily with 'materialists' is an involuntary witness to the consciousness of the human race. This witness shows that the human race is definitely aware of the difference between *idea* and *sensation,* even if philosophers have lost it.

come to see it as sharing in existence. In short, I intellectively perceive the body as one among possible *entia*, limited in a determined way by my senses.

Now I need none of this in order to have the *sensible visual species*: I need neither intellect (faculty of the intuition of being in all its universality) nor judgment (faculty of applying the idea of being in all its universality to particular things perceived by sense) nor even sense perception. All I need is my sight, which is common also to brute animals, without asociating with it any other sensation, operation or information.

974. Reid's error may have been caused by Aristotle's metaphorical expressions. Aristotle describes *sensible species*, *phantasms* and *intelligible species* or ideas as substantially the same thing, as if they were little images or statuettes which are gradually purified and spiritualised as they pass through the three powers of *sense*, *phantasy* and *intellect*, just as liquid or dust is refined as it passes through filters of varying density.[230]

975. Reid classed all these internal experiences under one general heading as *something in between* things and us, and by attacking them all, brought ruin to *ideas* as well as to *sensible species* and *phantasms*.

Consequently he speaks about Plato's *ideas* in the same way as he does about Aristotle's *sensible species*, as if the same arguments could be used about both, and both could be eliminated by the same reasoning. But this is impossible [*App.*, no. 41].

Article 5

Whether we perceive bodies through the principles of substance and cause

976. According to Descartes, the existence of bodies is made known to us through the principle of cause. This was the opinion of a great number of philosophers after Descartes and also (this is not a joke!) of Destutt-Tracy.

---

[230] *Essays on the Powers of the Human Mind*, Essay 1, c. 1. — Stewart, a disciple of Reid, repeats the same error in *Éléments de la philosophie de l'Esprit humain*, c. 1, sect. 1.

Galluppi denied that we know bodies through the principle of cause. He argued clearly and convincingly against Tracy: 'If the principle of causality makes us know objects, it cannot come from objects.'[231] Tracy had no reply to this observation, but my reply is: certainly the principle of cause cannot come from real things; it comes from the idea of being.

977. All Galluppi's other arguments against the principle of cause relative to the knowledge of the existence of external bodies are reduced to the following: 'If sense does not put us in direct communication with external objects, the principle of cause can only create an external world *a priori*. Idealism is therefore inevitable.'

This argument shows that while he was very concerned about the necessity of *sense perception*, he neglected to observe *intellective perception*.

978. I grant Galluppi an immediate communication of our spirit with the external world, but this implies the necessity of sense perception. Otherwise there would be no matter to which the principle of cause could be applied. If the principle is to act or produce anything, it must be applied to something. Apart from all this, there is still no *intellective perception* in which alone the *knowledge* of bodies consists.

Sense perception of bodies is direct;[232] it is a fact and needs no principle of the mind to form it. If we analyse the fact, we can easily distinguish in it, as Galluppi himself does, the act of perception and its object, and the intimate, necessary connection between these two — note, *object* here is understood as *term*, because sense itself has no real *object*.

The *intellective perception* of bodies is however a judgment. This judgment needs an intellective principle, or at least an *idea*, a *universal* which takes the form of principle when reduced to a proposition. This universal idea which makes us perceive bodies intellectively is the idea of existence, as I have explained throughout this work.

---

[231] *Saggio filosofico sulla critica della Conoscenza*, bk. 2, c. 1.

[232] Intellective perception can also be said to be *direct*, in the sense that it is done through a first judgment.

Article 6

Intellective perception was confused with sense perception
even in the case of internal feeling and *MYSELF*

979. Because philosophers confused external sense perception
with intellective perception, they made a single fact out of the
two.

The same confusio n and suppression of an element occurred
in the case of internal sensitivity or the perception of one's own
feeling. I pointed this out when discussing Malebranche (cf. 439
[443]).

To clarify the matter further, I will deal with the confusion
present at the very beginning of Descartes' doctrine.

'I think, therefore I exist'; this is the foundation stone of
Descartes' structure. But there is an easily recognisable and
insoluble objection to this principle, an objection that was naturally and quickly raised: If you say, 'I think, therefore I exist',
you must presuppose the knowledge that what thinks must
exist. In the very first line and at the start of your philosophy
you take for granted the notion of *existence*, which needs to be
explained.

980. If the objection had been calmly accepted and if the path
it indicated had been followed by people searching for the truth,
they would have been led directly to the beginning of all philosophy, the idea of existence.

But Descartes paid no attention to the objection. Instead he
maintained that the first words of his philosophy, 'I think,
therefore I exist', were meant to point to a truth directly perceived, not to something discovered by reasoning.[233] He did not
realise that the word 'therefore' gave the lie to his reply.

The great man was quite capable of seeing the force of the
objection, but could not bring himself to abandon the true part
of his thought. What is needed is the distinction between the
perception of *myself* as feeling and the *intellective perception* of
this same *myself*. The former is direct and simple, given by
nature; the latter is also direct but not simple because it presupposes a universal idea, the idea of existence. Failing to make this

[233] Cf. his reply to *Second Objections*.

distinction, Descartes attributed to intellective perception what was proper solely to feeling. Both he and his opponents were half right; none of them was fully right.

981. If we note the language he uses (because language is the portrait of ideas), we can see that he was speaking about intellective perception and attributed to it what pertained only to feeling. He says, 'I think, therefore I exist.' Surely there is some reasoning in these words? Surely the word 'therefore' expresses a consequence? 'Thinking' is certainly not the same as 'existing'. Thinking is the attribute, the predicate of an *ens*. And an *ens* cannot be intellectively conceived unless we know what *being* is in all its universality. In fact, the whole of the long first *Meditation*, in which the phrase 'I think, therefore I exist' occurs, is an example of continuous reasoning.

982. Discussing this principle, Galluppi says that Descartes' reasoning simply means 'that our existence is of such a kind that it is confirmed whether we deny it or doubt it'.[234] This is true, but knowing that our existence is confirmed by our denying or doubting it is itself an example of true reasoning, an indication that the act of denial and doubt is connected with *existence*. But this judgment or synthesis cannot be made, unless we know *existence* separately from the act of denial or doubt. If we perceived only denial and doubt, we could not carry out any mental act. In a simple perception where everything is individual, we cannot make distinctions and analyses without the help of some universal notion [*App.*, no. 42].

---

[234] *Saggio filosofico, etc.*

CHAPTER 16

The natural disharmonies between the perception of our body as co-subject, and as agent foreign to the subject

Article 1

The difference between the two principal ways of perceiving our body, that is, as co-subject and as an agent foreign to the subject

983. Our body is felt subjectively and extrasubjectively, like any other body.

It is the same entity felt by us in two ways. But what distinguishes extrasubjective from subjective perception?

When an ens is perceived as foreign to the *subject*, an *agent* is felt. But in the perception of an ens as *subject* or, to be more exact, as *co-subject*, the one *who has the experience* is felt, that is, feels himself in and with the subject.[235]

Now to be active and to be passive are contraries. The same nature, therefore, is perceived in both ways but in different and opposite respects. First, it is perceived as *something acting* that produces but does not feel sensations; second, as *something passive* that feels but does not produce sensations.

984. These two aspects are so opposed to each other that they have nothing in common. Consequently what is perceived in these two ways is presented as two entities, two different

---

[235] I refrain from saying 'as an object' because the body is only an object relatively to *intellective perception*, in which it is apprehended as an *ens*; *sense perception* perceives only an action foreign to the subject. Strictly speaking, the *object* of intellective perception cannot be said to be *active* but only *present*. We do indeed use our intellectual activity to perceive the object, but this activity produces nothing in the object except the act with which we perceive it. The perceived object, which we cannot change and over which we have no power, is what *forms* our cognition. Hence St. Thomas' statement: *Species intelligibilis principium formale est intellectualis operationis, sicut cuiuslibet forma agentis principium est propriae operationis* [The intelligible species is the formal principle of intellectual action, just as the form of any agent is the principle of its action] (*C. Gent.*, I, 46).

natures; they are not different levels but different *aspects* of the same thing, one of which directly excludes the other.

It is not simply the case of an idea of an acting body being the opposite of an idea of a passive body, but of the action and passivity particular to sense. If we consider our passive feeling, that is, our feeling of pleasure or pain, we have in the external principle producing the feeling the concept of an agent. If we consider the feeling in its term, that is, as terminated and experienced in itself, we have ourselves, modified and experiencing.

Article 2

The similarity between the impression of external things and the sensation that follows

985. An external body touching a sensitive part of our body produces movement in that part, that is, an *impression*.

This impression, caused by the external body, is either perceptible to our sight and touch or can be argued to. When a needle pricks my hand, I can see and touch the wound and notice the change in my body. If the impression is not large enough to be seen or touched, I can deduce it by analogy. Thus the impression made by light on my eye or the movement of my optic nerve is so minute and faint that I am not able to advert to the tiny particles of light with my sense of touch.[236] In the same way, the very faint impressions that the minute particles make on my organs of smell, taste and hearing cannot be noticed by sight and touch, and are perhaps too small for any microscope. But knowing the mechanical actions of bodies, I can reason that the minute particles must be acting on the eye, nostrils and palate, producing small irritations and alterations.

The idea that we have, therefore, of the *impression* of external bodies is the same as that of any impression, for example, on wax, or of a mark left behind or any movement stimulated in

---

[236] The movement of the iris under the action of light is not an effect of light only but depends on other physical principles and on the spontaneity of the soul.

[985]

any body. These effects are terms of our touch and eyes, like the changes of our body, and give rise to sensations.

986. It is my opinion that *impressions* like these do not have the least similarity with *sensations*, considered in their subjective part, even if sensations follow immediately upon the impressions. In fact there is a real, contrary opposition between them.

An imprint, a feature, a movement, an external body, perceived (with the touch) is an *agent* producing sensation in our organ. *Sensation* on the other hand is a kind of *passivity*; *the one who has the experience* is sensible to himself.

But *that which acts* is the opposite of *that which experiences an act* (cf. 983).

An *impression* made on a sensitive body, causing *sensations*, has no similarity at all with sensations in their subjective part. An impression is of its nature entirely the opposite of sensation; the one excludes the other just as 'yes' excludes 'no' and vice versa.

To make the difference clear, let us suppose a ball-bearing is pressed into a sensitive part of a person's body so that half of it forms a hemispherical impression in the skin. The person clearly feels two things: 1. the part of the body where the impression is made, and 2. the ball-bearing itself or agent.

The *feeling* in the affected part is different from the *perception* of the ball-bearing; they are two simultaneous feelings, referred to the same spot, but quite different.

For example, anyone who feels discomfort in his arm, *feels passively* what he is experiencing. When however he perceives the ball-bearing, he feels what *is acting*. These two feelings are opposites and cannot be confused.

The part of the arm he feels affected is the *concave* surface where the bearing is being pressed, so that a body of *concave* form is felt.

The part of the bearing he perceives is the convex surface pressing into the skin, so that a body of *convex* form is felt. A feeling is being experienced in the *concave surface* of the arm; a body undergoing an experience is felt. No sensation is referred to the *convex surface* of the bearing; it is not a body undergoing an experience but an insensitive body causing the experience.

In sensation therefore an external body (extrasubject) and our body (co-subject) are inconfusable opposites. The perception of the external body is the sensation itself but only as term of an action coming from outside.

Let us apply this distinction to *sensation* and *impression*.

The word 'impression' means something perceived by us as external *agent*; the word 'sensation' means something perceived by us as *subject*, in us. In the case of the ball-bearing, the impression (leaving the sensation aside for the moment) is perceived in exactly the same way as the bearing that in itself feels nothing. The person in our example, feeling discomfort, sees the hollow made by the bearing and then touches it with his finger; in this way he is seeing and touching the impression.

When he touches and sees the hollow, he certainly does not touch and see the *sensation* he has experienced and is experiencing as a result of the hollow. The sensation itself is neither visible nor touchable; it can be felt only through an internal feeling of the soul, only through itself.

After seeing and touching the hollow a few times, he says to those about him: 'Look at the impression the ball-bearing has left.' He calls an *impression* what he touches and sees or what is offered to his touch and sight. The meaning he is giving to the word 'impression' is that of a modification experienced by a body in the arrangement of its parts, a modification perceived by us with our sensories, particularly of sight and touch. This is not a sensation but an external term of our sensories.

Is what I see and touch, that is, an *impression* made on a body by the action of another body, similar in any way to the sensations of touch and sight with which it is perceived? All the by-standers do indeed perceive the *impression* with their touch and sight equally with the person receiving it, but he also experiences the *sensation* accompanying the impression.

987. Note carefully that when the person perceives the impression in his arm with his touch and eyes, new sensations take place, and these can be analysed in exactly the same way as the sensation of the ball-bearing. In fact when he touches the hollow in his arm, he has simultaneously a feeling composed of two basic parts or feelings:

1. a feeling of his finger, at the point where he is feeling with it, and

2. a feeling of the little hollow, which he is touching. We can say about this twofold feeling what we said previously

about the feeling of the arm and of the ball-bearing, that is, the finger is felt as *co-sentient*, and the hollow as *acting*.

He feels his finger with a sensation referred to a convex extension; he feels the hollow with a sensation referred to a concave extension.

The sensation he experiences by touching the hollow is not referred to the hollow but to his finger. Both his finger and his eye perceive the hollow as having no feeling; relative to his touch and eye, the hollow is only a term of action. His touch and eye is subject, or rather belongs to the subject. The hollow experiences no sensation but makes my eye and touch experience a sensation.

The hollow, as presented to the eye and external touch, is called an *impression* but in itself has no feeling. It is completely outside the sensations of touch and sight, and is in fact the opposite of sensation. Hence there is no similarity but only opposition between the *sensation* as subject and the *impression*. An impression therefore cannot be seen in any way as a degree of sensation, nor a sensation as a degree or kind of impression.

Article 3

Materialism rebutted

988. All materialistic arguments are based on the confusion between *impression* and *sensation*, because the opposite natures of these two things are not distinguished.

Materialists search for a similarity between them, explaining sensations by means of impressions or finding sensations in impressions.

They do not take into account the meaning given to names like 'impression', 'movement', etc., which as extrasubjective words indicate agents without feeling. These words have been coined to express things external to our senses and perceived by them, not things with feeling. Sensation is excluded by definition from things indicated by these words.

Materialists, and others inclined to the same error, try to explain sensation by reducing it to a *movement* of parts or an *impression*. This is to abuse terms and confuse ideas in a manifest contradiction. The *movement* of parts and *impressions* does indeed need *sensation* to be felt, but *sensation*, precisely because it is sensation, does not; sensation cannot be seen or touched or compared to anything seen and touched.

989. Epicurus thought sensation could be explained by imagining tiny statuettes emerging from bodies, flying through the air and reaching us. These perfect little images of bodies constituted our sensations. This explanation is a flight of fancy and explains nothing.

The error consists in turning what we know as the external term of our senses into a subjective sensation. The notion of the statuettes, a creation of Epicurus' phantasy, could come only from what we know with our senses, from things perfectly similar to what we touch and see. Nevertheless, instead of being able to touch and see them in reality, our phantasy imagines them to be so small that our sensories are too large to perceive them; our touch and sight would need to be more delicate. Sensation cannot be anything like this: it does not have a particle affecting our senses and capable of being seen with a microscope or touched with something more sensitive than our hand. Sensation could not be anything *extrasubjective*. It can be the act only of that which feels, the very opposite of what is extrasubjective and felt.[237]

990. Aristotle likened the sensation caused in us by external bodies to an imprint made in soft wax: the wax receives the form

[237] It would seem impossible to confuse the subjective perception of a body with the extrasubjective perception in the crude way we find in certain materialists. They allow themselves to be deluded by phantasy and believe they have explained something when they have joined together what is essentially opposite and irreconcilable. In a lecture he gave on light (Lect. 7), Robert Hook, a founding member of the Royal Society of London, to which he gave many lectures, makes ideas material substances. He thinks that the brain is composed of a certain matter capable of manufacturing the ideas of each sense. According to him, the ideas of sight are formed by a kind of matter similar to Bologna stone or some kind of phosphorous. The ideas of hearing are made from matter similar to violin strings, or to glass which receives a sound from vibrations of the air. The soul can construct hundreds of these ideas in a day. As soon as each idea is formed it is pushed away from the centre. All these ideas together with the last idea, which remains nearest the centre, form an unbroken chain. It seems impossible that a sane man can think things like this, worthy only of someone deranged!

of the seal but nothing of its matter. This likeness is false and materialist. When we speak about an impression made in wax, we are speaking about something we see with our eyes and touch with our hands, in other words, about something external to our senses. But sensation is not at all like this; it is not an external *agent*. It is an *experience* felt internally by our sensories, or better, something experienced by our sensitive principle. If an impression made in wax is to resemble the sensation, the impression would have to feel itself. In this case, we would not have explained the sensation but simply transferred it from our skin to the wax, and would still need to know what it is. The *impression* and the *sensation* in the wax would be foreign to each other, two incommunicable opposites, lacking any likeness.

991. Hume called *sensations* 'impressions'. Reid rightly points out that he should have told us whether this word meant the operation of the mind or the object of the mind.[238] Many sophists have founded their theories on this confused and improper use of the word.

992. Darwin defines idea as 'a contraction, movement or configuration of the fibres forming the immediate organ of sense';[239] sensation is 'an actuation or change of either the central parts of the sensory or all of the sensory. It begins from an extreme part of the sensory in the muscles or organs of sense'.[240] We clearly see here the gross confusion between the extrasubjective term of perception and the subjective sensation. The words 'contraction', 'movement' and 'configuration' were coined precisely to indicate terms of the experience of touch and sight, because words indicate things in so far as we perceive them. But *sensation* expresses the experience of the sentient subject itself and not a term. Hence, a *contraction*, *movement* and *configuration* can be touched, at least with a more delicate touch and eye than ours. But it is ridiculous and absurd to say that an *idea* is something that can be submitted to the observation of touch or sight, no matter how sharp these senses may be.

993. The same ambiguity, the same clumsy confusion, is

[238] *Essay on the Powers, etc.,* Essay 1, c. 1.

[239] Sect. 4, c. 3. — Darwin and all materialists do not know the real distinction between sensation and idea.

[240] Sect. 5, c. 1.

present everywhere in Cabanis, another materialist. Although he does not make *impression* and *sensation* altogether identical, he says that sensation consists in the reaction of the brain to an impression carried to it. He finds nothing strange in establishing an analogy between the stomach and the brain, and defining the brain as the bowel which digests thought! Yet he never ceases to call for the greatest exactitude in philosophical expressions! He claims to follow a precise, experimental method and to use a kind of surveyor's measure in the sequence of his propositions. The following is a sample of his strict, philosophical style:

> Someone may object that organic movements by which functions of the brain are carried out are unknown to us. But the action by which the stomach nerves determine the different operations constituting digestion and the way they use the gastric juices which have a very active solvent power do not invalidate our research in any way. We *see* nutrients enter the stomach and emerge with new qualities. We conclude that the stomach has brought about this alteration. We *also see* impressions that reach the brain by means of the nerves and then become isolated and incoherent. This bowel becomes active and acts upon them, and at once sends them back changed into ideas which are manifested externally by facial expression, gesture or verbal and written signs. With the *same certainty* we can conclude that the brain somehow digests impressions and organically produces the secretion of thought.[241]

We certainly cannot doubt that, simultaneously with the sensation felt in our consciousness, our eye perceives our organs in another configuration; it perceives impressions upon them and movements. But this means that although the order of our subjective modifications (that is, our own) is by nature totally unlike the order of the extrasubjective modifications (that is, of the external agent on our sensories, or of our organs themselves understood in a material sense), they are governed by a law of relationship which needs to be carefully observed and determined. We must therefore pay very close attention to and note the movements and shapes presented to our touch and sight in

---

[241] *Rapports du physique et du moral de l'homme etc.*, Mem. 2.

the affected organs when we are internally experiencing a sensation. At the same time however, the experienced sensation, because we cannot touch or see it (this itself is an absurd and unintelligible statement), must be distinguished from the movement and shapes observable by touch and sight, granted the shapes are large enough. In fact, shapes exist for us and are named solely because they are convenient terms of touch, sight and the other senses. They are not perceived by another faculty.

Cabanis would not have been subject to this strange mental confusion and obscurity if he had controlled his imagination and kept to the facts which he claimed to follow. It seemed clear to him that we *see* impressions come to the brain through the nerves in the same way that we *see* food enter the stomach. We *see* the brain change these impressions into ideas, judgments, etc., just as we *see* the stomach change food. I am well acquainted with Spallanzani's experiments on the digestion and force of the stomachs of chickens and other animals; I am aware that in opening many stomachs, he had the opportunity of allowing the senses to observe food in all the different states it passed through under the action of the bowels. But relative to the *digestion* of the brain, for which Cabanis says we have the *same certainty* as for the stomach, I honestly confess that I have never read of experiments by any scientist on the *impressions* transmitted by the nerves to the brain and then digested by the brain. It would indeed be profitable if various animals could be opened and we could follow these impressions on their way and extract them like food from the bowel or find them in the brain in various states of digestion, changed now into the state of ideas, now into that of judgments, now into other combinations. It would be helpful to be able to put these impressions under a microscope and submit them to any other experiment we choose, just as a mixture is extracted in different stages of digestion from the bowels and intestines of animals. Cabanis asks us to believe that these impressions are *seen* to enter the brain in the same way as food enters the stomach. I cannot say whether *he* has seen these impressions or not, but I know that I myself and others have never seen them. Moreover, I note that his very expressions contain the seed of his error. This superficial man supposes that everything we know is known through sight and touch and the other senses, and that only the external terms of these senses exist. According to this supposition, even *ideas* must be seen and touched, because we know them. His expressions, taken from the sense of sight and applied to feelings and ideas as well as to food in the stomach, are clear proof of this. But it is also clear from the following extract that he was unaware of *internal experience*, the other source of our cognitions, and reduced everything solely to the external experience of the senses:

> The only ideas we have of objects come from the observable phenomena they present us. Their nature and essence must be found solely in the composition of these phenomena.[242]

Because he excluded observation of the internal facts of feeling and consciousness, he inevitably fell into absurd, material *empiricism*. This was the result of very defective observation which forgets and excludes the series of sublime, noble facts of nature presented by the feeling, thinking subject to himself.

994. We must however acknowledge that the distinction between *subjective* and *extrasubjective* is not easily determined. We see this in authors of sound teaching who, unaware and unsuspecting, use inexact expressions which favour materialism and, like tiny roots which hold the teaching so firmly in the earth that it can never be uprooted or revealed, contribute to sad, ignoble teaching [*App.*, no. 43].

Article 4

The dividing line between physiology and psychology

995. The difference between *sensation* and *impression*, between our subjective feeling and what we see and touch or perceive *extrasubjectively*, establishes the dividing line between physiology and psychology.

Physiology and medicine are and can be only the product of *external observation*, that is, of observation made by touch, sight and the other senses. Psychology on the other hand is

---

[242] *Rapports du physique et du moral de l'homme etc.*, Mem. 2.

founded on *internal observation*, that is, of all that takes place in our consciousness.

Physiology and medicine deal with the body as an external *object* but the purpose of psychology is the spirit and what belongs to it as *subject*.

Physiology investigates the natural state of the human body, the different effects to which it is subject, the classification of these effects, their uniformity, that is to say, the laws of the body's operation. All these effects, movements, modifications and laws to which the body is subject, are only *terms* of touch, sight and the other senses, and objects of the understanding. Thus in these sciences the body is considered as something purely external and objective. The same can be said about medicine: it uses continual *external observation* to note the diseased changes or modifications in the human body and the remedies necessary for good health.

996. It is true that in these sciences we must pay attention to what takes place in our consciousness, but that is not their aim. If they turn their attention to human feelings, to the force that can be exercised on the body by an intense application of the spirit, they do so for the sole purpose of knowing the effects of such actions. If these sciences take into account the effect different habits of the body produce on the soul and on intellectual faculties, they do so to discover a way of restoring the body to that health which enables it to serve the spirit. In all these researches the physiologist and the doctor observe the body through external observation and therefore purely as *object*.

On the other hand the psychologist uses another kind of observation, internal observation. The facts of consciousness are the objects at which his observation stops; he considers *myself*, the subject. And if he concerns himself with the body as *object*, he does so only through the relationship between object and subject. But this science does not terminate in the object; its proper purpose and concern is the consciousness proper to the spirit, related to which all other things are only means and aids.

997. We can therefore conclude that even if the surgeon's knife were able to reveal the minutest fibres in animal bodies and if the most powerful microscopes imaginable had been invented to reveal the hidden structure of bodies more perfectly than ever before, it could never replace internal observation of

the facts of consciousness. The science of psychology would not profit in the least from these discoveries.

Article 5

Systems concerning the union of soul and body

998. It is impossible to find any likeness between body and soul as long as the former is restricted to its guise of term of our external senses. But without some likeness between the two, there is no possibility of mutual communication.

It is even possible to demonstrate the inherent repugnance of communication if the body is seen simply as the term of the external senses.

999. I note that it has always been customary to consider the body under this limited respect. As a result, great philosophers regarded as absurd and contradictory the opinion that the body as presented externally to our senses communicates with the spirit. They rejected physical influence and turned to other systems, the most famous of which is Malebranche's occasional causes and Leibniz's pre-established harmony.

The necessity of these systems, however, arose from defective observation of the body: the body was considered purely as it appears externally to our senses through which it makes itself partially known as something outside us.[243] But the problem requires the body to be considered as *co-subject*, that is, how is the body one subject with the soul?

1000. The union of the body with the soul was falsely imagined as an intermingling of two fluids or the close combination of two solids. They are things subject to external experience; we can examine them with our eyes, touch them and perform many sense experiments on them, except that the spirit was imagined to be so fine that it escaped external observation even by the most sensitive instruments. But all the time the spirit and its union with the body was considered to be and

---

[243] If everything we perceive with the senses is outside us, how could an action inside us be explained by what is essentially and by hypothesis outside us?

made to be like very small visible things and therefore subject to the observation of the senses if these were delicate enough to correspond to the extremely delicate intricacy of the objects.

1001. External observation, however, is not the only way in which we come to know our body. Interior observation also contributes to revealing the body in a very different light from that presented by the external senses. Through interior observation, we come to see its inner, *essential* properties. Thus it becomes *matter* and co-cause of the fundamental feeling.

In this way the body could be found in feeling itself, as St. Thomas thought, because action which has a *mode* and a *term* called *space* is done in the soul.

We need, therefore, to consider ourselves and the content of our awareness by reflecting upon *myself* without allowing our external imagination to intrude in any way. Our concept of the union between soul and body cannot arise from any other source.

1002. In the feeling of *myself*, therefore, we find a force different from *myself* itself, but felt by it. As *myself* feels this force, it diffuses its own sensation in an extended term. This feeling, to which *myself* is drawn by natural force (relative to which it is passive), is a fact. Consequently, the union of soul and body should have been considered as a *fact* derived from observation of our own experience. As a primal fact, constituting our very nature, its light dispels all difficulties we experience in admitting the existence of this union. These difficulties are inconceivable; they make no sense.

Article 6

The relationship between the *external* body and the body as *co-subject*

1003. Subjective and extrasubjective perception, therefore, provide two different and in some ways contrary concepts of the body as *co-subject* and *extrasubject*.

The opposition arises simply from the limitation of these mutually exclusive concepts which furnish contrary propositions about the body. For example: *the body is in the soul*, and *the soul is in the body*; both are true, but refer to opposite concepts of the body.

It is true that *the body is in the soul* in the concept of the subjective body, because in this case the body is only something *acting in myself* (in the soul).

It is true that *the soul is in the body*, when the body is considered as foreign to the subject and the soul is considered in the effects it produces in this extrasubjective element.

1004. We have to emphasise 'in the effects it produces' because the soul, considered in itself, is a *subject* which can never be a term of feeling, nor measured in relationship to space.

If the intelligent soul is considered in itself (as a subject) and compared with the body or with anything extended, we can add a third true statement: *the soul has no place* because it is simple.

These distinctions help to eliminate a great number of difficult questions to which there are no solutions except through determined efforts to clear up inexact language.

Article 7

Matter of the fundamental feeling

1005. When we dealt with the fundamental feeling, and with the subjective part of sensation as a modification of the fundamental feeling, we said that strictly speaking such a feeling can never have an *object*, but only some *matter* in which it terminates.

We perceive external *objects* and call them 'bodies' when thought is united with the operation of the senses, although we also realise that one of these perceived bodies, which we call 'my body' is the *matter* of our feeling.

What difference is there, however, between *object* and *matter*?

This problem requires careful investigation.

1006. Our body, whether in its natural state or modified, is the *matter* of our interior feeling in so far as it is felt by this feeling. It is *term* and *stimulus* of our individual sensories in so far as it is perceived by them; and it is also the *object* of our understanding. Consequently, the *matter* of feeling is something halfway between pure *subject* and the *term* of sense. It is not the sentient subject because it is itself felt, nor is it a pure *term* of sense because sense cannot exist without it.

1007. The first difference, therefore, between the *matter* and *object* of any potency is that the object is not necessary for the subsistence of the power while the matter is a constituent of the potency which, without it, could not be conceived mentally. It is true, for instance, that although there could be no sight without light, the eyes nevertheless subsist and can be thought of irrespective of light. The same is true, *mutatis mutandis*, for the other organs. The stimuli, therefore, are not *matter* of the organs, but simply *terms* of their acts, and *objects* when the understanding has perceived them.

1008. The difference between matter and object can only be understood through a correct concept of a *potency*. As we know, every potency is a *first act* which, given the necessary conditions, produces various other acts dependent upon differing conditions. The first, constant act is called potency relative to the secondary, transient acts. Every potency, therefore, is an activity held in check as it were, ready for action. With this in mind, it is easy to see that as every *second act* needs a term for it to take place, so a *potency* or *first act* needs its own internal term without which it could neither be nor be thought. Similarly, because a *potency* is something stable, while its operation is transient, it must have a stable term along with which it either remains in existence or perishes. If the term of its *operation* is removed, the potency remains; but if the term of the potency is removed, the potency ceases to exist.

1009. *Matter* is a stable term, proper to certain potencies, with which it forms a single reality. Because this term is joined with the potencies, it helps to constitute them and cannot be thought without them. This explains why it is not called simply *term* (a name common to everything in which the act finishes externally), but *matter*. Nevertheless, this characteristic of indivisibility from the potency is insufficient to constitute the *matter* of a potency because every potency has a term, but not matter.

1010. The second difference between the *object* and *matter* of a potency is that the object as such is neither receptive of action nor capable of being receptive of action.[244] On the other hand, the matter of any potency is mentally conceived as modifiable, that is, having no activity of its own relative to the potency. The objects of my cognitions do not stimulate my mind, but allow it to know by informing it; the impression of external light, on the other hand, is a forceful action, stimulus and term drawing my sensitivity to the act of sense perception. Generally speaking, objects of knowledge, which have no active state relative to cognitive potencies, are in a state of mere presence to them, an impassive state, while the terms of our practical potencies are definitely passive. Now if the term of the *first act*, which constitutes the potency itself, presents itself to us in an *impassive* state of simple presence to the potency which does nothing except receive it, I call it 'object', not just 'term', although it is such. I do not call it 'matter', because this word includes the concept of experiencing something, or modifiability. I also call it 'form' of the potency, that is, an object so contantly united with the subject that it places the subject in first act. This first act, the cause of many operations, is called *potency*. Hence I have called *the idea of universal being*, the *objective form* of the intellect. Our body, as felt, on the other hand, I have called *matter* of the feeling in so far as it is 'a stable term of the first act of our feeling, bereft of activity relative to the completed act of feeling.'

1011. However, the *matter* of the fundamental feeling has a third, truly noble characteristic. As we have said, it is a term without activity related to the completed feeling, and *capable* only of presenting itself to the feeling as a passive term. This capacity or *passive susceptibility*, however, is very imperfect because the matter resists, with a certain inertia, acceptance of the state that the activity of the feeling could offer it, and thus

[244] Normally speaking, we say that iron struck with a hammer is the object of the action of the hammer, and the same is true of every other term acted upon by any force or instrument. From an etymological point of view, this would appear correct (*ob-jectum* = thrown against), but this manner of speaking depends upon the way we conceive the fact and how the notion of object is added by the intelligence. But prescinding from this, the two material instruments have nothing outside themselves. Striking one another adventitiously, the two forces unite, contrast and modify one another, but there are no objects, the concept of which demands sameness and impassibility.

serves as a brake to the perfect operation of the feeling. Nevertheless, we cannot say that this inertia must be a force relative to
and in contrast with the feeling. We must note that readiness to
be moved easily denotes perfection when the movement improves the nature of what is moved. The capacity for receiving
improvement is an intrinsic activity. On the contrary, incapacity
for receiving improvement indicates a lack of what I would call
seminal activity, as it were, an activity and hidden potency without which development cannot take place. The lack itself is an
obstacle to the perfection that could be comunicated to an ens.
Matter, therefore, does not offer a real, active resistance to the
feeling, but incapacity or inertia.

It would not be correct to object that this is merely abstract
speculation. Observation provides the ground for such a description of the *matter* of the fundamental feeling because it
shows that this feeling does not expand in an 'empty' extension
(as it were), but in one where it experiences certain resistances,
and even changes and disturbance, according to stable laws
which constitute: 1. the relationship of the sensitive body with
external bodies; and 2. the relationship of the sensitive body
(matter) with *myself*, the act of feeling.

But we ought to reflect even more on the perfection of the
feeling than on that of the body. The feeling would be more perfect, the more it were capable of possessing a perfect body obedi-
ent to its will. If, therefore, harmful alterations take place in the
body and the feeling suffers as a result, we may indeed posit a
force in the body, but it will be such as to harm the feeling. As
we showed, the feeling with its matter forms a single thing, or a
single potency. The force of its matter is therefore the passive,
imperfect part of the potency, not its formal, perfect part. This is
the chief reason for calling our body, in so far as it is felt by us,
the *matter* of the fundamental feeling.[245]

1012. At this point, a difficulty presents itself. In this work, I
have described the body as something acting on the spirit, in

[245] We have to distinguish carefully between the principle of an act, and its
term. It is undeniable, although difficult to conceive, that the principle can be
simple, while its term is *multiple* or extended. The extension in which a
sensation is diffused with its term does not entail diminished simplicity in
myself as feeling principle. The reasons set out above (cf. 672–691) leave no
room for doubt about this [*App.*, no. 44].

which it causes and excites the fundamental feeling. How is it possible now to describe the *matter* of the fundamental feeling, which is the *body* itself, as passive and inert relative to the action of this feeling?

In the first place, we have to remember that the *matter* of the fundamental feeling is not the body with all its qualities. The fundamental feeling, in its matter, perceives the body only relatively to the special sensories in so far as the body offers itself as a passive and inert term of the feeling itself. The *activity* the body may possess for producing the feeling is not comprised in the *matter* of the feeling. But we have to reflect carefully to see how this is possible.

1013. 'A force working in a given way on an ens can draw this ens to an act terminating in the very force that has stimulated and encouraged it, so that the force becomes passive relative to the act which it caused. Moreover, it can stimulate an act terminating outside itself.' Let us examine the first of these two cases.

It is clear that I can put in motion a force producing some effect upon myself; for example, if I pick up a knife, I may easily cut myself. This truth can be seen even more clearly in the case of a spiritual agent which moves with remarkable spontaneity, as our experience shows. In fact, we only need an occasion, rather than a cause, to stimulate the spirit whose interior activity comes into play spontaneously, granted the necessary occasion and conditions. Our body may possess a force drawing the spirit to an act of feeling which, at the same time (because it also is an activity), may turn back on the body as on its necessary term. In fact, the laws according to which the spirit is first moved to feel are unknown, at least to me. Nevertheless, it is not absurd to conjecture that their hypothetical existence flows from the very nature of the spirit. In all the entia of which we have experience in the universe, we constantly find two things: 1. that they follow certain laws in their operations; 2. that these laws are not arbitrarily imposed upon them, but result from their nature.

If we apply the same observation to the spirit, it is not unreasonable to think that the active nature of the spirit is to operate under certain conditions. One necessary condition for the fundamental feeling, as we can see from our analysis of feeling itself, is the existence of an organised body. Given a body disposed in this way, it could happen that the union and feeling result from a law inherent in the very nature of the spirit. What is certain, however, is that the body can be passive relative to the fundamental feeling which it originated and encouraged, and of which it was undoubtedly a necessary condition. Considered under this respect alone, the body is called 'matter' of the fundamental feeling. The activity moving the spirit to feel is the *principle* of the feeling; the body enfolded by the spirit is its matter and term. And although reflection on our experience shows us that we are passive when we feel, because of the external agent acting in us, the activity itself cannot as such be the matter of our feeling. Following this line of thought, we may understand a little better the ancient distinction between *matter* and *body*.

1014. In the second place, we note that although the *body* is capable of receiving in itself the activity over the spirit of which we have spoken, this concealed activity is less noticed than other bodily qualities, especially *extension* and *inertia*. We shall understand this better by setting out in order the propositions we have already demonstrated.

1. The various ways of perceiving *bodies* offer such different perceptions that bodies appear to be *different entia*.

2. These *different entia* arise: *a*) partly because subjectivity plays a great role in the perception of bodies, causing them to exist as different *proximate terms* of our perception (the variation depends on the different 'mix' of subjectivity); *b*) partly because one kind of perception uncovers properties of a body that remain hidden in other kinds of perception (so that the body seems to be a different ens). Perceiving an external body with our organs, we obtain what we may call 'blind' qualities, rather than perceive the body's aptitude for being the matter of feeling, which we recognise only through our own feeling.

3. Consequently, the word 'body' takes various meanings as we use it to describe what we perceive in different ways.

4. The normal meaning attributed to 'body' depends upon what we perceive of external bodies with our five organs, because we easily advert to this *perception*, while perception

originating in the fundamental feeling or in the subjective sensation is very difficult *to reflect upon* and *distinguish*.[246]

Observations of this kind enable us to understand why 'body' is not used, commonly speaking, to indicate the intimate force with which it acts upon our spirit, causing the spirit to react and bring about union. Here, we may usefully observe what happens in acquired sensations from which we normally obtain the idea for which we invent the word 'body.'

1015. When an external body acts upon an organ, it simply produces a change in the sensitive form of the organ or, more generally speaking, causes movement in it. Given this movement, the spirit feels a new sensation which does not, however, stimulate it to some totally new activity. The law governing its feeling of the body is: 'The spirit feels the body in the sensitive state the spirit has as that moment' (cf. 705 ss.). When an external body acts upon a living body, therefore, it changes the living body's sensitive state while the sensitive principle, following it own action and the law governing this action, now feels the new state of the organ. But there has been no radically new action of the body on the spirit. The action here can be reduced to that between our own body and an external body whose mutual activity follows not particular laws but the mechanical, physical and chemical laws common to all inanimate bodies. The spirit does not unite itself to any new body while this is happening, and no new body acts upon it. Its own body's action, which it has not experienced in any new way, was present antecedently to what occurred. In an acquired sensation, therefore, all that can be perceived and noted of bodies is *external action* of the kind that external bodies exercise on one another. Because the action of our own body on the spirit is not comprised in this sensation, the action is not normally associated with the word 'body' which is generally reserved for the mutual extrasubjective action of bodies according to mechanical, physical and chemical laws. It is not difficult to see, therefore, how the word 'body' is void of any meaning indicating activity on the spirit.

1016. In the third place, the *activity* we have attributed to the

---

[246] Moreover, we have to reflect that with the external organs we perceive qualities absolutely necessary to a body, although unhelpful for discerning the nature of the *corporeal principle*.

body does not derive from the nature itself of the body, commonly so-called. This needs careful attention, and justifies common sense when it excludes from the meaning of 'body' the activity we have been examining. Generally speaking, therefore, the word 'body' offers no indication of activity, especially on our spirit.

1017. We can see this more clearly by examining the nature of the action of bodies among themselves and on our spirit.

I. *Movement*, which each body receives from outside, is not essential to bodies. However, the action done by *external* bodies on our organs seems to depend entirely upon movement. *Resistance* is simply the division of movement in the various parts of the body. *Adherence* between the parts only presents us with a law determining the number of parts amongst which movement has to be divided. The action of external bodies upon our own, therefore, as we normally experience it, is an activity received by the body but not essential and proper to it. Hence the body is truly *passive* relative to the activity of movement, because it only receives and communicates the movement.

1018. II. It seems evident, if we go on to speak about the action of our body on the spirit, that this action also is not comprised in the nature of the (extrasubjective) body, but is received by the body from some principle outside itself. If the aptitude for acting on the spirit were essential to our body as such, every body would have to be thought of as animated. But the normal concept of body tells us nothing of animation. Although the body *acts* on the spirit, it does not do so through an active principle demanded by its nature as body, but through an activity it has received. Relative to this activity, therefore, the body is an *inert, passive ens*, which receives but does not give.[247]

In the fourth place, (and the following observation seems to me the most important of all those made so far), the *body*, according to its common concept, does not as such act on the spirit, but receives this *activity*. But could it not receive this activity from the spirit itself? As we have already seen, 'One ens can stimulate activity in another, which can in its turn act upon

---

[247] Hence St. Thomas shows that the soul is something different from the body (*S.T.*, 1, q. 75, art. 1).

the ens which stimulates it.' We have already applied this to the action of the body, but could it not be applied much better to the action of the spirit?

1019. Meditation on this problem offers the following probable result:

I. For some kinds of action, the human spirit is determined by certain conditions, one of which is the existence of a body suitably organised for the spirit. This, however, requires no action on the part of the body, but depends upon a state of the body received from outside.

II. When such a perfectly organised body has been harmonised with the spirit, it seems that the spirit, now possessing the necessary condition for carrying out the action we have indicated, acts with this body, imparting to it the activity we call 'life', through which the body acquires the final properties of living bodies.

III. This activity received by the body is such that in its turn it reacts upon the spirit, drawing the spirit to the act called 'fundamental feeling.'

IV. The fundamental feeling pervades the body and makes it its *matter*, that is, its seat, its mode of being, its extension.

V. The body, as *matter* of the feeling, retains its inertia, remaining subject to the action of other external bodies. When the *matter which is felt* changes, the feeling changes, not however through any new action of the *matter* on the spirit, but through the law obliging the spirit to conclude its act in its matter, which is the passive term of the act.

PART SIX

Conclusion

CHAPTER 1
Epilogue of the Theory

1020. The original potencies of the soul are two senses, one for particular things, which constitutes the potency normally called 'sensitivity', and one for universal things,[248] which constitutes the potency normally called 'intellect'.[249]

1021. Every potency, is a particular first act, constituted by an inherent term essential to it. This term is called 'matter' if it is *passive* relative to the potency, and *form* if it is, as object, in a state of *mere presence* relative to the potency. This presence is such that it posits the subject in the act which constitutes the potency (cf. 1006 ss.).

[248] I have explained what must be understood by 'universal thing' (cf. vol. 1, 107ss.). Nothing can be universal in itself. Everything, in so far as it is, is singular and determined. A universal, therefore, is something through which many things, or rather an indefinite number of things, can be known. Universality is a mere relationship found only in ideas which, as we have seen, are things with which we know an indefinite number of other things. From this point of view, we call an idea a 'species'. It is true that at first sight there appears to be something besides ideas that can be called 'universal' and in this sense a portrait perhaps seems universal because it represents all its look-alikes. But this is misleading: the portrait is universal only in so far it is joined to an idea. It is only through the idea of the portrait that the mind is able to compare the portrait and the people it resembles, and to find the likeness which does not exist in the portrait but in the single idea with which the portrait and persons resembling it are thought. It is the unity of the idea which constitutes the likeness between similar things, as we see in our example of the portrait and the persons resembling it (cf. vol. 1, 177).

[249] We have reduced the power of understanding to a primal sense (cf. 553–558).

The essential term of sensitivity is its *matter*; the essential term of the intellect is its *object* and *form* (cf. 1010, 480–485).

1022. Sensitivity is *external* or *internal*. *External* sensitivity has body, that is, extended corporeal matter, as its essential term. *Internal* sensitivity has for its term the feeling of *myself* and the idea (cf. 473–479, 630–672).

The fundamental feeling of one's own body constitutes the potency of *external sensitivity* (cf. 721–728).

The simple feeling of *myself* constitutes the potency of *internal sensitivity* (cf. 692–720). The feeling that perceives the idea of being in all its universality constitutes the potency of the intellect (cf. 480–485).

1023. If the *matter* of sensitivity is removed, the *sensitive ens* no longer exists. If the *form* of the intellect is removed, the latter ceases, but the concept of *sensitive ens* remains intact. Hence, the *idea of being in all its universality* is a true, apprehended object, and distinct from the sensitive ens. But the term of sensitivity is constitutive of the sensitive ens and, because indistinguishable from it, cannot be called 'object' (cf. 1010 ss., 409–429).

1024. Perception and intuition require something distinct from the perceiving subject, and are therefore essentially extrasubjective; sensation requires only some *matter* (cf. 449, 742–752). Hence intellect is an *intuition*; sensitivity is simply a *primal feeling*.

1025. All these potencies exist in my fundamental feeling prior to their various operations, that is, in the feeling of myself together with my body (sensitivity) and my intellect.

This intimate, perfectly *one* feeling unites sensitivity and intellect. It also possesses an activity, which I would call 'spiritual sight' (rationality), by which it sees the relationship between sensitivity and intellect. This function constitutes the *primal synthesis* (cf. 528–555).

But if we consider more generally the activity originating from the intimate unity of the fundamental feeling, that is, if we consider *myself* as capable of seeing *relationships* in general, we call it *reason*, of which the *primal synthesis* becomes the first *function* (cf. 622, 480–482).

If we consider the same activity under the special respect of the union that it brings about between a predicate and a subject, it is called the *faculty of judgment* (cf. vol. 1, 337).

1026. The *primal synthesis* is the judgment with which *reason* acquires *intellective perception*.

But we cannot rise to any operation unless we are given some stimulus, or *mover*.

External sensitivity is the first potency drawn to operate by the stimuli of external bodies upon our organs (cf. 514 ss.). When *external sensitivity* has been aroused by these stimuli it informs our consciousness of a passivity coming not from our own body, but from a body separate from ourselves. This new feeling, that is, the modification of our fundamental feeling, becomes *sense perception* as the term of an external action, although previously it was simply feeling and a fundamental perception through which the soul is united to the body (cf. 630–691).

1027. The *first matter* of human cognitions ministered by *sensitivity* consists therefore in:

1. A feeling of *myself*, perceptive of the body (fundamental feeling).

2. The sensations or modifications of this feeling.

3. The sense perceptions of bodies.

1028. When reason considers these things in relationship with *being in all its universality*, and produces *intellective perceptions*, it adds *universality* to the particular changes experienced in our spirit, and under this aspect is called the *faculty of universalisation*. All *direct acts* of reason depend upon this special potency (cf. 490–500).

Reflective acts are proper to *reflection*, another *function* of *reason* (cf. 487–489).

1029. The objects of reflection are all acts of our spirit, in so far as it reasons, and terms of these acts. Thus, there is some impropriety in applying the word 'reflection' to the direct application of our understanding to sensations (cf. [*App.*, no. 12]). The *objects* of reflection, therefore, are:

1. A feeling of *myself* as perceptive of the idea of being in all its universality.

2. Acts of the faculty of universalisation.

3. Acts of reflection, and its terms or results.

Reflection has two operations, *synthesis* and *analysis*; it separates and unites (cf. 490 ss.). The faculty of *abstraction* (cf. 494 ss.) pertains to *analysis*.

1030. External stimuli excite *external sensitivity*. Physical instincts, by moving the phantasy initially, arouse the faculty of *universalisation*.

Corporeal images awake the potency for dividing ideas from perceptions.

Only language, received from society, can draw the faculty of *abstract ideas* into its act and furnish human beings with dominion over their own potencies, that is, with the use of *freedom* (cf. 483 ss.)

1031. *Free activity*, that is, dominion over one's own potencies acquired through abstract ideas furnished by language, provides the final impetus to the development of all one's potencies, and opens the way to the indefinite growth of the different human faculties.

[1031]

CHAPTER 2

The question concerning the origin of ideas

1032. There is *popular knowledge* and *philosophical knowledge*, as St. Thomas himself carefully distinguishes.

I have demonstrated the relationship between *popular knowledge* and this work, which is only, and only wants to be, the development of a popular opinion (cf. 1 ss.)

Whenever I have had the opportunity, I have also tried to show the relationship of the work to *philosophical knowledge*. I have indicated the sound cognitions of philosophers who preceded me and have profited from their teachings. But to do them greater justice, I want to add a few more words.

1033. Many wise thinkers, mentioned in the course of this work, have glimpsed the importance of the *idea of being* in all its universality and its intimate union with our mind. In modern philosophy Malebranche was, I think, one of those who best saw this important truth:

> The clear, intimate and necessary presence of ens, understood in a *undetermined* way, of ens *in general* present to the human mind, acts more forcefully in the mind than the presence of all finite things offered to the mind, and can never be banished by the mind.[250]

It is extraordinary to see how this outstanding Cartesian was aware that thinking of ens is more essential to our spirit than thinking of ourselves. This truth, which Descartes himself did not see [*App.*, no. 45], refutes the whole foundation of Cartesian philosophy. Malebranche adds:

> Persons may indeed not think of themselves for some time, but I do not believe that anyone can for a single instant not think of ens. On the contrary, even when we believe we are not thinking of anything, we are filled with the undetermined, general idea of ens.[251]

---

[250] Bk. 3, c. 8

[251] *Ibid.* — This observation was made by the author of the *Itinerarium*, as we have seen.

Moreover, Malebranche was not ignorant of the usual objection put by the uneducated and beginners in philosophy. Because they have reflected little on themselves, they easily say, 'If we thought ens continually, we would know it.' Malebranche gives the same answer as I, following the tradition of all antiquity. I showed that the objection arose from defective observation and from making one fact out of two very distinct facts of consciousness: 1. the act of our spirit; and 2 advertence to this act. Malebranche says the same immediately after the passage quoted above:

> Things which are very familiar to us and of little importance do not vividly stimulate our mind or motivate its attention. The idea of ens, although great, vast and true, is extremely familiar to us and stimulates us so little that we think we do not perceive it. Hence we do not turn our spirit to it; we hardly believe it exists, we draw its origin solely from the extreme confusion of all special ideas, even though we perceive all particular entia in and through it alone.[252]

He was indeed very close to finding the thread in the extremely intricate labyrinth of ideas: unknowingly, he had it in his hand. However, instead of saying, with St. Thomas, that the idea of ens is a created light, he makes it God himself. This was his mistake. Up to this point he had maintained an acute observation of human nature, applying accurate logic. But now he abandoned his method and, with his imagination, traversed the immense space between creature and Creator. He had said that the idea of ens is *vague* and *undetermined* and *ens in general*.[253] But the idea of God is not vague; God is infinite, not *undetermined*. Finally, God is not *being common* to all things, much less *being in general*, but first, certain, complete being outside all genera. This distinction between ideal, universal being and

[252] *Ibid.*

[253] St. Thomas and St. Bonaventura say very fittingly that God is not 'most common being', but 'supreme, absolute being'. We can easily see that Malebranche had received from his contemporaries a certain lack of esteem for the authors of this earlier period and, I would say, for authors before Descartes, with the exception of St. Augustine, on whom Descartes himself had drawn.

subsistent being is a truth preserved in the deposit of Christian tradition which should have been known and not neglected by such a great man.

1034. Malebranche and his system were preceded in France by Tommassini. At the same time, an Italian, Fr. Giovenale dell'Anaunia (Val di Non) in the Italian Tyrol, was reflecting on these matters. This little-known but learned Capuchin[254] published a book written in Latin in which he proposed the very system which, coming from the elegant pen of Malebranche, had resounding effect in the world. And for the sake of truth, I must say that in comparison with Malebranche's work, Fr. Giovenale's presents a more widely developed and moderate teaching. He is not ignorant of, and does not avoid the difficulties I have mentioned relative to Malebranche's system. He limits and adapts the meaning of his expressions in such a way that they do not oppose the great tradition of Catholic truth. Following the path of the Fathers, he continually seeks to reconcile the teachings of St. Augustine on this matter with the sentiments of St. Thomas.

1035. Previous to these authors, the Platonists who flourished in Tuscany under the Medici had come to sense the importance of the idea of being hidden in the remnants of ancient philosophy. Marsilio Ficino, whom we can consider as their head, clearly teaches that the notion of ens is present in all human beings, and his explanation of this truth is worth noting: 'All human beings *judge* that one being is not at all, that another is in a more imperfect way and that another is in a less imperfect way' [*App.*, no. 46]. The need of the idea of being for *making a*

---

[254] His work was printed in Augsburg under the title '*Solis intelligentiae, cui non succedit nox, lumen indeficiens ac inexstinguibile illuminans omnem hominem venientem in hunc mundum etc*', *per P. Juvenalem Anauniensem ord. Capuccinorum. Augustae Vindelicorum, Typis Simonis Uzschneideri reverendiss. ac altiss. Principis et Episcopi Augustani typographi, Anno MDCLXXXVI*. It is interesting that Fr. Giovenale died in 1713, just a short time before Malebranche. His book could be the first seed of the teachings developed and illustrated later by the Reformed Minors Fathers Ercolano and Filibert. Further information regarding Fr. Giovenale can be found in Jacopo Tartarotti's *Biblioteca Tirolese*, enlarged by Todeschini and printed in Venice, 1733, and also in Count Francesco Barbacovi's *Memorie storiche della Città e territorio di Trento*, vol. 1.

judgment is precisely the path I have followed to establish the co-created idea antecedent to all other ideas. However, Ficino does not take and develop this fertile thought. Instead he gives it the same importance as many other thoughts of lesser value. Moreover, Platonists generally fall into the confusion already mentioned between the idea of common being or being in potency and the idea of first, most actual being. They transform human reason into divine essence.

1036. The truths in question were not unknown to the scholastics, and I have shown this by the many places I have quoted from these authors. But I think they failed to investigate the connection binding the truths they knew. Consequently they failed to give to the system concerning the origin of ideas all its necessary simplicity and clarity. For many, our *first information* comes from a hidden, obscure source or a source which at best they described vaguely and metaphorically, or else declared it a species of instinct. This is how Dante understood the scholastic opinion, which he presented as follows:

> Every substantial form distinct from matter,
> but with matter united,
> has within itself specific virtue
> which when inactive is not felt
> nor ever shows itself except by its effects,
> as verdant leaf reveals life in the plant.
> So too we do not know whence comes
> our understanding of our first cognitions,
> nor whence affection for what we first desire.
> These things are to us
> as instinct to the bee for honey-making,
> — neither praised nor blamed.[255]

1037. This opinion that what we first know comes from an obscure source, from a blind instinct, from a law of human nature is the teaching finally taken up by the whole of modern philosophy, from Reid to Galluppi. Reid introduced a mysterious prompting on the part of nature; Kant, using the scholastic expression, introduced some forms in nature itself. These two opinions were revived a short time ago in France where two

[255] *Purg.* 18. — the image of the bee is taken from Arist. *Metaph.*, bk. 1, c. 10.

opposing parties seem intent on profitting from the same principle of blind, instinctive faith as the source of all that we first know. Finally, in Italy, Galluppi astutely refuted the error of these philosophers but still called ideas of *unity*, *identity*, etc., 'subjective', as if they emerged and drew existence from the subject himself. But if *what we first know* is not totally independent of the subject, and has no objective existence, the whole of human knowledge is, in my opinion, shaken to its foundations. Certainty is no longer possible, and scepticism, an impossible system, is inevitable. There is surely only one way to lay a firm foundation for human knowledge and certainty: we must accept that our thoughts do have an object which is necessary, universal and independent of human beings and every creature. This is the theory that I have explained of the con-created idea of being .

CHAPTER 3

Learning to understand what has been said about the origin of ideas

1038. However, it is not easy to grasp the theory I have developed about the origin of ideas. Reading about the theory is certainly insufficient; careful observation of one's own human nature is also required. Without such observation, it is possible to be misled about one's understanding of the book and to form a very mistaken view of what has been said.

But there is one helpful and fairly easy way to comprehend the argument. If four points are thoroughly examined and understood, the rest will follow. And although these four points are certainly not the most difficult and mysterious elements of human nature, they offer a path opening on to belief in the most wonderful truths. In a word, if we are prepared to accept as fact what has fallen under our own certain observation, even though it remains inexplicable and mysterious, we shall be able to penetrate ever deeper into the secrets of the intelligent spirit, secrets about which we shall no longer be able to doubt.

1039. The four points we have to make are four distinctions which will serve as a sign differentiating those who have understood the theory from others who have read but not grasped it. They are:

I. the distinction between *sensation* and *sense perception* (cf. 740–748);

II. the distinction between the *idea* of something and *judgment* about the thing's subsistence (cf. 402–409);

III. the distinction between *sense perception* and *intellective perception* (cf. 961 ss.);

IV. the distinction between *an act of the spirit*, and *advertence* to that act, for example, between feeling and adverting to feeling (cf. 548 ss.).

If these distinctions are noted carefully as facts concerning the human spirit, and their application becomes easy through constant use, the theory I have outlined will be faithfully understood and the effort made to write this book with all clarity will be rewarded not by infusing truth, which is impossible, but by helping others on the way to truth.

Appendix

1. (438)

[D'Alembert, Falletti and Galluppi on the feeling of *myself*]

D'Alembert in France and Falletti in Italy thought they could deduce the idea of existence in all its universality from the feeling of *myself*, that is, of the existence of ourselves. D'Alembert says:

> The abstract notion of existence is formed immediately by means of the feeling of *myself* which comes from our sensations and thoughts. We think that it is *possible* to separate this feeling of *myself* from the subject containing it without the subject's being destroyed. This gives us the abstract idea of existence which we then apply to entia different from us that seem to cause our sensations.
>
> (*Mélanges, éclaircissements sur ses éléments de philosophie*, §11)

The inaccuracies in this passage are almost impossible to list in a note. I will deal briefly with the principal errors:

1. The feeling of *myself* is confused with the idea of *myself*. These two things are totally different, as I will show in the next paragraph [439].

2. The feeling of *myself* is said to be acquired along with sensations and thoughts. If this were true, MYSELF would begin to exist only when I begin to be modified.

3. The subject containing the feeling of *myself* is said to be distinct from *myself* and considered divided from *myself* although *myself* alone is the *subject*.

4. Two things are therefore made out of one: the one subject *myself* is made into a non-subject *myself* and into a subject united with *myself*. The subject thus separated from *myself* (or rather created by the imagination), is said to be the same as the *idea of existence in all its universality*, although subject and existence are in fact two totally distinct things.

[*app.*, 1]

5. Finally a contradiction is gratuitously supposed as possible, namely that the *idea of universal ens* can be drawn from a *particular ens* (like *myself*), although what is universal is the contrary of what is particular and that which is does not in any way include that which is only possible.

Falletti, in his attempt to produce the idea of existence in all its universality from the feeling of *myself*, is more cautious and discerning than D'Alembert. He is aware that *myself*, as a fundamental feeling, must be essentially in us from the very first moment of our existence because *we* can never be without *ourselves*. He is also aware that, in his own words, 'the idea of *being in all its universality* must always be present to the soul' (*Saggio sopra l'origine delle umane cognizioni dell'abate Condillac, tradotto — colle osservazioni critiche di Tommaso Vincenzo Falletti*, Rome, 1784, vol. 1, p. 4). He supposes that the soul extracts this idea from itself through a primal, natural act. This is unsustainable because the soul, lacking the idea of existence in all its universality, cannot draw this idea from a particular ens such as *itself*. However, we see the extent to which Falletti sensed the truth which I have tried to explain at length in this work.

Among living Italian philosophers, Galluppi evidently agrees with these two thinkers, but his perspicacity sometimes puts him in opposition to them and draws him to cast doubt on the very doctrine he professes. For example, he says:

> Although the spirit begins its actions with the perception of *individual existences*, it cannot say 'I exist' unless it has acquired the most universal idea of existence. Thus when we see a fig tree or orange tree, we say it is a 'tree' only when we have acquired the general idea of 'tree', UNLESS WE WISH TO SAY THAT THE IDEA OF EXISTENCE IS IN-NATE IN US. But even in this hypothesis the spirit needs consciousness of reflection, of which I have spoken above, in order to be able to say 'I exist'
> (*Saggio sulla critica della Conoscenza*, Naples, 1819, vol. 1, p. 51)

In this passage Galluppi acutely touches the true system but lacks the courage to grasp it.

2. (442)
[St. Thomas on knowledge]

All this teaching may be found in the corpus of knowledge handed down to us by our predecessors. St. Thomas (*Contra Gent.*, III, q. 46) teaches that our soul needs an *intelligible species* in order to know itself, just as it does to know other things. 'Intelligible species', as I shall show later, is to be understood simply as a *universal idea* to which the soul (this particular ens) adheres as to its genus, or rather its major predicate. The soul, therefore, is known through the light of the *acting intellect* (the *idea of being*) in the same way as other beings. Here, too, St. Thomas distinguishes between the *matter* and *form* of knowledge. With its feeling of self, the soul provides only the matter of knowledge. This matter, informed through an innate light, becomes true knowledge. St. Thomas says:

> Natural knowledge is that which comes about through something placed in us by nature (*naturaliter nobis additum*). Of this kind are the indemonstrable principles known through the light of the acting intellect. If we knew the soul by means of the soul itself, this too would be natural knowledge. But in things known to us by nature, there is no error... Man does not err in his knowledge of principles. There would be no error, therefore, about the substance of the soul if this were known to us *per se*. But it is obviously false that the soul is known *per se*.

He goes on a little later:

> What is known *per se* must be known prior to everything known mediately. *Per se* knowledge, like first propositions related to conclusions, is the principle of knowledge related to mediate knowledge. But if the soul were to know its own substance through itself, it would be known *per se*, and consequently would be the first thing known and the principle of knowledge of everything else. But this is obviously false. The substance of the soul is not admitted and presumed as something already known. It has to be investigated and deduced from the principles.

These quotations show that: 1. St. Thomas admitted knowledge of the principles prior to particular knowledge of the soul; 2. knowledge of our own soul is impossible without knowledge of the principles; 3. the first principles are known *per se* and immediately through the innate light which, as we have shown elsewhere and go on repeating, can only be the *idea of being*; 4. the soul, known through the same principles governing our knowledge of other things, is neither what is *first known* nor the *principle of knowledge of other things*. It cannot, therefore, be the source whence we deduce universal ideas and principles, as Descartes and many others thought. Rather, knowledge of the soul has to be deduced from the universal principles.

Aristotle recognised this truth when he said that the possible intellect *knows itself in the same way* as it knows other things (*De Anima*, bk. 3, 45).

3. (453)

[Reid and analysis of sensation]

I think that these three events must be distinguished, but that Reid did not sufficiently describe the second (*sensation*). For him, sensation is simply a modification of the spirit so simple that the only notion we have of it is that of a relationship of the spirit with itself. More accurately, it is merely a different state of the spirit. But my analysis of sensation gives another result.

Sensation is an *experience* which on analysis always yields three elements: that which experiences; that which causes the experience; the experience itself. I note also that while a thing is indicated through *experience* relative to the one who experiences, the same thing is indicated through *action* relative to the agent. This difference in relationship with the one who experiences and the agent enables what is one thing to become two for our mind as a resuslt of the different relationship that the mind adds to it. And this single thing becomes two really different things relative to the terms to which it is referred. For the one who has the experience, the sensation is entirely different and contrary to that which it is to the agent.

It is now clear that *sensation*, as passive, is not a means of perceiving a single thing in itself devoid of relationships, but of perceiving it as experience, that is, related solely to the experiencer without reference to the thing's being as action, which is its very own being. In a *sensation*, the subject receiving the sensation, besides feeling itself, also experiences an event which does not come from itself (the experience it has), but which terminates in some other being as in its cause. It is true that the purely sentient subject does not perceive itself and what acts upon it as totally separate, but this does not prevent us from mentally distinguishing in the sensation: 1. a relationship with the sentient subject as sentient; 2. a relationship terminating not in the sentient subject, but in some other ens different from itself.

We have reserved the word *sensation* to indicate the sentient subject in so far as it senses, and the phrase *sense perception of bodies* to indicate sensation itself as a mere experience which, as such, is necessarily related with something extraneous to and different from the sentient subject.

Hence: 1. *sense perception of bodies*; 2. *intellective perception* (cf. 417, 418).

As I have said on several occasions, *sense perception* is subject to the action of our spirit, which *takes and envelops* bodies themselves. But we cannot say the same of *intellective perception*, except in so far as sense perception serves as *matter* for intellective perception.

According to this manner of speaking, Reid's error consisted in distinguishing only three things in the intellective perception of bodies. He should have distinguished four: 1. the mechanical *impression* on the organs; 2. *sensation* (considered in its sole relationship with the subject); 3. the *sense perception* of bodies (that is, our undergoing an experience caused by something outside us); and 4. the *intellective perception* of bodies (that is, acknowledgement of agents acting on us in a particular mode).

Because he failed to make this precise distinction, Reid confused *sense perception of bodies* with *intellective perception*, attributing to the former what applied to the latter. By making *intellective perception* and *sense perception* one thing only, he had to deny *ideas*, which he did not find in *sense perception*, although he did find the *perception of bodies*. He concluded therefore that the *perception of bodies* did not require *ideas*.

[*app.*, 3]

I grant that the *sense perception of bodies* does not require ideas, but we cannot have the *intellective perception* of bodies without at least the idea of existence.

Reid would have avoided this error if he had formed a clear idea of the *sense perception of bodies*. He would have seen that this kind of perception, which lacks anything intellectual, is not sufficient. It is certainly very difficult to form a clear notion of the *sense perception of bodies* precisely because in this perception we do not perceive bodies as such — we simply perceive them in and with us as terms of our *experience*, not as *agents*. Hence, I do not consider the phrase 'sense perception of bodies' accurate enough, since in this expression 'body' indicates something perceived intellectively. A more accurate expression, even if a little strange, would be 'corporeal sense perception'.

4. (453)
[Intellective and sense perception]

Intellective perception of bodies bears no likeness to *sensation*. But has *bodily sense perception* any likeness to the *intellective perception of bodies*? I maintain that there is a strict relationship between these two perceptions, but no relationship of likeness.

In *bodily sense perception*, it is not the body which is perceived, properly speaking, but an *experience* terminating in an outside agent. In *intellective perception of bodies*, the opposite is true: the *body itself* is perceived as an object acting in us. The two *perceptions* are contraries, just as *passive experience* and *action* are contraries.

Passive experience and *action* are opposed as such, but the understanding, when disregarding the particular, contrary relationships with the experiencer and agent, considers them as one and the same thing.

The nature of the understanding is to perceive things in themselves; it is not limited to perceiving their relationships. When the understanding has perceived the thing we are discussing (that is, the change taking place in us) as it is in itself, it also finds an association between *experience* and *action*; it has perceived their link, that is, the thing which is capable of two contrary relationships. This explains the association between *bodily sense perception* and the *intellective perception of bodies.*

Sense perception is an element (*matter*) of *intellective perception. Intellective perception*, composed of *matter* and *form*, cannot be said to resemble *sense perception* which is subordinate to and an element of intellective perception; it is neither equal to nor a copy of intellective perception. Thus, we do not normally say that a particular mouth is like the head containing the mouth, just as we do not normally say that the square shape of some particular object resembles the substance of the object, although the body is square in shape.

Nevertheless, the relationship between a *bodily sense perception* and the *intellective perception of that body* is so close that with each perception we perceive the same thing identically although in a different mode. With intellective perception we perceive in a universal mode what we perceive in a particular way with sense perception. The intellect adds being, that is, it adds the cause to the effect perceived by sense.

5. (453)

[Philosophy and mysteries]

Philosophy sometimes holds back from mysteries, and sometimes leads to them. Is philosophy, therefore, opposed only to certain mysteries and not to them all? I am speaking, of course, only of a tendency shown by a certain kind of philosophy — a tendency which to a great extent is independent of the individuals professing the philosophy. When I give my adhesion to a school or method of philosophy, I absorb its spirit without discerning clearly the nature of this spirit, which I follow blindly in the hope of reaching a happy conclusion. I say this in order to be fair to everyone, even while I indicate the nature and tendency of a certain kind of philosophy to avoid some mysteries and embrace others.

The mysteries it avoids are those which suppose the existence of something spiritual. Imagine now what happens when such a philosophy reaches a point beyond which it cannot go without recurring to something spiritual. It declares, 'No progress can be made here,' and creates a *mystery* by positing an inexplicable difficulty. At this point, our philosopher is quite capable of praising his own modesty, and of accusing others of presumption. He is governed, however, by a secret prejudice which excludes spirit as unnecessary, and reduces everything to matter.

What happens if a person begins from an unproven proposition which he accepts and loves absolutely to the exclusion of its contrary? He will proceed freely without turning to any 'elevated' notions until he can no longer advance without admitting something spiritual. Then he stops, and says that philosophical prudence requires him to retreat. Arbitrary, voluntary and humiliating limits of this nature, dependent upon a blind belief that what is disliked is unintelligible, first limits knowledge by forbidding human beings the free use of their reason, their highest faculty. They then go on to destroy philosophy and science by rendering human knowledge impossible. The more we meditate, the more we see that eliminating 'spirit' from the universe renders human wisdom vain and absurd. Intelligence, cut off from the divine, loses its human quality. Modern scepticism, indifference, selfishness and Epicureanism are the inevitable result of the philosophy we are speaking of. But even as *they boast of their status*, sceptics reason, cynics feel, egoists love and Epicureans rise from their baseness. Caught in this appalling contradiction, human beings stand self-condemned. Human nature, and the truth which mingles with it, cannot be filed away and forgotten.

6. (467)

[St. Thomas on union of the spirit with the idea of being]

We could ask what kind of union exists between the idea of being and our spirit. In some places, St Thomas seems to consider the union similar to that of ideas lying in our memory but not actually present in our thought; he says they form 'habitual knowledge' (*De Verit.*, q. 10, arts. 8–9). Similarly, St. Thomas' speculative and practical innate principles are *habitually* in us (*habitus principiorum*) and, on the occasion of sensations (*phantasmata*), are immediately drawn into act by the *acting*

[*app.*, 6]

intellect, as if we were recalling something. Note however that in addition to these innate notions *habitually* in us but not in *act*, St. Thomas posits an acting intellect which is truly in *act* and, with its *light*, makes everything actually present to thought. I believe that this *light* of the acting intellect, hidden under the metaphor and never (or very rarely and only fleetingly) uncovered by the ancient writers, is indeed the *idea of being*. This is certainly St. Bonaventure's opinion. One passage of St. Thomas could at first sight raise doubts about his opinion on this matter and about complete agreement with his great friend, St. Bonaventure. However I think the two great men can be reconciled by a careful understanding of St. Thomas' words. The passage I refer to states:

> Similarly, we must say that knowledge is acquired in the following way. Certain seeds of knowledge, that is, the first conceptions of the intellect, pre-exist in us. These are known immanently through the light of the acting intellect by means of the species abstracted from phantasms. It does not matter whether the phantasms are complex, as in the case of norms, or simple, as in the case of the concept of ENS (*ratio entis*) or ONE, or similar things which are soon apprehended by the intellect. All other principles come from these universal principles as from seminal reasons.
>
> (*De Verit.*, q. 11, art. 1)

This passage raises doubt about St. Thomas' opinion: he places the *concept of ens* among things directly seen by the acting intellect but on the occasion of phantasms. According to him therefore ens does not form the *acting intellect* itself, as in my conjecture. I would, however, suggest the following interpretation.

St. Thomas' words indicate that having the *concept of ens* (*ratio entis*) is one thing, having *ens* pure and simple is another. Having the concept of ens would mean understanding its force, that is, understanding how it can be applied and produce different cognitions in us from deep within itself. I, too, think that the force, fecundity and energy with which the idea of ens is applied cannot be known until we actually apply it on the occasion of sensations (phantasms). In this case, the idea is no longer solitary and inactive but operative. We consider it attentively and with new concentration, and become aware of its *notion* or intimate nature (*ratio entis*). However, whatever the case may be, we must grant that the idea of being adheres either actually or habitually to our spirit. When I have the idea, I can deduce from it every speculative and practical principle, and therefore explain the fact of human knowledge. When I lack the idea, either God must reveal it to me or I must create it for myself in the act of sensation. Both of these explanations are unacceptable.

Finally I note that St. Thomas himself uses the same expressions as I do and hence considers them true. For example, he says that the light of the acting intellect *formaliter inhaeret intellectui* [adheres formally to the intellect] (*S. T.*, I, q. 74, art. 4) and, speaking about the habitual knowledge which the soul has of itself, says *ipsa eius essentia intellectui nostro est praesens* [its essence is present to our intellect] and again, *anima per essentiam suam se videt* [the soul sees itself through its essence] (*De Verit.*, q. 10, art. 8) etc., although this seeing, for St. Thomas, is *habitual* not *actual* knowledge.

If I had time to explain more clearly, I could establish the following truth, which must seem obvious to those well accustomed to observing and reflecting upon themselves: 'Every act of our spirit is essentially unknown to itself.' The opinion that 'we have an actual vision of undetermined being at every moment of our existence', including the very first moments of which we have no memory at all, may indeed be difficult and awkward for some, but the difficulty would totally disappear and the opinion be accepted (even if with a certain wonder) without any recourse to *habitual* or dormant knowledge. However, because the mode of conceiving the union between the idea of being and ourselves is not of great relevance, I add nothing further provided the union itself is acknowledged.

7. (470)

[Plato and the idea of being]

These observations did not escape Plato, whose noble mind raised him high above ordinary people. He notes (and he himself experienced) that talking about things found in the human

spirit to someone who has not seen them gives rise to ridicule
and to the accusation of being a dreamer. For this reason, his
hidden or *esoteric* teaching (and that of the ancients before him)
was imparted only to a few initiates — giving it to the multitude
would only have invited contempt. The idea of *being*, the purest
of all ideas, is the last and most difficult idea to be noticed. Some
passages of Plato make me think either that he saw this idea but,
finding it too difficult, dealt with it only superficially, or as
Dante thinks (*Inferno*, 16: 124), presented it under the guise of
images and only in passing:

> No truth that seems a lie
> Should ever pass our lips
> If undeservèd blame's to be avoided.

I am speaking to a Christian world. I can therefore rightly
presume well of people and address them openly about these
difficult things. However, in order not to leave unproven what I
said about Plato, let me quote some passages of this great author
which confirm my judgment. In many places, Plato compares
the mind with the eye which sees only by means of the sun's
rays. This light, which for Plato illumines the mind but is lacking to the senses, is the idea of being or, in his words, of ens. I say
the *idea of ens* because according to Plato this light comes from
God (the ENS). In the *Republic* (book 6), however, he clearly
states that this light is not God, a distinction which Platonists
have abused. He says, 'The sun we see is not the sun itself,' and
then argues as follows:

> *Socrates*: Our eyes see whenever they are turned to things
> whose colours are illumined and manifested by daylight.
> But when we look at things in the dark, we see only
> vaguely and obscurely; our eyes seem almost totally blind,
> as if there were no pure sight in them.
> *Glaucon*: That is true.
> *Socrates*: But when our eyes look at things illumined by
> the sun, sight seems to be in the eyes themselves.
> *Glaucon*: Correct.
> *Socrates*: The same is true of the spirit. Applying itself to
> that in which the truth and ENS itself shines (that is, to *in-*
> *telligible* things), it understands and knows; it shows it has

intellect. But when it is drawn to what is mixed with darkness, to that which generates and corrupts (note how Plato
characterizes sensible things), its gaze is blurred; it forms
various opinions and seems to have no mind.

In the next dialogue (book 7), he uses an image to show how
difficult it is for us to rise from *sensible* things to the vision of
intelligible things and to *ens*. He imagines a straight cave deep
underground. At one end, there is an opening where a light
shines directly to the other end. There are people in the cave
bound in such a position that they can never turn their heads or
backs to see the opening and the light; they can look only at the
end wall. At the opening to the cave, vases and statues of people
and animals are placed in such a way that they cast their shadow
on this wall. As a result only the shadows can be seen by the
captives, who think that nothing else exists except the shadows.
If they heard speech, they might think the shadows were talking. But if they were released from their bonds and taken out
into the unaccustomed light, they would at first complain about
the novelty and the brightness of the light. Later, as they became
used to the situation, and came to appreciate the value of their
new state, of their vision of what is true and of light, they would
no longer wish to return underground to their prison. But if one
of them did go back (and returning into the darkness would
cause difficulties) and while down there

> began to speak about the shadows on the wall to those
> who had never been loosed from their chains and if, while
> still blinded and not yet accustomed to the great darkness
> (something that requires time), he gave his opinion about
> the shadows, would those wretches not ridicule him?
> Would they not scorn him as someone who after leaving
> has returned with his sight impaired? Would they not tell
> him he must never attempt to leave the cave? And would
> they not immediately kill anyone who tried to undo their
> bonds and lead them out?

This is the lot of wise people who open the eyes of others to
truths they cannot understand! Plato concludes:

> Let us suppose that someone with good sense remembers
> that the human eye can change in two ways and for two
> reasons: by passing from light into darkness and from

[*app.*, 7]

darkness into light. In the same way he will notice how the human spirit can be affected when disturbed and darkened in its discernment. Less inclined to mock, he will first investigate whether the person is overcome again by darkness as he comes from life in greater light or, when emerging from abysmal ignorance into brilliant light, faints before tremendous splendour. He will applaud those undergoing the second experience, and consider their life blessed; he will feel compassion for those suffering the first experience. However, if he wants to mock, he will not stupidly mock the first group but those who have descended from the light above.

Plato concludes with a passage very relevant to my purpose:

The eye cannot turn away from darkness to a shining object unless the whole body turns with the eye. Similarly we must with our whole mind turn from generation (that is, from things of sense) to what is called ENS, so that our gaze can pass to what is brightest of all.

According to Plato, therefore, *ens* is the lamp illuminating all other things.

The reader should compare Plato's cave with Locke's *camera obscura*, as Reid and Stewart do (*Éléments de la Philosophie, etc.*, vol. 1, c. 1, sect. 1). What a difference! Locke introduces the dark room to explain ideas, which he confuses with sensations; Plato introduces his cave to show the difference between shadows and reality, between sensations and ideas. To consider Locke's room on a par with Plato's cave, is like comparing a human head with a lump of wood because both are round!

8. (490)

[St. Thomas on intellect and phantasms]

St. Thomas' teaching seems to agree with this. But we must understand clearly his manner of speaking. He teaches: 1. sensible *phantasms* are only likenesses of things; 2. the intellect perceives things in their essence: 'The quiddity of a thing is the proper object of the intellect' (*quidditas rei est proprium objectum intellectus*: S.T., I, q. 85, art. 5). If the intellect finds only *likenesses* of things in the phantasms, but nevertheless perceives things themselves, not their *likenesses*, as St. Thomas says, the intellect must supply the *things*, the entia. The intellect, therefore, posits ens while sense, according to Thomas, posits only the likeness of beings. An attentive reading of the following passage would show that my interpretation is correct: 'Because phantasms are LIKENESSES of individuals' (they do not have the human intellect's mode of being) 'they have no power to imprint anything in the possible intellect.' Of themselves the phantasms cannot communicate anything to the intellect. But St. Thomas explains how they can be brought to do this: 'The acting intellect turns its attention to the phantasms and BY ITS POWER a certain likeness results in the possible intellect *(ex conversione intellectus agentis supra phantasmata)*; this likeness represents THE THINGS OF WHICH THEY ARE PHANTASMS, but in relationship to the nature of the species.' The *species* (idea) produced by the acting intellect does not represent the phantasms, likenesses or effects of the things — it represents the *things themselves*. If, therefore, the *things themselves* are not in the phantasms, the acting intellect must form the pure ideas of those things on the occasion of the phantasms by its own power *(virtute intellectus)*, through the innate light, because it sees ens (the nature of the thing) where the phantasms are, and thus the thing itself. The expression, 'the intellect turning its attention to the phantasms' *(converti supra phantasmata)*, can only mean 'to add ens to the phantasms received by the spirit.' We have sensations; we are conscious of them immediately and say: 'Some ens has produced these feelings in me.' Thus we turn to the phantasms and form the likeness or the *species*, not of the phantasms but of the ens that has produced the phantasms.

It may be claimed that for St. Thomas it is the acting intellect, not our spirit, that turns to the phantasms. But this way of speaking has its origin in the fact that the acting intellect supplies *being*, through which the *species* are made. Strictly speaking, this operation must be attributed to the human being himself. St. Thomas was in fact very careful about accuracy of speech and expressly points out that 'properly speaking, understanding is not a function of the intellect but of the soul through the intellect' *(Intelligere proprie loquendo, non est intellectus, sed animae per intellectum*) (*De Verit.*, q. 10, art. 9, ad 3 in contrar.). This expression is valid for all the operations of the soul's powers. Hence it is better to say that our spirit turns to the phantasms it feels, and, where they are, sees an ens (supplied by the acting intellect). The *species* or idea of the thing is formed by the primal synthesis, the first step taken by *reason*.

We should also note that this turning of the acting intellect to the phantasms has the same meaning as St. Thomas' other phrase, 'to illumine the phantasms' (*illuminare phantasmata*), that is, to envelop them with the *light* of the acting intellect which is precisely *being* (cf. *App.*, no. 9). Relative to my point, St. Thomas concludes: 'In the same way the intelligible species is said to be *abstracted* from the phantasms, [but this] is not because some form previously in the phantasms is afterwards numerically the same in the possible intellect (as though it were a body moved from one place to another' (*S. T.*, I, q. 85, art. 1, ad 1). According to St. Thomas, nothing is moved from the phantasms into the intellect; only on the occasion of the phantasms does the intellect form the *species* in itself. In other words, by the light of *being* which it possesses, it sees the *entia* which produce the phantasms.

9. (495)

[St. Thomas' illustrated phantasms]

St. Thomas often uses the phrases, *illustrari phantasmata, abstrahere phantasmata*, to indicate two operations of the *acting intellect* (*S. T.* I, q. 79, art. 4; I, q. 85, art. 1, ad 4). What is the proper meaning of the metaphorical expression, *illustrari phantasmata*? If I am not mistaken, it corresponds, as I have suggested, to *universalisation*, that is, the operation which forms ideas when phantasms present themselves, and thus enables sensile things to be understood. Undoubtedly *illustrating them* is a very happy way of describing the way our intelligence adds the idea of being to felt things which alone makes them intelligible, or clear, to the intellect. However, some passages of Aristotelian philosophers could render this interpretation doubtful, and lead us to believe that the two phrases do not always possess a clear, precise meaning. It would even seem that the phrase *to abstract* is often used to indicate the *universalisation* of ideas.

Nevertheless, careful consideration would seem to show that the passages in question can be given an adequate meaning. For example, this is how St. Thomas describes the two operations, *illustration* and *abstraction*: 'The phantasms are *illuminated* by the acting intellect, and the intelligible species *abstracted* from them by power of the acting intellect. They are *illuminated* by the acting intellect because its power is such that what is intelligible is abstracted from the phantasms, just as the sense part gains in strength from being joined to the intellect. The acting intellect *abstracts* the intelligible species from the phantasms in so far as, through the acting intellect, we can consider the *nature* of various species stripped of their individuality, in accordance with the likenesses informing the possible intellect' (*S.T.*, I, q. 85, art. 1, ad 4).

What does St. Thomas mean when he says that the sense part gains in strength (*efficitur virtuosior*) through being joined to the acting intellect, and moreover gains the power which renders the phantasms capable of undergoing the abstraction that provides the intelligible species, or ideas, of things? It is not difficult to recognise the nature of this power if we know what enables us to abstract the specific *natures* of things (the ideas), and I think I have shown what this is. As I said, the sensations or images (*phantasmata*) are united to the *idea of being* and to *judgment* on the thing's subsistence. In this way, *intellectual perception* is determined according to the individuals perceived by the sensations (*phantasmata*). The specific ideas of things are drawn precisely from the intellective perception (through a twofold type of abstraction: first, that by which the judgment indicating real things is removed; second, that by which *individual conditions* are set aside) in order to arrive at universal, pure and separate *ideas*. It seems clear that St. Thomas' *illustrated phantasms* correspond perfectly to what I have called *intellective perceptions*.

[Plato's species and genera]

It is certain, however, that in many places Plato spoke hesitatingly about his ideas. It seems that for him ideas were abstract, that is, ideas of things without accidents. But this way of speaking (for which I shall explain the reason later) does not detract from his basic thought. St. Thomas, in explaining Plato's work, uses words which hint at my own interpretation of Plato's ideas. For example, he says that Plato makes the species *substances of individual things* (in Aristotle's *Metaph.*, bk. 7, less. 16). Individual things considered in their perfection differ, and to each of them corresponds an idea, an exemplar, used by the creator of the thing to mould and form it, and to form and mould new individuals, provided these can be reduced to their unique common type. This interpretation of Plato seems to me to be confirmed by everything Aristotle says (in *Metaph.*, book 8, less. 16) about the way in which Plato arrived at his teaching.

Moreover, a statement of Plato about *species* and *genera* gives weight to the sense I attribute to him. He speaks about predicating something common to several entia, but in such a way that it is applicable first to one ens rather than another (*secundum prius et posterius*). In this case, what is common cannot exist *per se* and separately from the entia to which it is attributed; and this is proper to genus. But if what is common is predicated equally of several entia, it exists *per se* outside the beings to which it is attributed; and this is proper to *species*. According to Plato, therefore, individuals of a *species* must be perfectly equal, at least in their positive characteristics, without differing in dignity. I conclude that by his *species* Plato meant only *universal*, not abstract, *ideas*; these universal ideas contain all that is perceived in an individual except the reality of the individual, or the matter and, more generally speaking, the *subsistence* which is never contained in ideas, as I have shown (cf. 401–403).

If Plato's *species* are understood in this way, it seems to me that some of Aristotle's objections can be dismissed. For example, Aristotle's attempt to prove against Plato that the *matter* must form the *species* of things (*Metaph.* book 8) now appears a simple equivocation, a misunderstanding. When we think a corporeal thing, we certainly think of the matter composing the thing, but our idea of the matter is not the matter itself. If *species* means idea, *matter* does not enter into *species*. St. Thomas, in order to dispel the equivocation and in some way defend Aristotle, said that matter, which formed part of the species, was not the same matter as the *proper principle of the individual*, but a kind of *general matter* (that is, the *idea of matter*): 'Flesh and bones are found in the concept of human being, but not the flesh and bones of the living Socrates and Plato' *(Contra Gent.,* II, q. 92).

In any case, it seems that in other places Aristotle saw that the principle of *species* is the *universalisation* of an individual (I have already indicated this) and not the *abstraction*. Cf. book 8 of the *Metaphysics*, where he compares *species* to *numbers* and says that any unit increased in number immediately changes its species.

11. (507)

[Plato's ideas and Pythagoras' numbers]

To confirm my explanation of Plato's ideas and throw some light on an important point of ancient philosophical history, let me add an observation. Modern thinkers have discussed at length whether Pythagoras' *numbers* were the same as Plato's *ideas*. For our purpose we should note that *numbers* are *abstract ideas*, whereas Plato's *ideas*, which must serve as *exemplars*, can be only *specific*, not *abstract ideas* — Cicero writes, *nos recte* speciem *possumus dicere* [we can correctly say *species*] *(Academ.,* bk. 1). Pure *numbers* can never be exemplars of things, just as something totally abstract cannot be used by a sculptor as an exemplar for a statue. Plato, by substituting *ideas* for *numbers*, perfected the teaching glimpsed by Pythagoras, at least in the forms of its expression. The Pythagoreans themselves seem to have made some progress in perfecting the teaching according to certain passages in the *Timaeus*. It is extraordinary that modern authors (particularly Brucker) did not sense the difference which Plato himself had to some extent made clear. The fine Tuscan philosopher, Marsilio Ficino, mentions Plato's opinion: 'He (Plato) posits a first and a second intelligible. He places *ideas*, that is, the species and motions of the divine mind, other minds and souls in the first, and *numbers* and *shapes* in the second intelligible (*Thaeatetus*. Cf. also the end of the sixth dialogue of the *Republic*). We see here that exemplar *ideas* are separate from *numbers*. Ideas precede numbers because numbers are obtained from ideas by abstraction; numbers are a part of ideas, like all abstracts.

12. (511)

[Reflection]

If by reflection we mean the *aptitude possessed by the understanding for turning its attention toward the products of its own operations, universalisation* has no need of reflection. On the one hand, we have *sensation*, a direct act of our spirit; on the other hand, the intuition of being, another direct act. Between the two lies the unity of the spirit which has simultaneously the sensation and the idea. The subject's *awareness* of feeling sensation while intuiting the idea is *universalisation*, as it were whole and complete. But if reflection were to mean *an aptitude of the spirit for turning towards its own operations*, there could be partial *reflection* in the primal synthesis, and in the universalisation it contains. The subject, joining the idea of being to its sensations through the unity of its feeling, turns towards its *sensations*, but by means of a very different kind of act which of itself is direct and straightforward. In this case, one could distinguish between *reflection upon direct sensations* and *reflection upon ideas*. Reflection upon sensations is a direct act relative to the understanding to which alone it belongs, but a *reflective act* relative to the spirit, to which it belongs in equal manner, and to the sensations towards which it turns. I note this in order to avoid all ambiguity. For the rest, I generally use the word *reflection* to indicate reflection carried out by the understanding, not by the spirit.

The scholastics' 'reflection' must be understood in the second sense. For example, they say: 'The intellect knows individual things *per quandam reflexionem* [through a kind of reflection]' (cf. vol. 1, *App.*, no. 20). The whole weakness in this form of expression is use of the word 'intellect' instead of 'human spirit' which perceives *individual* sensations (by means of sense) and *universals* (by means of the intellect) and, uniting these two elements, produces for itself a single *perception*. We say that in this perception the spirit knows individual things (sensations), by reflecting upon them, and universals, by means of the direct act by which it sees ens. St. Thomas points to this interpretation of the scholastic dictum where he notes that we sometimes attribute incorrectly to the *intellect* what strictly speaking should be attributed to the *spirit*. Cf. *De Verit.*, q. 10, art. 9, ad 3.

13. (522)

[Language and abstract ideas]

It is impossible to invent a language for the human mind before the mind has *abstracts ideas*. No one can posit a *sign* for ideas they do not have. Rousseau's opinion that 'language cannot be invented without language' must be limited to the part of language dealing with abstract ideas. Because he did not make this distinction, he glimpsed a truth without demonstrating it. Indeed, as far as I know, no one since his time (including Bonald) has given a strict demonstration of this. But Rousseau's proposition, if restricted to ideas and abstract words, contains a basis of truth. First, no person cut off from the society of his fellows can invent a language. In this state he has no occasion to communicate his needs and thoughts to others, nor can they communicate theirs to him. Let us suppose that an individual person is living with other human beings who lack language. Two questions arise: could the others invent a language *before* forming some abstractions, or could they form these abstractions *before* inventing some kind of language or signs? My answer is 'No' to both questions. But to the question, 'Could these two things be done *simultaneously*, that is, discover some signs and by that act form abstractions?', I think the answer could be 'Yes' (cf. *Psychology*, vol. 2, *Development of the Human Soul*, 1456–1473).

[*app.*, 13]

14. (528)
[St. Thomas and natural and scientific knowledge]

In some passages of St. Thomas it could seem that the *matter* of our knowledge is supplied only by the exterior senses without any contribution from the internal feeling of *myself*. But if we compare the various observations he makes on the subject, his mind appears very clear: the matter of our knowledge comes from two sources, external sensations and the internal feeling of the soul itself.

St. Augustine had said: 'The mind knows itself through itself because it is incorporeal' (*De Trin.*, bk. 9, c. 3). Clearly he teaches that the soul has a feeling, or rather is itself a substantial feeling, and therefore supplies the understanding with some *matter* of knowledge that cannot in any way be furnished by the bodily senses. Aristotle, whom the scholastics had adopted as their guiding star (where he was not opposed to the Christian faith), took another view. According to him, 'The intellect understands nothing without corporeal phantasm' (*De Anima*, bk. 3, c. 30). St. Thomas' acute mind saw that Augustine's teaching was true from one point of view, and Aristotle's from another, and he tried to reconcile the two.

First, he established that no *species* offering a likeness of the soul could be drawn from phantasms; no idea of our soul, which is completely different from corporeal nature, could therefore be gained from corporeal phantasms: *anima non cognoscitur per speciem a sensibus abstractam, quasi intelligatur species illa esse animae similitudo* (*De Veri*, q. 10, art. 8). Secondly, he thought the best way of discovering how we know the nature of the soul was to examine the approach used by philosophers in their discussion about its properties. He observed that in meditating on the nature of the soul, they first examined its *acts*, especially its ideas. He says:

> Because the human soul knows the universal nature of each thing, they (the philosophers) noticed that the *species* (idea) with which the human being understands is immaterial. And because the intellectual species is immaterial, they realised that the intellect must be something independent

of matter. They went on from there to learn about the other properties of the intellective potency.

(Ibid.)

St. Thomas concludes that the abstract *species* (ideas) of material things were necessary to the philosophers' knowledge of the soul's nature not because the species could supply a likeness of the soul, *sed quia naturam speciei considerando, quae a sensibilibus abstrahitur, invenitur natura animae, in qua huiusmodi species recipitur* [but because, by considering the nature of the species abstracted from sensible things, we discover the nature of the soul in which this species is received] (*ibid.*). Thus it was not the sensible phantasms, but the species formed in us by the acting intellect, as we have seen, that provided information about the soul. This species, of a completely different nature from phantasms, supplies a starting point for discovering the nature of the soul.

This was *scientific* knowledge of the soul, reducible to a *definition*. But there is also a *natural* knowledge of the soul. Each of us is conscious of having, or rather being, an incommunicable, *personal feeling*, and of perceiving the feeling expressed in the word *myself*. We know that this feeling is not found in any way in the corporeal qualities of extension, and so on. These are all extrasubjective; *myself* is the subject itself.

This kind of knowledge did not, it seems to me, escape the attention of St. Thomas. To understand his mind, we must keep before us the expressions he uses to indicate the two kinds of knowledge I am discussing, *scientific* and *popular*. The former is founded on argued reasoning; the latter consists in immediate perception.

St. Thomas, therefore, declares that we cannot say we know the *nature* of anything if its specific or generic difference is unknown; only by means of this difference can we form a proposition containing the definition of the thing (*cum res speciali aut generali cognitione definitur*). Only scientific knowledge enables us to know the *nature* of the soul. But in speaking of what I would call *popular* or natural knowledge, St. Thomas calls it 'that by which the soul knows itself individually' (that is, *quantum ad id quod est ei proprium* [relative to what is proper to itself]). This kind of knowledge corresponds exactly to what

I call *perception of our soul*, which takes place for the first time when we say to ourselves: I AM. It is composed of the feeling of *myself* (matter) and of the idea of being in all its universality (form) and nothing more. We do not know expressly any differences it may have with other things, nor do we compare it with other objects. This kind of knowledge, according to St. Thomas, is such that it makes known only the *existence* of the soul, not its *essence* (*per hanc cognitionem cognoscitur an est anima; — per aliam vero — scitur quid est anima*).

Before proceeding, I would like to make an observation about calling *perception* 'knowledge by which we know the soul exists.' Aquinas himself puts the following objection: 'We cannot know that something exists unless we first know what it is' (*De Verit.*, q. 10, art. 12), and answers it: 'In order to know that something exists, it is not necessary to know what it is by *definition* (that is, to know it scientifically), but what is meant by its name.' Here St. Thomas is describing popular knowledge expressed by the way people name things. In our case, this knowledge is reduced to a global *perception* of the thing, without either comparison with other things or the realisation of the differences necessary for forming a perfect definition of it. I point this out to allow the reader to reflect that St. Thomas' knowledge 'by which something is known to be' (*qua scitur aliquid esse*) does not express the pure *existence* of the thing. We could not know the thing without sufficient information to distinguish it from all other things with which it shares existence.

We are now in a position to note the harmony between St. Thomas' teaching on knowledge *qua cognoscitur an est anima* [by which the soul is known to exist] and mine on *perceptive* or *natural and popular* knowledge.

Following the teaching of St. Augustine, St. Thomas affirms that 'the essence of the soul is always present to our intellect' (*ipsa ejus essentia intellectui nostro est praesens*). To perceive this essence, our understanding needs only to posit the act by which it perceives the essence of the soul. He concludes: *anima per essentiam suam se videt, id est, hoc ex ipso quod essentia sua est sibi praesens, est* potens *exire in actum cognitionis sui ipsius* [the soul sees itself through its essence, that is, it has the *ability* to arrive at knowledge of itself because its essence is present to itself] (*De Verit.*, 10, 8). He likens this knowledge to knowledge in our memory, saying that *sicut aliquis ex hoc quod habet alicujus scientiae habitum, ex ipsa praesentia habitus est potens percipere illa quae subsunt illi habitui* [someone who has a habit of knowledge, can perceive the things subject to the habit] (*ibid.*). And this direct knowledge that the soul has of itself without phantasms, he calls *habitual*.

For the understanding to come to *actual* knowledge of the soul (St. Thomas continues), a sufficient reason must be provided by the acts of the soul itself. 'Therefore I say that, as regards the actual knowledge by which anyone considers his soul in act, the soul is known only by its acts. A person perceives that he has a soul, that he lives and exists because he realises that he feels, knows, and performs other vital operations' (*ibid.*). No one can doubt this.

Let me conclude with an observation. Forget for a moment reflective knowledge of ourselves and remember that we are speaking only of direct, immediate knowledge, the perception of OURSELVES; our soul is only our own feeling of this OURSELVES. Now it is clear that we can perceive ourselves intellectively only by our acts. But some acts are essential, like feeling and the act xof the acting intellect (with which we perceive being) — both St. Thomas and Aristotle accept this last act. Because such acts are essential, we can never lack them. We could, therefore, have actual perception of ourselves even in the first moments of our existence if there were some stimulus to draw our attention to ourselves. But as long as such a stimulus is missing, we are left only with the power to acquire this knowledge: *est potens [anima] exire in actum cognitionis sui ipsius* [the soul has the capacity to produce an act of knowledge of itself].

15. (538)

[The *tabula rasa*]

This would seem to be the true interpretation of the *tabula rasa* of the ancients. Modern authors, driven by the desire to ridicule all antiquity, have not, it seems to me, understood it, and this opinion is strengthened by the following reasons:

1. The likeness of the *tabula rasa* excludes any particular

character written on our soul although a *tabula* exists on which anyone who wishes may write. This *smooth, flat tabula*, innate in our soul, is in my opinion *undetermined being* and capable of receiving any determination whatsoever.

2. The same likeness can be explained by another used by Aristotle, that of *light* and *colours*. According to Aristotle, there are no colours, only *innate light*, which is *per se* uniform (the evenness of the *tabula*) and capable of making visible all the colours of things.

3. If the *tabula rasa* is understood in the way I have explained, many passages of Aristotle, which are otherwise irreconcilable, can be reconciled.

4. The likeness is used by the ancients, and in certain passages the authors expressly say that the idea of being is innate. One example is St. Bonaventure (or whoever wrote the work I am referring to). He uses the likeness in the *Compendium theologicae veritatis*, bk. 2, c. 49. In c. 45 he says that all cognitions come from sense. But he certainly seems to posit the idea of *most actual being* as innate in the human being (*Itin. mentis in Deum*), that is, he posits more than I do — I posit only the *idea* of perfectly undetermined being as innate. We must conclude therefore that the likeness of the *tabula* was not understood in the mean-spirited way modern authors usually understand it.

16. (543)

[Logical impossibility in things]

Certain things contain a hidden *logical impossibility*, not immediately evident. This situation arises when the idea we have of something is defective because too extensive. We do not consider the thing in itself but take it indiscriminately as forming part of a genus or species. In this case, we have to sift it thoroughly by examining both the thing itself and its characteristics. It is not sufficient to consider only its common qualities in order to be sure of its possibility. A mathematical example may be useful here. 'What is the square root of 2, expressed in a finite series of numbers?' The answer to this problem seemed possible before mathematicians started to work on it. They concluded, however, that there could be no answer, and produced a demonstration of the impossibility of expressing the square root of 2 in a finite series of whole numbers or fractions. A similar demonstration is applicable to all *recurring* numbers. In our example, it was necessary to demonstrate the *impossibility* of the problem because the impossibility was hidden and not immediately obvious.

The reason for such mental imperfection, which obscures the impossibility of certain things and consequently impedes certainty about their *possibility*, lies in what we have said about the *undetermination* of the idea of being. This idea is a *tabula rasa*, in mere potency relative to determined beings. The mind cannot form a judgment about them or their possibility: 1. without thinking of determinations; and 2. without confronting the determinations with the idea of being, their supreme norm. In a word, the *rule* for judging the possibility of things is innate, but the *judgment* about their possibility, and the matter required for such a judgment, is not innate. The judgment has to be made, and often not without considerable difficulty

Kant, who had not noted that in itself *possibility* is simply a negative concept meaning 'the thing under discussion does not contradict the laws of thought and existence', also confused *possibility* with the danger we sometimes experience of judging it wrongly. This led him to deny that a thing can be judged possible provided we show that in it (in its idea) there is no repugnance, and made him require something more for the concept of possibility, as he does in his *Critique of Pure Reason*. This requirement distanced him even further from grasping the truth (cf. Part 1, bk. 2, c. 2, sect. 3, art. 4). However, there is some truth in what he says: the positive foundation of possibility is indeed in ideal being itself. In fact, everything we conceive has this proper characteristic: we conceive it as possible. *Conceiving something, therefore,* is the same as *conceiving it as possible.*

17. (548)

[Solid foundations needed in philosophy]

It would be poor method if I regulated my observation of nature by deciding to record only the most obvious facts. If I were to omit to verify observations requiring repeated, tedious experience and were satisfied with approximate results, I could rightly be accused of wanting to make a fool of nature and of those I am trying to instruct. It would be incredible presumption for me to attempt to construct theories without trying to lay solid foundations for them because facts were too difficult to ascertain or too obscure to clarify. This, however, is the method adopted by the materialist and sensist philosophers who have allied themselves with Locke, and it has even rubbed off on serious students like Bonnet, who prided himself on rigorous method. Bonnet dismisses feeling of our own existence for the following reason: 'It is not good to admit any feeling of our existence of which we cannot form an idea. There is no doubt that it is better to confine our attention to CLEAR MATTERS we can reason about.' (*Analyse abrégée de l'Essai analytique*, II). But affirming that we want to accept only what is altogether clear in nature is equivalent to admitting very little. Nature, as we know, is full of mystery and obscurity. And if we set out to look for what is *good* rather than what is *true*, who knows what each will take as matter for his philosophy. What is the *good* or the *better* to which we will confine our attention? In fact, it is the philosopher's responsibility to observe nature whole and entire, just as it is. Not only must he admit what is clear, he must accept and clarify, through hard work if necessary, what is *obscure*. The true philosopher, when faced with difficulties and mysteries, increases his efforts to penetrate the secrets of nature. If he still does not succeed in making progress, he admires the wisdom that has made nature so sublime and so profound. Certain questions cannot be neglected, whatever facile philosophy asserts. They must be faced courageously, and modestly. In particular, the fundamental feeling is a matter of such importance that its exclusion from philosophical observation on the grounds of its obscurity destroys any hope of progress in the theory of knowledge.

[*app.*, 17]

18. (554)

[St. Thomas on ideas and phantasms]

I would not want to argue with anyone who denied that the word *knowledge* could be applied to the unique idea placed in us by nature and then intuited directly by our spirit without the intervention of any judgment. This seems to have been Aquinas' view, and I hope to be able to throw some light upon it.

St. Thomas teaches that our mind understands and knows only through phantasms. Now it is very important to grasp what he means by this. He observes that it is proper to the human mind to know things themselves (*quidditas rei est objectum intellectus*). But the mind knows things through their *idea* or species. The intellect, therefore, knows real things, but through ideas which are the means of knowledge (*non quod cognoscit, sed quo cognoscit*). He can say, therefore, *ad cognitionem duo concurrere oportet, scilicet apprehensionem* (the idea), *et judicium* [two things are required for knowledge, namely apprehension (the idea) and judgment]. With the judgment, the intellect terminates in what is real (word of the mind). In this case, our simple apprehension, that is, the pure idea without any real, felt thing, would not be something we understood, but only the *means* of understanding. This is precisely the state of the mind which possesses only the idea of being without having received any phantasm through sense. It cannot be said to know anything because as yet it understands nothing; it has only a *potency* for knowing and understanding. As St. Thomas says:

> As a potency, it cannot know anything without turning to its object, just as vision is meaningless without colour. Phantasms, therefore, are related to the possible intellect as sensible things are related to sense. The intellect, although it may have some intelligible species, does not actually consider anything according to that species without turning to phantasms. Hence our intellect, in its present state, needs phantasms to really think.
> (*De Verit.*, q. 10, art. 2, ad 7)

St. Thomas admits that the intellect can have some *idea* or intellectual species antecedent to phantasms which, however, the mind needs in order *to know* in the restricted sense of the word.

19. (565)
[St. Thomas and innate principles]

Retinet [memoria] nihilominus scientiarum principia et dignitates ut sempiternalia et sempiternaliter, quia nunquam potest sic oblivisci eorum (dummodo ratione utatur), quin ea audita approbet, et eis assentiat, non tanquam de novo percipiat, sed tanquam SIBI INNATA et familiaria recognoscat [(The memory) retains forever the principles and standards of systematic knowledge because of their everlasting quality. It can never forget them (as long as it uses reason) because in giving them its approval and assent it recognises them as INNATE and familiar. These principles are never something newly perceived] (*Itin. mentis etc.* c. 3). This is a very acute *observation of fact,* of the type neglected by modern sensists, despite their lip-service to facts which, even if neglected, can never be entirely ignored.

St. Thomas is of the same opinion as the author of the *Itinerarium. Prima principia, QUORUM COGNITIO EST NOBIS INNATA,* sunt quaedam similitudines increatae veritatis [The first principles, KNOWLEDGE OF WHICH IS INNATE IN US, are certain likenesses of uncreated truth] (*De Verit.,* q. 10, art. 6, ad 6). He often repeats this teaching, as in the following passage: *In eo qui docetur, scientia praeexistebat, non quidem in actu completo, sed quasi in rationibus seminalibus secundum quod universales conceptiones, quarum cognitio est NOBIS NATURALITER INSITA, sunt quasi semina quaedam omnium sequentium cognitorum* [Knowledge is already present in the student, but not completely. It lies there in seminal notions because the universal conceptions whose knowledge IS NATURALLY PRESENT TO US are like seeds containing all that we shall ever know] (*De Verit.,* q. 11, art. 1, ad 5).

My interpretation of these passages requires that 'innate' and 'naturally present to us' be understood in the sense that the first principles are present in our first acts of reason or (and it comes to the same thing) when we first use *the idea of being,* which alone is innate strictly speaking and corresponds to St. Thomas' *acting intellect*. In order to see the truth of my interpretation it is sufficient to compare what St. Thomas says above with the following: *In lumine intellectus agentis nobis est quodammodo omnis scientia originaliter indita, mediantibus universalibus conceptionibus, quae statim LUMINE INTELLECTUS AGENTIS cognoscuntur, per quas sicut per universalia principia judicamus de aliis, et ea praecognoscimus in ipsis* [All knowledge is placed within us originally in the light of the acting intellect, through universal conceptions which are known immediately BY THE LIGHT OF THE ACTING INTELLECT. These universal conceptions are as it were universal principles through which we judge of other things, which we know beforehand in them] (*De Verit.*, q. 10, art. 6).

20. (621)

[St. Thomas on substance]

St. Thomas deduces the idea of substance in the same way as I do. First, he establishes that the proper object of the intellect is *ens or common truth (objectum intellectus est ens, vel verum commune)*. He concludes that everything is knowable in so far as it is, in so far as it has an existence of its own. This is my conclusion also. It is in fact absurd that what is not, could be understood: *Unumquodque autem in quantum habet DE ESSE, in tantum est cognoscibile* [Each thing is knowable in so far as it has wherewith TO BE] (*S.T.*, I, q. 16, art. 3). It follows that things are understood through their *substance* because substance is that by which they are *entia*. This accounts for St. Thomas' other declaration where he states that *substance* is the object of the intellect precisely because the object of the intellect is ens: *Quidditas rei est proprium objectum intellectus* [The proper object of the intellect is what makes a thing what it is] (*S.T.*, I, q. 85, art. 5). Another acute observation, drawn from this very principle, is that the *truth* in things is their *substance* and their very being: *Verum autem quod est in rebus, convertitur cum ente secundum substantiam* [What is true in things is interchanged with being in the realm of substance] (*S.T.*, I, q. 16, art

3). The truth of things is their relationship with ideas in the intellect, which however can only be of their substance, because this is the object of the intellect. It follows that truth, in so far as it is shared by things, is their substance. Note that *quidditas*, in the quotation above, has been equated with *substance* because of the meaning given it by St. Thomas in this place; it is always true that the quiddity or essence of accidents can only be understood related to substantial quiddity or essence.

21. (622)

[The action of St. Thomas' *acting intellect*]

I would like to add a few more words about St. Thomas' teaching. It is important that the philosophical principles on which he bases religious teaching, so profoundly needed by human nature, should be understood perfectly.

I have already noted that the intellect cannot be the power which *universalises* sensations; only the soul can do this through its *unity* and *simplicity*. On the one hand, the soul experiences sensations; on the other, it possesses the vision of being and unites these two things in itself. If we examine the use made of the *acting intellect* by St. Thomas, we shall see that the power of the soul uniting these two things is what he calls the *acting intellect*. Consequently, the *acting intellect* corresponds to what I have called *the faculty of primal synthesis* or the first function of *reason*. St. Thomas also notes a *particular reason*, which he calls the *cogitative force*, whose power lies in descending to particular matters and regulating them: *mens regit inferiores, et sic singularibus se immiscet movente* ratione particulari*, quae est potentia quaedam individualis quae alio nomine dicitur cogitativa* [The mind governs the inferior faculties, and thus influences individual things with its own *particular reasoning power*, that is, with a certain individual potency we call *cogitative*] (*De Ver.*, q. 10, art. 5).

As he says, *reason* is the power of the soul that, after coming into possession of sensations and phantasms on the one side, and possession of ens on the other, joins these two extremes. This energy of the soul then becomes St. Thomas' *particular reason* or *cogitative force* when considered relative to the particulars which it has to regulate. But if it is considered as a power for forming ideas in the way described, that is, by universalising phantasms, then it corresponds to St. Thomas' *acting intellect* which he rightly calls *virtus quaedam animae nostrae* [a certain power of our soul] (*S.T.*, I, q. 89, art. 4). St. Thomas' teaching will be understood more clearly if we are allowed the following observations.

St. Thomas first establishes that neither sensations as such nor corporeal images (*phantasmata*) are ideas; the *acting intellect* has to *illustrate* them in order to render them such. I have already shown how this illustration, or illumination, is simply their *universalisation* brought about by adding to them the *light of the acting intellect*, that is, *possibility* or *ideal being*. The soul considers the sensations it experiences as infinitely renewable, and hence views them in their possible or general existence, rather than in their *individual existence. Formae sensibiles non possunt agere in mentem nostram, nisi quatenus per* lumen *intellectus agentis immateriales redduntur, et sic efficiuntur quodammodo homogeneae intellectui possibili, in quem agunt* [Sensible forms cannot act relatively to our mind unless they are rendered immaterial through the *light* of the acting intellect and thus made compatible with the possible intellect in which they act] (*De Ver.*, q. 10, art. 6). He concludes that the principal agent in the formation of ideas is neither *sense* nor *phantasms*, but the acting intellect with its innate light.

My own comment is this. If the acting intellect renders the phantasms immaterial (universalises them), it must act upon them and, according to St. Thomas' own phrase, 'turn towards them'. The acting intellect, therefore, can only be the power possessed by the soul of beholding, in possible being which it intuits, the sensations it experiences. The following passage shows clearly that the nature of the *acting intellect* is as I have described it. St. Thomas shows that the *acting intellect* makes phantasms immaterial. This takes place through the *unity* of the subject, that is, of the soul which on the one side has the phantasms, on the other the power of the intellect. He says: 'Although the intellective soul is immaterial in act, it is in potency to DETERMINED species of things.' This *immateriality* in act on the part of the intellective soul indicates its intuition of being in a universal act, free from corporeal limitations and determinations. St. Thomas does in fact teach that we know the immateriality of the soul by its ideas which we find to be universal (*De Ver.*, q. 10, art. 8) and therefore immaterial. He continues: 'The phantasms, although certainly likenesses of some species in act, are only potentially immaterial', that is, they are not universal, although they can be universalised by our spirit. 'There is nothing to prevent a SINGLE, IDENTICAL SOUL which is immaterial in act', that is, in so far as it has the idea of possible being, 'from possessing a certain power enabling it to render immaterial in act (to universalise) the phantasms by abstracting from the individual conditions imposed by matter. THIS POWER IS CALLED THE ACTING INTELLECT. At the same time, the one, identical soul may possess another receptive power called *possible intellect* because it is capable of accepting such universalised species' (*S.T.*, I, q. 79, art. 4). These words show clearly that for St. Thomas the *acting intellect* is the power by which the soul *applies ens* to sensations, and hence is proper to the soul in so far as it feels both its sensations and the completely universal idea of being.

We can now reach some conclusions about the nature of the acting and possible intellects. The soul possesses an innate *light* which is the idea of being in all its universality. This *idea* can be considered in two relationships. First, the soul uses and applies it in order to universalise sensations. In this respect, it forms the *acting intellect*. Second, the intelligent spirit beholds it continually as the idea transforms itself in all other ideas (all possible ideas are only the idea of being furnished with various determinations). This capacity for auto-transformation enables the idea to form the *possible intellect*. These considerations explain clearly the truth of the Aristotelian distinction between the two intellects: 'The soul possesses an intellect that *becomes* all things (the possible intellect), and an intellect that *makes* all things (the acting intellect)': *Est quidam intellectus talis qui omnia fiat, et quidam qui omnia faciat (De Anima*, bk. 3, lect. 10). As I said, the *idea* of being becomes all ideas: this is the *possible intellect*; and through the *idea of being* the soul forms all ideas: this is the *acting intellect*.

22. (667)

[Sensations and the meaning of words]

Reid noticed and tried to explain at length that in ordinary language 'odour', 'colour', 'taste', etc. have two totally distinct meanings. They first mean *sensations in us*, and secondly *perceptions* of the corresponding powers, present in bodies, to produce these sensations. But he has difficulty in explaining this double meaning because words receive their sense from the general consent of people, a consent which can never, or very rarely, be accused of error. He attempts to explain as follows the lack of clarity he finds in words:

> Neither ought he [the reader] to expect that the *sensation* and its corresponding *perception*, should be distinguished in common language, because the purposes of common life do not require it. Language is made to serve the purposes of ordinary conversation; and we have no reason to expect that it should make distinctions that are not of common use. Hence it happens that a quality perceived, and the sensation corresponding to that perception, often go under the same name.
> (*Essays on the Powers of the Human Mind*, vol. 1)

Although this explanation may be satisfactory at first glance, examined more closely it is not altogether satisfactory for the following reasons:

1. We do not use words simply to express our *purposes* but rather to express our *knowledge* of things. When we see two different things we give them two names without further ado. What we think as distinct and separate we naturally express and indicate with different words, which are images of our thoughts. In fact our first *purpose* is precisely for natural truth in our words, that is, that they express faithfully what we conceive in our minds.

2. If Reid's distinction between *sensations* and *perceptions* of sensible qualities really exists, how does he show that we gain nothing by expressing the distinction in words, and that confusing the two things does no harm? The confusion would give rise to an infinite number of equivocations: every time we spoke of what we are experiencing, we could mean

bodies and not ourselves, or vice versa. Surely this would be a great insult to intelligence and mutual conversation?

Galluppi gives another explanation for making one name serve two ideas. He maintains that every sensation is naturally *objective* and that consequently we do not mentally *jump* from the *sensation* to the corresponding *sensible quality* in the external body, nor make this jump by a *suggestion of nature*, as Reid says. Galluppi denies this arbitrary passage suggested by Reid. He establishes an essential connection between *sensation* and *sensible quality* so that the two are in themselves indivisible and form a single thing which he calls *objective sensation*. The theory is ingenious and would explain the assignment of one word to two things, *sensation* and *sensible quality*, or rather, one word would signify only a single thing, present in nature but divided and broken down into two by analysis and abstraction.

I believe however that Galluppi, by retaining Reid's language about the ambiguity of the use of words, failed to maintain sufficient propriety of expression to be coherent with himself. He says:

> The difficulty arises from *ambiguity* in the word 'taste'. This word can denote both a sensation of the soul and the *object* of this sensation. The object is a quality of the sapid body. If we consider it as a sensation, it cannot denote an external quality in the act in which the sapid body is seen as lacking sensibility.
> (*Saggio filosofico sulla critica della conoscenza*, bk. 2, c. 6, §113)

In my opinion, after establishing *objective sensation* (which really means *extrasubjective* sensation, that is, containing something outside the subject), Galluppi could have denied Reid's claim that these words are ambiguous and affirmed that by their nature they indicate a single *sensation* which is both subjective and extrasubjective. In this way the words could be fittingly applied at one moment to the subject, at another to something foreign to the subject.

I will make another observation about Galluppi's system. I accept *extrasubjective sensation* but call it *sense perception* in so far as it is such. However, it seems to me that Galluppi in establishing his opinion has taken a step in which I cannot follow him. His whole theory rests on two propositions:

1. 'All sensations are objective', that is, I perceive something outside me but perceive it intimately united with MYSELF; I cannot perceive it when it is separated from MYSELF.

2. 'Perception of MYSELF is simultaneous with perception of its modifications', that is, I cannot perceive myself in isolation from my modifications (external sensations).

I grant the first proposition but not the word 'objective', which is proper to the intellect alone, a fact hidden from Galluppi by his *subjectivism*. I would substitute 'extrasubjective'. In other words, I admit that the qualities of bodies cannot be perceived by me without the perception of MYSELF. Consequently there is a fact which is simultaneously *subjective* and *extrasubjective*.

I do not grant the second proposition that MYSELF cannot be perceived separate from external sensations. Moreover it is not necessary for the first proposition. I hold that in MYSELF there is a fundamental feeling which may be difficult to observe but is *per se* perceptible.

Finally I note with St. Thomas himself that the intimate union of foreign substance and subject results in a single thing. St. Thomas makes one thing out of the felt body and sentient organ. According to him the organ is the *potency*, and the felt body the *act* of the potency: *corpus sensibile est nobilius organo animalis, secundem hoc quod comparatur ad ipsum, ut ens in actu ad ens in potentia: sicut coloratum in actu ad pupillam, quae colorata est in potentia* [the sensible body is more noble than the organ of the animal in so far as, compared with it, the body is ens in act relative to ens in potency, in the way that what is coloured is in act relative to the pupil which is coloured in potency] (*S.T.*, I, q. 84, art. 6, ad 2). In another place he says that the actual *sensible* thing is simply *sense* itself in act: *sensibile in actu est sensus in actu* (*C. Gent.*, I, c. 51). However, this teaching, according to St. Thomas, is verified only in the act itself of sensation, when the foreign felt force and the sentient subject are united in such a way that they become a single thing. Whenever the sensible body and the sentient organ are considered separate from each other, they are two distinct things. He writes, 'The *actual sensible* thing is *sense in act*. But if they are considered

[*app.*, 22]

separate from each other, they are each in potency. The visual
organ is not sight in act, nor is what is visible actually seen,
unless sight is informed by the visible species. IN THIS WAY SIGHT
AND WHAT IS VISIBLE BECOME A SINGLE THING': *Sensibile in actu
est sensus in actu: secundum vero quod (sensibile) ab (sensu)
distinguitur, est utrumque in potentia —; neque enim visus est
videns actu, neque visibile videtur actu nisi cum visus
informatur visibili specie, UT SIC EX VISIBILI ET VISU UNUM FIAT*
(*C. Gent.*, I, q. 51).

This union of the sentient (subject) with what is felt (foreign
force) is certainly mysterious and obscure. If it had been proposed forty or fifty years ago, when modern philosophy was
still at its initial stage among us and in France, it would probably have been treated with derision and rejected as a quirk of
scholasticism.

But modern philosophy has now made progress in France
and Italy. We have learnt what Reid thought in Scotland, and
Kant in Germany. Their serious meditations, although a little
late, attracted our attention and exposed the whole weakness of
current doctrine (Condillac's). These new meditations spawned
others; philosophy expanded and improved. One of the best
contributions was Galluppi's here in Italy. He established that
something foreign to the subject entered into *sensation*,
although he incorrectly called this foreign element 'object'.
These many years of rigorous meditation, aimed at advancing
and maturing philosophy, had finally resulted in an *observation*
made by our ancestors six centuries ago! The arrogant philosophy of the past century despised and ignored this observation, which a more mature, humble philosophy now accepts as
necessary. It is true that we are deterred by the stern appearance
of certain difficult truths, but only for a time. And even if we do
neglect them, we take them up again when we finally see our
absolute need of them, and we courageously plumb their
depths.

I must now make an observation about the difficult truth
which initiated this footnote, that is, the perfect *unity* between
what feels and *what is felt*.

This mysterious unity is found not only between an ens that
feels and an ens that is felt, but also in any action by which one
ens affects another, when one is passive and the other active. We

must carefully observe the fact as it is; I do not wish to enter into an explanation of it. It will be found that the fact happens as follows.

What is being *experienced* is the *term* of action of another ens. Now, although the experience, purely as experience, is in the passive ens, it is also *term* of the action. Considered as term of the *action*, it is in the active *ens*. It is impossible to posit two *terms* of action, one outside, the other inside the agent, as though this were a fact, rather than a product of the imagination. The experience is the *effect* produced by the agent; an agent must be *acting* precisely where there is an effect and nowhere else; the agent's action properly terminates in the effect. The term of the action is necessarily joined to the action in precisely the same way as the term or limit of a stick is in the stick. The *acting ens* is indeed separate from the effect it produces in the *experiencing* ens, but this occurs when its action ceases. Now, we are considering the ens at the moment of its action. What for one ens (the experiencer) is an experience, is for the other, at that moment, a *term* of action; the same thing is joined and belongs to two entia in one act, having its own direct relation to each. It is a concept of two entia touching each other, as it were — a difficult, unique concept but nevertheless true. Like any *fact*, it cannot be dismissed, much less denied; on the contrary, it should be investigated and verified with greater care.

As regards the fact of sensation, which Galluppi found to be composed of two elements, one *subjective*, the other *objective* (*extrasubjective*), I must indicate the sense in which I accept the fusion of these two elements into one single fact. I refer the reader to the footnotes to 453 [cf. *App*. nos. 3, 4, 5] where I have shown how *reflection* can break down *sensation* into two elements, *subjective* and *extrasubjective*. Sensation can properly be called *sensation* in so far as it is subjective, and *corporeal sense perception* in so far as it is extrasubjective or term of an action outside us. All this demonstrates how *extrasubjective sensation*, which I admit, must never be confused with *intellective perception* or with the *idea* of bodies, because this is formed not only through sense but also through the intellect endowed with the *idea of being*.

Finally I point out that 'smell', 'taste', 'sound', etc. are words indicating mainly the *subjective* element, while names of the first qualities of bodies, like extension, indicate solely the *extrasubjective* element. But later I will have the opportunity to discuss all this at greater length.

23. (685)

[St. Thomas and Locke on reflection]

St. Thomas, who is unjustly confused with modern sensists, carefully distinguished the faculty of *reflection* from the faculty of *feeling*. He stripped feeling of all *reflection* upon itself; reflection appertained to *intellect*. This distinction was sufficient to divide the two faculties and prevent any intermingling. 'No feeling knows itself or its action,' he writes. 'Sight does not in any way see itself, nor see its seeing; this is proper to a superior power. — The intellect knows itself and knows its knowing. *Intellect* and *feeling* are not therefore the same thing' (*C. Gentes*, II, 66). This teaching, founded on Aristotle's (*De Anima*, bk. 3), confirms my interpretation of that *judgment* which Aristotle incorrectly attributes to *feeling* (cf. vol. 1, *App.*, no. 16). If feeling cannot return upon itself, much less can it, properly speaking, *judge* what it feels.

Locke, however, did distinguish reflection in some way, although he was incoherent in denying the idea of substance on the one hand, while sometimes feeling obliged to grant a vague notion of it on the other. After him, his successors confused everything by making reflection coalesce with sensation. In Italy, Gallini, professor of physiology at Padua University, seems to acknowledge only one difference between direct and reflective ideas: there is a lesser degree of intension in the attention we give to the impressions made on our sensories. This difference alone explains greater or lesser clarity in our ideas. Unfortunately he did not see that the act of *reflection* is another act, inconfusable with the act of *direct attention*, just as *direct attention* of the intellect is something essentially different from instinctive or *sensitive tension* (cf. Dr. Stefano Gallini's article, *Considerazioni filosofiche sul senso del Bello*, etc., in *Esercitazioni dell'Ateneo di Venezia*, vol. 1).

[*app.*, 23]

24. (685)

[Locke and the philosophy of sensation]

A small, almost imperceptible error in the priinciples of a system will without doubt develop in the course of time. All errors, even contradictory errors, will emerge from this one seed and spread so widely that the system itself which produced them will be held in horror. In the light of the results, the tiny, fatal seed will be removed, the system healed, and philosophy perfected. This observation is confirmed by the history of Locke's system. Locke's tiny error lay in the unsustainable vagueness of his *reflection* which did not provide a firm foundation for the existence of reflection.

This error was sufficient to eliminate such a vague faculty, and force a return to *sensation* (a more positive faculty) as the origin of cognitions. This change seemed nothing, and even appeared necessary to Locke's system. The result, however, was total upheaval and a new system. Locke, while admitting reflection in some way, was moving from internal evidence; but with reflection removed and sensation alone retained, philosophy began solely from what is external, and finished there. Condillac, in reducing philosophy to sensation, was unaware of what he was doing. He believed himself to be Locke's interpreter, but all unawares changed the entire character and nature of Locke's system.

In our time, when we can view the teaching of these two authors at a distance and feel the improvement compared with the myopia of thirty and forty years ago, we can see the difference between them. In the French *Globe* of 3 January 1829, we read:

> It is sufficient to read the first pages of the *Traité des sensations* and compare them with the beginning of the second book of *An Essay concerning Human Understanding*, to be convinced of Condillac's extraordinary illusion in believing himself a disciple of Locke. Although the same formulas are frequently found in both works, the two men did not understand each other, despite Locke's good sense and Condillac's love of clarity; their points of view are totally different. On the one hand, Locke, shut up within

himself, allows the images of the external world to come to him. On the other, Condillac places himself outside, next to his statue, and forms a soul for it out of the sensations which he grants successively to it. What is certain for Locke is *myself*, which he does not question and about which he allows no discussion. What is irrefutable for Condillac, and raises no problem whatsoever for him, is the external world. Locke is concerned with knowing how *myself* knows the external world; Condillac is concerned with discovering how the external world, acting on our senses, develops what he calls *the phenomena of intellect and will* in the *statue's* feeling. Locke solves his problem by declaring that we know the external world only through *the ideas of the world transmitted to us by the senses*. Condillac solves his difficulty by protesting that everything in the statue is solely a *transformation of sensation*. Locke is always *inside*, Condillac *outside*, just as they were at the start of their journey. For Locke there is no *going out* to see bodies; these must be found solely in the internal fact of ideas. For Condillac, there is *no entrance* which allows knowledge of the phenomena of the soul, which must be deduced from the external fact of sensation.

Condillac simply perfected Locke's error, and having perfected it, turned Locke's teaching upside down. Locke's teaching was a clear invitation to thought to reduce all ideas to sensation. We can see this from its development in both England and France, although the work was carried out independently in both countries. The philosophy of *sensation* did in fact appear in England at the same time and in the same way as in France.

What were the results of the philosophy of *sensation*?

As I said, it developed independently in England and France. This is confirmed by the fact that each country, after coming more or less to the same result (the philosophy of *sensation*), then began to go its own way and draw away by a different path. In France the theory of *sensation* developed into the *materialism* of Cabanis and Tracy; in England, it developed into the *idealism* of Berkeley and Hume.

How could such contradictory systems arise from the same principle? As I have said, the answer is: an error of itself propagates even more contradictory errors.

[*app.*, 24]

On the one hand, if human beings are reduced to pure *corporeal feeling*, and the body is necessary for feeling, each human being is a corporeal faculty. At this point it is easy to believe that the body is the sole cause of the faculty which perishes with the body. This is pure materialism.

On the other hand, if sensation is found solely in a sentient subject, and if only pure sensations exist, there is nothing outside the sentient subject. This is idealism. Hence, Pasquale Galluppi was able to show the link between Condillac's system and transcendental idealism. By making Kant begin from the foundations laid by the French philosopher, Galluppi discovered Kant's hidden path which clearly led him to his own strange system (cf. Galluppi's *Lettere filosofiche*, letter 4, Messina, 1827).

25. (708)

[Extrasubjective perception of bodies]

When we had to establish the first, substantial difference between our own body and bodies different from our own, we found that the former was perceived along with us as sentient *subject*, while the latter were perceived simply as forces different from the subject. This difference was proved by: 1. a *fact* revealed by consciousness — when we say 'fact' we mean 'something self-evident', and therefore 'certain'; 2. use of the theory of *perception* already outlined (cf. 528–536), and of the *principles of substance and cause* (cf. 567–569).

However, our body can be perceived *extrasubjectively*, just as any other body can be. In this case, if we perceive our body as an *extrasubjective* term of our sense-faculty, we can discover secondary, but nevertheless important differences, enabling us once again to distinguish it from external bodies. This way of distinguishing our own body (considered as different from us as subject) from external bodies, supposes the truth about an *extrasubjective* term of our sense-faculty. There was, however, no need of this as long as the distinction between our own and other bodies depended upon the substantial difference between *subject* and *that which is extrasubjective*.

[*app.*, 25]

Three differences may be noted between the *extrasubjective* perception of our own and external bodies. These differences show that our own body is quite distinct from any external body. Galluppi sets out the differences as follows:

First difference:

If your right hand is warm, and your left cold, and you bring them into contact, you will feel the same 'self' in them both. *Myself* which feels the warmth of the right hand is the same as that which feels the cold of the left. *Myself*, therefore, seems to exist in both hands. But if you touch a lump of metal with one hand, you will feel *myself* in the hand without feeling it in the metal. It does not seem to exist in the lump of metal, which is extraneous to *myself*. Contact between the two hands furnishes two sensations; contact with the metal only one. *Myself* looks upon right and left hands as parts of its *own* body because it has a touch-feeling in both; it looks upon the lump of metal as an *external body* because it has a touch-feeling *of* the metal, but not *in* the metal. *Myself* regards as its *own* the body which it feels, and in which it seems to feel or to exist; it regards as *external* to itself a body which it feels, but in which it does not seem to feel or exist.

Second difference:

If you want to move your arm, you do so from within, immanently. But the lump of metal will not move simply because you want it to. First, you have to move your hand towards it, and then move the lump by moving your hand. *Myself* regards as its *own* the body which it can move by willing to do so; it regards as *external* any body whose movement does not depend upon its act of will.

Third difference:

You can move the lump of metal to a place where it no longer acts upon any of your senses. But you cannot do this with your own body. At least while you are awake, it is impossible to avoid its action. *Myself* regards as its *own*, therefore, that body which is unceasingly present to it; it regards as *external* any body ceasing to modify it or not present to it.

(*Elementi di filosofia ecc.*, vol. 3, c. 3, §29)

Galluppi concludes from these observations that we can

distinguish our own from external bodies by means of *sight* and *touch*. But both senses perceive *extrasubjectively*, and I am not satisfied with showing a difference between our *own body* and *external bodies* as differing terms of sight and touch. We must also recognise that our own body pertains to ourselves as subject, while external bodies are purely *extrasubjective*. This is the basic difference beteen them.

Nevertheless, the three facts indicated by Galluppi do help considerably to underline the distinction between a *subject* and something *different from the subject*, if we take their analysis one step further. In the first of the three differences, where the *hand* feels itself as sentient, we find a *subject*, while the *lump of metal* which is only felt and does not feel itself, is indicative of *something different from the subject*. In the second difference, the movement that I want to carry out through my hand can be perceived not only with sight and touch, but principally through interior feeling and consciousness, which draw attention to the *subject*. The movement I impart to the lump of metal is clearly noted only through sight and touch indicating *something different from the subject*. In the third difference, I feel my body united with me wherever I go, not because I see it or touch it, but principally through interior consciousness, which indicates me as its *subject*. The distance of external bodies is brought home to me by touch or the other senses indicating that these bodies are *extrasubjective terms* of my feeling powers.

26. (fn. 126)

[St. Thomas and phantasms]

Understanding this [the chronological order of feelings and of thought] enables us to reconcile different passages of St. Thomas Aquinas on the need for *phantasms* if we are to think.

Sometimes he is adamant about the necessity of *phantasms* in our thought (*S.T.*, I, q. 86, art. 7), affirming: *quidditas rei materialis est proprium objectum intellectus* [the proper object of the intellect is that which makes material things what they are] (*S.T.*, I, q. 85, art. 5) or *natura rei materialis est objectum intellectus* [the object of the intellect is the nature of material things] (*S.T.*, q. 87, art. 2). He then concludes that *habits* are not *objects* of the intellect, but are present *ut quibus intellectus intelligit* [as things enabling the intellect to understand].

Taken by itself, this teaching appears the opposite of that attributed to St. Thomas in this book, and proved with his own words (cf. fn. 24 and *App.*, no. 14) that is, that the *matter* of our cognitions is furnished by the interior feeling as well as by the external *sensations*. Although presenting some difficulty, St. Thomas' teaching about two sources is of great importance, and should be evaluated carefully. Let us try to explain St. Thomas with St. Thomas.

According to him, the *material thing* is not the *sole* object of the intellect, but simply *first* in *chronological* order. This is precisely what I am saying. St. Thomas asks (*S.T.*, I, q. 87, art. 3) 'whether the intellect knows its own act,' which is certainly not material, and replies affirmatively. He adds, however, that it does so *after* knowing *material things*. In this, the human being differs, according to Aquinas, from angels who with their first act understand both themselves and the act with which they understand themselves. He says: 'Another intellect exists, the human one, which does not furnish its own understanding (as the divine intellect does). The essence of this intellect is not the *first* object of understanding' (as happens with the angels, according to St. Thomas). 'Its *first* object is something external, that is, the nature of material things. Hence, the *first* thing known by the human intellect is a material object. Only *secondarily* does the human intellect know the act with which it knows the object, and through this second knowledge comes to know itself' (*Est autem alius intellectus, scilicet humanus, qui nec est suum intelligere, nec sui intelligere est OBJECTUM PRIMUM ipsa eius essentia, sed aliquid extrinsecum, scilicet natura materialis rei. Et ideo id quod PRIMO cognoscitur ab intellectu humano, est hujusmodi objectum, et SECUNDARIO cognoscitur ipse actus, quo cognoscitur objectum: et per actum cognoscitur ipse intellectus*). He says the same thing more clearly shortly afterwards in summing up his teaching: 'The object of the intellect is something common, that is, ENS and TRUTH, included in which is the act itself of understanding. The intellect, therefore, can know its own act, but not as its FIRST object which, in our present state, is not any ens and truth, but ens and truth considered in material things' *(S.T.,* I, corp. ad 1). He confirms this with a phrase from Aristotle: 'Objects are known BEFORE acts (*PRAECOGNOS-CUNTUR*), and acts BEFORE powers' (*De Anima*, bk. 2, test. 33). It is clear that we are dealing with priority in *time* alone, and this is precisely what I have been saying.

But I also observed that in order to reach the state of intellectual development necessary for reflection on one's own interior feeling, it is not enough to know bodily things *first*. It is also necessary to arrive at abstract thoughts (which is normally impossible without the use of language) and through them obtain dominion over one's attention which can then be directed at will. Only after this can a human being reflect upon himself, and advert to his interior acts. *First* amongst these acts, as we have said, is the fundamental feeling which, however, is reflected upon *last*, after advertence to its accidental acts. The *chronological* order of our *advertence* runs as follows: 1. we advert to what is sensible in a bodily sense; 2. form *abstract thoughts*; 3. advert to our *act of feeling* (sensations) and our act of understanding; 4. finally advert to the *fundamental feeling*, the first act and common root of both sense and intelligence.

It is now very easy to reconcile other passages of St. Thomas in which he makes it clear that the sources of our cognitions are not the senses alone. Some examples may be useful.

'Sensitive knowledge is not the whole cause (*TOTA CAUSA*) of intellective knowledge. We should not be surprised, therefore, if intellective knowledge extends beyond sensitive knowledge (*ultra sensitivam se extendit*)' *(S.T.,* I, q. 84, art. 6). Amongst these things which go beyond sense knowledge, and to which only intellective knowledge reaches out, first place belongs to all that is in our understanding. *Quod intellectualiter cognoscitur, per se est notum, et ad ipsum cognoscendum natura cognoscentis sufficit ABSQUE EXTERIORI MEDIO* [What is known intellectually is known of itself, and the nature of the person who knows is sufficient, WITHOUT ANY EXTERIOR MEANS, as a means of knowing it] (*Contra Gent.,* I, q. 57). For example, we cannot know where our affections lie except by consulting our heart. External, material things can tell us nothing about them: *Etsi fides non cognoscatur per EXTERIORES CORPORIS MOTUS, percipitur tamen etiam ab eo in quo est per INTERIOREM ACTUM CORDIS* [Although faith is not known through EXTERIOR

MOVEMENTS OF OUR BODY, it is perceived by the person possessing it through AN INTERIOR ACT OF THE HEART] (*S.T.*, I, 87, q. 2). Again, if we knew only *material things*, we could not form any idea about *spirits*, knowledge of which has to be drawn from our own soul, as Thomas says, following Augustine: *Ex illa auctoritate Augustini haberi potest quod illud, quod mens nostra de cognitione incorporalium rerum accipit, PER SEIPSAM cognoscere possit. Et hoc adeo verum est, ut etiam apud Philosophum dicatur, quod scientia de anima est PRINCIPIUM quoddam ad cognoscendum substantias separatas* (De Anima, bk. I, test. 2). *Per hoc enim quod anima nostra cognoscit seipsam, pertingit ad cognitionem aliquam habendam de substantiis incorporeis, qualem eam contingit habere* [We have Augustine's authority for saying that the mind can know THROUGH ITSELF the knowledge it receives about incorporeal things. Indeed, even Aristotle says that knowledge of our soul is a certain PRINCIPLE enabling us to know separated substances (*De Anima*, bk. 1, test.2). Hence the knowledge our soul has of itself is an element in the knowledge of incorporeal substances as our soul must have it] (*S.T.*, I, q. 88, ad 1).

27. (732)

[Galluppi and sensation of distant bodies]

At this point I part company with Galluppi. He says that the eye sees distant bodies directly. He likens the tiny units of light successively striking the retina to the different parts of a walking stick felt successively by a hand. But the two facts differ: the hand moves, the eye does not. The length of the walking stick is revealed by *movement*. If the stick passed over a motionless hand, the hand by itself would not, in my opinion, perceive its length, except possibly through habit and memory. I grant that the eye also senses what is outside itself, but only in so far as the eye is touch; it never senses distance but only something *different* from itself, or if preferred, something *outside* itself (because the eye is already felt by the fundamental feeling). This 'outside itself' would indeed be something different from the eye but nevertheless adhering to it.

Galluppi's opinion receives favourable support from the cata-
ract operation performed by the oculist, Giovanni Janin, on a
young man. It is also supported by Professor Luigi de'
Gregoris' success in restoring partial sight to some people born
blind, none of whom, it is said, thought that bodies adhered to
their eyes but were things directly seen outside them (cf *Delle
cateratte de' ciechi nati, osservazioni teorico-chimiche del
Professore di chimica e di oftalmia Luigi de Gregoris romano*,
Rome, 1826). On the other hand Cheselden's experiment is so
impressive and so well corroborated that, despite the above
evidence, it cannot be immediately refuted. Indeed, the experiment was repeated very carefully in Italy by Professor Jacobi of
Pavia and confirmed in every respect.

28. (806)

[Idea relative to subsistence of things]

I take the opportunity of resolving a possible doubt about the
distinction between an *idea* and *judgment on the subsistence of
things.* I said (cf. 398–401) that any object whatsoever could be
mentally conceived as endowed with all its essential and accidental characteristics, and still not subsist. Judgment of its subsistence, therefore, adds nothing to the idea we have of it. But
are not place and time characteristics of a thing, and added to it
when we judge that the thing subsists? If so, the judgment does
add something that was not previously present in the idea of the
thing.

I would deny that place and time are characteristics of a thing.
Wherever and whenever a thing subsists, it is always itself, neither more nor less. There is no change, no addition to its nature.
This needs careful consideration, and proof of it may be found
in experience undergone by sensitive *entia* transported thousands of miles without feeling the change. This occurs because
being in one place or another (and the same may be said about
time) has no effect on their nature which remains exactly what it
was. Place and time do not enter, therefore, into the idea of a
thing.

When, however, judgment on the subsistence of a corporeal

thing depends upon sense perception, such judgment determines its *place*. If I perceive a body with my senses, I must perceive it in a determined place. But what is this *place* occupied by the perceived body? *Place*, we maintain, is something appertaining to *reality* precisely because it is foreign to the idea but at home in the judgment together with the *subsistence* of the thing of which, in corporeal matters, it forms an element.

An immediate objection springs to mind: what of the *idea* of place? It is of course true that we have such an idea, but in the same way as we have the *idea of subsistence* which, like all other ideas, is universal because it is only the *possibility* that an ens subsists. Where, however, we are dealing with the particular subsistence of an ens, the subsistence we think of is the idea of *subsistence* focused through a judgment on an individual. The same is true about our idea of a place. This idea is the *possibility* that an extended ens exists in that place. But when we perceive a subsistent, extended ens, we determine the *idea* of that extended thing by a judgment affirming its subsistence and, together with its subsistence, the place it occupies. The difference between subsistence and *place* is that the former is the act itself of the ens while *place* is an abstract, that is, the *mode of the subsistence* of the ens we call body.

The distinction between the content of an *idea* or *essence* and the judgment which makes known something about it (the particular subsistence), was known to early philosophers, but often forgotten (it is in fact very difficult to keep before the mind). As a result, questions insoluble without it were tackled by means of other distinctions resembling it. This resulted in serious embarrassment for science by multipying entia without necessity under the guise of such distinctions. One of these distinctions, which we have already mentioned, is that between *general* and *particular matter*. It was thought that the former, but not the latter, was necessary for corporeal things. In fact, it is not true that these two kinds of matter exist. What exists is: 1. particular matter; and 2. the *idea* of particular matter. The latter is simply particular matter in so far as it is thought possible. Because what is possible is universal, it seems to be universal matter. The same kind of distinction was made by early philosophers between universal and particular quantity, and here too the same observation is relevant: universal quantity is only the *idea* of quantity.

The term *intelligible quantity* used by these philosophers shows they had some notion of this. In book 4 of Aristotle's *Physics*, Simplicius says: 'I think it is better to say that we have a *specific* extension' (the Greek has κατ'εἶδος, that is, 'according to the idea', as I have been suggesting) 'which can be seen in *exemplars*, and another extension conceived mentally by passive discernment of an indivisible substance without parts.' *Intelligible* quantity is that described as *according to the idea*, which is seen in *exemplars*, that is, in first ideas. It is therefore the *idea of quantity*, or, if you prefer, the quantity thought in the idea, which is the same as possible or universal quantity.

29. (810)

[Judgment about the identity of a body]

Generally speaking, we can show that when we touch bodies with different parts of our own body we do not perceive their identity. Different perceptions of external things correspond to different affected parts of our body, and the bodies (agents acting on us) seem as many as the perceptions we have in different parts of our body, especially if the perceptions take place simultaneously. Nevertheless, when we are touched in (phenomenally) continuous space, touch gives notice of several bodies forming a continuum amongst themselves, as happens with solids. On the other hand, if we have non-continuous sensations, for instance, when we are touched by a body on our hand and again on our foot, we can only think that two bodies have touched us. Only the use of sight, or the continuity of touch, as I said, and habit, enables us to judge the unity of a body.

The judgment that we make about the identity of a body touching us simultaneously on several parts of our body is an *habitual* judgment, dependent upon experience, and as such can sometimes deceive us. For example, if I touch a button with two fingers crossed one over the other, I feel two buttons because I feel two sensations in different parts of my fingers where I am not accustomed to be touched simultaneously by a single body. The natural position of my fingers, when I touch a body, is straight out and flat so that the sensations produced by an external body are close together. On the other hand, when my fingers are crossed, one sensation takes place at a distance from the other and at a part of the tip opposite to where it normally happens.

In our case of the pencil tip running along the arm, we have the (phenomenal) continuity of a sliding sensation which makes us believe that the body touching me is the same although different parts of the arm are touched. Nevertheless, simple touch tells us that only similar sensations succeed one another without noticeable interruption. This is certainly not sufficient to prove the movement of the external body. On the contrary, when I take a body in my hand and carry it from one place to another, the identity of the body is proved by the continuity of its perception, unmoved relative to my hand grasping the body. In this case, I would perceive the movement not with simple touch, but with touch assisted by interior awareness of my arm which I move.

30. (846)
[Extension misunderstood]

Philosophy has come down to us not through one but many channels, and has nearly come to grief in the limitless ocean of modern scepticism. I have traced the history of this system (which is really a negation of system) through Locke, Berkeley, Hume, Reid and Kant, as well as through Condillac and the French sceptics. The same philosophical destruction came to us through another channel: Descartes, Bayle and Kant. Descartes, who had made famous and universally acceptable Galileo's opinion that the secondary properties of bodies were only in the subject, posited the essence of bodies in extension. His error consisted in his failure to observe that all our sensations (colour, taste, sound, odour, etc.), although subjective, necessarily contain an *extrasubjective* part.

When Bayle came on the scene, this extrasubjective part had been forgotten, and all the above-mentioned sensations were taken as subjective. Bayle applied the arguments which

Descartes had used for secondary qualities and showed that primary qualities, one of which was *extension*, were subjective. His argument was simple in the extreme and *ad hominem*: we perceive extension only through a sensation; but sensations are subjective, therefore extension is subjective.

Kant, beginning from this point, needed only to invent the name 'form of external sense' for the subject's aptitude for perceiving space. He had now entered the domain of critical philosophy. He took a few steps in this territory, on to which he had been thrown, as it were, by the shipwreck of his time, and found himself on the sad terrain of transcendental philosophy. After Descartes' small error in missing the *extrasubjective* element intermingled with all our subjective sensations, *extension* could no longer be defended.

31. (851)

[Reid and the concept of body]

If the concept I have given of body is borne in mind, we can see how unreasonable the following words of Reid are:

> We ought not, therefore, to conclude that such bodily organs are, in their own nature, necessary to *perception*; but rather that, by the will of God, our power of *perceiving external objects* is limited and circumscribed by our organs of sense; so that we perceive objects in a certain manner, and in certain circumstances, and in no other.
>
> (*Essays on the powers etc.*, vol. 1, p. 71)

It is certainly true that in entia which lack corporeal organs *knowledge* of bodies can be more perfect than ours, but the opinion that the *sense perception* of bodies can be better without organs is sustainable only by those who have not made a perfect analysis of this perception. I have shown that what we call *body* is precisely what we perceive with our organs. Organs are just as necessary as corporeal nature for the sense perception of corporeal nature. Reid's words clearly show that according to him and all modern philosophers after him, bodies are an idea of something unknown and mysterious. This vague, confused and totally mysterious idea of bodies allowed thinkers to phantasise as they wished. It gave rise, in fact, to all the extraordinary theories of modern philosophy, particularly idealism. But the only thing the word *body* expresses and can express is that which we know and perceive sensibly. Hence our notion of bodies is conditioned by and strictly bound with our organs. In this respect Reid's error was the opposite of Newton's. Newton considered it necessary to attribute infinite space to God as a sensory, but Reid considered that extended organs were unnecesaary to divine *knowledge*. The majority of these faults can be avoided if *sensation* and *sense perception* are clearly distinguished from the *idea* and *word* of the understanding.

32. (895)
[Tradition and the subjectivity of sensations]

Some believe that before Descartes the *subjectivity* of sensation had never been observed, but it was familiar to all antiquity. In fact the sophists misused it by denying every truth except what is subjective or relative to the human being. In this way they created a universal scepticism. The sceptics were followed by the Epicureans. Lucretius, for example, denied colour to first bodies, that is, to corporeal essence:

> Material bodies entirely lack colour;
> It is neither becomes nor unbecomes things.

Similarly, he denies cold, heat, sound, odour and taste:

> But think not haply that primal bodies
> Remain despoiled alone of colour: they also
> Are from warmth dissevered and from cold
> And from hot exhalations; they move,
> Soundless and sweatless; and throw
> No odour from the body that is theirs.

He proves this with beautiful observations (2, 729–863).

The tradition of this truth was not lost when scholasticism flourished. St. Thomas expressly teaches that the phrase, 'The sun is hot', must not be understand to mean that we attribute the sensation of heat to the sun, but to mean that the sun is the cause of this sensation. It has the same sense as 'Medicine is healthy', that is, medicine contains neither health nor illness but causes health in us (*C. Gent.*, I, qq. 29 and 31). This teaching of St. Thomas stamps the two periods of scholastic philosophy: the first, brilliant period, when Aquinas and other sublime minds flourished; the second, final period, when scholasticism, like all human things, declined. Providence then placed the promotion of philosophical truth in other hands. It was Galileo who restored the truth we are discussing, and a quotation from his fine words will be helpful:

> I do not think that external bodies require anything more than size, shape, number and movement (slow or rapid) to stimulate taste, odour and sound. If we remove ears, tongue and nose, I am certain that shape, number and movement remain but not odour, taste and sound which, outside a living animal, are simply words, just as tickling and titillation are mere names when the armpits and the skin around the nose are removed (where tickling is initiated by touch).

He applies the same teaching to heat:

> I am very much of the opinion that heat is of this kind. The things which produce and make us feel heat and are generally called 'fire', are a quantity of very tiny particles of a particular shape which move at a particular speed. They are so fine that when they strike our body, they penetrate it and, as they pass through and touch our substance, we feel them. This feeling is the experience we call heat, pleasant or unpleasant according to their number and the relative speed with which the particles penetrate us. This penetration is pleasant when it helps our insensible, necessary perspiration, but unpleasant when it causes too great a division and disruption of our substance. In short, the action of fire is simply the movement by which it penetrates all bodies with its estreme fineness. It breaks the bodies down slowly or rapidly, depending on the number and speed of the fiery particles and on the degree of density of the bodies' matter. Most of these disintegrating bodies change into other fiery particles and continue the dissolution as long as they encounter dissoluble matter. But I do

not think that in fire there is any other quality which may be warm. Only shape, number, movement, penetration and touch are present. In other words, fire is such a part of ourselves that if the animated, sensitive body is removed, heat is nothing more than a word.

(Cf. *Il Saggiatore*)

33. (897)

[Advertence and senses]

The following observations offer further confirmation that many things attributed to the different grades of perfection of our senses should in fact be attributed to levels of perfection of our *advertence* or attention to sensations.

Observation shows that the hand is not the most sensitive part of our body; other parts contain more nerves and are more sensitive. In fact we can say that the skin is more sensitive in all other parts of our body than in the hand where nature has wisely reduced sensitivity so that we can use the hand freely without being frequently troubled by pain. Continual use hardens our hand still more. Increase in the hand's sensitivity, therefore, is not brought about by its use except for greater effectivity and alertness of the nerves in the parts that are used more; and I have no doubt that this comes into play here. This, however, only proves the need for a greater attention or at least *sensitive* effectivity. My concern, on the other hand, is to know which part of our body can more easily make us perceive and distinguish the tiniest particles, the little inequalities of rough, uneven bodies and all their tactile differences. The answer must be the hand.

This ability does not come from greater, natural sensitivity of touch in the hand but from our habit of using the hand for that purpose and from our habit of *adverting* to minute differences in the hand's sensations. Normally, we do not learn to *advert* to them in other parts of our body. But extraordinary things are done by people who have lost their hands. Long education has taught them to be attentive to the sensations in their feet, accurately noting and differentiating every sensation. Such evidence does not lead me to think that sensitivity in their feet has increased. Rather, they have learnt to direct their attention to the sensations in their feet and note what takes place. Other people pay little or no attention at all to these sensations.

A good doctor with long experience notices the least change of pulse in a sick person; others do not. His sense of touch has not been refined specifically for taking pulses; any other person could have taken the pulse and learnt nothing. If the constant taking of pulses actually refines the doctor's touch, why does contact at the place of the vein rather than elsewhere render the nerves of the doctor's hand more sensitive? Why is the doctor's touch so sensitive to pulses but dull and coarse to the delicate engravings of an object worked in gold. If feeling the differences of pulse depended on the physical sensitivity of the skin and not on the acquired ability to advert to what is felt, the same sensitive touch could be used for everything; those born blind would not have to learn to determine the pulse by practice since they would already have a very sensitive touch.

All this is explained by *advertence* to our sensations, which is being continually improved and increases much more than the senses themselves. Our senses might improve a little even physically by use but certainly not enough to explain the great difference between senses that have been used meaningfully and senses that have not been so used. The physical refinement of a sense, which depends on the texture of the organ, is given by nature and cannot be markedly changed. The sense of sight, it seems, can be improved and sharpened by practice, but we must remember that what this sense tells us about distant bodies is due to *habitual judgments* (as we shall show later); it is our ability to make these judgments that is perfected. And what sight tells us about surfaces is to a large extent due to the practice of observation. The jeweller's sharp eye, the doctor's capacity to tell at a glance how a person feels, other people's insight into character, all depend upon sharpened observation. The very subtle differences painters see in colours and pictures obviously involves skill in discerning the variations which others also see but do not advert to.

The same is true about music and the practised ear, which seems to hear much more than the ears of others in an orchestral piece. In both cases the same sounds are perceived but with

different mental attention. Another example is the acute sense
of smell of tribesmen who, it is said, could identify the tracks of
the Spaniards by smelling the ground. But we should be much
more amazed by their constant practice in sensing minute sensations of smell and their differences.

Again, the taste buds of the palate undergo little change from
frequent contact with different foods but what amazing sensitivity gourmets acquire, compared with other people, in judging different tastes! Perhaps Juvenal's glutton had dulled his
palate by continual use of spices and dainty foods, but nevertheless, by applying the greatest attention to food, had so developed his sense of taste for oysters that one gulp could tell him
from which sea they had come.

The benefit the reader can draw from all these observations is
to be convinced of the great difference between *sensation* and
advertence, and to be persuaded that we feel an infinity of
things without being in the least aware of them.

34. (901)

[Indication and perception in sensation]

Hearing and smell indicate distant bodies, but I am not considering these senses under this aspect. I am discussing them
only in so far as they receive the direct sensation of sound and
smell. In the following chapter [12], I will deal with sight in so
far as it indicates distant bodies, but not with hearing and smell
because it is easy to apply the same observations to them as to
sight. It is sufficient to observe here that one of the greatest
sources of error in discussing the senses is to confuse direct perception with the *indication* given by perception, and to claim
that perception gives what in fact is given only by indication,
just as it is erroneous to confuse the knowledge we obtain about
bodies from different senses. Reid, for example, in his attempt
to rebut Locke's teaching that the primary qualities we perceive
of bodies are likenesses of the bodies themselves, argues as
follows:

Taking it for granted that, by the ideas of primary and

secondary qualities, he [Locke] means the sensations they excite in us, I observe that it appears strange, that sensation should be the idea of a quality in body, to which it is acknowledged to bear no resemblance. If the sensation of sound be the idea of that vibration of the sounding which occasions it, a surfeit may, for the same reason, be the idea of a feast.

(Essays on the Powers, etc.)

I do not know what Locke might have replied to these words, but in my opinion they are foreign to the discussion. We need to bear in mind:

1. The sensation of sound is direct. On the other hand, we do not in any way perceive the vibration of the sonorous body with our hearing except as a result of an association of ideas through which, when we hear the sound, we remember the oscillation of the strings or of the sonorous body which we have perceived at other times with touch and sight. It is therefore impossible for sound to represent and imitate what it merely arouses in our memory. When I say that the perceived primary qualities of a body resemble the body, I am indicating something totally different from what Reid is saying here.

2. The primary qualities are perceived only confusedly by hearing, smell and taste. We cannot therefore appeal to these senses to discover the likeness of which I am speaking.

3. It is false to say that the first qualities, when perceived, are sensation; they are only a part of sensations, the *extra-subjective part.*

4. Finally, it is totally inexact and false to say that a sensation is an idea of a thing. Such language may have been tolerated by Locke, but in itself it can lay no claim to tolerance. As I have shown, there is an infinite distance between ideas and sensations.

35. (902)

[Primary and secondary qualities]

Reid glimpsed this truth when he posited the difference

[*app.*, 35]

between the *primary* and *secondary* qualities of bodies. He saw that the primary qualities give us *distinct* notions, the secondary, *confused* notions. His observation is true but he was unable to explain it. To the question whether the distinction is real, he replies:

> I answer, That there appears to me to be a real foundation for the distinction; and it is this — that our senses give us a direct notion of the primary qualities, and inform us of what they are in themselves. But of the secondary qualities, our sense gives only a relative and obscure notion — they inform us only, that they are qualities that affect us in a certain manner — that is, produce in us a certain sensation; but as to what they are in themselves, our senses leave us in the dark.
>
> (*Essays on the Powers*, etc.)

For Locke, the distinction between the *primary* and *secondary* qualities lies in this: primary qualities, and certainly not the secondary, are *likenesses* of bodies. Reid completely rejected this opinion of Locke. He might not have done so if he had carefully noted the true principle from which the distinction between the primary and secondary qualities of matter must be drawn. According to this principle, sensation is composed of two parts, one subjective, the other extrasubjective. As we have seen, the *extrasubjective* element is the perception of the primary qualities, which are truly extrasubjective. From this point of view we can say that *sensation* is a likeness of the external agents because it has in common with them the qualities of multiplicity and continuity; having common qualities is the same as having likeness. Here I agree with Locke's opinion which, however, I limit and explain. In fact I believe that pyrrhonism relative to sensible things is inevitable when all likeness between bodies and sensations is rejected. Moreover, there could be no reply to Bayle's objections about primary qualities. All his objections arise from his failure to observe the extrasubjectivity of primary qualities, and his consequent attempt to make them subjective like other qualities.

36. (925)

[Error and habitual judgment]

Most common errors, it would seem, depend upon habitual judgments formed almost involuntarily and irresistibly by the mass of people. Judgments become habitual because experience indicates an almost constant connection between the inability of ordinary people to take note of infrequent exceptions and their tendency to judge immediately; they pass from 'often' to 'always' without suspending judgment when necessary. For example, everyone said that the sun moved around the earth, although the eye told us nothing of the real movement of the sun. People as a whole judged on the basis of their sight-sensation; they would have avoided error if they had suspended their judgment. But was this possible in the light of almost general experience which showed apparent movement to be accompanied by real movement of what was seen? It is true that this law of experience showed various anomalies, some of which are common to everybody's experience. For example, to a man in a moving boat the banks seem to be moving. But individual examples are powerless to help the mass of people suspend their judgment. When people as a whole are ready to make certain kinds of conclusions, to urge them to suspend their judgment is like trying to prevent an avalanche on a mountain — you may foresee it, but you will be unable to stop it. Such judgments are amended only after centuries. First, some extraordinary person shows that they are wrong, only to be eliminated for his pains by public opinion. But his martyrdom does not sweep away what he has discovered. The grain of truth gradually forces its way to the surface and conquers the multitude itself which comes finally to realise its errors, to repent and to blush at the thought of its stupid presumption and cruel, ignorant pride.

37. (938)

[Sight relative to touch]

Condillac and Buffon said that objects seen upside down by

the eye are put right by touch. It is extraordinary to see how this prejudice has been copied and repeated by one author after another. Hauy (*Traité élémentaire de physique*, vol. 2), Foderé (*Physiologie positive*, vol. 3) and Algarotti together with the whole band of our most recent authors have simply repeated the same thing. However, Melchiorre Gioia must be exempted. Despite numerous errors he made the following sound observation:

> It seems absolutely false that sensations of touch can correct the impressions of sight. In fact, although touch assures us that a stick protruding from the water in a pond is straight, we see it bent and always see it bent, even if we touch it a thousand times. Again, although touch tells us that the image we see of ourselves in a mirror does not exist suspended in the air, our eye tells us that the image does exist, and we see it. An artist who has painted a sphere on canvas is certain that the sphere lies on a flat surface. His eye however tells him that a good part of the sphere emerges from the canvas towards him.
>
> If we accept the explanation of physiologists that touch corrects the impressions of sight, objects should appear inverted until touch has removed the delusion. But this is not the case: people born with a cataract see objects the right way up, not inverted, when the cataract is removed. Finally, animals that lack practically all touch should see objects inverted, but their behaviour makes us believe the opposite: they see objects the right way up, as we do.
>
> (*Esercizio logico sugli errori d'Ideologia e Zoologia, ecc.*, pp. 98 ss.)

38. (947)

[Erroneous judgments about sensations]

The idealists in particular have abused this impropriety. As we can see in Hume, they drew one of their arguments from the changing size of bodies as distance changes.

Aristotle is a good example of the antiquity of this deception which attributes to all the senses in general what pertains only to sight. He says that size and movement are *common sensible* qualities, and that our sense is deceived much more by these qualities than by the sensible qualities proper to each sense. His reason is that sizes and movements change as distances change. That which is proper only to the eye, which Aristotle calls the *greatest sense* (*De Anima*, bk 3), is attributed to the senses in general. But he should really have said that applying colours to bodies is a far more frequent error, because colours in fact are only sensations in the optic nerve. Evidently Aristotle did not notice this; he too accepted the general error.

I will use this opportunity to add another observation about the defects, as they seem to me, in Aristotle's analysis of sensations. Apparently he was not always aware of the *habitual judgments* we continually mix with sensations. Like people in general, he confused them with sensations. For example, he says, 'Only on *very few occasions* does sense mistake its proper objects.' The explanation commonly given of 'very few occasions' (the context and Aristotle's style of language do not allow any doubt) is that sense mistakes its *proper objects* only on the very rare occasions when it is infirm. But note, *infirm sense* in itself does not err; error is caused by the judgment we add to sense. Thus sense, even when infirm, does not mistake its proper objects. The error lies in our judgment, which is the source of every error. Aristotle's teaching must give place to that of St. Augustine who says: *si omnes corporis sensus ita nuntiant ut afficiuntur, quid ab eis amplius exigere debeamus, ignoro* [If all the senses of the body tell us in this way that they have been affected, what more can we possibly require from them?] (*De Vera Religione*, c. 33).

39. (952)

[Reid on judgment and sensation]

It seems to me that here Reid is not perfectly coherent with himself, or at least that his explanation is somewhat obscure. On the one hand, he says that *perception* is of its nature totally different from *sensation*: perception is made by means of a *natural judgment* which affirms external bodies; sensation does not extend beyond the soul which feels itself modified. In other words, perception and sensation are evidently different powers. He seems to affirm this even more clearly where he speaks of perception as a mysterious faculty within the spirit, that is, something definitely different from sensation. On the other hand, he says that *sense* does not exist without *judgment*; the word 'sense' in everyday language, to which he appeals, always expresses an ability to judge. It was philosophers who mistakenly divided these two things (sense and judgment) and made two faculties of them (*Essays on the Powers of the Human Mind, etc.*, vol. 2, p. 176).

We see that Reid finds contradictions in philosophers but cannot determine the cause. According to him, they define sense as a power giving us ideas without judgment, and judgment as a power to compare the ideas given us by sense. Granted this, he says, philosophers are forced to define sense in the same way as they describe judgment (if ideas are to come from sense). As proof of this he takes an example from the second chapter of Locke's fourth book where Locke calls the eyes *judges* of colour and thus attributes the faculty of judgment to sense.

Although this observation is totally true, Reid, who notes the incoherence of philosophers, is unable to determine the cause.

His inability results from the failure of philosophers to distinguish carefully between the nature of *sensation* and that of *intellection* or idea. They failed to observe that ideas can be obtained only by means of a judgment, and that *sensations* are received in us without a judgment.

They saw on the one hand that 1. sense is not judgment, and on the other, 2. thought that *sensation* and *idea* were more or less the same thing, although idea did not exist without judgment. This led them to describe sense as if it were a judgment, without their being aware of the contradiction between the conclusion and the distinction they had already made between the faculty of feeling and that of judgment.

Reid tried to remove the contradiction by suggesting that *sense* must not be defined as different from *judgment* but as a judgment itself. He appeals to common sense and thinks he has determined common opinion by investigating the use of words, which are depositaries of commonly held beliefs. He finds that the words 'sense' and 'feeling' are used to mean *judgment*, and

454   *A New Essay concerning the Origin of Ideas*

therefore concludes that people in general consider judgment to be the same as feeling.

But these thoughts of Reid simply inform us that we are not safe from error when we say, 'I intend to follow common sense'. Common sense, like a book written by a very learned person, must be read with great attention and interpreted with great wisdom.

Indeed, if it were true that people in general confuse feeling with judgment, as Reid maintains, this must surely be a general error rather than a general truth. The reasons I have given to demonstrate the necessary distinction between *sense* and *judgment* cannot, it seems to me, leave any doubt about the distinction (cf. several places in volume 1, particularly 218 ss.). If the expression, 'The senses judge', is to be excused, it must be understood as a summary expression for 'Judgment follows sense'. In my opinion however, this manner of speaking is often misunderstood by people in general who have never analysed the operations of their own spirit nor distinguished the two very closely united operations of sense and of judgment accompanying sense. When they do reflect, they fail to see the distinction and fall into the error of judging the two things as one.

I have no difficulty in accepting other expressions such as 'This person has this feeling', 'I feel in this way', etc., I have no difficulty in accepting them as good and true when they are used to express actions pertaining to intelligence. There is in fact an intellectual sense which is the principle and source of every intellective action (cf. 553). As St. Augustine says, *est enim sensus et mentis* [For there is a sense proper to the mind also] (*Retract.*, bk. 1, c. 1). This intellectual sense however must not be confused with our bodily senses.

40. (966)
[Ideas and need of intellectual activity]

Tradition has uninterruptedly passed down from the earliest times the truth that some *activity* of the understanding is necessary for the formation of ideas. For Plato, separate ideas were necessary, as well as subjective activity. Aristotle posited activity in the human being which resulted in the concept of understanding which possessed a primal, essential act. This activity of the understanding, necessary for forming ideas from sensations, is manifest in everything said by the Fathers of the Church. St. Augustine speaks powerfully about it: *Et quia illa corpora sunt, quae foris per sensus carnis adamavit, eorumque diuturna quadam familiaritate implicata est, nec secum potest introrsum tamquam in regionem incorporeae naturae ipsa corpora inferre, imagines eorum convolvit, et rapit factas in semetipsa de semetipsa. Dat enim* EIS FORMANDIS QUIDDAM SUBSTANTIAE SUAE [These things which [the soul] loved externally through the carnal senses are bodies with which it has become entangled by a kind of daily familiarity, but which it cannot transport within, into the region, as it were, of incorporeal nature. It shapes certain images of them, therefore, and draws within itself what it has itself made. IT GIVES TO THEIR FORMATION SOMETHING OF ITS OWN SUBSTANCE] (*De Trinit.*, bk. 10, c. 5). We see here the extent of the activity attributed by Augustine to the soul in the formation of ideas. Surely this truth could not be missed in the centuries of barbarism? Anyone uncorrupted by false systems could not fail to see how the understanding acts in the formation of its ideas on the occasion of sensations.

Another witness comes from the eighth century: Charlemagne. Describing the origin of ideas, he uses expressions which clearly indicate intellectual activity —Alcuin writes, '*Nunc autem consideremus miram velocitatem animae in formandis rebus quas percipit per carnales sensus, a quibus quasi per quosdam nuntios quicquid rerum sensibilium*' (note, he says *sensible* not *all* things) '*cognitarum vel incognitarum percipit, mox in seipsa earum ineffabili celeritate format figuras, informatasque in suae thesauro memoriae recondit*' [Let us now consider how extraordinarily quickly the soul forms things which it perceives through the bodily senses. Through these, as if they were messengers, it perceives something of sensible things (note, he says *sensible* not *all* things), both known and unknown. Immediately and with the utmost speed, the soul forms images of them and stores these in the treasury of its memory]. A little further on he gives the following definition of the soul: '*Anima, seu animus, est spiritus intellectualis, rationalis,* SEMPER IN MOTU, *semper vivens, bonae malaeque voluntatis capax'* [The soul, or spirit, is an intellectual, rational spirit, ALWAYS IN MOVEMENT, always alive, and capable of both good and evil will]. Concerning its activity he says: '*Nec etiam aliquis potest satis admirari, quod sensus ille vivus atque coelestis, qui mens, vel animus nuncupatur, tantae mobilitatis est, ut ne tum quidem, cum sopitus est conquiescat'* [Nor should anyone be surprised at the great mobility of this living, heavenly sense called mind or spirit which, even in sleep, does not rest] (*De Animae ratione ad Eulaliam virginem*).

Five centuries later, St. Thomas and others like him taught the same doctrine about the necessity of an intellectual activity, if sensible things were to be suitable for the understanding to perceive. Elsewhere I have given clear demonstrations of this. It is indeed extraordinary that St. Thomas not only denies to *sensations* the aptitude for being *per se* perceptions of the mind, but does not even accept them as *abstractions* unless they are *universalised* by the intellect. He expressly teaches: '*Formae sensibiles,* VEL A SENSIBILIBUS ABSTRACTAE, *non possunt agere in mentem nostram, nisi quatenus per lumen intellectus agentis immateriales redduntur, et sic efficiuntur quodammodo homogeneae intellectui possibili, in quem agunt'* [Sensible forms, OR FORMS ABSTRACTED FROM SENSIBLE THINGS, cannot act in our mind without their being made immaterial through the light of the acting intellect and becoming in some way homogenous to the possible intellect in which they act] (*De Verit.*, 10, art. 6, ad 2). We can therefore say that all centuries have acknowledged the fact 'that an activity of the understanding is necessary for the acquisition of ideas'.

41. (975)

[Reid and the meaning of idea]

Reid claims that 'idea' has two meanings, one for philosophers and the other for people in general. He wants us to reject the philosophers' meaning and keep the popular meaning. But, as I have said (cf. vol. 1, 99 ss.), I do not think he is in fact following common sense in this. What are the two claimed meanings of the word 'idea'? In philosophy, it means *something in between* us and objects, so that through ideas we know objects. For ordinary people, it means an *operation* of our mind with which we directly think of the objects themselves. To prove the existence of this second meaning, Reid argues as follows:

> In common speech, 'to think of a thing' and 'to have the idea of a thing' mean exactly the same thing. But 'to think' is an active verb, expressing the operation of the mind; 'to have an idea' therefore also expresses the activity of the mind.
> (*Essay on the Powers of the Human Mind, etc.*, London, 1812, vol. 1, p. 20 ss.)

But if he can draw this conclusion from noting the meaning of 'to think of a thing', I can draw an opposite conclusion from noting the meaning of 'to have an idea'. According to me, this phrase expresses simply possession of a thing; the verb 'to have' expresses nothing more than possession. Consequently, 'to have an idea' expresses only a *state* of the mind which has the idea but not an operation of the mind. Now, if it is erroneous for me to draw the meaning of 'to think of a thing' from the meaning of 'to have an idea', it seems unreasonable to obtain the meaning 'to have an idea' from the meaning of 'to think of a thing'. I grant that the verb 'to think' expresses the *operation* of our spirit but this is precisely why I deny that the two phrases have the same meaning. I can have an idea without actually thinking of the thing of which I have the *idea*. The *operation* of the mind thinking of a thing is quite different from simply *having the idea of the thing*, that is, when the thing is not necessarily being thought of. Note, all languages, as far as I know, contain the two different expressions, 'to think of a thing' and 'to have the idea of a thing'. According to Reid's principles, this would not be the case if the common sense of people had not really intended to express two different things. If a language constantly makes a distinction by two words or phrases, the distinction must really exist. Reid himself uses this argument to counter Hume's inappropriate way of speaking (*Essay on the Powers of the Human Mind, etc.*, Essay 1, c. 1, p. 20 ss.).

But does Reid's teaching on the exclusion of ideas contain

anything solid? I think so. I agree with Reid when he says that philosophers generally erred not by accepting *ideas* as distinct from the *operation* of the spirit when it is thinking of things, but by the notion they gave to these ideas.

He distinguishes three things in human thought:

> This expression ['thinking of it'] implies a mind that thinks, an act of that mind we call thinking, and an object about which we think. But, besides these three, the philosopher conceives that there is a fourth — to wit, the *idea*, which is the immediate object....I believe that *idea*, taken in this sense, to be a mere fiction of philosophers.

Some philosophers have certainly formed a concept of *idea* as the sole, perfect *means* through which we know real things. This is an error. The *idea* of a thing does not make anything real known to us; it presents only mere possibility. Idea is not the *perfect, total means* for knowing real things, as St. Thomas notes in many places; something else is needed for this information. Corporeal things therefore need a *corporeal sense*, with which we perceive directly the experience effected in us by the external powers we call bodies. The two elements of our *perception* and knowledge of *bodies* are the *sensation* of the bodies joined with the *idea*.

We must not think that we know subsistent bodies by means of ideas, as if these were *perfect images* of the bodies; this is a false concept of *ideas*. Bodies are powers acting directly on us, and our sense receives their action, but this individual perception is not the intellectual knowledge of them. We first form the intellectual perception and then separate the *idea* from this perception. This *idea* therefore, whose initial element and matter is the experienced *sense* of *bodies themselves*, is that which makes them known to us in a universal or intellectual way.

I think that the scholastics meant this when they said that the *idea* abstracts from *matter*, that is, the idea does not present to us the real, subsistent thing of which it is not an adequate *image*; *sensation* is needed to give us knowledge of real bodies. In this sense, I myself accept that an idea is a kind of *image* or *likeness*, as I have explained in volume 1 [*App.*, no. 2].

I certainly do not accept in the general sense of touch a *sensible species* in addition to and really distinct from *sensation*. Any distinction lies solely in the different ways *sensation* is considered.

The observations made so far show how necessary it is to be more careful in determining the opinions of philosophers than Reid was, if opinions are not to be attributed them which they do not hold. For example, Garve, as a result of his further study of Plato's expressions, thinks that the relationship between ideas and objects established by Plato is not the relationship described by Reid, that is, making the idea a *middle term* between the mind and objects (cf. *Legendorum philosophorum veterum praecepta nonnulla et exempla*).

Nevertheless, I give Reid some merit for saying that to call the idea a *means* of knowing things is somewhat equivocal. In fact, like Reid, I say that the intellectual perception of bodies is *direct* (that is, *reasoning* is not a means of perception, as he says) (*Essay on the Powers, etc.*, Essay 2, p. 100). As soon as our *sense* perceives a body, our *understanding* also perceives it directly and makes a first judgment without any intermediary. Sense and understanding are therefore two powers which directly and as it were *pari passu* co-operate in the perception of a body. The pure *idea* of a body follows on the *perception* in so far as in the idea we abstract from the actual existence of the body. On the other hand, in *perception*, we still think of the *presence* or *subsistence* of a body as an agent acting on us. In this sense, the *idea* of a body is not a *means* but an *element* of the *perception* of bodies.

42. (982)

[Galluppi's and Descartes' perception of self]

The thrust of all Galluppi's arguments is to prove that the *perception of myself* is direct. But this perception, I must add, can be considered either simply as *feeling* or as an *intellective act*. In the first case, it does not have the nature of intellective perception because an *intellective perception of myself* requires a synthesis; it requires a judgment between *myself* as *feeling* and the idea of *existence*. By making the judgment, 'I exist', I have an intellective perception because I have perceived not only myself in particular but myself as an *ens*, in a relationship with universal existence. Granted the possession of this intellective perception of *myself*, I must now take another step and *advert* to the perception. I am drawn to this act of *advertence*, which is itself another reflection on myself, by an unusual, vivid modification of my active feeling; it is precisely this feeling which attracts my attention —in other words, I am drawn by my acts. This is the starting point of Descartes' philosophy: 'I think, therefore I exist', which has the same force as: 'I am *aware* of my existence through my thoughts'. The argument is valid for *awareness* but not for intellective *perception*, and much less for *sense perception*. Intellective perception can and must be the starting point of philosophy. We are certainly not thinking and definitely not beginning to philosophise when we have nothing more than sense perceptions. When we have intellective perceptions, we think but do not reflect that we think; this is the level of intellectual life of the mass of people. The time comes however when we reflect that we are thinking; philosophy begins here. But the starting point for our mind can only be the state in which it finds itself. Those who begin to philosophise are in the state of reflection and advertence, and begin there. Descartes himself began there when he said, 'I think, therefore I exist'. However, previous to this state, are the states of direct knowledge and of advertence. It was natural therefore that Locke's philosophy should follow Descartes', that is, philosophy regressed from the examination of thought to the analysis of sensation, upon which thought is founded. By pursuing this course, it was easy to jump the stage of first, direct knowledge, because this stage is very difficult to observe and advert to, for the many reasons I have indicated. In fact Descartes and Locke jumped it intentionally: Descartes began from *reflection*; Locke investigated sensation. They both omitted the analysis of *simple knowledge*, which lies between the phenomena of reflection and sensation and serves as their key to both. In this work I have tried as well as I can to supply for the omission.

[*app.*, 42]

43. (994)

[Reid's censure of other philosophers]

Reid deserves great merit for his censure of some philosophical *expressions* which are fundamentally inexact and result in materialism. For example, to say that sensation is due to the *impulse* of the nerve in the spirit expresses hypothetical, material imagery. Speaking about Locke he says: 'Mr. Locke affirms with great certainty that the ideas of external objects are produced in our minds *through impulse* because this is the only way we can conceive the possibility of bodies acting', and then goes on to show how gratuitous Locke's expression is. Note however that Reid acknowledges that Locke retracted this opinion in his first letter to the bishop of Worcester and promised to correct the passage in the next edition of his *Essay*. Nevertheless Reid comments: 'Either through the author's forgetfulness or the printer's neglect, the passage remains in all the following editions I have seen' (*Essays on the Powers, etc.*, vol. 2, p. 88). Reid also notes the ambiguity contained in 'outside or inside the mind' and other expressions, which are apply to the extrasubjective perception of bodies. If 'outside or inside the soul' is to have exact meaning, it cannot mean ideas of place; it can only mean that ideas are or are not *in the subject*. However sometimes I think Dr. Reid is too severe in his censure of some expressions. There are expressions which, as far as I can see, have a true meaning even when taken in their proper sense, for example, 'representation' applied to the mind —this word generally means what is placed and drawn up in space before our eyes. But I note that when I am immersed in my own thought, I can and must conceive that whatever my intelligent spirit thinks is *represented* to it. My spirit has no power over the object of its thought; it cannot pervade the thing it is thinking or become one with it; my spirit remains distinct. The thing I am thinking is in my spirit in such a way that it cannot be confused with my spirit. This mode of presence is, it seems to me, well expressed by 'representation' and similar words. For the same reason I think that certain expressions used in connection with the sense of sight also have a proper, not a metaphorical sense relative to the understanding. Although sight and understanding are by nature two totally different faculties, there is nevertheless a kind of analogy between them.

44. (fn. 245)
[Malebranche's basic difficulty]

This observation [about the distinction between the simplicity of the principle and extension of the term] escaped Malebranche's notice. Consequently he did not see the possibility of communication between soul and body. Arnald, in his dispute with Malebranche, made the following fine observation where, however, we see the usual confusion of concepts concerning sensations and ideas, that is, concerning sense perception and intellective perception:

> Nothing seems stranger to me than saying that bodies are too large to be seen directly by the soul. If it were a question of making bodies *know*, we would be justified in bringing forward their size and imperfection, but if they are only *to be known*, the imperfections of material things cause no problems. *Knowledge* is clearly a great perfection in anyone who knows: the lowest level of intellective nature is incomparably greater and more admirable than what is most perfect in corporeal nature. But *to be known* is simply a name for a known object. Provided the object is not pure nothingness, which is incapable of being known, it is sufficient that it exist. To be knowable is an inseparable property of existence, like the properties of *unity, truth* and *goodness*; indeed, to be knowable is the same thing as to be *true*.
>
> (*Des vraies et des fausses idées*, c. 10)

The basic difficulty in Malebranche's teaching consisted more in considering bodies as *sense-perceived* rather than as *known*. Nevertheless Arnald's opinion can have some validity for sensation in a sensitive, intelligent ens.

45. (1033)

[Descartes' mistaken criterion of certainty]

Descartes was correctly taxed with begging the question when he established his criterion of certainty. He first says: 'Clear perception is the criterion of certainty', and uses this *criterion* to arrive at the existence of God. But he then says: 'Clear perception could deceive me, but the existence of God is the reason why the perception cannot deceive me. It comes from God who cannot deceive me' It seems impossible that his brilliant mind did not see the vicious circle here. But as his error becomes more obvious and necessary, the claim that his system is erroneous acquires greater validity. He knew that the perception of himself as subject needed something else for the perception to be authoritative, because in itself the perception was not necessarily infallible. What was needed was the *idea of being*, which contains *objectivity* and *necessity*. However, because he did not know this truth, he had recourse to the idea of God. He erred therefore in two ways: 1. he argued in a vicious circle because he deduced from *perception* the very thing necessary to prove perception; and 2. he precluded recourse to *common being* because he had recourse to the idea of *first, subsistent being*. The second error set him on the way to his *a priori* proof of the divine existence. His argument, in the way he presented it, was erroneous: he equivocated by taking the idea of being as subsistent being. However, his efforts and errors prove the necessity of the *idea of being* (a necessity which I accept), just as much as his authority would have proved this necessity if he had clearly asserted it.

46. (1035)

[Being in potency and in act]

Above all, Cardinal di Cusa's book, *De apice theoriae*, should be read. Tommassini drew upon Ficino in support of his opinions. Both held the following doctrine, in full agreement with mine: '*Being* shines so brilliantly that it is impossible to think it does not exist — OTHER THINGS ARE KNOWN THROUGH BEING, BUT BEING IS KNOWN THROUGH ITSELF' (Tommass., *Tract. De Deo Deique propriet.*, bk. 1, c. 14, art. 1). Cardinal Gerdil expresses the same opinion in his well-known work against Locke and in defence of Fr. Malebranche. But the thing that has escaped all these authors is, it seems to me, the great distinction between *being in potency* (idea, essence of being) and *being in act* (cf. 530 ss.). St. Thomas uses this distinction to show that God is not among things known through themselves (*S.T.*, 1, q. 2, art. 1). What these authors are saying is, 'Being cannot be thought without being. Therefore being exists.' Here the word 'being' is equivocal: if it means *ideal being*, this certainly cannot be thought unless it is and is necessarily, but it must not be confused with *subsistent being*. There is however a true, profound element in Ficino's and Tommassini's reasoning, which is also that of Descartes and St. Anselm. Traces of it can also be found in St. Augustine and many other ancient authors. But I will discuss this argument in the right place.

Index of Persons

*Numbers in roman indicate paragraphs or, where stated, the appendix (app.);
numbers in italic indicate footnotes*

Alcuin, *app.* no. 40
Algarotti, *app.* no. 37
Anselm (St.), *app.* no. 46
Arabs, 461–462
Araldi, Michele, *119*
Aristotle, 461, 948, 951, 974–975, 990; *18,
    27, 34, 51, 53, 58, 222; app.* nos. 2, 10,
    14–15, 21, 23, 26, 28, 38, 40
Arnald, *app.* no. 44
Augustine (St.), 485, 579–582, 1034; *24,
    29, 47, 49, 85; app.* nos. 14, 26, 38–40, 46

Bayle, *app.* nos. 30, 35
Berkeley, 608, 634–635, 639, 660, 683–686,
    689, 692, 749; *229; app.* nos. 24, 30
Boethius, 222
Bonald, *app.* no. 13
Bonaventure (St.), 472, 483, 485, 565; *14,
    23, 152; app.* nos. 6, 15
Bonnet, *app.* no. 17
Boscovich, *140*
Brucker, *app.* no. 11
Buffon, *app.* no. 37

Cabanis, 993; *200; app.* no. 24
Caldani, Leopoldo, *119*
Charlemagne, *app.* no. 40
Cheselden, *app.* no. 27
Cicero, *app.* no. 11
Condillac, 387, 410, 449, 458, 749; *1, 109;
    app.* nos. 22, 24, 30, 37
Cousin, 601; *72*

D'Alembert, *app.* no. 1
Dante, 549, 850, 1036; *188; app.* no. 7
Darwin, 992
De' Gregoris, Luigi, *app.* no. 27
Descartes, 750, 976, 979–982, 1033; *1; app.*
    nos. 2, 30, 32, 42, 45–46
Destutt-Tracy, 976; *app.* no. 24
Di Cusa, Cardinal, *app.* no. 46

Epicurus, 989

Falletti, T. V., *app.* no. 1
Ficino, Marsilio, 1035; *app.* nos. 11, 46
Foderé, *app.* no. 37

Galileo, *app.* nos. 30, 32
Gallini, S., *app.* no. 23
Galluppi, P., 671, 953–955 (title), 967–968,
    970–971, 976–978, 982, 1037; *78, 124,
    203, 210; app.* nos. 1, 22, 25, 27, 42
Garve, *app.* no. 41
Gerdil, Cardinal, *app.* no. 46
Gioia, Melchiorre, *app.* no. 37
Giovenale dell'Anaunia (Val di Non),
    1034

Haller, Albert, *119*
Hauy, *app.* no. 37
Hume, 608–611, 614, 632–633, 635, 660,
    685, 991; *229; app.* nos. 24, 30, 38, 41

Idealists, 848, 879; *229*

Jacobi, *app.* no. 27
Janin, Giovanni, *27*
Juvenal, *app.* no. 33

Kant, 389, 393, 395, 430, 461, 463, 470,
    599, 789, 1037; *app.* nos. 16, 22, 30

Laromiguière, 967, 970–971
Leibniz, 389, 392–393, 469, 710, 750, 847,
    869; *195*
Locke, 386–388, 410, 444–450, 469, 539,
    685, 710, 966–967, 969, 971; *24, 229;
    app.* nos. 7, 17, 23–24, 30, 34–35, 39,
    42–43, 46
Lucretius, *app.* no. 32

Malebranche, 443, 750, 979, 1033–1034; *1, 52, 158*; *app.* nos. 44, 46
Materialists, *229*
Molineux, *195*

Newton, *21*; *app.* no. 31
Norris, *52*

Plato, 389, 391, 393, 432, 500–501, 506, 647, 975; *34, 49 app.* nos. 7, 10–11, 40–41
Pythagoras, *app.* no. 11

Reid, 388, 452–454, 951–954, 969–975, 991, 1037; *app.* nos. 3, 7, 22, 30–31, 34–35, 39, 41, 43
Rousseau, *app.* no. 13
Royer-Collard, *160*

Sceptics, *73*
Scholastics,, 478, 491, 609, 611, 948, 1036; *26, 48, 50*; *app.* nos. 12, 14, 41
Sensists, 386
Simplicius, *app.* no. 28
Spallanzi, 993
Spinoza, *98*
Stewart, 388, 946; *230*; *app.* no. 7

Thomas Aquinas (St.), 385 (title), 477–478, 483–484, 565, 720, 830, 1001, 1032–1034; *22, 32–34, 46–48, 50–51, 54, 58, 138, 151–152*; *app.* nos. 2, 6, 8–10, 12, 14, 18–23, 26, 32, 40–41, 46
Tommassini, 1034; *app.* no. 46
Transcendentalists, 848

General Index

Numbers in roman indicate paragraphs or, where stated, an appendix (app.);
numbers in italic indicate footnotes

Abstraction
analysis and, 1029
forms of, 654–656
generic ideas and, 653
ideas and, 508, 510, 517, 519, 653
perceptions and, 519
phantasms and, 517
reflection and, 489, 512–513, 519
signs causing, 521
thoughts and, 588
universalisation and, 490–499, 652

Absurdity
mystery and, 973

Accident(s)
dependence of, 688
effects and, 568
happenings and, 568
idea of, 610–612
mental or dialectical, 655
subject and, 637
substance and, 610–613; *90*
variability of, 612–613

Act
first, 1008, 1010; *87*
force and, 1013
human spirit and, 436, 1019
potency as, 1008
principle and term of, *245*
second, 649, 1008

Action(s)
cause and, 631, 623
composite, 782
ens and, 530, 621, 795
fact and, 616
first, 530

idea of, 618
intensity and duration of, 766–767, 770-773
life and, *146*
observation of, 784
passive experiences and, 774; *app.* no. 4
succession and, 797
successive duration, 767–768, 784
unity of recipient and, *168*
see also **Duration**

Activity
ens exerting, 1018
idea of, 666
stimulation of, 524–525

Advertence, Attention, Awareness
act of spirit and, 1033, 1039
attention and, 928
change necessary for, 710
chronological order of, *app.* no. 26
extension and, 813
feeling and, 710, 715, 968; *174*
idea and, 470, 548–551
intellect and, *17, 188*
intellectual and sensible, 449
law governing, 928
perceptions and, 929, 945–947
philosophy and, *app.* no. 42
reflection and, 488
sensations and, 664–665, 897–899, 927; *203; app.* no. 33

Amputated Limb
feeling and, 762; *173*

Analysis
abstraction and, 1029
synthesis and, 489; *15*

Animal(s)
  instinct and, 487
  lack of speech, 710
  nerves and, *189*
  sensations and, 487
  space and, *199*

Attention, *see* **Advertence**

Awareness, *see* **Advertence**

Baby
  idea of being and, 470

Beauty
  aesthetics and, 571
  idea of, 629

Being
  divine, 658
  ens and, *25*
  essential, *49*
  human spirit and, 521
  ideal, 555–556, 1033
  intellect and, 481–482
  intuition of, 548–552
  light of, 397
  possible, 396–397, 426–427, 437
  real, 479, 555
  sense and, 476
  subsistence and, 479
  subsistent, 1033
  thought by human beings, 398–399
  understanding and, 620
  universal, 398–399
  vision of, *app.* no. 6
    see also **Ens, Idea of Being**

Belief
  perception and, 528
  word of the mind and, *45*

Birds
  touch and measurement in, *166*

Blind People
  idea of mathematical and physical
    body in, 875
  mathematics and, 839
  movement and, 812
  perception of space by, 839
  sensation in recovered sight, 910
  touch and, 897

Body/Bodies
  activity and, 1015–1019
  agent and, 855
  concept of, 397
  continuous extension of elementary,
    869–870
  corporeal principle and, 855–856
  co-subject with soul, 999, 1003–1004
  defined, 667, 749–753, 820, 871
  essence of, 708, 754, 843
  existence of, 683–684, 754–759,
    876–877
  extension and, 750, 842–846, 858–860,
    862; *132*
  extrasubjective, 1003
  feeling and, 750, 1005–1006
  first knowledge of, *115*
  force and, 872
  forms of elementary bodies, *176, 178*
  idea of, 672–673
  idea of mathematical, 874–875
  idea of physical body, 875
  idea of solid, 872–873
  identity of extension of our own and
    external, 842–844
  identity of external, *app.* no. 29
  intellective perception of, 458, 691
  limited ens, 680
  meaning of, 667, 673, 1014; *178*
  movement and, 801–802, 872–873,
    1017
  moving our own, 821
  multiplicity and, 847–848, 854,
    857–858
  observation and, 1001
  origin of idea of, summarised, 690
  our own body and external, 708–709,
    753, 842–845; *app.* no. 25
  perception of, 517, 529, 627, 707, 713,
    723, 755, 802, 831–832, 844,
    872–873, 876, 956–960, 1015
  pleasure or pain and, 757
  power and substance of, 858
  properties of, 692–693, 886
  relationship between, 693–694
  relationship with our spirit, 693,
    695–697
  sensations and external, 722–723,
    831–832, 835–836, 956
  sensible representation of, 713
  sensitive, 696–700
  separate thing, 688
  size of, 862, 922–924
  soul and, 720–721, 955, 998–1004
  surface of, as likeness of body, 950

touch and idea of, 832
unity of, *63*; *app.* no. 29
  see also **Human Body**

Brain
  sensitivity and, *123*
  unity of body and, 850

Callology
  principle of, 629

Cause
  common sense and, 615
  idea of, 615–621
  principle of, 567–569, 977–978
  proposition concerning, 616–617
  subject and, 637–638
  substance and, 622
  ultimate, 686

Certainty,
  human knowledge and, 1037

Change
  awareness and, 710

Child
  judging subsistent entia, *43*
  language and, 522
  philosophy and, 470
  size of things and, *200*

Classification
  general idea and, 448

Cognition
  first matter of, 1027
  principle of, 565, 567
    see also **Knowledge**

Colour(s)
  distance and, 918
  movement and, 917
  qualities of things and, *196*
  sizes of things and, 912, 918
  subjective part of sensation, 914

Common Sense, *see* **People**

Concept(s)
  analysis of, 611
  elementary, 575–578
  first, *83*
  non-pure, 397
  pure, 397

Consciousness
  action on us and, 880
  two facts of, 1033

Contemplation
  unnoticed, *56*

Continuum, Continuity
  contradiction in, 790
  definition, 826
  fundamental feeling and, *164*
  idea of, *158*
  in space, 823–830
  in succesion, 790, 794, 815
  infinitely divisible, 830
  mathematical points and, 864–865
  meaning of, 825
  of elementary sensations, 864–869
  of movement, 813–819
  of time, 781–799
  real, 824
  simple, 794
  touch and phenomenal, 863, 899

Contradiction,
  principle of, 559–567, 605

Definitions
  understanding and, *179*

Distance
  sight and, 910, 917–919, 924–925

Dream
  life as, 763

Duration
  action, ens, essence and, 795
  continuum of, 794–796
  God, human soul and, 796
  successive, 767–768, 784
    see also **Time**

Ecstasy
  state of, 549

Energy
  existence and, *74*
  sensations and, 677, 683–684, 689,
    691–692, 860
  substance and, 589–590
  two sorts of, 708
    see also **Force**

Ens
action and, 530, 621
being and, 25
force and, 676
idea of, *app*. no. 6
meaning of, 620
sensitivity and, 1023
thought and, 649
understanding and, 620, 632–624
unity of active and passive, *app*. no. 22
see also **Being**

Entia
laws of, 1013
material, 420
spiritual, 401

Essence
defined, 646
first concept and, *83*
generic, 647, 653–656
most universal, 647
specific, 647–652, 657–659

Ethics
justice and, 571

Evil
good and, 648

Existence
energy and, *74*
meaning of, 530
perception of self and first moments of, *app*. no. 14
substance and, 589–590, 607, 610

Experience
action and, *app*. no. 4
judgment and, *app*. no. 36
passive, 663
sensation and, *app*. no. 3

Extension
as abstraction, 820
body and, 750, 842–846, 858–860; *132*
continuous, 869, 882
corporeal pleasure and pain and, 728–731
corporeal properties and, 885
extrasubjective, *135*
four senses and, 902
fundamental feeling and, 729–731,

735–739, 752, 841, 844–845, 922–923; *132, 156*
limitless, 821–822
mode of feeling, 730–731, 758; *142*
multiplicity and, *170*
observation and, 813
our body, external body and identity of, 842–845; *182*
real, continuous, 858–860
sensation and, 426; *156*
spirit and, 718
subjective, 728–731, 735; *137*
touch and, 896–900, 903
see also **Space**

Extrasubjective
and subjective perception, 983–984, 994
meaning of, 627
perception of body, 701, 712
qualities, *171*
touch as, 750; *139*
see also **Subjective**

Fact(s)
action as, 616
active and passive, 666
meaning of, *app*. no. 25
observation and, *app*. no. 17
possibility and, 783
reason and, 815

Faculty
effects and, 410
integrative, *95*

Fathers of the Church
human mind and, *152*
idea of being and, 471–472

Feeling
amputated limb and, 762; *173*
awareness and, 710, 715; *174*
bodies and, 750, 1006, 1010
brain and, 732–734
chronological order of feelings, *126*
different from pleasure and pain, *162*
extension and, 728–731; *132*
ideas and faculty of, *3*
reflection and, 968
sensitivity and, 1024
subsistence and, 528
sudden existence of, 718
term of, 962
term of intelligence and, 516

union of felt with, *app.* no. 22
unity of, 887–888
  see also **Fundamental Feeling**

Force
  act and, 1013
  bodies and, 720, 876, 882–883
  diffusion of, 817–818, 870
  ens and, 676
  feeling and, 627
  instinctive, animal, 449
  perception and, 845
  senses and, 901
  vital, *119*
    see also **Energy**

Form
  matter and, 1021
  of intellect and, 1023

France
  ideas and, *1*
  philosophy of sensation in, *app.* no.
    24

Freedom
  human faculties and, 1031
  language and, 1030

Fundamental Feeling
  attention and, 737
  characteristics of, 752, 762
  continuum and, *164*
  defined, 726
  described, 710–714
  existence of, 715–719
  extension and, 729–731, 735–739, 752,
    758, 842–845, 922–923; *132, 156*
  human body and, 696, 701–707, 843,
    963; *154*
  intellect and, 1025
  life and, 698–700, 753, 955
  matter of the, 1005–1019
  mode of, 730
  modification(s) of, 702–704, 724–725,
    727, 889–892
  movement and, 739, 803
  myself and, 719
  parts of, *205*
  perception of a body and, *211*
  pleasure and, 725
  sensation and, 735–739, 955
  sensitivity and, 1025
  space and, 840–841; *221*
  time and, *146*

touch and, 746
  see also **Feeling**

Genera
  real, mental and nominal, 654–655
  universalisation and, 499

God
  being and, 1033
  bodies and, 682
  duration of, 796
  sensations and, 681, 686
  ultimate cause, 686
    see also **Being**

Good
  evil and, 648

Hand
  sensitivity of, *app.* no. 33

Happening
  cause and, 615–616

Hearing
  distance and, *app.* no. 34
  functions of, 948
  language and, 921
  movement and, 812
  perceptions of, 742
  sight and, 920–921
  touch and, 920
    see also **Sounds**

Human Beings
  internal feelings and, 625

Human Body
  error about part of our, 761–762
  external bodies and, 708–709, 753,
    760
  extrasubjective perception of our
    own, *app.* no. 25
  fundamental feeling and, *154*
  multiplicity of feeling of, 852–853
  perceived in two ways, 701–704, 706,
    712, 747–748
  union with spirit, 706
  unity and unicity of, 849–852
    see also **Body/Bodies**

Human Race
  ideas and, 227
    see also **Masses (The), People**

Idea(s)
    abstract, 508–509, 519, 521, 524–526,
        578, 620, 650–651, 820, 1030
    abstract, specific, 651; *96*
    apparent, 585
    attention to, 548
    awareness of, 470
    classes of, 508
    complete, specific, 650; *96*
    composite, 504, 507–510; *38*
    composition of, 474
    determined, 511
    elementary, 575–578
    elements of, 432
    essential being and, *49*
    France and, *1*
    full, 509
    full, specific, 518; *96*
    generic, 653–655
    Germany and, *1*
    idea of being and other, 471, 476, 486
    innate, 389–391, 393, 396; *58*
    intellective operation and, 968
    intellective perception and, 973; *app.*
        no. 41
    Italy and, *1*
    judgment and, 385–388, 402–407,
        455–456; *33*
    language and, *85*
    meaning of, 416–417
    modes of, 506–509, 649–650
    non-pure, 630
    numbers and, *app.* no. 11
    persuasion and, *77*
    place, time and, *app.* no. 28
    possibility and, 431, 783; *app.* no. 41
    possible being and, 397
    pure, 435, 517, 630, 965
    sensation and, 419–422, 518; *app.* no.
        39
    signs and, 521
    specific, 649–652
    subsistence and, 402–407
    synthesis of, 508
    thing and its idea, *44*
    undetermined, 401
    universality of, 387
    word of the mind and, 534
        see also **Concepts, Idea of Being**

Idea of Being
    as a principle, 569
    awareness of, 469–470
    characteristics of, 415–416, 423,
        426–429, 431

    co-created, 1035
    elementary ideas and, 576–577
    elements of, 424, 437
    existing ens and, 530
    Fathers of the Church and, 471–472
    feeling of existence and, 438–443
    form of cognitions, 601
    ideas and, 471, 473, 486
    immutability and eternity of, 433
    innate, 467–468, 539
    intellect and, 1010, 1022–1023
    intuition of, 541
    judgment and, 1035
    knowledge and, *app.* no. 18
    light of soul, 537, 556; *app.* no. 6
    Locke's reflection and, 444–450
    most universal, 409
    nature of, 555–557
    objectivity of, 415–422, 464–465
    other ideas and, 412
    philosophy's steps towards, 971
    possibility and, 408–409, 423–425
    predicate, 530, 546
    principle of contradiction and, 565,
        605
    produced by act of perception,
        451–466
    sensations and, 414–437, 451
    sensible image and, 400, 423
    simplicity of, 426
    spirit (human) and, 557
    subject and, 463–465
    subsistence and, 408–409, 495
    summary of theory of, 1020–1031
    thought and, 399, 410–411
    truth and, *29*
    understanding the theory of,
        1038–1039
    undetermination of, 434–436; *app.* no.
        16
    unity or identity of, 427
    universality and necessity of, 428–432
    wise philosophers and 1033–1037
        see also **Being, Idea(s)**

Idealism
    Hume's, 609
    sensations and, *app.* no. 24
    transcendental, *4*

Image
    ideas and sensible, 400–401; *app.* no.
        41
    nature of, 928
    sensations and, *22*

sight and, 944, 949
things and corporeal, 517, 520

Imagination
as intellection, *36*

Impossibility
hidden, *app.* no. 16
logical, 561
physical, 543
see also **Possibility**

Impression
external body and, 985
materialists and, 988
sensation and, 986–988, 990

Improvement
capacity for, 1011

Individual
origin of idea of, 591
perception of, 597

Insight
spiritual, 1025

Instinct
animal and, 487
judgment and, 388
rational, 524
sensation and, 449
sense-instinct, 524

Integration
species and, 652; *37*

Intellect
being and, 482, 564
defined, 481
faculty of, 973; *79*
form of, 1023
idea of being and, 1010
intuition and, 1024
reflection and, *17*
time and, 799
see also **Intellective Perception,
Intelligence, Mind,
Understanding**

Intellection
classification of, 505–509
defined, 505

Intellective (Intellectual) Perception
direct, *232*
ens and, 632–624
explained, 528-530
four things in, *app.* no. 3
idea and, 973, 978
necessity of, 535–536
object of, *235*
of bodies, 458, 528, 962–965, 970, 973,
978; *app.* no. 41
of self, 528
philosophy and, *app.* no. 42
primal synthesis and, 1026
real things and, 415–422, 495, 507
sensations and, 454, 491, 517–518;
app. nos. 4, 22
sense perception and, 418, 623–624,
961-982; *58*; *app.* nos. 3, 4
three parts of, 454

Intelligence
as sense, 553
being and, 564
essentially thinking, 537
law of, 535–536
tabula rasa, 538
see also **Intellect, Mind,
Understanding**

Intuition
defined, 548
idea and, 541, 548–551
intellect and, 1024
judgment and, 552
subject and, 1024

Judgment
constitutive law of, 456
error and, *app.* no. 38
faculty of, 973, 1025
habitual, 733; *143, 173, 212; app.* nos.
29, 33, 36–37
idea and, 385–388, 402–407, 455–456;
33; app. nos. 28, 39
idea of being and, 569
instinct and, 388
intuition and, 552
knowledge and, 386
nature of, 541
universal idea and, 970

Justice
ethics and, 571
idea of, 629

Knowledge
  a posteriori, 474
  a priori, 430, 437 (title)
  certainty and, 1037
  entia without organs and, *app*. no. 31
  formal part of, 394, 396, 474, 480
  idea of being and, *app*. no. 18
  judgment and, 386
  matter of, 474, 480
  naturally immutable, *60*
  passivity and, *84*
  popular and philosophical, 1032
  positive and negative, *114*
  progress of, *179*
  scientific and popular, *app*. no. 14
  self, 710
      see also **Cognition**

Language(s)
  abstract ideas and, 521–522, 527,
      1030; *app*. no. 13
  animals and, 710
  hearing and, 921
  ideas and, *85*
  negative and positive beings and, 543
  society and, 919; *app*. no. 13
  synthetical and analytical methods, *15*
  use of, 605
  word of the mind and, 533
  words, ideas and, 918
      see also **Word(s)**

Leap
  passage and, 817

Life
  as dream, 763
  first action, *146*
  fundamental feeling and, 698–700,
      753
  nature of, 696, 698
  pleasure and, 755

Light
  idea of being as, 537, 556; *app*. no. 6

Likeness (Species)
  idea and, *248*; *app*. no. 41
  sensation and, 948–951, 960
  sight and, 948–951, 956, 973

Logic
  principle of, 629

Many
  one and, *64*

Masses, The
  reflection and, *app*. no. 42
  thought and opinion of, *226*
      see also **Human Race**

Materialism
  corporeal feeling and, *app*. no. 24
  rebutted, 988–994

Mathematics
  blind people and, 839
  principles and, 559

Matter
  general and particular, *app*. no. 28
  object and, 1005–1010
  potencies and, 1009–1010

Meditation
  ideas, feelings and, 968

Memory
  as intellection, *36*

Mind
  eternal things and, *152*
  object conceived by, *4*
  regular shapes and, *190*
  thoughts and, 586
  three operations of, 510
  truth and, *70*
      see also **Intellect**

Moral Science
  principle of, 629

Movement
  active, 800, 802–803, 805
  awareness of, 804, 806
  bodies and, 801–802, 872–873, 1017
  colours and, 917–919
  concept of, 397
  continuity of, 813–819
  fundamental feeling and, 739
  hearing and, 812
  idea of, 800–819
  insensible, 806
  observation and continuity of, 814
  passive, 800, 802, 804–805
  sensation and, 809
  sense-organs and, 807–808
  sight and, 811

smell and, 812
subjective perception of body and, 764–765
taste and, 812
touch and, 810
velocity, 770

Multiplicity
corporeal nature and, 847–849, 882, 884
body and, 852–854, 857–858; *99*
extension and, *170*
shallow-thinking people and, *64*
unity and, 847

Myself
active and passive effects (facts) in, 662–666
body and, 668
corporeal substance and, 662–669
feeling, thinking subject, 668; *app.* no. 14
force and feeling of, 1002
fundamental feeling and, 719
idea and feeling of, 439
idea of, 669
idea of being and, 442–443, 465
intellective perception of, 980
movement and, 739
particular existence and, 440–441
perception of, 980; *100*; *app.* nos. 14, 22, 42
relationships and, 1025
sensations and, 640–642, 739; *220*
sensitivity and, 1022

Mystery
absurdity and, 973
philosophy and, *app.* no. 5

Names
perception and, 855

Nature
leaps in, 816–817
mysterious facts in, 793
observation of, *app.* no. 17
subtleties of, 813

Nerves
animals and, *189*
duration of sensation and, *183*
images and, 521
pleasant sensation and, *193*

sensitivity and, 698–699, 702, 707, 715, 823; *119*
smell and olfactory, 743
sympathetic (diffused) sensation and, 904
touch and, 841; *163*

Nouns
syntheses, *15*

Number(s)
Augustine (St.) on, 579–581
ideas and, *app.* no. 11
undetermined, 780

Object
characteristic of, 554
intellective perception and, *235*
matter and, 1005–1010
mind and, *4*
subject and, *59–60*, 103
understanding and, 602–603, 606

Observation
actions and, 784
body and, 1001
matters of fact and, 783
movement and, 814
nature and, *app.* no. 17
nature of, *203*
origin of ideas and, 1038

Pain
attention and, 665
existence of body and, 757
see also **Pleasure**

Passivity
idea of, 666
knowledge and, 617

People
idea of sensible qualities and of internal feeling, 634
judgment and, *app.* nos. 36, 39
reared outside society, 518, 522
sensations and, 635
see also **Human Race**

Perception
belief differs from, 528
corporeal, 958–960, 963
extrasubjective, 841, 845, 983–984, 1024
idea of being and act of, 451–466

indication and, *app.* no. 34
of bodies, 529; *app.* no. 41
of our own body, 701, 706, 712,
    747–748
of solid space, 839–841
reflection, reason and, 487
senses and, 833–836
subjective, 983–984
two kinds of, *31*
    see also **Intellective Perception,**
    Sense Perception

Perspective
art of, 931

Persuasion
ideas and, *77*
subsistence and, 405, 408, 517, 520,
    592; *3, 49*

Phantasms
abstraction and, 517
external bodies and, *186*
rational instinct and, 524

Philosopher
nature and, *app.* no. 17

Philosophy
child and, 470
error and system of, *app.* no. 24
mysteries and, *app.* no. 5
Scholasticism and, 611
starting point of, *app.* no. 42

Physiology
psychology and, 995–997

Place
idea and, *app.* no. 28

Pleasure
attention and, 448, 665
corporeal, *727–729*
existence of body and, 757
feelings and, *162*
fundamental feeling and, 725, 752,
    889
instinct and, 449
organ and, 741
    see also **Pain**

Points
mathematical, 864–868
simple, 870

Possibility
concept of, 546; *app.* no. 16
facts and, 783
idea and, 533; *app.* no. 41
idea of being and, 408–409, 423–425,
    821
indefinite reproduction of things and,
    786, 821
logical, 543
probability and, 543-546
pure idea and, 431
rule and judgment about, *app.* no. 16
universality, necessity and, 431, 491
    see also **Impossibility**

Potency
first act, 1008, 1021
form of, 1021
matter and, 1009–1010, 1021
soul and, 1020

Predicate
idea of being as, 546
subject and, 530

Principle(s)
corporeal, 855–856, 869; *246*
first, *app.* no. 19
judgment and, 565
of cause, 567–569
of cognition, 565
of contradiction, 561–567, 605
of ethics, 571
of reasoning, 558–560, 570
of substance, 567–568
origin of, 574
propositions and, 559, 565
scientific, 570–574

Probability
possibility and, 543–546

Propositions
analyses, *15*
judgment and, 560
principles as, 559

Psycholoy
physiology and, 995–997

Qualities
extrasubjective, *171*
primary, *app.* no. 34–35
secondary, *app.* no. 35
    see also **Sensible Qualities**

Quantity
  intelligible, *app*. no. 28

Rationality
  spiritual insight, 1025

Reason
  idea of being and, 482
  defined, 481
  facts and, 815
  first principles and, *app*. no. 19
  perception and, 487
  primal synthesis and, 1025
  reflection and, 487, 1028
  univerality and, 1028
    see also **Reasoning**

Reasoning
  concepts conditioning, 575
  consciousness of, *100*
  deduction and, 570
  faculty of, 514
  first principles of, 397
  idea of being and, 566, 569
    see also **Reason**

Reflection
  abstraction and, 489, 512, 519
  attention and, 488, 549–550
  ideas and, 968; *app*. no. 12
  ideas of relationship and, 488
  intellect and, *17*
  Locke's, 444–450
  objects of, 1029
  operations of, 1029
  perception, reason and, 487
  philosophy and, *app*. no. 42
  requirements for, *app*. no. 26
  sensations and, *app*. no. 12
  will and, 513

Relationship
  as abstract idea, 525–526
  between two things, 645

Representation
  thought and, *app*. no. 43

Scholasticism
  philosophy and, 611

Sciences
  classifying, 573
  principles of, 570–574

Sensation(s)
  accidentality of, 429
  advertence and, *app*. no. 33
  animal and, 487
  awareness and, 897–899; *203*
  bodily parts and, 889–895
  consciousness and, 882
  continuous, 864–868
  determined. 435
  duration of, *183*
  elements of, 689, 723, 831, 841, 879; *183*; *app*. no. 22
  energy and, 677, 687, 691–692
  experience and, 990; *app*. no. 3
  extension, 426; 156
  external, *155*
  external bodies and, 722–723, 831–832, 835–836, 956, 960; *app*. no. 35
  extrasubjective, 740, 878, 881–883; *196*; *app*. nos. 22, 30
  first action and, 530
  fundamental feeling and, 701, 705–706, 717–719, 735–739, 955; *183*
  God and, 681, 686
  human spirit and, 516, 664
  idea and, 419–422, 518; *app*. no. 39
  idea of being and, 414–437, 451
  idea of body and, 674
  images and, *22*
  immateriality of, 989
  impression and, 986–988, 990
  instinct and, 449
  intellective perception and, 454, 517; *app*. no. 4
  location and, 427, 865
  meaning of, 416–417; *130*
  modes of, 736
  myself and, 640–642, 664–665
  nerves and pleasant, *193*
  our own organs and, 737–743, 901–905
  particularity of, 428, 436
  perception of bodies and, 517, 707; *app*. no. 41
  sensitive parts and, 861
  size of body and, 862
  special, 894–895
  species of things and, 948–950
  stimulus and, *174*
  subject of, 640–643
  subjective, 740, 878, 881–883, 887–895; *196*; *app*. nos. 22, 30
  substance and, 640, 643, 675–676, 858

sympathetic, 860, 904
things and, 416, 423, 841
touch and awareness of, 897–899
twofold quality of, 703–704
understanding and, 710, 902; *188*
unified by space, 941–944
unnoticed, *56*

Sense
action of bodies and, *63*
being and, 476
error and, *app*. no. 38
ideas and, 478–479
instinctive expectation of, 963
intellectual, 553–554; *app*. no. 39
meaning of, *24*
see also **Feeling, Senses (human)**

Senses (human)
as touch, 744–745, 908
force and, 901
perception by, 833–836, 956–960
sensation in the four, 901–905
species and, 948–951

Sense Perception
clarity of, 929
corporeal, 691, 740–743; *13; app*. no. 3
defined, 417
intellective perception and, 417–422,
518, 623–624, 961-982; *58; app*. nos.
3, 4
modification of fundamental feeling
and, 1026
of bodies, 674, 963–982, 978; *235*
organs and, *app*. no. 31
sensation and, 703; *app*. no. 22

Sensible Qualities
body and, 667
capacities, 690
common sense and, 635
defined, 645
subject of, 644–645
substance and, 607–610, 613–614,
623–625, 627, 660

Sensitivity
ens and, 1023
external, 1022, 1026, 1030
feeling and, 1024
internal, 1022
judgment and, 387
myself and, 1022

Shape(s)
mind and regular, *190*
of bodies, 939
sight and, 940, 993
space and, *206*
touch and, 900, 993
see also **Touch**

Sight
coloured surface and, 906–912, 919
distance and, 911–913, 917–919,
924–925; *app*. no. 27
erroneous influence of, 946
functions of, 948
hearing, smell and, 920–921
illusion about distant objects,
930–931
images and, 944, 949
inverted image and, 932–938
movement and, 811, 911–912,
917–919
perception of bodies and, 945–947
perceptions relative to, 741
shapes, 940, 943–944
size of things and, 910, 912–916,
924–929
species and, 948–949
three dimensional space and, 911
touch and, 811, 914–916, 924,
926–927, 929; *195; app*. no. 37

Signs
abstract ideas and, 521
colours as, *196*
free will and, 524
things signed and, 925; *198*
words as, 918

Smell
distance and, *app*. no. 34
functions of, 948
movement and, 812
perceptions and, 741
sight and, 920–921
size of things and, 941
touch and, 920

Soul
always thinking, 537
body and, 720–721, 955, 998–1004
duration of, 796
light of, 537, 556
potencies of, 1020
see also **Spirit**

Sounds
language and, 942
size of things and, 942
see also **Hearing**

Space
body and, 820
concept of, 397
continuum in, 794, 823–830
fundamental feeling and, 803,
840–841
idea of, 820–830
limitless, 821–822
perception of indefinite, 839–841
sensations unified by, 941–944
shape and, *206*
subjective perception of body and,
764–765
thought of, 840
three dimensional, 838
see also **Extension**

Species
abstract, 652
complete, 507
full, 652; *37*
integration and, 652; *37*
meaning of, *35*
perfect, *37*
universalisation and, 499
see also **Likeness**

Spirit (human)
act and, *app*. no. 6
activity of, 1013
being and, 521
body and, 706, 1016
corporeal pleasure and pain and, *134*
extension and, 718
forces acting on, 708
incorporeal, 670–671
instinct and, 518
light of, 556
myself as, 669
perception and, 515
sensations and, 516–518
term limiting, 515
thing thought and, *app*. no. 43
thoughts caused by, 637
universalisation and, 513
see also **Soul**

Spiritual Entia
subsistence and, 401

Spontaneity
meaning of, *41*

Stimuli
abstracts and, 514–527
instinctive, 524

Subject
cause and, 637–638
co-subject and, 983, 999, 1003
idea of being and, 464–465
object and, *59–60, 103*
predicate and, 530
sensations and 640–643

Subjective
and extrasubjective perception,
983–984, 994
perception of body, 701–704
touch as, 750; *139*
unity of extrasubjective and, *134*; *app*.
no. 22
see also **Extrasubjective**

Subsistence
being and, 479
defined, 406
feeling and, 528
idea and judgment about, 402–407,
431, 495, 592–593; *app*. no. 28
idea of being and, 408–409
persuasion of, 405, 408, 517, 520; *3, 49*

Substance
accidents and, 610–613; *90*
cause and, 622
concept of, 588
defined, 587, 657, 660, 686; *83*
dependence of, 687
existence and, 589–590, 607, 610
first cause and, 687
generic idea of, 589–590
idea of being and, 601
ideas and subsistence of, 592–593
ideas of, 583–614
invariability of, 612–613
our own, 625–628
principle of, 567–568
sensations and, 640, 643, 660, 675–676
sensible qualities and, 607–610,
613–614, 623–625, 627, 660
specific idea of, 589–590
systems dealing with idea of, 599–601
truth and, *app*. no. 20

Succession
actions and, 797
continuity of, 790, 815
duration, 767–768, 784
time and, 767–768, 784; *153*

Superstitions
religious instruction and, 947

Synthesis
analysis and, 489, 968; *15*
primal, 513, 690, 965, 1025
universal ideas and, 968

Tabula Rasa
undetermined being and, 538; *app.*
nos. 15–16

Taste
movement and, 812
size of things and, 941
touch and, 920
two different functions of, 948

Term
activity of, 515

Things
essence of, 572
idea of, *44*
perception of, 415
sensation and, 416, 423

Thought(s)
ens and, 649
idea of being and, 410–411
mind and, 586
principle of contradiction and,
561–564
representation and, *app.* no. 43
space and, 840
spirit as cause of, 637
three series of, 401

Time
action of others and, 774
all that happens and, 779–780
concept of, 397
continuity in, 781–799
fundamental feeling and, *146*
idea and, *app.* no. 28
idea of, 764–799
idea of being and, 797–799
idea of pure, indefinitely long,
776–778, 785–788

indefinite divisibility of, 787–788
intellect and, 799
measure of, 768–769, 777
observation and, 782
our own actions and, 766–773
passive experiences and, 774
phenomenal idea of continuity of,
789–790
pure idea of, 775–776, 785
subjective perception of body and,
764–765
successive duration, 767–768, 784
uniformity of, 772, 777

Touch
as corporeal perception, 958–960
blind people and, 897
double nature of, 752; *139*
extension and, 896–900, 903
external bodies and, 872–873,
956–960, 963
idea of bodies and, 831–873
identity of a body and, *app.* no. 29
liquids and, *191*
measuring distance, *166*
movement and, 810
origin of, 746
phenomenal continuity and, 863
shape of bodies and, 939
sight and, 811, 914–916, 926–927, 929;
195; *app.* no. 37
size of body and, 862, 922–924
smell, hearing, taste and, 920
surfaces and, 837, 872
three dimensional space and, 838
union of bodies in, 908; *182*
universal sense, 744–745, 948

Truth
human mind and, *70*
idea of, 629
idea of being and, *29*
substance and, *app.* no. 20

Understanding
direct act of, 713
ens and, 620, 632–624
faculty of, 602, 1030
idea of cause and, 621
integrative faculty of, 624
object and, 602–603, 606
perception of bodies and, 964; *app.*
nos. 4, 41
primal sense, *249*
qualities perceived by, 607

reflection and, *app.* no. 12
sensation and, 710, 902; *188*
single act of, 551
  see also **Intellect, Intelligence,
  Mind**

Unity
multiplicity and, 847
of action and recipient, *168*
of our body, 849–850

Universalisation
abstraction and, 490–499, 652
faculty of, 1028
feeling, idea and, *app.* no. 12
ideas and, 508, 510–511, 653; *app.* no.
  9
spirit moving to, 513
  see also **Universality**

Universality
explained, *248*

reason and, 1028
  see also **Universalisation**

Will
free, 524–526

Word(s)
essential being and, *49*
ideas and, 521–522, 918
language and, 605, 679
meaning of, 678–679
mental, 531–534; *33, 45*
naming a thing, 678
real thing and, *177*
use of, 679, 855; *app.* no. 22
written, *196*
  see also **Language(s)**

Writing
sight sensations and, *207*